Instant *Office 2000 Answers ...*

For Saving Time

To Do This	In	Select This	Or Click This	Or Press
Create new document	All	File | New		...N
Create or run macros	All except Access	Tools | Macro		8
Display all open windows	All	Window | Arran...		
Remove the selected item to the clipboard	All	Edit | Cut		...X
Repeat the last action	All	Edit | Redo		CTRL+Y
Replace text in a document	All	Edit | Replace		CTRL+H
Reverse the last action	All	Edit | Undo		CTRL+Z
Save the current document	All	File | Save		CTRL+S
Save with a new name	All	File | Save As		
See how a page will print	All except PowerPoint	File | Print Preview		
Select an entire document/slide/records/page	All except Excel	Edit | Select All		CTRL+A
Switch to a different open document	All	Window | select document		
Transmit a document via e-mail	All	File | Send To | Mail Recipient		
Use Help	All	Help | Help		F1
Display context-sensitive Help	All	Help | What's This		SHIFT+F1
Find similar records	Access	Records | Filter | Filter By Selection		
Set an area to print	Excel	File | Print Area | Set Print Area		
Display a slide show	PowerPoint	View | Slide Show		F5
Create or insert AutoText	Word	Insert | AutoText | select text or type text and select Add		
Save as a separate version	Word	File | Versions		

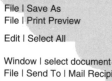

For Navigating Office

To Do This	In	Select This	Or Click This	Or Press This
Close an application and return to Windows	All	File | Exit		CTRL+F4
Close the current document	All	File | Close		ALT+F4
Find text in a document or file	All	Edit | Find		CTRL+F
Go to a page, section, line, etc.	All	Edit | Go To		CTRL+G
Open an existing document	All	File | Open		CRTL+O
Print an area or selected page	All	File | Print		CTRL+P

For Customizing Office

To Do This	In	Select This	Or Click This	Or Press This
Add buttons to or delete buttons from toolbars	All	Tools | Customize | Commands		
Attach templates or use wizards	All	Tools | Add-Ins		
Change the size of the screen display	All	View | Zoom | select magnification		
Choose the types of errors to be corrected	All	Tools | AutoCorrect | select types		
Display a toolbar	All	View | Toolbars | select toolbar		
Display data without page formatting	All except Access	View | Normal		
Duplicate a window	All except Access	Window | New Windows		
Set defaults for various functions	All	Tools | Options		
Set document properties	All	File | Properties		
Set page features	All	File | Page Setup		
Hide columns	Access	Format | Hide Columns		
Protect a database	Access	Tools | Security | select protection type		
Hide a row, column, or sheet	Excel	Format | Row/Column/Sheet | Hide		
Protect or share a workbook or sheet	Excel	Tools | Protection | select item		
Protect a file	Word	Tools | Protect Document | Enter a password		

Instant *Office 2000* Answers ...

For Integrating Office

To Do This	In	Select This	Or Click This	Or Press This
Edit a linked or embedded object	All	Edit | Links		
Edit a selected object	All except Access	Edit | Object		
Get help from the Internet	All	Help | Office On The Web | select item		
Save as a web page	All except Access	File | Save As Web Page		
Choose a format for exporting a file	Access	File | Export		
Produce large mailings	Access	Tools | Office Links | Merge It With MS Word		
Produce large mailings	Word	Tools | Mail Merge		

For Enhancing a Document

To Do This	In	Select This	Or Click This	Or Press This
Add a comment	All except Access	Insert | Comment	☐	
Check spelling	All	Tools | Spelling	☐	F7
Choose a font type and size	All	Format | Font		
Copy a hyperlink	All	Edit | Paste As Hyperlink		
Copy the clipboard contents to the current insertion point	All	Edit | Paste	☐	CTRL+V
Copy an OLE object	All	Edit | Paste Special		
Copy a selected item to the clipboard	All	Edit | Copy	☐	CTRL+C
Create or edit headers and footers	All except Access	View | Header And Footer		
Delete a selection	All except Access	Edit | Clear | Contents		DELETE
Insert a hyperlink to a URL or document	All	Insert | Hyperlink	☐	CTRL+K
Insert a picture	All except Access	Insert | Picture | select picture type		
Insert an object to be embedded	All	Insert | Object | select object or link		
Delete a row (record)	Access	Edit | Delete Record	☐	
Enter field names and data in tables	Access	View | Design View		
Insert a new record	Access	Insert | Record	☐	
Sort records	Access	Records | Sort | select A-Z or Z-A	☐	
Adjust page breaks	Excel	View | Page Break Preview		
Apply formatting to selected cells	Excel	Format | Cells | select format(s)	☐	CTRL+1
Create a PivotTable	Excel	Data | PivotTable And PivotChart Report		
Create a chart	Excel	Insert | Chart	☐	
Sort selected data	Excel	Data | Sort	☐	
Apply a style to selected text	Excel or Word	Format | Style | select style		
Apply automatic formatting	Excel or Word	Format | AutoFormat | select style		
Mark edits	Excel or Word	Tools | Track Changes | Highlight Changes		
Add a new slide to a presentation	PowerPoint	Insert | New Slide | select layout	☐	CTRL+M
Choose a new slide layout	PowerPoint	Format | Slide Layout	☐	
Sort slides	PowerPoint	View | Slide Sorter	☐	
Add borders and shading to paragraphs and pages	Word	Format | Borders And Shading | select borders and/or shading		
Add bullets or numbering to text	Word	Format | Bullets And Numbering	☐	
Address envelopes and labels	Word	Tools | Envelopes And Labels		
Change selected text to a table	Word	Table | Convert | Text To Table		
Format text in newspaper-type columns	Word	Format | Columns | select columns	☐	
Look up synonyms and antonyms	Word	Tools | Language | Thesaurus		SHIFT+F7
Sort paragraphs in a table or selection	Word	Table | Sort	☐	
Insert a date or time	Word or PowerPoint	Insert | Date And Time | select format		
Type text in an object	Word or PowerPoint	Insert | Text Box	☐	

Office 2000

Answers!

Office 2000

Answers!

Martin S. Matthews
Carole Boggs Matthews

Osborne/**McGraw-Hill**

Berkeley • New York • St. Louis • San Francisco
Auckland • Bogotá • Hamburg • London
Madrid • Mexico City • Milan • Montreal
New Delhi • Panama City • Paris • São Paulo
Singapore • Sydney • Tokyo • Toronto

Osborne/**McGraw-Hill**
2600 Tenth Street
Berkeley, California 94710
U.S.A.

For information on translations or book distributors outside the U.S.A., or to arrange bulk purchase discounts for sales promotions, premiums, or fund-raisers, please contact Osborne/**McGraw-Hill** at the above address.

Office 2000 Answers!

1234567890 DOC DOC 90198765432109

ISBN 0-07-211888-1

Publisher
Brandon A. Nordin

**Associate Publisher and
Editor-in-Chief**
Scott Rogers

Acquisitions Editor
Joanne Cuthbertson

Project Editor
Emily Rader

Editorial Assistant
Stephane Thomas

Technical Editor
John Cronin

Copy Editor
Andy Carroll

Proofreader
Linda Medoff

Indexer
Rebecca Plunkett

Computer Designers
Jani Beckwith
Roberta Steele
Gary Corrigan

Illustrators
Brian Wells
Beth Young
Robert Hansen

Series Design
Michelle Galicia

This book was published with Corel Ventura.

Contents

Acknowledgments

Patricia Shepard and John Cronan did significant amounts of writing for this book. Pat wrote Chapters 3 and 8, while John wrote Chapters 5 and 6. John also technically reviewed all parts of the book that he didn't write. Both Pat and John are authors in their own right, and we are very lucky to have had them work on this project. For this, for the ease with which we were able to work with them, and for their willingness to do whatever was necessary, we are most grateful. Thanks Pat and John!

The crew at Osborne, ably led by Joanne Cuthbertson in Acquisitions and Emily Rader in Editorial, with strong support from Stephane Thomas as Editorial Assistant, as always, made the project as easy as possible and in many instances even fun. Thanks Joanne, Emily, and Stephane!

Carole and Marty Matthews
April, 1999

Introduction

The Office suite not only includes from five to eight full-featured productivity applications (depending on the version), but also a number of utilities, all with many features, commands, and options. Office 2000 represents a new level of sophistication and maturity in many of its components. It is therefore natural that you'll have many questions about how to use what is there, as well as how to handle situations when things don't go quite right. Between almost nonexistent documentation, online Help that never quite answers the question you are asking, and the hours you can spend waiting on a toll phone line to get tech support from Microsoft, there is a great disparity between the questions being asked and the answers that are available. The purpose of this book is to fill that void.

The many real-world questions that are answered here came from a combination of the authors' and their associates' many years of using Office, plus many months of using Office 2000 beta and release candidates, in addition to Stream International's experience in providing tech support to Office 97 users since the release of Office 97. The authors have delved into virtually every nook and cranny of the product and experienced a great many of the problems first hand. As a result, they have located practically every source of answers and have referenced many of them here.

The book combines the "on the firing line" experience of a company providing tech support for Office 97 (and shortly for Office 2000) with about as much depth of experience in researching and using the product as you can have without actually being one of the programmers who wrote Office 2000 (and the authors have spent a lot of time talking to the people behind Office 2000).

Office 2000 Answers! is divided into 11 chapters, each of which covers a major subject. Within each chapter, the questions and answers are further divided into topics. To find a particular answer, use the Table of Contents to find the

central topic of your question. Then go right to that chapter and look at the headings and lists of specific question topics at the beginning of the chapter. You can also use the Index to alphabetically locate a topic that doesn't pop out at you in the Answer Topics at the beginning of each chapter.

Besides the questions and answers, there are many Tips, Notes, and supplementary sidebars throughout the book that give you insight into how best to do something that only considerable experience would otherwise bring. In addition to the Tips, Notes, and sidebars, there are a number of Cautions that point out actions that can cause considerable problems if you are not careful to avoid them. Each chapter has an introductory section labeled "@ a Glance." This section gives you an introduction to the chapter's subject and how to address the issues related to it. Reading all of the "@ a Glance" sections will give you a broad understanding of Office 2000 and answer many of your questions before you ask them.

CONVENTIONS USED IN THIS BOOK

Office 2000 Answers! uses several conventions designed to make the book easier for you to follow. Among these are the following:

- **Bold type** is used for text that you are to type from the keyboard.
- *Italic type* is used for terms or phrases that deserve special emphasis.
- Small capital letters are used for keys on the keyboard such as ENTER and SHIFT.

When you are expected to enter a command, you are told to press the key(s). If you are to enter text or numbers, you are told to type them.

Chapter 1

Top 10 Frequently Asked Questions

Answers Topics!

Top 10 FAQs @ a Glance

 This chapter presents ten of the most common questions that are asked about Outlook 2000. The questions address everyday tasks, as well as questions on new features.

1. How do I turn off the Office Assistant?

In Office 97, the Office Assistant could be disabled or hidden, but pressing F1 or using Help would bring it back. In Office 2000, the Office Assistant allows you to select when the Assistant will appear. Follow these steps:

1. Right-click the Office Assistant and select Options from the context menu, as shown here:

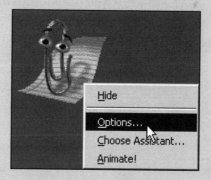

2. Select the Options tab. You will see the dialog box shown here:

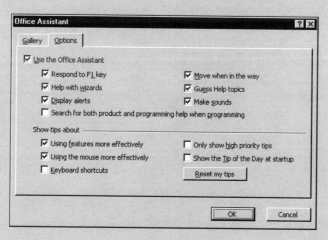

3. Remove the check marks next to the situations for which you do not want the Office Assistant to appear.

4. Click OK when you have finished.

✚   ***Tip:***   *To completely hide the Office Assistant, clear the Use The Office Assistant check box. You can turn the Assistant back on by selecting Show Office Assistant from the Help menu.*

2. Whenever I type text that follows a period or text that I want to display in a list in lowercase only, the first character is automatically capitalized. Why is this? How can I avoid automatic capitalization?

The default setting is uppercase for the initial character in text at the beginning of sentences and text at the beginning of lines. This is a feature of AutoCorrect. To turn off this feature, follow these steps:

1. Choose AutoCorrect from the Tools menu.

2. Select the AutoCorrect tab.

3. Click the option Capitalize First Letter of Sentence (or Sentences, in Word) to remove the check mark from the box, as shown here, and click OK.

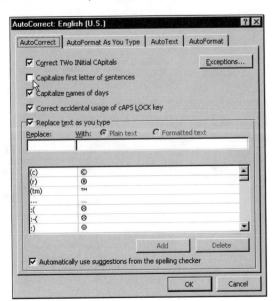

3. When I click a menu, some of the commands are not shown, and then they appear after I have held the menu open for a few seconds. Why don't all the commands on a menu appear when the menu is first opened?

A new feature of Office 2000 personalizes menus by "learning" which menu commands you use most often and placing those commands most prominently on the menu. When you first open a menu, you will see the commands you use most often. If you hold the menu open for a few seconds, or if you place the mouse pointer or click the double down arrows on the bottom of the menu, as shown here:

the menu will expand, showing the rest of the commands, as shown here:

You can change this behavior with the steps listed next.

1. Right-click a menu bar or toolbar, and select Customize from the menu. Click the Options tab, as shown here:

2. To void the new menu personalization feature, clear the check mark before Menus Show Recently Used Commands First.

3. To only show the most recently used commands until the double arrow is clicked, clear the check mark before Show Full Menus After A Short Delay.

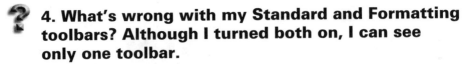

4. What's wrong with my Standard and Formatting toolbars? Although I turned both on, I can see only one toolbar.

Even though you may have selected to display both toolbars in the View | Toolbars dialog box, a new default in Office 2000 combines the two toolbars to give you more space to display your document. However, in doing so, more of the toolbar buttons are hidden, available by clicking the down arrow at the end of the toolbar. If you use many of the toolbar buttons, you may prefer to display the two toolbars separately to have more buttons showing. To turn off the sharing of the toolbars, follow these steps:

1. Click View | Toolbars | Customize and click the Options tab.

2. Remove the check mark before Standard And Formatting Toolbars Share One Row.

5. How does Excel 2000 treat Y2K dates?

Years can be expressed either with four digits, such as 2001, or with two digits, such as 01. Excel makes assumptions when handling dates. Excel assumes the two-digit years 00 through 29 are the years 2000 through 2029. Excel assumes the two-digit years 30 through 99 are the years 1930 through 1999. So the date 03/17/44 will be March 17, 1944, while 04/05/10 will be April 05, 2010. To ensure that your dates are handled accurately, use four-digit years, such as 2025.

Note: *If you are using Windows 95 or earlier, or Windows NT 4.0 or earlier, you can have your system administrator change Excel's date assumptions by specifying the earliest date that belongs to the 1900s. The 30 through 99 can be changed to 50 through 99, for instance. This information is in the Microsoft Office Resource Kit. If you have Windows 98 or Windows 2000, you can change it yourself. Select Start | Settings | Control Panel. Double-click Regional Settings (in Windows 2000, double-click Regional Options) and click the Date tab. Then enter the upper limit for the century next to When A Two-Digit Year Is Entered, Interpret As A Year Between box.*

In dealing with inexact dates, such as *September 9*, Excel assumes that the numbers 1 through 31 are days of the month, so this example will be interpreted as September 9 of the current year, not September 2009. However, numbers greater than 31 are treated as years, so September 50 becomes September 1, 1950.

6. How does Access 2000 convert files from and to different versions?

To create an environment in which multiple versions of Access can operate at the same time, Access 2000 allows you either to read but not edit an older version of an Access database or to convert the older database to Access 2000. To

read it only, open the file using File | Open and then find and select the file. You will be informed that you must convert the file in order to edit it. When you click OK to acknowledge the message, shown here, the older database will be available for you to look at.

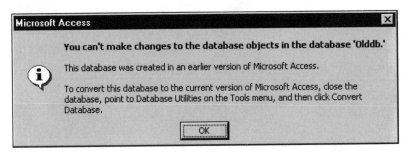

To convert a previous version of an Access database to Access 2000, follow these steps:

1. Select Tools | Database Utilities | Convert Database | To Current Access Database Version.

2. Find the file to be converted, click it, and click Convert. You may be told to enter a new name. Click OK.

3. In the Convert Database Into dialog box, type the new filename and click Save. Depending on the size, it may take several minutes to convert the database. You will know it has finished when the hourglass icon returns to the pointer icon.

4. Select File | Open. Select the new filename and click Open. The new database will be opened. You can now use the database with all the features of Access 2000.

When converting to a previous version, Access 2000 will only convert a database to Access 97, one previous version. You perform this with similar steps: select Tools | Database Utilities | Convert Database. Then select To Prior Access Database Version. Again, you'll be prompted to provide a location to save it to, and you'll be prompted for a different name—you can't use the same name as the Access 2000

version of the database if you save it in the same file folder. You can use the same name, however, if you change the folder name.

You should be aware that when you convert to an older version, some features will not be supported. Access 97, for example, does not support data access pages in the same way that Access 2000 does. Access 97 requires that you install either the Microsoft Personal Web Server (MSPWS) or Internet Information Service (IIS), as well as Active Server Pages (ASP) on your computer before you can create data access pages, Access 2000's name for active server pages. The pages are not stored directly in the database, so you will be unable to view or manipulate them in the same way you do in Access 2000. This technology was still new at the time Access 97 was released and many of the kinks had not been worked out, so the process of creating them in Access 97 is both more complicated and less stable.

Also, any code you have in your database may not function properly after converting it. This can happen because you referred to objects or files not stored or existing on your system, such as functions that come from other databases or dynamic link libraries (DLLs). This can complicate the process of converting the database, and there is no easy way to work around it. You may need to fix the code as it breaks, line by line. Fortunately, the tools Access 97 has for working with code are efficient and should help with this process.

7. I see a new item on the Help menus called Detect and Repair. What does it do?

The Detect and Repair function performs a check of the active program files, searching for corrupted, outdated, or missing files. Although the programs also perform self-checking as they are loaded, Detect and Repair is more thorough. Here's how you use it:

1. From the expanded Help menu, select Detect and Repair. The dialog box shown here will be displayed.

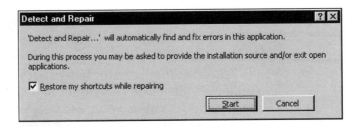

2. Click Start and the whole application will be scanned for problems.

3. You may be asked for the source of Office 2000—your CD-ROM, for instance. You may also be asked to close certain features or programs that are open.

3. When the Detect and Repair operation is finished, you will be asked to restart your computer. Click Yes to restart it now, or No if you want to do it later.

 Tip: *You can also repair program files from Start | Settings | Control Panel. You then double-click Add / Remove Programs, select Microsoft Office 2000 from the list of options, click Add / Remove, and click Repair Office.*

8. I've gotten my Office applications to look and work the way that's best for me. Will installing Office 2000 overwrite all my settings?

The Office 2000 setup program will do its best to retain your user settings. It compares the original default settings against your current settings, analyzes the differences, and carries them over to Office 2000. Settings that have not changed will be replaced with the new defaults for them in Office 2000.

9. If I give or send a Word or Excel 2000 file to someone who has Office 97, will they be able to open it?

Yes. With the exception of Access, Office 97 programs can read Office 2000 documents without converters. Access 2000 files will have to be saved as Access 97 files from Access 2000 to be read by Access 97 (see the earlier question "How does Access 2000 convert files from and to different versions?").

Office 2000 is backward compatible with Office 97 and uses the same file structure. However, any new features in Office 2000 will not be available when you open that file in Office 97, although features will be matched as closely as possible. Also, if you send an Office 2000 file to someone with an Office version prior to 97, he or she will be unable to open it.

To read a Word or Excel 2000 document with a version prior to Office 97, you must first save it in the earlier format, such as Word 6.0/95 (*.doc) format. An alternative is to install a Word or Excel 2000 converter that will allow you to open and edit documents created in either Word or Excel 2000 or Word or Excel 97. Some converters can be found on the Office 2000 CD.

To get a Word or Excel converter from the CD, follow these steps:

1. Select Start | Settings | Control Panel and double-click Add/Remove Programs.

2. Select Microsoft Office 2000 from the listed software on the Install/Uninstall tab. Click Add/Remove.

3. On the Microsoft Office 2000 Maintenance Mode dialog box, click Add Or Remove Features.

4. Beside Converters And Filters, click the plus sign (+) to get a list of the converters and filters available on the CD. Click Text Converters to display another list, as shown here:

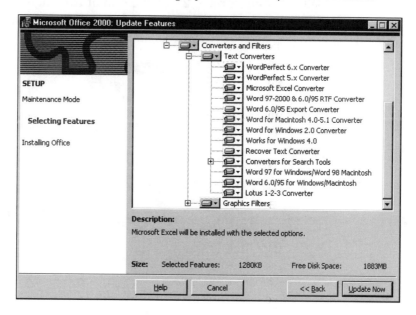

5. Click the converter you want to install, and select the method you want to use to install it: Run From My Computer, Run All From My Computer, Run From CD, Run All From CD, or Installed On First Use.

6. Click Update Now.

7. Click OK when the installation is complete and click OK again to clear the Add/Remove Programs Properties dialog box.

Tip: *Other converters can be found on the Office On The Web site accessible from your Help menu.*

10. In Word, how do I print just one page in landscape orientation? Only page 3 of my document should be printed that way, and all the others should print in portrait orientation.

To print only one page with a different orientation, you must insert a continuous page break on the page preceding the change and then redefine the page orientation for the page with the different orientation. Follow these steps to do it:

1. On the page before the landscape orientation (in this case, page 2), at the end of the page, select Break from the Insert menu, and then Continuous under Section Break Types, as shown here:

2. Click OK.

3. On the page to be printed in landscape (page 3, in this case), select Page Setup from the File menu, and then click the Paper Size tab.

4. Click Landscape, as shown here, and click OK.

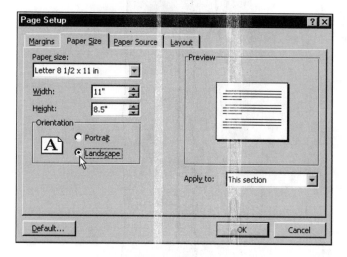

 Tip: *To view the landscape orientation onscreen, select Print Layout from the View menu. The header and footer for that page will remain the same as for the pages in portrait orientation.*

Chapter 2

Getting Started with Office 2000

Answer Topics!

Getting Started with Office 2000 @ a Glance

You will find that Office 2000 provides many new and useful features, such as its ability to save a document in HTML format, thereby enabling anyone with a browser to view it, and then to edit it in HTML format with Word 2000. Each of the Office 2000 components can now access information more directly and with greater facility. New tools, such as the PivotTable and PivotChart, tie together data from Excel, Access, and SQL Server so that data can be analyzed and manipulated with greater ease. Other new features enhance your ability to manage data, such as Collect and Paste, which lets you copy or cut 12 different objects onto the Clipboard and then paste them individually or as a group; Self-Repairing installation, which automatically repairs missing or accidentally deleted files for you; and Floating Tables, with which you can wrap text around tables placed where you need them. This chapter explores the questions you will most likely ask in these areas:

Office 2000 Comes in Four Versions outlines the four Office 2000 packages that are available (the Premium, Small Business, Professional, and Standard Editions) and the programs that each package comes with.

Installing Office 2000 describes situations you may encounter while you are installing Office 2000, and answers questions you may have about the implications of installing it.

Customizing User Interfaces covers some ways that you can change Office 2000 to match your own personal needs.

File Handling and Compatibility describes how you can ensure your older files are compatible with Office 2000.

Using Help and the Office Assistant explains ways that you can make the most out of the Help system in Office 2000.

Miscellaneous describes two situations involving recording macros and creating a custom dictionary that you may encounter.

OFFICE 2000 COMES IN FOUR VERSIONS

You can now choose between four versions of Office 2000: Premium Edition, Small Business Edition, Professional Edition, and Standard Edition. Table 2-1 shows the contents of each edition. You would choose the Standard Edition for the basic applications of Word 2000 for word processing, Excel 2000 for spreadsheets, Outlook 2000 for e-mail and messaging, and PowerPoint 2000 for creating presentations. The Small Business Edition is the same as the Standard Edition except that PowerPoint 2000 is replaced by Publisher 2000 for desktop publishing. With the Professional Edition, you'll find all the standard applications of the Standard Edition, as well as Access 2000 for databases and Publisher 2000, but not PhotoDraw 2000 for graphics or FrontPage 2000 for web design. Finally, the Premium Edition includes all applications within Office 2000, including FrontPage 2000 and PhotoDraw 2000.

Office 2000 contains up to eight applications:

- **Word 2000**　Used for word processing tasks, such as writing letters, brochures, manuals, reports, or other text-related documents. There are too many new features included in Office 2000 to list them all; however, some of the more exciting are as follows: more integration with Outlook and web technology so that documents sent as e-mail are HTML compatible and thereby are capable of being saved to a web site or read by a browser; automatic formatting, which lets you double-click on a page and begin typing while Word 2000 corrects the paragraph and space formatting; automatic page sizing, which lets you print pages to scale for different sizes of paper; personalized menus that revise themselves by placing more frequently used commands in the more accessible locations; Collect and Paste, which allows you to collect up to 12 different cut or copied objects and paste them all at once or singularly; text wraparound graphics; and the ability to treat tables as floating, nested, and side by side.

- **Excel 2000**　Used for spreadsheet tasks, in which working with columns and rows of data allows you to more easily analyze, sort, chart, and otherwise work with numbers.

Application	Standard Edition	Small Business Edition	Professional Edition	Premium Edition
Microsoft Word 2000 for word processing	Yes	Yes	Yes	Yes
Microsoft Excel 2000 for creating spreadsheets	Yes	Yes	Yes	Yes
Microsoft Outlook 2000 for messaging and network collaboration	Yes	Yes	Yes	Yes
Microsoft Publisher 2000 for desktop publishing	No	Yes	Yes	Yes
Microsoft PowerPoint 2000 for creating presentation programs	Yes	No	Yes	Yes
Microsoft Access 2000 for creating and managing databases	No	No	Yes	Yes
Microsoft FrontPage 2000 for creating and handling web sites	No	No	No	Yes
Microsoft PhotoDraw 2000 for creating graphics	No	No	No	Yes

Table 2-1   Contents of Office 2000 Editions

New with Office 2000 is the ability to save Excel files in HTML format so that users can view them with a browser. With enhanced web support, you can drag and drop table data from a browser into Excel 2000 and back again. You can save the data as a web page for interactive or static viewing. Improved PivotTable features allow you to drag fields from a worksheet to a PivotTable, format it, and create refreshable charts with PivotChart. The AutoFill feature automatically fills in formats and formulas as data is added to a list. Other improvements include year 2000 enhancements, AutoFill lists, different cursors for visual aids about the worksheet, and improved charts.

● **Access 2000**   Used for database tasks, when you must organize data—either simple lists or very complex relational databases involving multiple linked tables and databases. New in Access 2000 is the ability to save database data into HTML files, which can be manipulated with Access 2000 and then saved, edited,

and reported using a web browser. Using *data access pages*, a new feature in Access 2000, you can create a web page that retrieves data from a database. SQL Server support has been enhanced; for example, Access 2000 can be used as the interface to a SQL Server database, and server-side objects (such as tables, views, and database diagrams) can be created and handled using Access. Other enhancements include the ability to compact databases as they are closed and to drag and drop Access objects into Excel, support for earlier versions of Access, global AutoCorrect for field name changes, and conditional formatting (such as less than, greater than, equal to, and between). (Access 2000 is available only with the Premium and Professional Editions.)

● **Outlook 2000** Outlook is an information manager for organizing your appointments, calls, messages, name lists, and tasks. It provides a central place where faxes and intranet and Internet messages can be viewed; provides a scheduling calendar that reminds you of appointments and to-do tasks; and includes a place to store address files, which can be grouped and organized according to your needs. E-mail messages can be sent as HTML text so they can be easily read with any HTML-compliant reader (including Microsoft Outlook Express, Eudora, and some Lotus and Netscape products). A preview pane can be used to quickly look inside attachments and hyperlinks in HTML. Calendar and scheduling features now can publish team calendars as a web page; show free and busy times in contrasting colors; print daily, weekly, and monthly appointments; and allow you to pick times from free time schedule slots with an improved meeting planner. The Contacts feature allows you to view all activity related to one person, such as e-mail, tasks, appointments, and documents. An enhanced mail merge allows you to filter Outlook 2000 contacts for use in Microsoft Word 2000 mail merges. Finally, you can include shortcuts to any file, folder, or web page in the Outlook bar.

● **PowerPoint 2000**   A multimedia tool for creating presentations, from simple overhead slides to powerful sound and video presentations with animated graphics. PowerPoint 2000 includes a slide finder for finding slides in other presentations, speaker notes for providing notes to accompany individual slides, enhanced animation tools for creating custom motion effects, custom shows for displaying selected slides within a presentation, action buttons that let you jump to any slide, narration features for recording voices slide by slide, the ability to play CDs during presentations, and more.

● **FrontPage 2000**   Available for the first time in the Premium and Professional Editions, this tool is used for creating and managing web sites. In addition to its integration with other applications, it offers enhanced web features for collaboration with others. It has many new features, including the following: added control over web pages with custom themes; dynamic hypertext markup language (DHTML) animation; precise positioning and layering of graphics, text, and other objects, and custom colors; added HTML editing; and integration with Access 2000 data. FrontPage 2000 makes use of the new web components (Spreadsheet, PivotTable, and Chart). It also uses the Microsoft Script Editor for working with scripts, including JavaScript and Microsoft Visual Basic Scripting Edition.

● **PhotoDraw 2000**   Used for creating business graphics by both novices and sophisticated users. The graphics can be used in FrontPage, PowerPoint, Word, Publisher, or other programs. They can be used with TWAIN digital cameras and scanners, and PhotoDraw allows you to export and import in many different formats.

● **Publisher 2000**   Allows you to create brochures, manuscripts, and other documents for publishing. It includes over 2000 design templates to help you produce a range of publications, from the quick and easy one-page flyer, to a sophisticated multipage publication.

The power of Office 2000 lies not only in the comprehensiveness of each application, but in how they

are integrated. Some of the ways this integration is achieved are listed here:

- *Common user interfaces,* including common keyboard commands and similar-looking menus, shortcuts, and toolbars, tie the applications together. When you have learned one application, you know much about how to use the others. Office 2000 offers personalized menus wherein the most frequently used commands are displayed on the menus. All the toolbars can be customized, placing the commands you want where you want them.

- *Web integration* has been really improved in Office 2000. Using Office 2000 and the web interface, you can create and maintain documents, procedures, and other objects using the Internet or an intranet, saving you time, effort, and resources. However, this is just the beginning. You'll find that the web becomes a part of the way you do business, whether it is scheduling meetings, sharing documents (such as an internal procedures manual), or collaborating on a project or presentation. By creating hypertext markup language (HTML) documents from any of the Office 2000 applications, you can immediately post them on a web site making them available to anyone using a web browser. New web components (Spreadsheet, PivotTables, and Chart) add functionality and simplicity to the process of creating and maintaining web sites. A Web Page Preview command lets you see how your document will look with a browser before you save it.

- *Shared tools* also give a common feel to the separate applications. For instance, Spelling Checker and AutoCorrect allow you to specify custom settings that are available to all the applications. The Clip Gallery and Graph packages provide common clipart and graphing features to Office applications, just as Office Art gives consistent drawing and art capability to Word, Excel, and PowerPoint. These are just some of the shared tools in Office 2000.

- *Data compatibility* enables you to cut and copy data from one application and paste it into another. The new Collect and Paste feature lets you copy up to 12 groups of text or graphics and then paste them all together or individually into another application— this applies to documents, spreadsheets, e-mail, web pages, presentations, or other files. For example, you can copy an Excel chart and an Access table from the Office Clipboard into a Word document or a PowerPoint presentation concurrently.

- *Comprehensive help* comes in several flavors. First is the typical Help system available with each application for looking up subjects. The HTML-based Office Assistant Help system is enhanced in Office 2000; it monitors what you are doing, tries to guess what you are trying to do, and offers tips on how to proceed. If you don't see the tip you need, you can type your own question and get a list of options as it tries to interpret what you have asked. Finally, you can ask for online Help directly from Microsoft's Home Page. You are given a list of destinations for the most likely topics you might seek online Help for.

- *Linking and embedding data,* another way of integrating the applications, allows you to share data between files. Linking connects one file, or object within a file, to another. The connected file or object is displayed as part of the other file. The displayed object is actually the original file or object, not a copy. Therefore, when a linked file is updated, the updates are automatically reflected in the file containing the link. For instance, if you link a spreadsheet to a Word document, you don't have to remember to update the numbers in both documents. Embedding, on the other hand, inserts a copy of another object. When the original of that object is updated, the embedded copy is not updated.

- *Office Binder* lets you keep all the files related to the project in a binder that is available to all members of a project team. The binder contents can be revised and

contributed to by many individuals, each uniquely identified. Schedules can be tracked and the project's progress can be monitored, because all team members share the contents of the binder. The Office Binder is not part of the Typical Installation and must be installed manually.

 Visual Basic for Applications, the macro and programming language, can be used throughout Office to build short macros or complex applications based on the powerful Office applications.

INSTALLING OFFICE 2000

How much disk space do I need to install Office 2000?

The space you need for Office 2000 will vary depending on the product you select and the installation process you use. Here are the requirements:

Installation Process	Disk Space Required	RAM Required
Standard Edition	189MB for Word, Excel, Outlook, and PowerPoint	4MB to run each individual application simultaneously; 8MB for Outlook
Small Business Edition, Typical	178MB for Word, Excel, Outlook; 182MB for Publisher and Small Business Tools	4MB to run each individual application simultaneously; 8MB for Outlook
Professional Edition, Typical	217MB for Word Excel, Outlook, PowerPoint, and Access; 174MB for Publisher and Small Business Tools	4MB to run each individual application simultaneously; 8MB for Outlook or Access

Installation Process	Disk Space Required	RAM Required
Premium Edition, Typical	252MB for Word, Excel, Outlook, PowerPoint, Access, and FrontPage; 174MB for Publisher and Small Business Tools; and 100MB for PhotoDraw (plus an additional 100MB of free hard disk space for graphics and temporary image caches) is recommended	4MB to run each individual application simultaneously; 8MB for Outlook, Access, and FrontPage; and 16MB for PhotoDraw

By using a custom installation, you can decrease the disk space requirements to some extent, depending on which applications and components you really need. If you are low on disk space, you can experiment with selecting different components. You might, for example, delay installing components you are not sure you'll use until you really need them, and then install them using Add/Remove Programs on the Control Panel.

Note: *You will also need up to 100MB of free disk space for temporary storage on an ongoing basis in order for Office 2000 to operate optimally.*

When you choose a custom installation (and if you later seek to reinstall some or all the options), you will be given the chance to selectively install applications in several ways. The choices you have are shown in Figure 2-1 (the network choices are only available if you are connected to a network):

● **Run From My Computer**   Install the programs for this feature on your hard disk where it will be available for use.

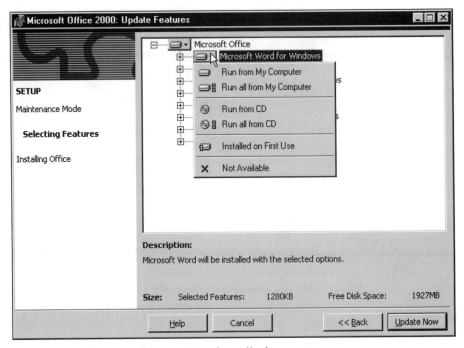

Figure 2-1   Choices in a custom installation

- **Run All From My Computer**   Install the programs for this feature and its subfeatures on your hard disk where they will be available for use.

- **Run From Network**   Set this option to run from the network server. The programs will not be written to your hard disk. Rather, when you use this feature, it will be retrieved from the network server, which will have to remain available.

- **Run All From Network**—Set this option and its subfeatures to run from the network server. The programs will not be written to your hard disk. Rather, when you use this feature, it will be retrieved from the network server, which will have to remain available.

- **Run From CD**   Set this feature to run from a CD. This option requires that the CD was originally used to install Office 2000. The programs for this feature will not be written on your hard disk. When you need this feature, it will be accessed from the CD, not your disk.

- **Run All From CD**   Set this feature and all its subfeatures to run from a CD. This option requires that the CD was originally used to install Office 2000. The programs for this feature and its subfeatures will not be written on your hard disk. When you need this feature, it will be accessed from the CD, not your disk.

- **Installed On First Use**   Install this option later when you first try to use it. This is not available for all features, and when you want to install it later, you will need either the CD or access to the network server on which you originally got Office 2000.

- **Not Available**   Do not install. You can, however, install this option at a later date.

Tip: *If you are really short on disk space, you can run Office from the CD, albeit more slowly. To do this, select Run From CD as the type of installation when you select the custom installation specifics.*

I installed too much. Now my disk space is too cramped and I have several Office components, such as the Equation Editor, that I never use. How can I remove some of the Office components without affecting the others?

You will need to run Setup again and allow Microsoft Office to uninstall the components you do not want. To do this, follow these steps:

Tip: *If you have Office applications running, you should close them before continuing. If you don't, Setup will halt the process to suggest that you do.*

1. From the Start menu, select Settings and then Control Panel.

2. Double-click Add/Remove Programs. The Add/Remove Programs Properties dialog box will be displayed.

3. On the Install/Uninstall tab, select the Microsoft Office 2000 program, as shown here:

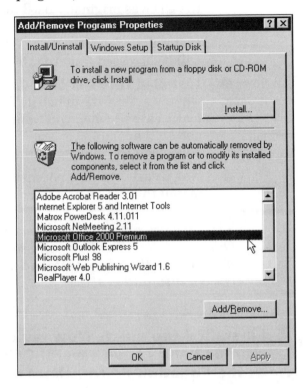

Click Add/Remove. The Microsoft Office 2000 Setup will begin.

4. Click Add Or Remove Features in the Microsoft Office 2000 Maintenance Mode dialog box to get a list of installed components.

5. In the Microsoft Office 2000:Update Features dialog box, click the plus (+) sign to the left of the feature you want, such as Office Tools (shown here), to get a list of the components:

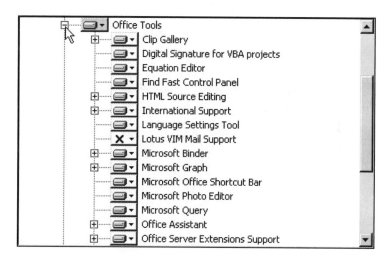

6. Click the symbol next to the item you want to delete, such as the Equation Editor. Select Not Available to remove it from your installed options. An × will replace the symbol of the installed feature.

7. When you have finished selecting all of the features to be removed, click Update Now. You will soon see a message that Office 2000 Setup completed successfully.

8. Click OK. Click OK again to close the Add/Remove dialog box.

Is Office 2000 Y2K compliant?

Yes. Specifically, Microsoft says that the Office 2000 office suite meets "Microsoft standards" for year-2000 issues. Read about what this entails and how you can prepare at http://www.microsoft.com/magazine/guide2000/ms/y2k-res.htm or at http://officeupdate.microsoft.com/default.htm.

 Our company is using several versions of Word (Word 6, 95, and 97). We want to start using Office 2000 but are concerned about losing files created in these earlier versions of Word. How do we handle this?

Documents created with earlier versions of Word are handled in these ways:

- Word 2000 can read all of these earlier versions with no problems. All formatting is retained while it is being read.

- Word 2000 can save these documents in their original formats, or can change them to the Word 2000 format, depending on how you save them. You request the Save As Type that you want when you save it. When you save the document in its original format, the formatting that has been added by Word 2000 is replaced with formatting supported by the original versions.

- Documents saved as Word 2000 format can still be read by Word 97, but not by Word 95 or Word 6.

- To read a Word 2000 document with Word 95 or 6 that has been opened and edited by Word 2000, you must first save it in Word 6.0/95 (*.doc) format. An alternative is to install a Word 2000 converter that will allow you to open and edit documents created in either Word 2000 or Word 97. The Word 2000 converter can be found on the Office 2000 CD.

 Note: *If you have files created by a different version of the same program, you may need a converter to open and work with the document. If you don't have Office at all, you can use a viewer to read the Office documents. You can find instructions for downloading converters and viewers from the web site in the "I need to transmit some of my Office documents to someone who doesn't have Office installed . . ." question, later in this chapter under "File Handling and Compatibility."*

To get a converter from the CD-ROM, follow these steps:

1. From the Start menu, select Settings and then Control Panel.

2. Double-click Add/Remove Programs.

3. Select Microsoft Office 2000 from the listed software on the Install/Uninstall tab. Click Add/Remove.

4. On the Microsoft Office 2000 Maintenance Mode dialog box, click Add Or Remove Features.

5. Beside Converters And Filters, click the plus sign (+) to get a list of the converters and filters available on the CD, as shown in Figure 2-2. Click Text Converters to get a further list.

6. Click the converter you want to install, and select the method you want to use to install it: Run From My Computer, Run All From My Computer, Run From CD, Run All From CD, or Installed On First Use.

Proceed by following the installation instructions that are displayed.

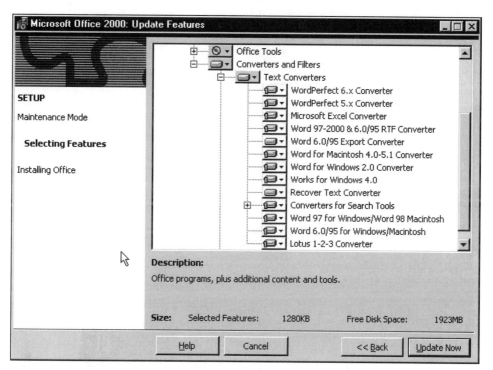

Figure 2-2 Converters available from the Office 2000 CD-ROM

 I need to continue using a prior version of Microsoft Office with some of my documents. Will Office 2000 overwrite my older version?

Only if you want it to. The default location for both Office 97 and 2000 is C:\Program Files\Microsoft Office, and for Office 95 it is C:\Msoffice. During installation, you will be asked if you want to change the folder name for storing Office programs, as shown in Figure 2-3. You can specify a folder name that is different from the previous installation. If you do not change the folder name, after pressing Next you will see a list of the programs that Setup will remove from your computer. If you want to retain the programs, press Back and change the folder name, and then press Next again. If you

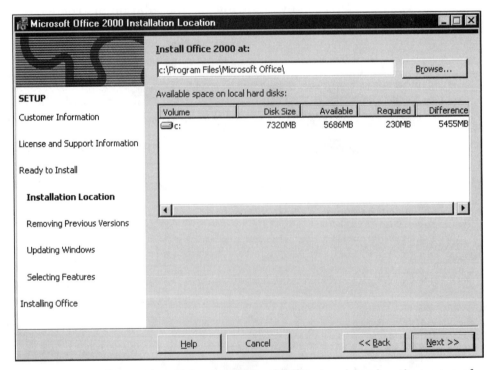

Figure 2-3 Preserving older versions of Office by changing the name of the folder that will contain Office 2000

choose not to change the folder name, your previous Office programs will be removed and replaced with Office 2000. Your data files will remain unchanged regardless of the method you use.

Caution: *The default (and the recommended way to install) is for Office 2000 to replace any older versions of Office, preserving the data files and user settings such as those in AutoCorrect. If you want to retain a previous installation of Office, you must change the folder name when asked.*

I have Windows 3.1. Must I upgrade to Windows 98 to install Office 2000?

Yes. Office 2000 only works with Windows 95, 98, NT 4, and 2000. However, if you are using Windows 95 or Windows NT Workstation 4, you must download service pack #3 or later, which will give you the full capability of Office 2000. You can do this by clicking Help | Office On The Web and then selecting the appropriate choice.

Tip: *Disable any virus-detection utilities you may have before installing Office 2000. These programs often use changes in system files to activate corrective procedures. If they detect a program being installed, they could halt or otherwise disrupt the installation procedure.*

CUSTOMIZING USER INTERFACES

How can I create a new menu on my menu bar for tasks I do repeatedly for a project I'm working on?

To create a menu and place it on the menu bar, follow these steps:

1. Open the Office application that you want to add the new menu to.

2. Right-click the menu bar or any toolbar (except the Office toolbar), and choose Customize from the context menu:

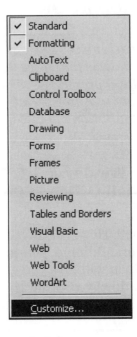

3. Select the Commands tab.

4. Select New Menu from the Categories list, and then select New Menu in the Commands list, as shown here:

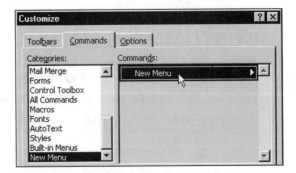

5. Drag the New Menu item to the menu bar on which you want the new menu.

6. To rename the menu, right-click the new menu and drag the cursor over the New Menu name. Type in the name you want.

7. In the Categories side of the Customize dialog box, select the items you want on the menu (for a list of macros, select Macros, and so on). Drag the specific commands you want from the Commands list on the right side of the dialog box and place them in the menu where you want them.

8. When you have finished placing the menu items, click Close. Here is an example of a custom menu named Web Tasks that was created this way:

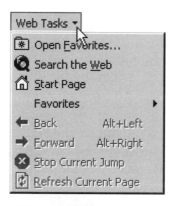

Tip: *You can move the menu's items from one spot to another by dragging them. First make sure that the Customize dialog box is open, and then click the pointer on the item, wait for a second until a rectangle appears, and move the rectangle to where you want the item placed.*

I want to create a new toolbar for my own tasks. How do I do this?

To customize or create a new toolbar for Office, follow these steps:

1. Right-click one of the toolbars or the menu bar and choose Customize from the context menu. (You can also select Customize from the Tools menu.)

2. On the Toolbars tab, click New to create a new toolbar.

3. In the New Toolbar dialog box, shown next, type a name for the toolbar. (In Word, you also need to select the template you want to attach it to.) Click OK.

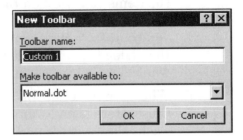

4. Drag the toolbar to where you want it on the menu bar or toolbar.

5. Click the Commands tab of the Customize dialog box to select the buttons you want to add to the toolbar.

6. To select a button, click one of the Categories on the left of the dialog box and then one of the Commands listed on the right. When you select a command, you can see its description by clicking the Description button, as shown here:

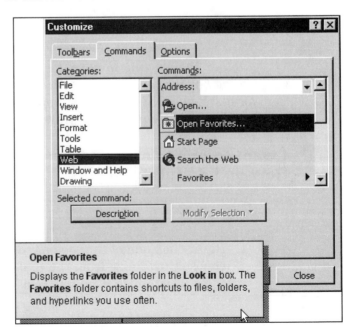

7. To modify the toolbar, you can perform any of these actions:

- To add a button, drag the button from the Commands list to the toolbar.

- To delete a button from the toolbar, drag it off the toolbar and release the mouse button, making sure you don't drop it onto another toolbar.

- To copy a button on the toolbar to another toolbar, press CTRL while dragging the button to another toolbar.

- To change the appearance of a button, either click the button and then click the Modify Selection button on the Commands tab, or right-click the button. Choose either Edit Button Image or Change Button Image to alter its appearance. (See the following explanation in "Modifying a Toolbar Button" for more details.)

- To change the size of a toolbar, place the mouse pointer on the edge of the toolbar and drag it to the size you want.

8. When you have finished changing the toolbar, click Close.

Modifying a Toolbar Button

When you select Modify Selection from the Customize dialog box, or right-click a button, a menu is displayed with options for changing buttons on a toolbar, as shown in Figure 2-4.

- **Reset**   Restores the original buttons to a toolbar, if it has been modified.

- **Delete**   Removes a button from the toolbar.

- **Name**   Allows you to type over and change the displayed name of the toolbar.

- **Copy Button Image**   Copies the image of the button into the Clipboard.

- **Paste Button Image**   Places the image on the Clipboard onto the selected button.

- **Reset Button Image**   Restores the original image to the button.

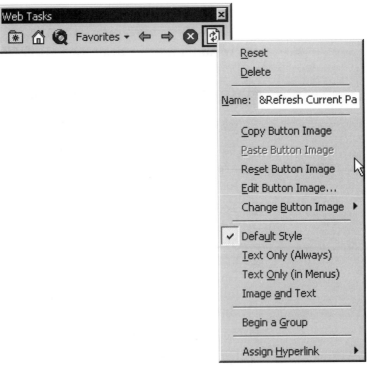

Figure 2-4 The Modify Selection context menu offers choices for changing toolbars

● **Edit Button Image** Changes the appearance of a button directly by altering the pixels of the image, as shown here:

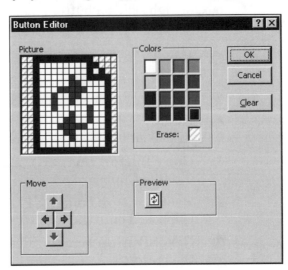

You can change the color by clicking a color under the Colors label, and then clicking the Picture "pixels" that you want to be that color. You can remove the colors from the pixels, one at a time, by clicking Erase and then clicking the pixels. You can clear all the pixels by clicking Clear. (If you click Cancel, the Button Editor closes and the button returns to its original image.) You can move the entire design up, down, right, or left by clicking the arrow keys in the Move box. Preview shows you what the button will look like in its normal size on the toolbar.

- **Change Button Image**   Displays a selection of images, as shown next. You can choose one of these images for a button by clicking the image to select it.

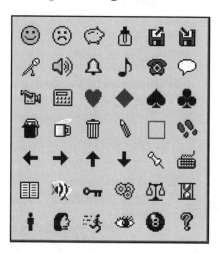

- **Default Style**   Displays the button in the default style, usually an image.

- **Text Only (Always)**   Always displays a text label for the button in toolbars or menus.

- **Text Only (In Menus)**   Always displays a text label for the button in menus.

- **Image And Text**   Displays both an image and text.

- **Begin A Group**   Groups menu commands together by placing a divider on the toolbar, to the left of the button.

- **Assign Hypertext**   Allows you to assign a web address to the selected button.

● **Assign Macro** In Excel only, opens the Assign Macro dialog box so that you can choose a macro for the toolbar.

● **Properties** In Access only, opens the toolbar's Control Properties dialog box, which lists properties for each selected button (or control) in the toolbar.

How do I make a toolbar button for an existing macro?

Placing an existing macro on a currently displayed toolbar involves several steps, depending on the application.

Placing a Macro Button on a Toolbar in Excel

In Excel, you must first place an unassigned macro icon on the toolbar, and then assign the icon to the macro of your choice. Then you can modify the icon's appearance as you wish. Follow these steps:

1. Make sure the toolbar you want to modify is currently displayed on the screen. If it isn't, display it by selecting Toolbars from the View menu, and clicking the name of the toolbar you want to display.

2. From the Tools menu, select Customize.

3. On the Commands tab, find Macros in the Categories list box, shown here:

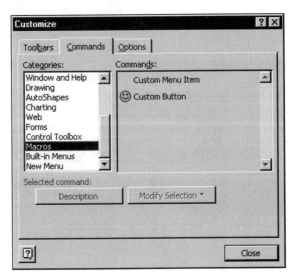

4. Drag the smiley-face macro icon from the Commands list to a blank spot on the toolbar where you want your own macro icon to appear; the mouse pointer will appear to be dragging a small rectangle. A plus sign in the rectangle signals that you can now drop the image, as shown here, while an × tells you that you cannot place the image at the current site:

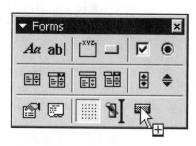

5. After you have dropped the image, the Modify Selection button will be available on the Commands tab (if it is not, click on the smiley-face icon on the toolbar). Click Modify Selection, and a menu will appear.

6. To change the name of the custom icon, select the &Custom Button name and type in your own macro name.

7. Select Assign Macro to transfer your own macro functions to the custom button. A list of your macros will be displayed. Select the one you want for the button, and click OK.

8. To change the appearance of the macro icon, click the Modify Selection button to display the menu again. Select from the following options to change the appearance:

   ● **Text Only**   Displays only the label on the button

   ● **Edit Button Image**   Allows you to directly modify the smiley-face image

   ● **Change Button Image**   Allows you to select another image supplied with Office 2000

9. When you are finished, click Close to clear the dialog box from the window.

Placing a Macro Button on a Toolbar in Word

In Word, the procedure is slightly different. You first define a macro, place it on the toolbar, and then modify its appearance. Follow these steps:

1. After displaying the toolbar to be modified, record your macro as usual, making sure you click Assign Macro To Toolbars in the Record Macro dialog box.

2. Right-click a toolbar, and select the Customize option. Select the Commands tab.

3. Under Categories, find Macros. A list of the existing macros will be listed under Commands, as shown here (your own list of macros may be different from ours):

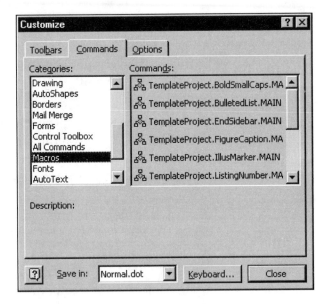

4. In the Commands list box, select the macro you want to add to the toolbar, and drag it to the toolbar (you will see an I-beam appear where the icon will be inserted). The whole name of the macro will appear on the button.

5. To change the name and appearance of the macro, right-click the button to display the Modify Selection menu.

6. To change the image on the button, use the guidelines listed in the question "I want to create a new toolbar for my own tasks. How do I do this?," earlier in this chapter.

Tip: *You can also change toolbar buttons and menus by choosing Customize from the Tools menu.*

How do I get the Office Shortcut bar to appear on my screen, and then make it go away when I am working in one of the Office applications. Is there a way to display it but not see it when I don't need it?

You bet. Office 2000 no longer places the Shortcut bar on the screen automatically. You must install it from the CD or network server. If you insert your CD in the CD drive, you can start the installation from there. Otherwise, here's how you install it:

1. From the Start menu, select Settings and then Control Panel.

2. Double-click Add/Remove Programs.

3. On the Install/Uninstall tab, select Microsoft Office 2000 and then click Add/Remove. You may be instructed to insert the CD-ROM. Click Add Or Remove Features.

4. Click the plus sign (+) beside Office Tools.

5. Click the down arrow beside Microsoft Office Shortcut Bar, and select Run From My Computer to install the Shortcut bar on your hard disk, as shown here:

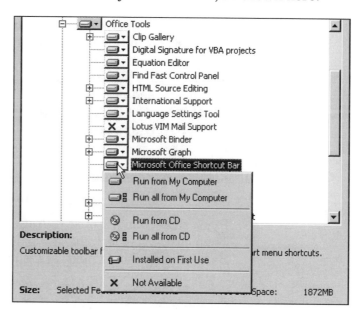

 Note: *You will probably initially see an × symbol beside Microsoft Office Shortcut Bar, indicating that it has not been installed. You might also see a hard drive icon with the number 1 as a symbol, which indicates that Office will install the Shortcut bar on first use (it is not yet installed on your computer). If you see any other symbol, the Shortcut bar is already installed, and you can skip ahead to step 8.*

6. Click Update Now. The Shortcut bar will be installed on your hard disk.

7. Click OK again on the Install/Uninstall dialog box to close it.

The Shortcut bar is now installed, but you still need to instruct Office 2000 to display it.

1. Select Start | Programs | Microsoft Office Tools | Microsoft Office Shortcut Bar.

2. A dialog box will ask whether you want the Office Shortcut Bar to always be displayed on the desktop. Click Yes or No. If your answer is No, you might also want to click the Please Do Not Ask Me This Question Again. Regardless of how you answered, the Shortcut bar will be displayed.

You can cause the Shortcut bar to be hidden most of the time. One way to do this is to dock the Shortcut bar by dragging it to a toolbar or the edge of the screen. Then right-click it and select AutoHide from the context menu to hide it in its docked position. When you want it to display again, just move the mouse pointer over the blank space where it normally appears, and it will reappear. Here's how to set this up:

1. Right-click an empty spot on the Shortcut bar.

2. Select Customize from the context menu.

3. Place a check mark next to Auto Hide Between Uses. Then clear the check mark next to Auto Fit Into Title Bar Area, as shown next, and click OK.

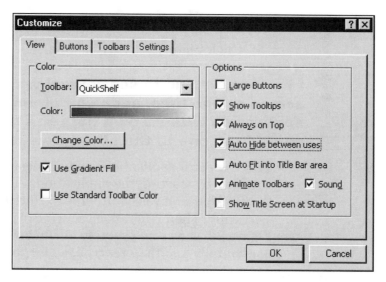

Tip: *To close the Shortcut bar altogether, double-click the control menu icon—the leftmost (or topmost) button on the bar. The Shortcut bar will reappear the next time Windows is started if you have selected that option. To redisplay the Shortcut bar in the current session of Windows, select Start | Programs | Microsoft Office Tools | Microsoft Office Shortcut Bar.*

A previous employee modified a toolbar. We would like to restore the original toolbar. How do we do that?

You can restore Office's default toolbar buttons by following these steps:

1. Right-click an empty space on the toolbar, and select Customize.

2. In the Toolbars list, select the toolbar to be restored.

3. Click Reset. In Word, you can make the change to a specific document or template, or to all documents (Normal.dot).

4. Click OK if the Assistant asks for verification.

5. Click Close.

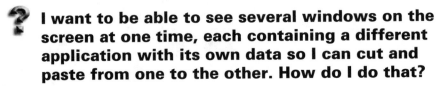 **I want to be able to see several windows on the screen at one time, each containing a different application with its own data so I can cut and paste from one to the other. How do I do that?**

To see several applications simultaneously, open the different windows by starting the applications. Then simply right-click the Taskbar and select either Tile Horizontally or Tile Vertically. Then rearrange the windows as you want them. Figure 2-5 shows an example of windows that were tiled horizontally and then rearranged for convenience.

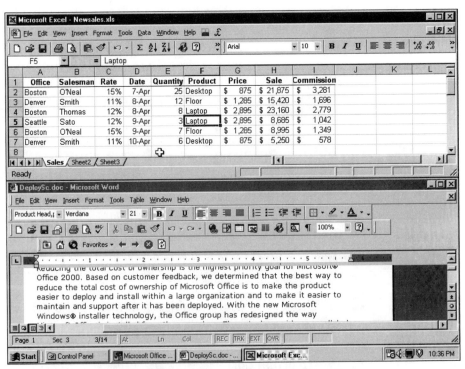

Figure 2-5 Tiled windows running different applications

FILE HANDLING AND COMPATIBILITY

I have multiple name and address files, with some duplicated names. For example, I have an investment club list in Word, a customer list in Access, and my e-mail contacts in Outlook. How do I decide the best application to use for my name lists?

Having multiple name and address files is not necessarily bad, depending on how they are used. However, there are some guidelines as to when to use one application rather than another for names and addresses. Word is probably not a good choice for name and address lists unless it is a very trivial list, and small and stable. The three tools for name lists within Office 2000 are Outlook (the primary tool), Access, and Excel.

- Use Outlook for contacts when you want to manage multiple phone numbers, e-mail addresses, fax numbers, and addresses in one central location.

- Use Access for larger files when you are working with multiple, complex data files; for example, a customer database that is linked to purchase and accounts receivable files. Access works well if you have several people working on these files simultaneously in a networked environment and reporting is important; for example, you need to generate Orders Outstanding reports or Overdue Accounts reports.

- Use Excel for situations in which a spreadsheet provides the best tools for analyzing the data related to a file. For example, perhaps you want to calculate sales commissions by geographic area for the current quarter.

Tip: *You can export and import lists among Word, Outlook, Excel, and Access by saving them as delimited files and then importing them into the desired application.*

 How can I quickly create a copy of an Office file?

By right-clicking the filename in Windows Explorer, you can choose Copy and then right-click on another folder and choose Paste. Another option is to open a copy of a file rather than opening the original. Follow these steps:

1. In Windows Explorer, right-click the filename.

2. Select New from the context menu (for an Access file, you will have to save the file under a new name), as shown here. A new window will open, containing the document but untitled.

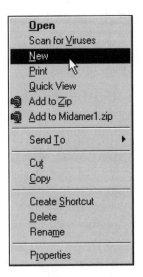

3. Save the copy under a new name with File | Save As. You now have an open copy of the Office file.

 Tip: *You can also create a copy of a file by right-clicking a filename in the Open, Save, or Save As dialog boxes.*

I must retain both Office 2000 and a previous version of Office on my computer, and documents created with Office 2000 must sometimes be saved in the older version's format. What happens to the formatting created with features not in the earlier version?

Office 2000 re-creates the new features using the older version's tools. Although it may not be a perfect reproduction, it will be mapped as closely as possible. Some formatting may be lost.

When I install Office 2000, do I need to worry about my older data files that were created with a previous version of Microsoft Office?

Office 2000 strives for compatibility between Office versions, so there is not much cause for worry. Here are some of the compatibility features of Office 2000:

● If you install Office 2000 over an earlier version of Office, the data files will be preserved.

● Office 2000 can open data files created with previous versions of Office.

● All data is saved from the Outlook components, such as Calendar, Task, and Contact files, and e-mail sent and received.

● With Office 2000, you can elect to save files in either the new format or an older one. So, not only can you preserve the older file formats, but you can duplicate them with the newer formatting of Office 2000.

I need to transmit some of my Word documents to someone who doesn't have Word installed on her computer. Is there a way she can read Word documents without Word?

Since Word 2000 and Word 97 have the same file format, you can use the Word 97 viewer, which is downloadable from the Office web site. You can find this viewer by selecting

Help | Office On The Web. Using this viewer allows you to read Word 97 or Word 2000 documents without the Word 97 or Word 2000 program. Converters are also available to enable you to open files created with a different version of Office than you have. The Office Update web page contains several converters, viewers, and other helpful utilities for Word, Excel, Outlook, Access, and PowerPoint.

USING HELP AND THE OFFICE ASSISTANT

The Help system has changed in the Office Assistant. Where is the Index feature so that I can look up the item I want by searching through an index?

The primary Help system is now available through the Office Assistant and through the web site, although you can still find the Index by following these steps:

1. Click the Help menu and select Microsoft Word Help (or select Help for another application). The Office Assistant will appear.

2. Type the words describing what you are seeking (for example, Help index, as shown here), and click Search:

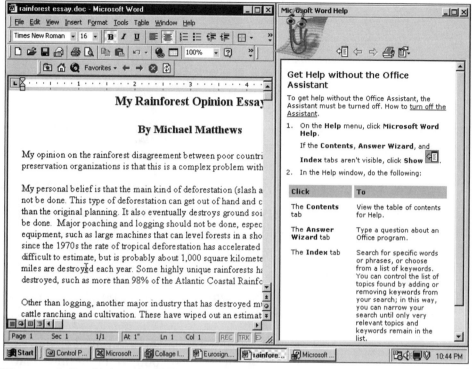

Figure 2-6 Using the Office Assistant

3. You may have to click the down arrow at the bottom of the list of topics to find Get Help Without The Assistant. Click it and the screen shown in Figure 2-6 will appear.

4. Click the Show icon above the topic content, and click the Index tab.

I would really like another Office Assistant animated icon. The paper clip is driving me nuts!

Easy to do! Office 2000 comes with additional Office Assistant animated icons. To select another Assistant, follow these steps:

1. If the Office Assistant is displayed on the screen, right-click to display a context menu, as shown next.

2. Select Choose Assistant and then select the Gallery tab.

3. Using the Next and Back commands, find the animated icon you prefer from the choices offered.

4. Click OK to select one.

5. If the Assistant is not already installed, you will be asked if you want to install it now. Respond as guided to install it.

If you do not like any of the animated Office Assistant icons available with Office 2000, you can download other animated and inanimate Office Assistants from the Microsoft Office web site.

Sometimes the Office Assistant is on the screen and sometimes not. How can I display the Office Assistant when I want it?

On the right of the Standard toolbar is the Office Assistant icon, the question mark. After you have hidden the Office Assistant, you can use this icon to redisplay it, hide it, or turn it off. Click the icon and the Office Assistant will appear, along with some helpful hints, as shown in the following illustration.

Tip: *After using the Office Assistant, you can hide it by right-clicking it and selecting Hide from the context menu.*

When I place my cursor on an icon in a toolbar, I see no label showing what the icon does. I know this feature exists. How do I get it for Office 2000?

You must turn on the Toolbar ScreenTips with these steps:

1. From the View menu, select Toolbars, and then Customize. Click the Options tab.

2. Click Show ScreenTips On Toolbars to turn on the feature, as shown next.

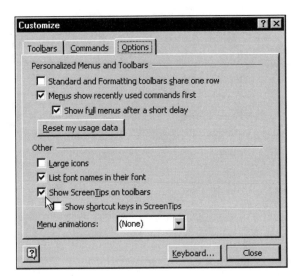

3. Click Close.

Tip: *If you would like to see the shortcut keys on the screen icon labels, click the Show Shortcut Keys In ScreenTips option in the same Customize dialog box.*

 I am finding that the Office Assistant frequently gets in the way. It is always asking to help when I don't want help, although there are times when I do find it useful. How can I better control when the Office Assistant appears?

Office Assistant allows you to select some of the times when the Assistant is to appear. Follow these steps:

1. Right-click the Office Assistant and select Options from the context menu.

2. Select the Options tab. You will see the dialog box shown in Figure 2-7.

3. Remove the check marks next to the situations in which you do not want the Office Assistant to appear.

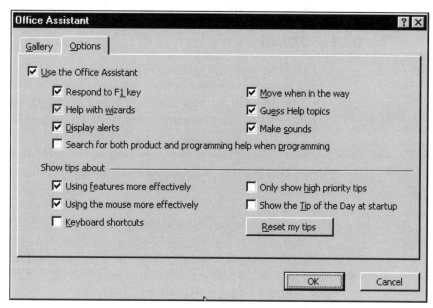

Figure 2-7 Modifying the Office Assistant's behavior

MISCELLANEOUS

Sometimes I get a beep when recording a macro using the mouse. What's the problem?

The macro recorder cannot record some mouse movements. When you hear the error sound, try using keyboard commands instead of the mouse.

I thought the Spelling Checker was a shared component of Office; but when I add a new word to my custom spelling dictionary and then use another application, the second application does not recognize the word added to the dictionary.

You must close the first application before the added word can be recognized by other Office applications. The custom dictionary is updated with new words when the application is closed.

 ## How do I enable the language capability in Office 2000?

Office 2000's language capability enables you to work with other languages in a variety of ways. For example, you can create and edit documents in other languages, using spell checking, a thesaurus, and grammar checking. You can specify that Office's user interface be in another language, with adjustments for time and currency differences. Features for working with other languages differ for the type of language: European, East Asian, or right-to-left languages. You even can pick an English version that is specific to the United Kingdom, Canada, or Australia.

You can find the enabling function in the Start menu under Microsoft Office Tools. The Microsoft Office Language Settings will enable the language capability. You may have to install this feature from the CD-ROM.

Chapter 3

Writing with Word

Answer Topics!

Writing with Word @ a Glance

Word is the application in the Office Professional 2000 package that is used for word processing. This chapter answers a large number of questions about Word that have been grouped into the following areas:

 Word Features explains the features available to you in Word and the types of documents they enable you to produce.

Creating and Saving Documents and Templates shows you how to recover files, create online forms, create and change templates, choose between templates and wizards, and create a template toolbar.

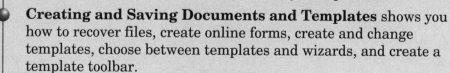

- **Entering and Editing Text** describes how to quickly change misspelled words, use click and type, prevent Word from making grammatical errors, edit in Print Preview, and delete blank lines with Replace.

- **Formatting Text** discusses how to avoid AutoFormat's "overcorrections," keep Word from formatting e-mail addresses as hyperlinks, use the mouse to change margins, control bulleted and numbered lists, and transfer styles to other documents.

- **Inserting Pictures and Objects** presents ways to move existing text into linked text boxes, remove a border around a text box, add text within an AutoShape, and wrap text around a text box.

- **Using Tables and Borders** explains how to use automatic border and table formatting, center a table, convert text to a table, and display the results of formulas.

- **Using Macros** talks about the use of macros, how to assign a shortcut key to a macro, and how to enable macros in a document.

- **Mail and Other Merging** looks at how to automatically insert a return address, add a new field to a data source, print custom-sized labels, print envelopes, select only certain addresses in a merge, and start the merge function.

- **Working with Large Documents** discusses how to create subdocuments, combine several documents in a master document, move outline levels from one subdocument to another, and work with page numbering in separate documents.

- **Collaborative Editing** describes how to compare different versions of the same document, preserve an original version of a document, mark edits as they are added to a document, prevent unwanted changes to shared documents, and share Word 2000 documents with Word 97 users.

WORD FEATURES

Word is a sophisticated program that helps you produce the following:

● *Documents,* which can be created using automatic features, such as AutoText, AutoCorrect, and AutoFormat. *AutoText* on the Insert menu allows you to save a block of text that you use frequently (for example, an address or a closing), and then insert it automatically by typing the name you gave the block and pressing F3. *AutoCorrect* on the Tools menu corrects misspelled words automatically as you type. When you press the SPACEBAR after misspelling a word, the word is corrected automatically. Only words listed in the AutoCorrect dialog box are corrected; however, you can add your own words to this list. *AutoFormat* on the Format menu is used in two ways. You can format an entire document automatically, or you can automatically add formatting such as bullets, numbering, tables, bold, and underlining to text as you type.

   Creating a document consists of typing text, inserting graphics or other objects, creating tables, formatting text with borders, and adding any other formatting that you want. The document is then named and saved by clicking the Save button on the toolbar, typing a filename, and clicking the Save button. If you want to save an existing document with a different filename, choose Save As from the File menu, type a new filename, and click the Save button.

● *Templates,* which are files that contain styles, graphics, and text that can be used to create documents. To create a template, choose New from the File menu, select the Blank Document icon, click Template in the Create New box, and click OK. In the Template window, you can create styles, insert graphic objects, and enter text. Save the template the same way you save a document, except save it as a Document Template rather than as a Word Document. Templates are stored by default in Windows\Application Data\Microsoft\Templates.

- *Letters, labels, and envelopes,* which can be produced using the Mail Merge function. Choose Mail Merge from the Tools menu, and the Mail Merge Helper will help you produce any of these. You can also create labels and envelopes without using the merge function by choosing Envelopes and Labels from the Tools menu.

- *Newsletters, brochures, and flyers,* which can be enhanced by inserting a variety of pictures, ClipArt, WordArt, and automatic shapes.

- *Master document files,* which can combine several smaller files. For example, if you are writing a book and you save each chapter in a separate file, you can then combine these files in a master document in order to produce a table of contents and index that includes topics from all the chapters. The master document function also allows several people on a network to work on documents simultaneously. In Word 2000, the master document feature is available on the Outlining toolbar when in Outline view.

- *Tracking,* which allows you to mark text, add highlighting, and insert comments. You can then save several edited versions of the same document, compare the versions, and quickly select or accept the marked changes. The Track Changes option is listed on the Tools menu.

CREATING AND SAVING DOCUMENTS AND TEMPLATES

 How do I know if the automatically recovered files are saved? I looked in the Save tab in the Options dialog box and confirmed that AutoRecover and background save were turned on, but I didn't see my files being saved as they were in earlier versions.

You were right to check the Save tab to make sure these features were turned on. Also, click the File Locations tab in the Options dialog box to see the name of the folder that has been assigned for the AutoRecover files. You can assign a different folder for these files, if you like. Follow these steps:

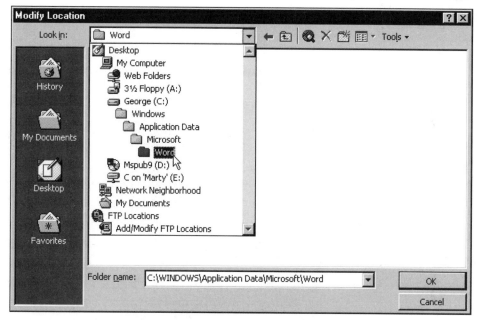

Figure 3-1 3333333The Modify Location dialog box

1. Choose Options from the Tools menu.

2. Click the File Locations tab.

3. Select AutoRecover Files and click Modify to go to the Modify Location dialog box.

4. Click the down arrow in the Look In list box and select the folder in which you want the files to be saved. See the example in Figure 3-1.

5. When you are done, click OK to return to the File Locations tab and click Close to return to the document.

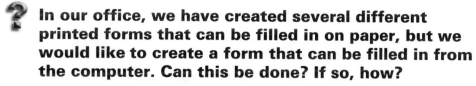

In our office, we have created several different printed forms that can be filled in on paper, but we would like to create a form that can be filled in from the computer. Can this be done? If so, how?

Creating an electronic form is very similar to creating a printed form that is filled in on paper, except that an electronic form should be created as a template rather than as a document. This allows users to fill in the form without changing the original design.

To create a template, follow these steps:

1. Choose New from the File menu and click the General tab.

2. In the Create New section, select Template, as shown in Figure 3-2.

3. Click OK.

4. Create the form as usual, entering whatever text, graphics, borders, and tables are needed, and inserting fields that make it easy to fill in the form on the computer. For a detailed explanation of how to insert these fields, see the sidebar "Inserting Form Fields."

5. Display the Forms toolbar and click any of the form field buttons to insert the fields you want. These are the types of form fields that can be inserted:

● Text form fields, in which users can type text when filling in the form. You can also enter default text so users do not have to type in text.

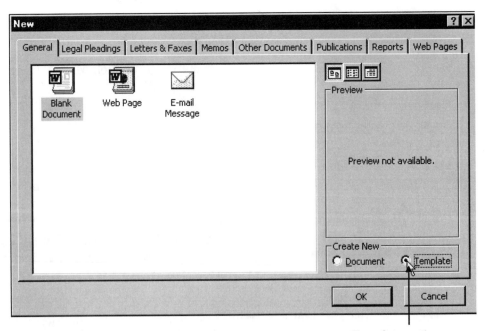

Template option

Figure 3-2 The New dialog box

- Drop-down form fields, which display a series of choices. Users can scroll through the list to see all options and select the one they want.

- Check box form fields, which allow the person filling in the form to click a check box to turn it on.

6. When you are done, click the Protect Form button to prevent changes from being made.

7. Save and close the template.

To use a form, follow these steps:

1. Open a new document and select the form template as you would any other template. If Protect Form was turned on when the form was created, your insertion point will be automatically positioned in the first field.

2. Fill in the field and press TAB to move to the next field, continuing until the form is filled in.

- When you are in a text box, type the text appropriate for that field. The box will expand to accommodate the text.

- When you come to a check box, type a character (x, for example) to fill in the box.

- When you come to a drop-down menu, click the down arrow to see all of the available choices and select the one you want.

3. When you are done, print the form. You can then save it as a document if you like, or you can close it without saving.

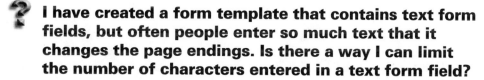

I have created a form template that contains text form fields, but often people enter so much text that it changes the page endings. Is there a way I can limit the number of characters entered in a text form field?

Yes, you can control the length of the text form field. Do the following.

1. Open the template containing the field or create a new template.

Inserting Form Fields

Display the Forms toolbar by clicking any toolbar with the right mouse button and selecting Forms.

Inserting a Text Form Field

1. Move the insertion point to the spot where you want to place the field.

 2. Click the Text Form Field button. A shaded box will be displayed. The size of the box will change as text is inserted when you use the form.

Inserting a Drop-Down Form Field

1. Move the insertion point to the spot where you want to place the field.

 2. Click the Drop-Down Field Form button. A shaded box will be displayed.

3. Double-click the shaded box to open the Drop-Down Form Field Options dialog box.

4. Type an entry in the Drop-Down Item box and click Add. The entry will be displayed in the Items In Drop-Down List box to the right.

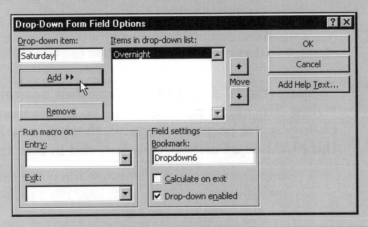

5. Repeat step 4 as often as needed to add your items to the list.

6. When you are done, click OK. The first entry will be displayed in the box. When the form template is being filled in, the drop-down list will be displayed when the down arrow at the right end of the box is clicked.

Inserting a Check Box Form Field

1. Move the insertion point to the location where you want to place the field.

 2. Click Check Box Form Field, as shown here. A shaded box will be inserted. The default size of the box is 10 points, and the default value for the box is not checked.

 Tip: *See the next question for specific information about opening and changing an existing template or creating a new template.*

2. Display the Forms toolbar. To do this, right-click any toolbar and click Forms.

3. Select the text form field to be limited; or, if you are creating a new template, insert a text form field and then select it.

 4. On the Forms toolbar, click the Form Field Options button. The Text Form Field Options dialog box will be displayed (see Figure 3-3).

5. In the Maximum Length box, click the up or down arrow to select the number of characters that can be typed in the field. Then click OK.

6. Repeat steps 3 through 5 for additional text form fields.

7. When you are done, click the Protect Form button on the Forms toolbar.

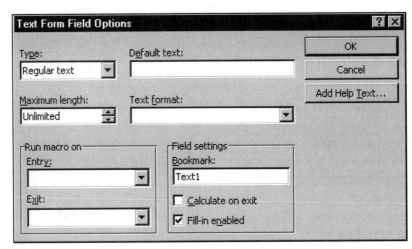

Figure 3-3 The Text Form Field Options dialog box

 Note: *If you do not protect the form, the limit on the field length will not be in effect.*

8. Save the template and close it.

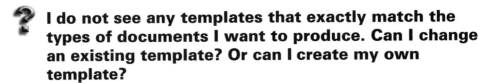

I do not see any templates that exactly match the types of documents I want to produce. Can I change an existing template? Or can I create my own template?

You can do both. To edit an existing template, use the following steps:

1. Choose Open from the File menu. Select Document Templates in the Files Of Type box, select the template to be changed, and click Open.

 Note: *If you do not see any templates listed in the dialog box, select the following path in the Look In box: Windows\ Application Data\Microsoft\Templates.*

2. Make your changes to the template and save and close the file.

To create a new template, do the following:

1. Choose New from the File menu.

2. Select Blank Document, click Template in the Create New section, and click OK. A new template window is opened, containing only the styles from the Normal.dot template. The title bar now shows you are working in a template window rather than a document window.

3. Create your styles and enter any text and graphics that you may want.

4. When you are done, choose Save from the File menu.

5. Name the template and click the Save button. The template will now appear in the General tab in the New dialog box.

Is it possible to create a toolbar for a new template that I created?

Yes, it is. To do this, open a document based on the template to which you want to add a toolbar, and then do the following:

1. Choose Customize from the Tools menu.

2. Click the Toolbars tab and click New. The New Toolbar dialog box will be displayed.

3. Type a name for the toolbar or accept the suggested name; and in the Make Toolbar Available To list box, select where you want to assign the toolbar. You can choose the template currently being used, the Normal template, or just the current document.

4. Click OK when you are done. A small toolbar will be displayed in the document window. See Figure 3-4.

5. Click the Commands tab, scroll through the Categories list, and select a category of commands. The commands for that category will be displayed in the Commands box, as shown in Figure 3-4.

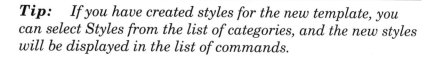

Tip: *If you have created styles for the new template, you can select Styles from the list of categories, and the new styles will be displayed in the list of commands.*

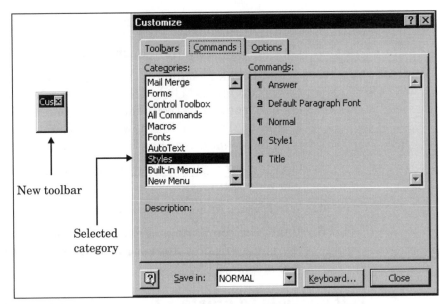

New toolbar

Selected
category

Figure 3-4 The Customize dialog box and the new toolbar

6. Select a command and drag it to the toolbar to create a new toolbar button for that command.

7. Repeat steps 5 and 6 to add more commands to the new toolbar.

 Note: *You can select a new toolbar button, click Modify Selection, and make changes to the button's appearance, including changing the text. To change the text, open the Modify Selection menu and type the new name in the Name text box. See Figure 3-5.*

8. When you are done, click Close and drag the new toolbar to an appropriate position. If you move the floating toolbar to the top of the window below existing toolbars, you can *dock* it and then adjust its position by clicking the vertical line at the left side of the toolbar and dragging it to the left or right, as shown here:

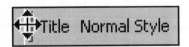

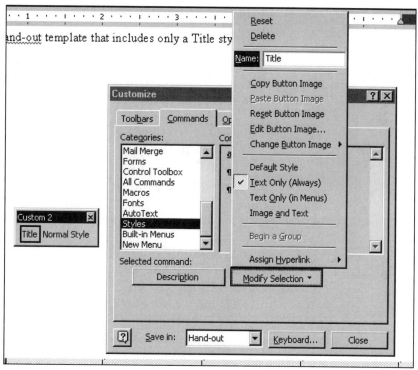

Figure 3-5   The Modify Selection menu

    Note: *When you close the document, you will be prompted to save both the document and the template.*

 How can I change the default folder for my Word documents?

The default folder for all Office 2000 documents is the My Documents folder on drive C; however, depending on how you work, you may want to change it by doing the following:

1. Choose Options from the Tools menu.

2. Click the File Locations tab to display the list of items and the folders in which they are currently stored.

3. Select Documents in the File Types list, if it is not already selected.

4. Click Modify to go to the Modify Location dialog box (shown in Figure 3-1).

5. Click the down arrow in the Look In box and select the folder you want.

Tip: *If you double-click a drive, all the folders in that drive will be displayed. Then you can double-click a folder to display any folders and the files within it.*

6. Click OK to return to the File Locations tab and click Close to return to the document window.

Note: *Changing the default folder for documents in Word does not change the default folder for other Office 2000 files. The default folder for other documents remains My Documents.*

If you want to create a new folder while you are in the Modify Location dialog box, use it to select the folder in which the new folder will be created. Then click the Create New Folder button, type a name for the folder, and click OK. To make this new folder the default folder for Word documents, select the new folder, click OK to return to the File Locations tab, and click Close to return to the document window.

I keep having to click the double arrows on drop-down menus to display all the options. Is there a way that I can display the entire drop-down menu more easily?

If the Show Full Menus After A Short Delay option is not checked, you will have to click the double arrows to display the entire menu. To activate this option:

1. Choose Customize from the Tools menu.

2. Click the Options tab and click Show Full Menus After A Short Delay to check the box.

3. Click Close to return to the document. Now when a menu is opened, the full menu will be displayed after several seconds.

Tip: *If you have displayed one full menu, and move your pointer to another menu, it will be immediately displayed in its entirety.*

In Word 2000, the Formatting toolbar is displayed in the same row as the Standard toolbar. Is there a way to display the toolbars in separate rows?

Yes, there is. Do the following:

1. Choose Customize from the Tools menu.
2. Click the Options tab and then click Standard And Formatting Toolbars Share One Row to remove the check mark in the box.
3. Click Close.

Why are document names now displayed in the Taskbar in Word 2000?

This is a new feature in Word 2000. Each time a new document is opened, Word 2000 is also opened, which results in the application and the document name being displayed in the Taskbar. This makes working with multiple documents much more intuitive. All you have to do to switch to a different opened document is click its button in the Taskbar. Also, you can immediately see which documents are currently open without going to the Window menu. You do, however, have to close each document separately when you end a word processing session.

Should I use a template or a wizard to create a document? It seems to me that wizards are much easier to use.

Using a template is faster than using a wizard, and with a wizard you are sometimes limited in your choices for opening a document. When you open a new document with a template, you go directly to the document window and can begin creating your document.

The wizard leads you through creating the document step by step, which can be very helpful. It provides you with choices of styles, layouts, and information to be included. When you are done with the step-by-step procedure, click Finish and the new document is opened. The document will be laid out according to the choices you made, and new styles will be available if you chose them. You can make any changes you

want to the document after the wizard is finished, and then save the document as you usually do.

Templates and wizards are located on various tabs in the New dialog box when you choose New from the File menu. Click a tab to select the category you want, select the template or wizard to be used with the new document, and click OK.

ENTERING AND EDITING TEXT

 Is there a way to quickly change misspelled words that have been marked by Word?

You can do one of two things, both of which are fairly quick:

● Right-click the misspelled word to display the list of spelling and grammar options that pertain to this word, and select the spelling you want.

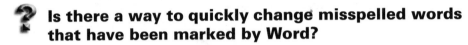 ● Move the insertion point to the misspelled word and double-click the Spelling & Grammar Status button on the status bar. A list of options will be displayed, and you can select the one you want.

➕ ***Tip:*** *If you frequently misspell a word that is not included in the AutoCorrect list, you can easily add it to the list. Then when you misspell the word, it will be corrected automatically when the SPACEBAR is pressed after typing the word. See the Sidebar, "Adding Words to the AutoCorrect List."*

 I have heard that Word 2000 has a new feature called click and type; however, I don't see anything different in the document window. What is it and how can I use it?

Click and type allows you to move your insertion point to any position in the document window (in Print Layout view), even areas where no text has yet been entered, and then double-click and start typing. If you do not see anything different in your document window, then the click-and-type function is not turned on or your text is formatted in columns. Click and type does not work with column formatting.

Adding Words to the AutoCorrect List

To add a frequently misspelled word:

1. Choose AutoCorrect from the Tools menu.

2. Type the incorrect spelling of the word in the Replace box, as shown here:

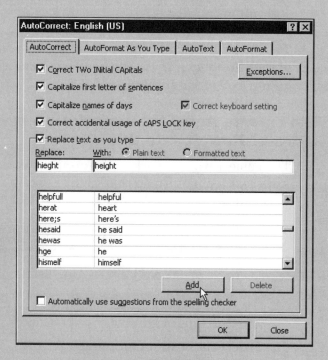

3. Tab to the With box and type the correct spelling.

4. Click Add and click Close.

To turn on click and type, follow these steps:

1. Choose Options from the Tools menu.

2. Click the Edit tab, and click Enable Click And Type.

3. Click OK to return to the document window, and then switch to Print Layout view. Now when you move the

insertion point to a blank area, you will see lines indicating the type of alignment—left, right, or center—as shown here:

4. Double-click and start typing. Your text will be aligned automatically.

Tip: *To center text, move the insertion point near the center of your document; to right-align text, move the insertion point all the way to the right.*

Can I create AutoText items for my own logo and address? How do I do this?

The easiest way to work with AutoText is to first display the AutoText toolbar. To do this, right-click any toolbar and select AutoText. The AutoText toolbar looks like this:

To create your own item in AutoText:

1. Type the text and, if you like, insert any picture, WordArt, or other type of graphic.

2. Select the text and graphic.

3. Click New on the AutoText toolbar to display the Create AutoText dialog box:

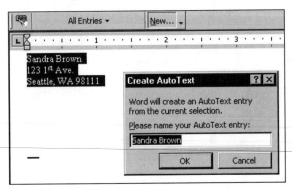

✚   ***Tip:*** *Another way to display the Create AutoText dialog box is to choose AutoText from the Insert menu and click New.*

4. The first several words of the selected text will be displayed in the dialog box as a default name; however, if the selection begins with a logo or other graphic, the text box will be blank. Either accept the suggested name that is displayed by clicking OK, or type a short name for the AutoText entry, and then click OK. See the next question for information about inserting AutoText.

Is there a way to insert AutoText quickly?

A quick way to insert an AutoText entry is to move the insertion point to the place where you want to enter it, type the name of the entry, and press F3. If you are not sure of the name, display the AutoText toolbar, click All Entries, and select Normal. A list of the entries you have created will be displayed; click the one you want. Or you can choose AutoText from the Insert menu, select Normal, and click the entry you want.

I like the feature of having misspelled words marked as I type, but I do not always want to mark grammatical errors. Is there any way I can avoid this?

The fastest way is to right-click the Spelling & Grammar Status icon on the status bar and then click Hide Grammatical Errors. Or you can select Options from this shortcut menu, and the dialog box in Figure 3-6 will be displayed. (This is the same Spelling & Grammar tab you see by clicking Tools I Options I Spelling & Grammar tab.) The options that can be turned off or on are shown here. Click Check Grammar As You Type to turn it off, and click OK. If you turn off both the spelling and grammar checking as you type, the Spelling and Grammar Status icon will not be displayed on the status bar.

Another way is to choose Spelling and Grammar from the Tools menu, and click Options in the Spelling and Grammar dialog box; however, if there are no errors in your document, the Spelling and Grammar dialog box will not be displayed.

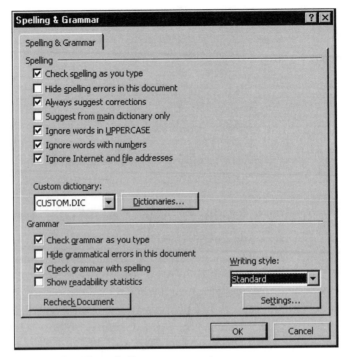

Figure 3-6 The Spelling & Grammar options

 I work with large documents and would like to move quickly through them to see topics that are included; however, I do not usually use Outline view. I have heard that Word 2000 has other ways to move around in a document easily. What are they and how do I use them?

Document Map is one of the features you can use to move quickly around in a document, and the Select Browse Object button and scroll box in the vertical scroll bar are also available.

 To use the Document Map, click Document Map on the Standard toolbar. When it is selected, an additional pane is displayed to the left of the document, as shown in Figure 3-7. This pane contains the current headings in the document. You can click any heading in this pane to move directly to that location in the document.

Tip: *You can resize the document pane the way other windows can be resized. Just point to the side of the pane until the pointer shows a double arrow, and drag to the size you want.*

You can also change the display of headings in the pane:

● To collapse subheadings, click the minus sign that is displayed next to the heading.

● To expand subheadings, click the plus sign next to the heading.

● To determine what levels of headings are displayed, right-click the Document Map pane and select the level from the shortcut menu. All levels up to and including the level you choose will be displayed.

To remove the pane from view, click the Document Map button again.

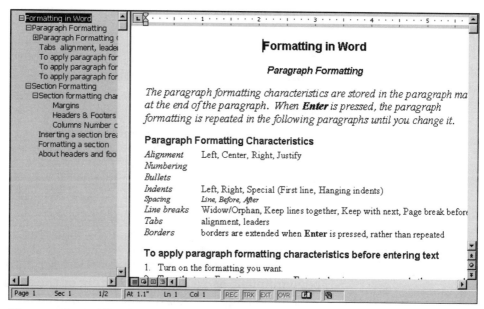

Figure 3-7   The Document Map pane

 Note: *If you have formatted paragraphs in your document with styles other than heading levels, these paragraphs may also be displayed in the Document Map pane.*

To use the Select Browse Object button to quickly move through the document, do this:

1. Click Select Browse Object on the vertical scroll bar at the right of the document window. A box showing various options will be displayed:

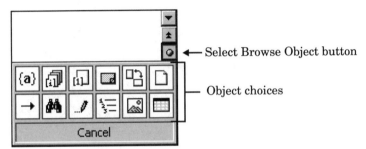

2. Move your pointer across each of the pictures to display a description of each type of object.

3. Click the one you want.

4. Click the Previous or Next buttons, shown here, to move immediately to that type of object:

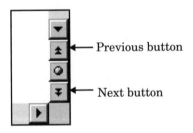

To use the scroll box, do either of the following.

● Drag the box up or down in the vertical scroll bar. A page number, as well as the heading or the section in which the page is located, will be displayed as you drag up or down.

● Click above or below the scroll box to move up or down one screen length.

Note: *In Word 2000, the Previous and Next buttons on the vertical scroll bar are available in all views. In previous versions of Word, these buttons were not available in Normal view.*

How is Print Layout view different from Page Layout view?

Print Layout view is a new term in Word 2000 that replaces the term Page Layout view in previous versions. It is essentially the same as Page Layout view, but better describes the type of view. When you are in Print Layout view you see columns as they will be printed. Headers and footers and graphics are displayed and can be edited easily, and margins can be changed by dragging them to different positions.

I like to see my document in Print Preview to confirm the overall layout of my document because I can see up to six pages at once. However, I wish I could make changes there, such as adjusting page endings, rather than in Print Layout view, which only shows two pages at a time. Can I use Print Preview to edit text?

Yes, you can. In the Print Preview window, click Magnifier to turn it off. Turning off the magnifier changes the mouse pointer to an I-beam. Then you can make any editing changes you want. Click Magnifier again to leave editing and return to magnification.

I created a document in which I pressed ENTER three times to insert two blank lines after each paragraph. Later I decided the document would look better if there were only one blank line after each paragraph. Is there any way I can use the Replace function to make this change quickly?

Yes, you can replace special characters by doing the following:

1. Choose Find from the Edit menu and click the Replace tab; or if the entire Edit menu is displayed, you can choose Replace.

2. Click More to display the Special button.

3. With your insertion point in the Find What box, click Special and select Paragraph Mark. Do this three times to insert three characters in the Find What box, as shown in Figure 3-8.

 Note: *The Special button is also available in the Find tab.*

4. Tab to the Replace With text box, click Special, and select Paragraph Mark twice.

 Tip: *Once you know how any of the special characters appear in the Find What box after you have selected them from the Special menu, you can type them in directly—for example,* **^P** *(SHIFT-6, P) for each time ENTER was pressed.*

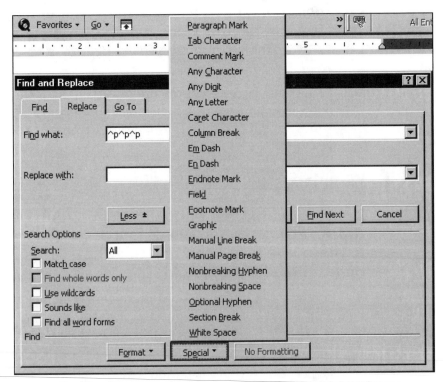

Figure 3-8   The Replace tab showing the list of Special options

5. Click Find Next, and click Replace. If you are certain that you want this replacement throughout the document, click Replace All.

Tip: *If you want to find or replace only formatting, click Format in the Find And Replace dialog box, and select the type of formatting you want. You can also instruct Word to find or replace text when it is formatted in a certain way. For example, if you wanted to locate a word only when it is formatted in bold, enter the word in the Find What box, click the Format button, and choose the type of formatting from one of the options on the menu. The formatting characteristic will appear in the area below the Find What box.*

FORMATTING TEXT

I am confused about using AutoFormat. When I choose AutoFormat on the Format menu and click Options in the AutoFormat dialog box, Automatic Bulleted Lists is selected in both the AutoFormat tab and in the AutoFormat As You Type tab. However, when I type items in a list, they are not automatically formatted with bullets. How do I do this without using the bullet button?

Type any of the characters listed below, press TAB, type some text, and press ENTER. Depending upon the character that you typed, a different type of bullet will be inserted when ENTER is pressed. The list below shows the results of typing different characters:

● Type an asterisk (*) to display a round bullet.

■ Type two hyphens (--) to display a boxed bullet.

- Type one hyphen (-) to display a hyphen.

➢ Type a greater than sign (>) to display a pointer.

➔ Type a hyphen and a greater than sign (->) to display an arrow.

⇨ Type an equal sign and a greater than sign (=>) to display an outline arrow.

 Note: *The AutoFormat tab is used to turn on or off the features that are included in AutoFormatting, which automatically formats the entire document. The AutoFormat As You Type tab is used to turn on or off the features that are automatically formatted as you enter text in a document.*

I am having a problem with some of AutoFormat's "overcorrections"; for example, typing text that begins with a capital letter followed by a period, a tab, and descriptive text. If I type "B. (TAB) Birth date" and press ENTER, Word displays a "C." On the following line. I want the next line after B. to be M. (TAB) Married. How do I do this?

Typing a period following the capital letter automatically formats text in an outline form. You can do one of two things to avoid this:

●   If you do not type a period following the letter, a subsequent letter will not be displayed when you press ENTER.

●   If you want to keep the period, you can make changes to the AutoFormat options.

To turn off options that automatically format text:

1. Choose AutoFormat from the Format menu.

2. Click Options in the AutoFormat dialog box.

3. Click the AutoFormat As You Type tab.

4. Turn off Automatic Numbered Lists, click OK, and click Close.

 Tip: *If you want to end the automatic formatting quickly on the following line, press CTRL-Q to restore the default paragraph formatting characteristics—left align, single space, and no indents or spacing before and after the paragraph. This will not, however, prevent automatic formatting unless you have turned off the specific feature in the AutoFormat As You Type tab.*

There are times when I want to avoid formatting an e-mail address as a hyperlink. Is there a way I can do this?

Yes, there is. Just choose AutoCorrect from the Tools menu, click the AutoFormat As You Type tab, and click Internet And Network Paths With Hyperlinks to remove the check mark. Then click OK.

I tried to use the mouse to change margins in the ruler, but I couldn't move anything but the indent markers. Can I do this? If so, how?

You cannot change margins using the mouse when you are in Normal view. You need to be in either Print Layout view or in Print Preview.

- To change margins in Print Layout view, point to the margin you want to change. A double-sided arrow will be displayed, as well as a ScreenTip that identifies the margin. Drag the margin to a new position. Notice that in Print Layout view a vertical ruler is displayed, which allows you to change the top and bottom margins, as well as a horizontal ruler to change the left and right margins.

- To change margins in Print Preview, click the View Ruler button if rulers are not displayed:

Then point to the margin—a double-headed arrow will be displayed. Drag the margin to a new position.

I have a list of numbered paragraphs. If I insert a note or comment that is not numbered, and I apply the numbering to the paragraph following the note, the numbering will begin with the number 1. Is there a way to change numbers in numbered lists?

Yes. Do the following:

1. Move your insertion point to the item with the number you want to change.

2. Choose Bullets And Numbering from the Format menu to open the Bullets And Numbering dialog box.

 Tip: *You can also open the Bullets And Numbering dialog box by right-clicking any bulleted or numbered item—a shortcut menu will be displayed, and you can choose Bullets And Numbering.*

3. In the Bullets And Numbering dialog box, click the Numbered tab and select the type of numbering you are using, if it is not already selected.

4. Click Continue Previous List.

 Tip: *You can also click Customize at this point; and in the Start At box, select a different starting number, if you like. Also, you can format the numbers with a different font, style, size, or other attributes in the Customize Numbered List dialog box.*

5. Click OK to return to the document window.

 I would like some lists to be spaced differently than the normal paragraph text. Is there a way to control the spacing in bulleted or numbered lists?

Yes, there is. It can be done easily using the following steps.

1. Type the bulleted or numbered lists using the current document spacing.

2. Select the list and choose Paragraph from the Format menu.

3. Under Spacing, click the down spinner and set Before and After to Auto.

4. Click OK to return to the document.

 I have problems using the indent markers. If I inadvertently drag them too far to the left or right, they change the position of my text. Is it possible to restore it? How?

The quickest way is to click the Undo button if you haven't made any other edits after moving the markers. Or you can press CTRL-Q to restore the default paragraph characteristics, which would return the indent markers to the left margin; however, you would then have to reapply any formatting that you had for that paragraph. A third way is to drag the indent markers back to the position you want. After doing any of these, your display of text may still need to be adjusted. To do this, click the left or right arrow on the ends of the horizontal scroll bar or drag the scroll box as shown here:

Left scroll   Scroll box   Right scroll
arrow   arrow

I frequently use the Shrink To Fit option in Print Preview, but there are times when the formatting changes are not what I want. For example, sometimes the font that is selected in Shrink To Fit is too small to be practical. How can I change back to the original formatting?

In either Print Preview or the document window, choose Undo Shrink To Fit from the Edit menu. However, you must do this before saving the changes; otherwise, the Undo Shrink To Fit option will not be available. If this option is not available, you will have to select the text and make any formatting changes that you want by using the Format menu.

Shrink To Fit is a feature available in the Print Preview window that automatically reformats your document so that it fits on a page. For example, if you have a document with text that extends to a second page, but you want it to be on one page, you can go to Print Preview and click Shrink To Fit.

The formatting changes that are necessary to accomplish this shrinking are automatically applied to your document. If you have three pages, Shrink To Fit will reformat it so that the text will fit on two pages.

 I created several styles to use in a document, and I would like to use these same styles in a different document, but I did not create a new template for the first document. Is there any way I can transfer styles in the Normal.dot template to other documents?

Open the document that does contain the styles you want to use, and do the following:

1. Choose Style from the Format menu, and click Organizer.

2. In the Organizer dialog box, shown in Figure 3-9, a list of styles in the opened document is displayed at the left, and the styles in the Normal.dot template are displayed

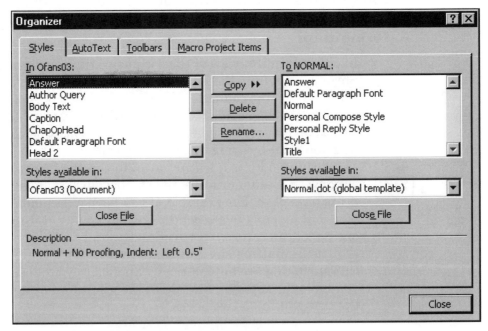

Figure 3-9   The Organizer dialog box

at the right. Select the styles in the box at the left and click Copy to add them to the Normal.dot template.

3. Click Close. When you open a new document window using the Normal.dot template, the added styles will be included.

Note: *The styles that are added to the Normal.dot template will remain there throughout the current word processing session; however, when you exit Word, you will be prompted to save the changes to the Normal.dot template file if you want to keep those styles.*

INSERTING PICTURES AND OBJECTS

I have created a document that contains linked text boxes with text continuing from one text box to the next one on a different page. I also entered other text in the document, but now I want to place some of it in linked text boxes, too. Is it possible to move existing text into linked text boxes? If so, how do you do it?

Yes, you can do this. Use the following steps:

1. Choose Text Box from the Insert menu. You will automatically switch to Print Layout View.

2. Draw the first box approximately where you want it. Then choose Text Box from the Insert menu again and draw a second text box at a different position.

Note: *The text boxes may be displayed in front of text. Refer to the question that begins "I inserted a text box in my document . . .," later in this section, which gives specific steps for wrapping text around text boxes.*

3. Move the insertion point to the first text box to display the Text Box toolbar. Click Link on the Text Box toolbar, as shown here:

Link button

4. The pointer becomes a pitcher. Click the up or down arrows in the vertical scroll bar (do not use the Next Page or Previous Page buttons—you will lose the link) to go to the second text box, and click it to create the link. The pitcher "pours its contents" into the second text box.

5. Select the text to be placed in the text boxes and choose Cut or Copy from the Edit menu, depending on what you want to do. Then move the insertion point to the first box and choose Paste from the Edit menu. It may take a few seconds for the text to be inserted in both linked boxes.

6. To adjust the placement of the text boxes, point to their borders to show four-sided arrows, and drag each box to an appropriate position; or, to resize the boxes, drag any of the eight sizing handles around the boxes.

How do I remove a border around a text box?

You can easily remove the border, as follows:

1. Select the text box and double-click any border, or choose Text Box from the Format menu.

2. Click the Colors And Lines tab.

3. In the Line section, click the down arrow in the Color box to display a list of options. See Figure 3-10.

4. Click No Line and click OK to return to the document window. Your box is now formatted without the border around it. When you move your insertion point away from the text box, you will not see the box; but if you

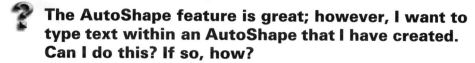

Figure 3-10 The Format Text Box dialog box

click the area where it is located, the selection border
and sizing handles will be displayed.

The AutoShape feature is great; however, I want to type text within an AutoShape that I have created. Can I do this? If so, how?

First, insert the AutoShape you want. See the sidebar "Inserting
an AutoShape" for specific instructions for doing this. Then use
the following steps to insert text in the AutoShape.

1. Right-click the AutoShape to show the shortcut menu.
   See Figure 3-11.

Inserting an AutoShape

1. Choose Picture from the Insert menu, and click AutoShapes. The AutoShapes toolbar is displayed, as well as the Drawing toolbar at the bottom of the window.

    Tip: *You can also right-click any toolbar to display the toolbar menu and select Drawing.*

2. You can use either of the following methods to select a shape:

    - If you use the AutoShapes toolbar, click a category and select a shape.

    - If you use the Drawing toolbar, click the AutoShapes button to display a list of categories. Select a category, and click the AutoShape you want to insert.

    You are automatically placed in Print Layout view, and the pointer becomes a crosshair. Point to where you want to insert the shape, and drag to the size you want.

    Note: *To change the size of the AutoShape, select it to display the sizing handles—these are eight small squares surrounding the shape. Point to any of them and drag a side or corner to the size you want.*

2. Click Add Text and type text in the shape. You can type text in any AutoShape except a line or a freeform shape.

    To edit the text, just right-click the AutoShape (not the text) to show the shortcut menu, and select Edit Text.

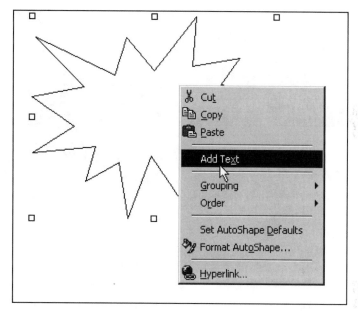

Figure 3-11 The shortcut menu for an AutoShape

I inserted a text box in my document and it was on top of existing text. I want to wrap the text around the text box. How do I do this?

You need to select the type of layout that you want for the text box. Use the following steps to do this:

1. Select the text box and double-click any border, or select the text box and choose Text Box from the Format menu. The Format Text Box dialog box will be displayed.

2. Click the Layout tab, as shown in Figure 3-12.

3. Click the type of wrapping style that you want. Also click a type of horizontal alignment, if you like.

4. Click OK.

Refer to the sidebar "Wrapping Text Around Other Objects" for more information.

Wrapping Text Around Other Objects

There are different ways of wrapping text around inserted objects other than text boxes.

Wrapping Text Around a Picture

Pictures are inserted inline with text, but you can change this if you like by doing the following:

1. Select the picture. The Picture toolbar will be displayed (if not, select it from the View | Toolbars | Picture option).

2. Click Text Wrapping and select the wrapping style you want.

Wrapping Text Around WordArt

When WordArt is inserted in a document, it will probably be located above the existing text, and you can wrap the text around it using the same procedure used to wrap text around a picture.

1. Select the WordArt object. The WordArt toolbar will be displayed.

2. Click Text Wrapping and select the wrapping style you want.

Wrapping Text Around an AutoShape

The procedure used to wrap text around an AutoShape is similar to wrapping text around a text box.

1. Double-click the AutoShape; or you can select the AutoShape and choose AutoShape from the Format menu.

2. Click the Layout tab and click the wrapping style you want.

3. Click OK to return to the document window.

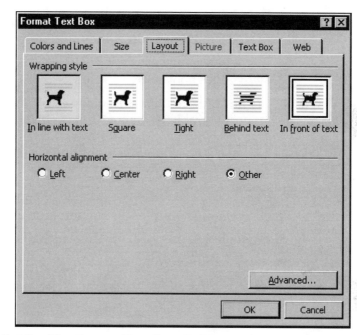

Figure 3-12 The Format Text Box dialog box

USING TABLES AND BORDERS

When I choose AutoFormat from the Format menu and click Options, I notice that Borders and Tables in AutoFormat As You Type are both turned on. How do you use these features?

To insert borders as you type, enter any of the following at the beginning of a paragraph:

● Type three or more hyphens (-) and press ENTER to place a line above a paragraph.

● Type three or more underscores (_) and press ENTER to place a thick line above a paragraph.

● Type three or more asterisks (*) and press ENTER to place a dotted line above a paragraph.

● Type three or more number signs (#) and press ENTER to place a decorative line above a paragraph.

● Type three or more tildes (~) and press ENTER to place a wavy line above a paragraph.

● Type three or more equal signs (=) and press ENTER to place a double line above a paragraph.

Examples of each are shown in Figure 3-13.

To insert a table automatically as you type, do the following.

1. Type a plus sign (+) for the left side of the table.

2. Type hyphens (------) for the width of the first column.

3. Type a plus sign to begin the second column.

4. Type hyphens for the width of the second column.

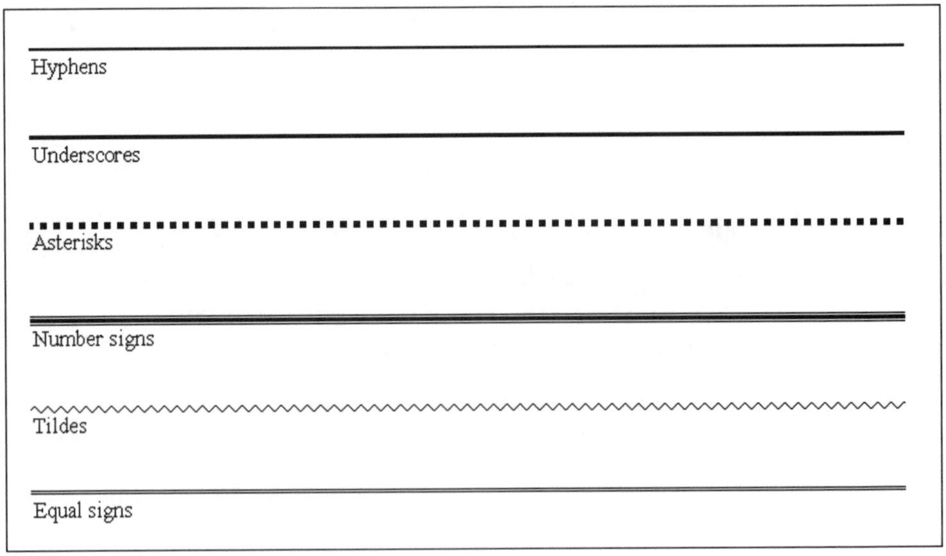

Hyphens

Underscores

Asterisks

Number signs

Tildes

Equal signs

Figure 3-13   Borders created with automatic formatting

5. Repeat steps 3 and 4 for as many columns as you want.

6. To end the table AutoFormatting, type a plus sign and press ENTER. For example, if you were to type

this is what the resulting table would look like:

Drag to move the table to a different position

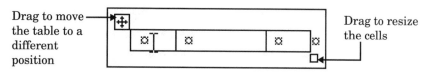

Drag to resize the cells

 Tip: *The items identified in the preceding illustration are used to drag or resize tables and are also available in other tables that you create using the Insert Table button (▦); the Draw Table button (✐); located on the Tables And Borders toolbar; or the Table menu. These sizing and dragging tools are only displayed, however, when you are in Print Layout view and when the insertion point is in the table.*

Note: *To add additional rows to the table, move the insertion point to the last cell at the right, and press TAB.*

I used the Insert Table button to create a table; and after reducing the width of the columns in the table, I wanted to center it across the page. I selected it and clicked the Center button on the Standard toolbar, but that only centered the text in each cell. How can I center an entire table quickly?

Right-click the table and choose Table Properties from the menu. Click the Table tab and click Center in the Alignment section of the dialog box, as shown next.

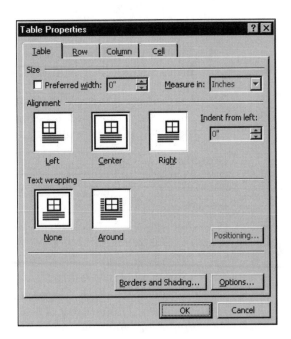

Click OK to return to the document window. Your table will be centered between the left and right margins.

Recently, before converting text to a table, I selected several paragraphs. I wanted each paragraph to be in its own cell; however, the text was divided into many cells. How can I avoid this?

To convert paragraph text to a table so that each entire paragraph is in a cell, follow these steps:

1. Select all of the paragraph text that you want in a table.

2. Choose Convert from the Table menu and select Text To Table.

3. Select the number of columns you want, if you want more than one.

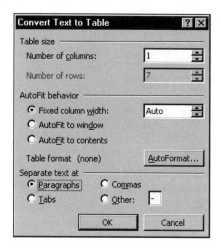

4. In the Convert Text To Table dialog box, there are several options in the Separate Text At box. To keep each paragraph in one cell, click the Paragraphs option:

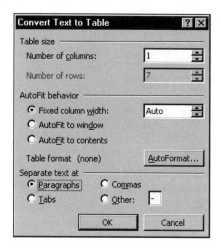

5. Click OK.

I created a template that included a table with formulas that would multiply a value in one cell by the value in another cell. When I used this template and entered values in various cells, I did not see the results of the calculation when I moved to the cell that contained the formula. What did I do wrong that prevented the formula from performing the calculation?

To see the results of the calculation, move the insertion point to the cell containing the formula and press F9. If the cells containing formulas are in the same row or in the same column, you can select all of them and press F9. See the sidebar "Entering Formulas in a Table" for more information.

Entering Formulas in a Table

1. Move the insertion point to the place where you want to insert the formula.

2. Choose Formula from the Table menu. The SUM function, which adds values in cells, may be displayed in the Formula box. Delete the function, if that is not the one you want.

3. Click the down arrow in the Paste Function box and select the function that you want; it is immediately displayed in the Formula box, as shown here:

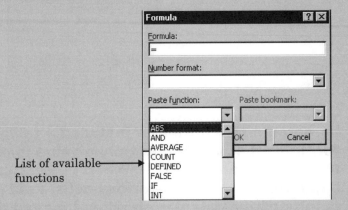

List of available functions

4. Enter the cells that are to be included in the formula. For example, to multiply the value in cell A1 by the value in cell C1, type **(a1,c1)** immediately following the function. Also, be sure the formula begins with an equal sign (=). Example: =PRODUCT(a1,c1).

Note: *Cells are numbered and lettered starting at the upper left with A1. Columns are lettered from A to Z, left to right. Rows are numbered down. A cell address is the intersection of a column letter and a row number.*

5. You can then click the down arrow in the Number Format box and select the format you want.

6. Click OK when you are done to return to the table. The calculation will be displayed in the appropriate cell.

Tip: *If you only want to add values in a row or column, display the Tables And Borders toolbar; move the insertion point to the cell in which the results are to be inserted; and click AutoSum, shown here. The result will be displayed immediately.*

AutoSum button

 Note: *You can insert an Excel worksheet in a Word document, which allows you to enter formulas easily in various cells, and you can enter text just as you do in a Word table. See Chapter 8 for more information about copying objects between Office applications.*

USING MACROS

I created a macro and neglected to assign a shortcut key to run it. Can I assign a shortcut key to a macro after I have created the macro?

Yes, you can use the Customize option in the Tools menu, or you can create the macro again and assign shortcut keys to it. The fastest way is to use the Customize option.

1. Choose Customize from the Tools menu.

2. In any tab, click Keyboard, shown here:

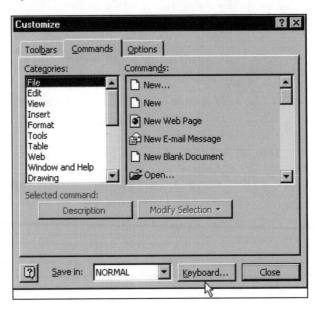

3. In the Categories list, scroll down and choose Macros. Your macros will then be displayed in the Macros box.

4. Select the macro to which you want to assign a shortcut key.

5. Move the insertion point to the Press New Shortcut Key box and press the keys you want. If they are already assigned to a function, that information will be displayed below the text box.

6. Click Assign. The new keys will then be displayed in the Current Keys box.

7. Click Close and Close again. See the sidebar, "Creating a Macro," for more information.

 I tried to use one of the Word command macros; however, I got a message saying that my macros are disabled. How can I enable macros so they will run in my documents?

Since there are a number of viruses that depend on Word or Excel macros, Microsoft has established security levels that determine whether or not macros will work.

Creating a Macro

1. Choose Macro from the Tools menu.

2. Click Record New Macro. The Record Macro dialog box will be displayed, as shown here:

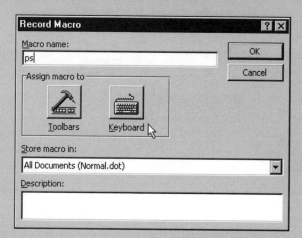

3. Type a name for the macro.

Note: *If you are creating a macro a second time to assign shortcut keys to it, type the same name as the old macro and follow the prompts.*

4. Click Keyboard if you want to assign shortcut keys; and with the insertion point in the Press New Shortcut Key box, press the keys you want to run the macro. Then click Assign and Close. The mouse pointer will look like an arrow with an attached cassette tape when the macro recorder is turned on.

Note: *If the shortcut keys are already assigned, the Currently Assigned To area will tell you that.*

Tip: *You can also assign the macro to a toolbar, if you like. Click Toolbars and follow the prompts.*

5. You can now create a macro by entering the keystrokes and commands and options that you want to be recorded in the macro. You can use the mouse to select menus and options; however, you cannot use the mouse to move around in the document or to select text that is to be copied or cut. You will have to use the keyboard for these actions.

6. When you have finished, click the Stop Recording button in the Macro toolbar, shown here:

Stop Recording ⟶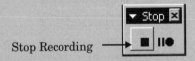

To run the macro, press the shortcut keys assigned to it; or choose Macro from the Tools menu, click Macros, select the macro you want, and click Run.

If you select the Low security level, you will be able to open documents that have macros without being prompted. If you select the Medium security level, you will be prompted to Enable Macros each time a document that contains macros opens. If you select the High security level, macros will be enabled when the document is opened only if the macros are signed from a trusted source. If the document contains macros that are unsigned, the macros will be disabled. If the macros are signed by an unknown author, the user can enable the macros if they believe the author to be a trusted source.

To change the security level for your documents, follow these steps:

1. Choose Macros from the Tools menu.

2. Click Security to display the Security dialog box shown in Figure 3-14.

3. Click Low to select the least security.

4. Click OK to return to the document.

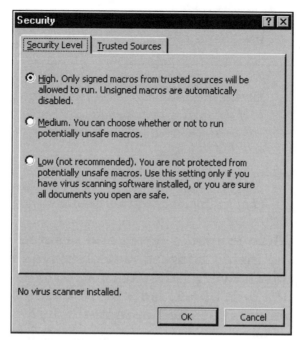

Figure 3-14   Security dialog box

5. Close the file and reopen it for the new security level to take effect. You can then rerun the macro. If Low security was selected, the macro will run directly. If you selected Medium, a dialog box will ask you to click Enable Macros to continue. If you selected High, the response you get will depend on the validity of the signature for the macro.

MAIL AND OTHER MERGING

 I want to print an organization name in uppercase in a merged document, but I want it in lowercase with initial caps elsewhere. I tried to format the merge field in uppercase; but each time I merged, the formatting immediately changed back to lowercase. How can I format a field in uppercase?

Select the field and be sure to include the chevrons. Then choose Font from the Format menu, click All Caps, and click

OK. The Change Case option in the Format menu cannot be used here.

 Note: *When you select a field in order to change the formatting, drag across the field to include the chevrons. Notice that the field is then a shade darker than if you click it once, or if you double-click it. The darker shade indicates that you have selected it.*

 Note: *Refer to the sidebar, "Mail Merge Helper," later in this chapter, for detailed instructions for using the Merge function.*

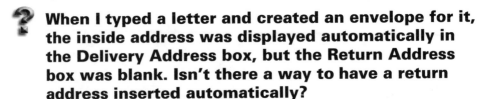

 When I typed a letter and created an envelope for it, the inside address was displayed automatically in the Delivery Address box, but the Return Address box was blank. Isn't there a way to have a return address inserted automatically?

To insert your address automatically in the Return Address box, choose Options from the Tools menu, click the User Information tab, and type your address in the Mailing Address box. Then, each time you create an envelope, your address will be in the Return Address box.

I want to insert a new field in my data source; however, I don't see a way to do this in the data form window. Is it possible to add a new field?

Yes it is, but you have to add the new field in the data source window that displays the table, rather than in the data form window. To do this, follow these steps:

 1. Open the main document (the data source that is attached is also opened automatically); click the Edit Data Source button in the Mail Merge toolbar, shown here, to switch to the data form; and click View Source. The table containing the data will be displayed.

 2. In the data source window, click the Manage Fields button on the Database toolbar.

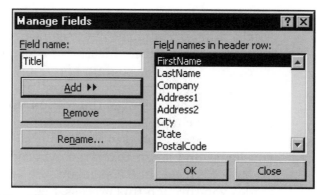

Figure 3-15   The Manage Fields dialog box

a. The Manage Fields dialog box will be displayed, as shown in Figure 3-15. Type a name for the new field and click Add.

b. When you're done, click OK to return to the data source window. Type appropriate information in the new field(s) and save the changes.

Note: *You can also add a field by going to the data file (table), selecting the column that you want to be adjacent to the new column, choosing Insert from the Table menu, and clicking either Columns To The Left or Columns To The Right. A column will then be inserted. Type a field name in the first row in the new column, and save the file.*

You can move a new field (column) to a different position by selecting the entire column and dragging it to a different position. To select an entire column quickly, point to the top of the column to display the wide black arrow, and click.

I saved my merge output to a document file and then tried to open it using the Merge Documents option on the Tools menu, but I saw a prompt: "The merge documents contain unmarked changes. Do you want to merge up to the first untracked changes?" What does this have to do with merged documents?

Nothing. The Merge Documents option is used to combine into one document the edits of documents that have been

reviewed by several users. Generally, these edited documents will be different versions of the same document that have been saved as separate files. These documents contain editing marks, and may also contain highlighted text and comments. There is more information about editing and saving different versions of a document in the section "Collaborative Editing," later in this chapter.

Mail Merge is used to send boilerplate documents, envelopes, and labels to a large mailing list. When you choose Mail Merge from the Tools menu, the Mail Merge Helper guides you through this process. See the "Mail Merge Helper" sidebar for more information.

Mail Merge Helper

To use the Mail Merge Helper, follow these steps:

1. Open a new document window, if necessary, and choose Mail Merge from the Tools menu. The Mail Merge Helper is displayed, as shown here:

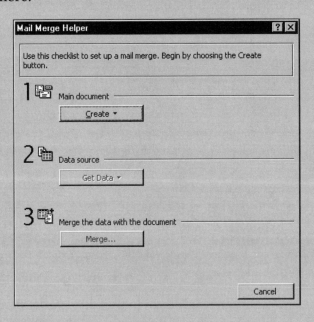

2. Click Create under Main Document and select the type of document you want to create.

3. Click Active Window to use the current window for the main document. If you click New Main Document, a new document window will be opened. The Get Data button will now be available.

4. Click Get Data and select Create Data Source if you need to create a new data document. If you already have a data document available, click Open Data Source and select the document you want. Or, to extract data from one of several address books you might have, choose Use Address Book.

5. If you click Create Data Source, a list of field names is displayed at the right. They will automatically be included in your data document; however, you can remove any of them. To do this, select the field you do not want and click Remove Field Name. To add a new field name, type the name in the Field Name box at the left and click Add Field Name. If you enter a space in a field name, you will not be able to use it—no spaces in field names are allowed.

6. When you are done, click OK. The Save As dialog box is displayed. Type a filename for the data document and click Save.

7. You can now go to either the data file or the main document; however, for our purposes here, click Edit Data Source. A data form will be displayed, and you can enter personal information for each record. Press ENTER after each entry, and also press ENTER after completing the last entry in the first record to go to the next record. The number of records is displayed at the bottom of the dialog box. When you have typed in all the entries, click OK.

8. You are now in the main document window. Choose Save from the File menu, type a filename, and click Save.

9. Now you can type the boilerplate text in the main document and insert fields where you need them. For example, if you are creating a form letter, move the insertion point to the place where the inside

address will be printed, click Insert Merge Field on the Mail Merge toolbar shown here, and click Title to insert the title field:

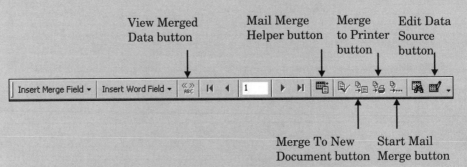

Press the SPACEBAR once and repeat to insert the field FirstName, and so on. You can insert fields just as you do text—separate them by spaces and press ENTER to move another line. Also, you can insert one field as many times as necessary in the main document. When you are done, save your changes.

10. You can click Edit Data Source to switch to the data form. If you want to see the entire table, click View Source in the Data Form dialog box. When you are in the data source table, you can click the Mail Merge Main Document button, as shown here, to switch to that window:

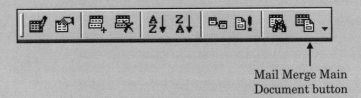

11. In the main document, you can click View Merged Data, shown in step 9, to see what the merged output will look like. Click this button again to see the fields. This is not the actual merge.

12. To produce the merged output, you can do one of the following:

- Click the Merge To New Document button to merge the data document with the main document and see the output in a new

document window. You can then print the output from there and save the document as a new file. However, if you have a large database, this takes up a lot of disk space; saving the output is not necessary as long as you have the main document and the data document.

● Click the Merge To Printer button to send the merged output directly to the printer.

● Click the Merge button. This allows you to customize your merge with the following choices. When you are done, click Merge again.

   ● Select Records To Be Merged to merge only certain records. For example, you can merge only records 10 through 20 using this option. Select From and type **10** in the first box and **20** in the second box.

   ● Click Query Options to enter specifications for a query or to sort the data based on selected fields. The question that begins "I opened my data document. . .," later in this chapter, gives more information on how to perform queries.

   ● Specify whether you want to print or not print blank lines that may be inserted if a field is empty.

13. When the merge is complete, save and close the main document and the data document.

To perform another merge using the same documents, open the main document. When you do this, the data document will be opened too, because it was attached when you created the main document. If you want to select a different data document, open the main document, click the Mail Merge Helper button, click Get Data, select Open A Data Source, and select a different data document.

 I do not see any labels that are the size of the ones I usually use in mailings. How can I print custom-sized labels that are not included in Word 2000's label list?

Word has a custom label facility that allows you to create a custom label by doing the following:

1. Select Envelopes And Labels from the Tools menu and click the Labels tab.

2. Click Options and then click New Label to go to the New Custom dialog box shown in Figure 3-16.

3. Type a label name and, in the various boxes, enter new measurements for the label size you want. Notice that the Preview changes as you enter new measurements.

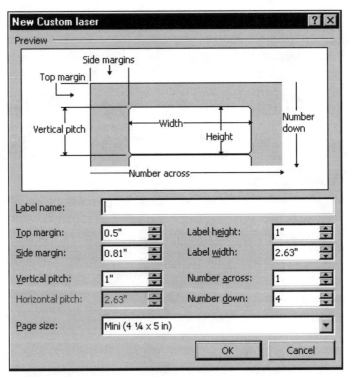

Figure 3-16   The New Custom dialog box

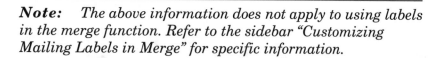

Be sure to select an appropriate paper size. A Horizontal Pitch is available only when you have more than one label across the page.

4. Click OK when you are done to return to the Label Options dialog box.

5. Select the new custom label now listed in the Product Number box, and click OK. At this point you can enter an address for the label; and in the Print area of the Envelopes And Labels dialog box, choose whether to print a full page of the same label or to print only one label.

6. Click Print.

Note: *The above information does not apply to using labels in the merge function. Refer to the sidebar "Customizing Mailing Labels in Merge" for specific information.*

Tip: *If you are not using merge to produce labels and you want to print a page of labels with different addresses on each label, choose Envelopes And Labels from the Tools menu, click Options, and select the type of label you want. Click OK and click New Document in the Label tab. The blank labels will be shown in a new document window, and you can enter addresses in each. Press TAB to move from one label to the next.*

When I print envelopes, I have to place each one in the center of the manual feed tray. There is not a precise guide on the tray, and many times the addresses are not placed correctly on the envelope. Can anything be done about this?

You can make changes to the way the envelope is inserted. Follow these steps:

1. Choose Envelopes And Labels from the Tools menu.

2. Choose the Envelopes tab and click Options.

3. Click the Printing Options tab, shown next.

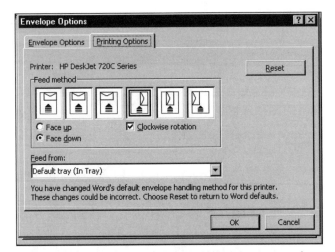

Customizing Mailing Labels in Merge

To customize mailing labels in merge, do the following:

1. Choose Mail Merge from the Tools menu.
2. Click Create under Main Document and select Mailing Labels.
3. Click Active Window to use the current document window for the main document.
4. Click Get Data under Data Source and create or open a data source. Then click Set Up Main Document. The Label Options dialog box is displayed.
5. Click New Label.
6. Type a label name, enter the measurements as needed, and click OK. Click OK again to go to the Create Labels window.
7. Click Insert Merge Fields and select the fields for the address.
8. Click OK when you have finished, and click Close to remove the Mail Merge Helper from the window and to see your labels.
9. You can now complete the merge by clicking the Merge To Document, Merge To Printer, or Merge button on the Mail Merge toolbar to use query options.

Which default feed method is selected depends on the printer you are using.

4. Select a different feed method, and click OK to return to the Envelope tab.

5. Click Print.

Tip: *Depending on the type of printer you are using, you may have to try several feed methods to find the one that works best for you.*

I opened my data document and wanted to perform a query to select only certain addresses (those in one city) to use in a merge. How can I do this?

You can only perform a query in the Word data document if the main document that it is attached to is also open. Open the main document first, and then do the following:

1. Click Merge on the Mail Merge toolbar.

2. Click Query Options and select the Filter Records tab, shown in Figure 3-17.

3. Click the down arrow under Field and select the field for the query (see Figure 3-17).

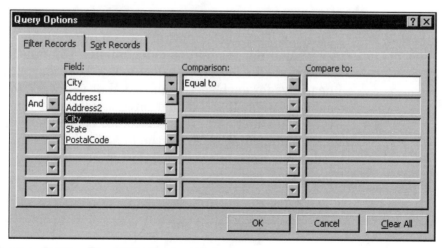

Figure 3-17 The Filter Records tab

4. Select the type of Comparison, if necessary.

5. Move to the Compare To box and type the data to be selected for the query. You can repeat steps 3, 4, and 5 for additional fields, if you like.

6. Click OK and then click Merge.

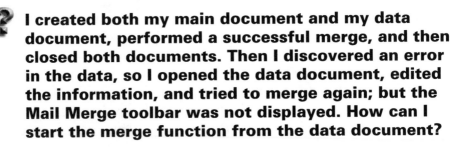 **I created both my main document and my data document, performed a successful merge, and then closed both documents. Then I discovered an error in the data, so I opened the data document, edited the information, and tried to merge again; but the Mail Merge toolbar was not displayed. How can I start the merge function from the data document?**

You can't. You always have to open the main document to begin a merge. Once the main document and the data document are created, the main document has the data document attached to it automatically. See the sidebar "Mail Merge Helper," earlier in this chapter, for information about using Mail Merge.

WORKING WITH LARGE DOCUMENTS

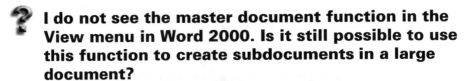 **I do not see the master document function in the View menu in Word 2000. Is it still possible to use this function to create subdocuments in a large document?**

Yes it is. The master document is now available in Outline view. In order to create subdocuments, you must first have an outline for the master document. That is, you must have headings for each section of text that you want to create as a subdocument. If you do not have headings in your document, type a heading and press ENTER for each subdocument. Then assign a heading style for the headings. You can then use the following steps to create subdocuments based on the headings.

1. Click the Outline View button at the left of the horizontal scroll bar.

2. Select the headings and text that you want in subdocuments. For example, if you select text beginning with a Heading 2 style, a subdocument will be created at each heading formatted with a Heading 2 style.

3. Click the Create Subdocument button. Each section beginning with a Heading 2 style is a subdocument. When you save the master document, each subdocument is saved as a separate file, using the heading text for the filename. A continuous section break separates each file in the master document.

 Note: *If you collapse the subdocuments before naming and saving the master document, you will be prompted to save.*

 I know how to divide a large document into subdocuments using the Master Document feature. However, now I would like to combine several documents in a master document. Can I do this? If so, how?

Open a new document window and switch to Outline view. The Outlining toolbar will be displayed. To insert existing documents in the master document, do the following:

1. Click the Insert Subdocument button.

2. The Insert Subdocument dialog box will open. Select the file you want to insert, and click the Open button. The file is inserted in the master document at the insertion point, followed by a section break.

3. Repeat steps 1 and 2 to select additional documents.

4. When you are done, choose Save from the File menu, type a filename for the master document, and click Save.

 Tip: *If you decide to collapse the subdocuments before saving, you will be prompted to save.*

 Can I use a concordance file in Word 2000 the same way I used it in earlier versions of Word?

Yes, the concordance file is still available and is used to automatically mark text for index entries. To use it, do the following:

1. Create the concordance file. (See the sidebar, "Creating a Concordance File," later in this chapter, for specific steps.)

2. Open the document to be marked for index entries, and choose Index And Tables from the Insert menu. Click the Index tab, shown here:

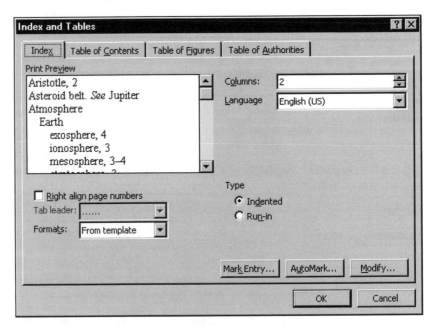

3. Click AutoMark, select the file that you are using as a concordance file to automatically mark text for the index, and click Open. The entries will then be marked automatically for the index.

Tip: *If Show / Hide (the paragraph mark in the Standard toolbar) is turned on, the index marks will be displayed in the text; otherwise, you will not see them.*

4. Move the insertion point to the place where you want to insert the index.

5. Choose Index And Tables from the Insert menu, go to the Index tab again, and click OK to create the index.

 Tip: *In the Index tab, you can change the alignment of page numbers, select a leader character, select a special format, choose the number of columns, and otherwise customize the way the index will be formatted.*

Can I move outline levels from one subdocument to another in Outline view? If I do this, will it change my original documents?

You can easily move a section of text in a master document. Click the Expand Subdocuments button if the subdocument text is not displayed.

Then do the following:

1. To select the block of text that is to be moved, click the plus sign to the left of the heading and the text.

 Tip: *If you double-click the plus sign, the text below the heading will be collapsed, making it easier to move.*

2. Click the plus sign and drag it to the position where you want to move the text. As you drag, a horizontal line will be displayed, indicating the position of the block of text.

3. Release the mouse button when the text is where you want it.

Creating a Concordance File

A concordance file contains a list of words or phrases that you want to include in an index. It is used to automatically mark these words as index entries. When the index is created, they are inserted automatically with their corresponding page numbers. To create this file, follow these steps:

1. Open a new document file.

2. Insert a two-column table, and in the left column type the words to be included in the index exactly as they appear in the document, including the same capitalization. In the right column, type the entries as you want them to appear in the index. Here's an example:

Creating·a·document	Document:Create
Saving·a·document	Document:Save
options	Options
mouse	Mouse
keyboard	Keyboard
characters	Characters
show·all	Characters:Show·all
hide·all	Characters:Hide·all

> *Note:* *If you want an item to be displayed in the Index as a subentry, type the main entry text followed by a colon (no spaces), and then type the subentry text, as shown in the preceding illustration.*

3. Choose Save from the File menu, name the document, and click Save.

4. Close the file.

> *Tip:* *You can also create a concordance without a table by pressing TAB after typing the word to be marked, and then type the entry the way you want it to appear in the index. However, it is much easier to use a table; if the entries are in a table, you can easily rearrange them, edit them, or select only certain ones.*

If you save the changes made by moving text from one subdocument to another, this will change the original documents. When you open one of the subdocuments as a file by itself, you will see the changes.

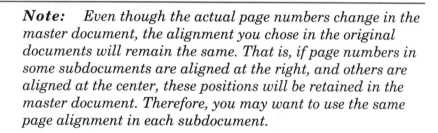

I inserted page numbers in separate subdocuments that I have now combined in a master document. What happens to these page numbers when I create a table of contents in the master document?

Appropriate page numbers will be assigned to each page in the master document, and the table of contents will show them. You can save the master document, and these page numbers will remain in the master document. However, when you open each subdocument individually, you will find that the original page numbers have not been changed. For example, if the last document had page numbering starting with the number 1, it will remain that way when that document is opened by itself, rather than as part of the master document.

Note: *Even though the actual page numbers change in the master document, the alignment you chose in the original documents will remain the same. That is, if page numbers in some subdocuments are aligned at the right, and others are aligned at the center, these positions will be retained in the master document. Therefore, you may want to use the same page alignment in each subdocument.*

COLLABORATIVE EDITING

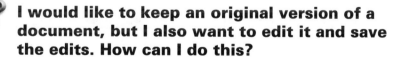

I would like to keep an original version of a document, but I also want to edit it and save the edits. How can I do this?

You can save several versions in the same document file by using the following steps.

1. Open the document; display the Reviewing toolbar; and, if necessary, choose Track Changes from the Tools

menu, select Highlight Changes, and click Track Changes While Editing. You can also click Highlight Changes On Screen, which will make it easy to identify edits.

 2. Edit the document, and then click the Save Version button on the Reviewing toolbar. The Save Version dialog box will be displayed.

 Tip: *If the Reviewing toolbar is not displayed, right-click any toolbar and click Reviewing.*

3. Enter comments if you like, but this is not necessary. Click OK.

4. After saving the edited text as a new version, reject all of the edits in the original document. To do this, right-click on any edit, and click Accept Or Reject Changes. The Accept Or Reject Changes dialog box will be displayed, as shown in Figure 3-18. Click Reject All and then Yes to confirm. Click Close.

5. Save and close the document. When you open the original document, it will not contain the edits. They are saved in the new version.

 Note: *You can also choose Versions from the File menu, enter comments if you like, and click OK.*

Figure 3-18   The Accept Or Reject Changes dialog box

Another way to keep the original version is as follows:

1. Open the document, display the Reviewing toolbar, and click Save Version; or, if the Reviewing toolbar is not displayed, choose Versions from the File menu, and click Save Now. The Save Version dialog box is displayed.

2. If you like, enter a comment such as "original version," and click OK.

3. Edit the document and save the edits.

4. Double-click the Versions icon on the status bar, select the first version, and click Open. Both versions will be displayed. You can close either window and work on the version you want.

 Note: *It is not necessary to track the changes; however, if the edits are highlighted on the screen, it is obviously easier to identify them.*

 I would like to compare a document version created with Word's File | Versions option with the orginal document. Can I do this?

In order to compare the original document with a version created with Word's version feature, as described in the previous question, you have to save the version you want to compare with a different filename. To do this,

1. Open the document containing saved versions, and double-click the Versions icon on the status bar, or select Versions from the File menu.

2. Select the file version you want, and click the Open button.

3. Save the document with a different filename, and click Close on the File menu.

4. In the document that is saved with multiple versions, choose Track Changes from the Tools menu, and click Compare Documents.

5. Select the newly saved file and click Open. Click Yes if prompted. The original document will now display the edits that have been saved in the different version.

I have been told that reviewers can mark edits as they are added to documents. How do you do this?

To mark edits as they are entered, follow these steps:

1. Choose Track Changes from the Tools menu.

2. Select Highlight Changes to display the Highlight Changes dialog box shown here:

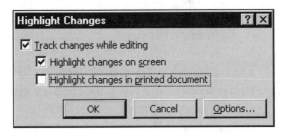

3. Turn on both Track Changes While Editing and Highlight Changes On Screen. You can leave Highlight Changes In Printed Document turned on, if you like, or you can turn it off.

4. Click OK.

Another way to mark text, if Highlight Changes On Screen is turned on, is as follows:

1. Display the Reviewing toolbar. To do this, right-click any toolbar and select Reviewing.

2. Click the Track Changes button, shown here. TRK will be turned on in the status bar:

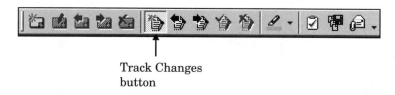

Track Changes
button

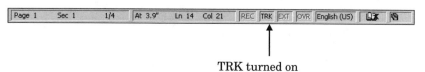

TRK turned on

3. Type any new text. It will be underlined to indicate added edits. If you delete text, it will be formatted with a strikethrough to indicate a suggested deletion.

See the sidebar "Revision Marks, Highlighting, and Comments" for more detailed information on these features.

Our office produces large documents that include files created by several people. We lock the subdocuments, but anyone can open the master document and remove the lock on the subdocuments. Is there any other way to prevent unwanted changes to subdocuments?

The best way to prevent unwanted changes to documents is to save each subdocument with a password. First, open a subdocument. You can do this by either opening it as a separate document, or, in the master document, collapsing all documents and clicking the subdocument that you want to open. Then do the following:

1. Choose Save As from the File menu.

2. Click Tools and click General Options.

Revision Marks, Highlighting, and Comments

If you want others to review your document, they can suggest edits without changing the original document. Any or all of the following features can be used.

- Revision marks can be added to edits as they are entered, as discussed in the answer to the preceding question, "I have been told that reviewers can mark edits as they are added to documents. How do you do this?"

- Highlighting can be added to text to call attention to it.

- Comments can be inserted. Comments do not change the text but are ideas or suggestions by a reviewer.

Adding Highlighting to Text

 1. Click Highlight on the Formatting toolbar. The pointer becomes a drawing tool.

> *Tip:* *If the Highlight button is not displayed on the Formatting toolbar, display the Reviewing toolbar.*

2. Drag the drawing tool across all of the text that you want to highlight.

3. When you are done, click the Highlight button again to return the mouse pointer to an I-beam.

> *Tip:* *You can change the color of the highlighting. Click the down arrow at the right of the Highlight button. A palette is displayed, and you can select the color you want.*

4. If you want to remove highlighting, click Highlight on the Formatting toolbar to turn it on and drag across the highlighted text.

Inserting a Comment

1. Display the Reviewing toolbar.

2. Move the insertion point to the place where you want to add a comment.

 3. Click the Insert Comment button.

4. Text will be highlighted and followed by your initials and a number in brackets. A comments pane appears at the bottom of the document window, as shown here:

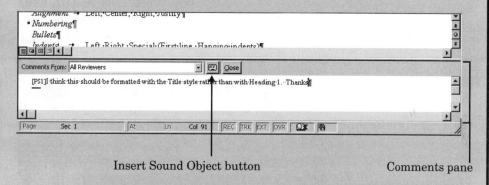

Insert Sound Object button   Comments pane

5. Type your comments in this pane, and click Close when you are done.

Tip: *If you have a microphone and speakers, you can click Insert Sound Object and enter your comments verbally.*

Reading a Comment in a Document

Move the pointer over the highlighted text. The comment and the author's name will be displayed automatically, as shown here:

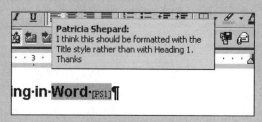

Removing a Comment

1. Display the Reviewing toolbar.
2. Click the highlighted text.

 3. Click the Delete Comment button on the Reviewing toolbar.

> *Tip:* *Another way to remove the comment is to right-click the comment's highlighted text and click Delete Comment.*

3. Type a password in the Password To Modify box and click OK. The Confirm Password dialog box, shown here, will be displayed:

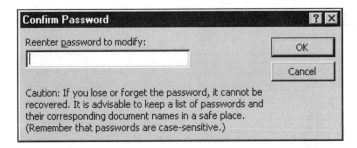

4. Type the password a second time, and click OK.

 Caution: *Be sure you remember the password. It is a good idea to write down the passwords for documents that you are using and keep them in a safe place. If several people are going to be working on the same document, make sure each of them knows the password for the document. They will have to enter the password before the document can be opened.*

5. Click Save.

 Note: *If others review the documents, but you want to control the types of changes they can make, turn on Protect Document and specify the type of changes allowed. To do this, choose Protect Document from the Tools menu. A dialog box is displayed, in which you can turn on any of the following to allow only certain changes: Tracked Changes, Comments, or Forms. You can also enter a password that will be required to open the document.*

You can save the master document with the Read-Only Recommended option turned on; however, this will not prevent the subdocuments in the master document from being opened and edited by anyone on the network. To save the master document as read-only, do this:

1. Choose Save As from the File menu.
2. Click Tools and click General Options.
3. Click Read-Only Recommended.

File sharing options for "Formatting"
Password to open: Password to modify:

☑ Read-only recommended

4. Click OK and then click Save.

 Note: To turn off read-only or remove a password, open the document, choose Save As from the File menu, click Tools, and click General Options. Delete the password in the applicable Password box and click Read-Only Recommended to remove the check mark. Click OK and then click Save.

 When I open a document that I know contains several versions, I open only the original version. How do I know what other versions of a document have been saved, and how can I open them?

 Open the document and double-click the Versions icon on the status bar. A Versions In dialog box will be displayed, as shown in Figure 3-19. You will see the date and time each version was saved, who saved it, and any comments that were entered. Select the version you want to see, and click Open.

 Note: If no versions have been saved, the Versions icon will not be displayed.

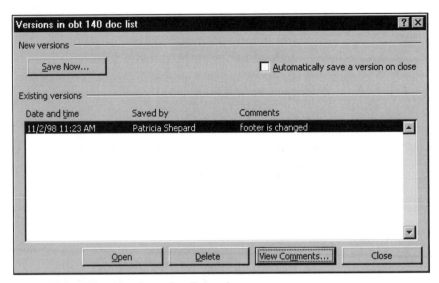

Figure 3-19   The Versions In dialog box

 Tip: *If the status bar is not displayed, you can choose Versions from the File menu to see the versions that have been saved. If you want to display the status bar, choose Options from the Tools menu and click the View tab. Click Status Bar to turn it on, and click OK.*

 Is there a way that I can share documents created in Word 2000 with others who use Word 97?

Yes, you can. The features in Word 2000 that are not supported by Word 97 can be disabled. To do this, follow these steps:

1. Choose Options from the Tools menu.

2. Click the Save tab, and check Disable Features Not Supported By Word 97.

3. Click OK.

Chapter 4

Analyzing with Excel

Answer Topics!

Analyzing with Excel @ a Glance

This chapter covers Excel, the spreadsheet application within Office. It will offer revealing insights in the following areas:

Excel Functions provides an overview of the functions performed by Excel. It will help you understand the complexities of this powerful program.

Using and Changing a Worksheet addresses how to work with the worksheet itself and its tools and elements, whether they are keys, functions, toolbars, or multiple pages of a worksheet. You can change some defaults that may not work for you.

Entering and Changing Information discusses easy ways to handle basic tasks, such as changing the way the ENTER key works or deleting data. This section also discusses ways of handling numbers as text, working with a series of numbers, and inserting special characters.

Entering and Using Formulas and Functions tackles one of the most confusing tasks: handling formulas and functions. In this section, you will see how to make them more readable and accurate. Also, you will learn how to find information about using them more quickly and how to manipulate the formulas to use them more effectively.

Copying and Moving Information covers the simple, but important, tasks of moving and copying data in ways that are not typical, such as working with relative formulas and inserting cells above or to the left of existing cells.

Adding Formatting, Patterns, and Borders helps you work with worksheets, formatting your data to make it more readable or professional looking. You will learn how to insert special symbols, apply patterns or fancy formatting very simply, reuse formatting in other worksheets, split cells, and rotate text.

Creating and Formatting Charts presents some interesting and helpful tidbits, such as how to add callouts to a chart or change labels after a chart has already been created. You will get some pointers on what kind of chart can be most helpful, and how to use data ranges, data series, data labels, and data markers most effectively.

Sorting, Filtering, and Summarizing Data addresses how to sift through data by creating handy input forms, importing other databases, selecting certain records from the spreadsheet, sorting on more than three levels, and creating subtotals in a sorted list.

Working with PivotTables and PivotCharts discusses how you create and work with Pivot Tables and Pivot Charts to work with the data table that is the source of the chart data, to reset the automatic totaling on rows in the Pivot Table, to reorder data in the Pivot Table, to change dollars to a count on the PivotTable, and to find missing data tables.

EXCEL FUNCTIONS

Excel is considered the worksheet component of Office, yet Excel can perform three separate functions:

- The *worksheet* function, which displays and analyzes text and numbers in rows and columns

- *The database* function, which manipulates lists of information

- *The chart* function, which produces charts that graphically depict data

Each function is really just a different way of looking at and interacting with data that has a common structure based on *rows* and *columns*. This common structure is the worksheet.

The worksheet function of Excel, shown in Figure 4-1, provides for as many sheets as you can hold in memory, each containing 256 columns and 65,536 rows. The intersection of a row and a column on a single sheet is a *cell*, which can contain up to 32,767 characters.

Excel's worksheets are stored in *files* called *workbooks* (*books,* for short). Think of a workbook as a file of worksheets (*sheets,* for short), although it can also contain charts and programming pages. The three-dimensional structure of rows, columns, and sheets provides a powerful framework for financial analysis. Consider a company's financial plan or budget, an example of which is shown in Figure 4-2:

- Each row is an account—an element of revenue or expense.

- Each column is a period of time—months, quarters, or years.

- Each sheet is a unit of the company—a store, plant, office, or division.

- Summing across columns, you get the total for an account.

- Summing down rows, you get the total for a time period.

- Summing through the sheets, you get the total for the company.

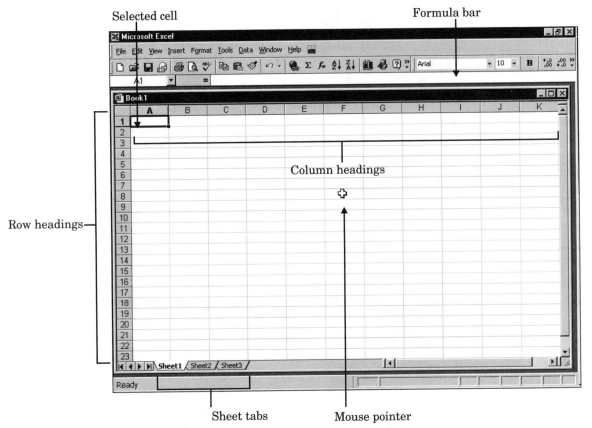

Figure 4-1 Excel's Worksheet window

Excel identifies where information is located on a worksheet with the following notation:

- Rows are numbered 1 through 65,536.
- The 256 columns are labeled A through IV (A through Z, then AA through AZ, BA through BZ, and so on through IV).
- Sheets are identified initially as Sheet1 through however many sheets you have, but you can rename them anything you want, within the 31-character limit.

When information is entered on a sheet, it is stored in a specific cell or location. You refer to that location by the

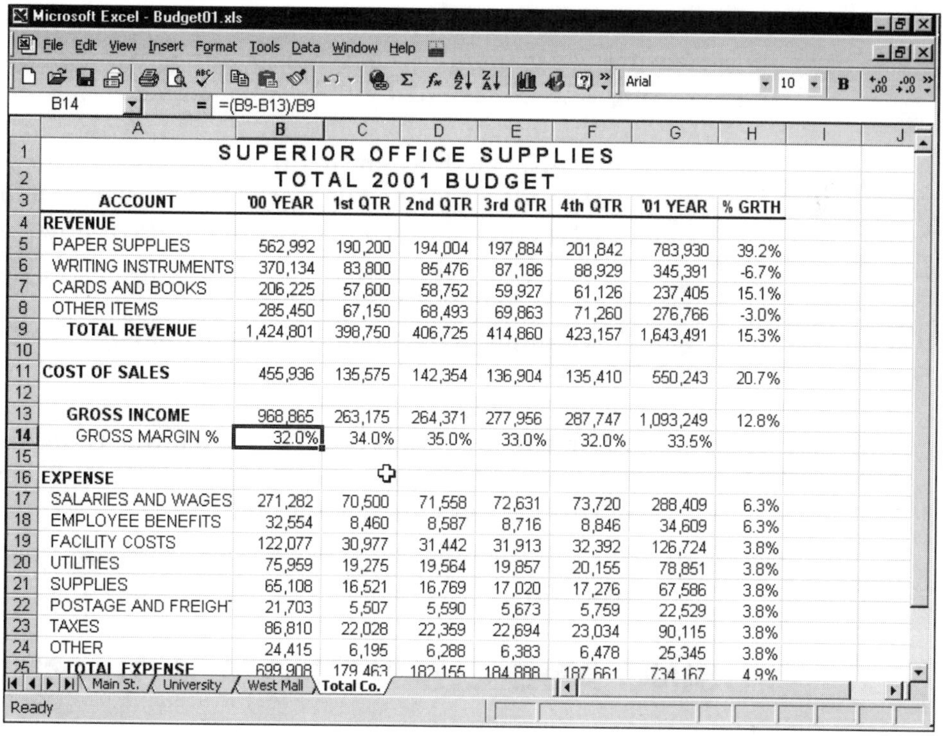

	A	B	C	D	E	F	G	H
1	SUPERIOR OFFICE SUPPLIES							
2	TOTAL 2001 BUDGET							
3	ACCOUNT	'00 YEAR	1st QTR	2nd QTR	3rd QTR	4th QTR	'01 YEAR	% GRTH
4	REVENUE							
5	PAPER SUPPLIES	562,992	190,200	194,004	197,884	201,842	783,930	39.2%
6	WRITING INSTRUMENTS	370,134	83,800	85,476	87,186	88,929	345,391	-6.7%
7	CARDS AND BOOKS	206,225	57,600	58,752	59,927	61,126	237,405	15.1%
8	OTHER ITEMS	285,450	67,150	68,493	69,863	71,260	276,766	-3.0%
9	TOTAL REVENUE	1,424,801	398,750	406,725	414,860	423,157	1,643,491	15.3%
10								
11	COST OF SALES	455,936	135,575	142,354	136,904	135,410	550,243	20.7%
12								
13	GROSS INCOME	968,865	263,175	264,371	277,956	287,747	1,093,249	12.8%
14	GROSS MARGIN %	32.0%	34.0%	35.0%	33.0%	32.0%	33.5%	
15								
16	EXPENSE							
17	SALARIES AND WAGES	271,282	70,500	71,558	72,631	73,720	288,409	6.3%
18	EMPLOYEE BENEFITS	32,554	8,460	8,587	8,716	8,846	34,609	6.3%
19	FACILITY COSTS	122,077	30,977	31,442	31,913	32,392	126,724	3.8%
20	UTILITIES	75,959	19,275	19,564	19,857	20,155	78,851	3.8%
21	SUPPLIES	65,108	16,521	16,769	17,020	17,276	67,586	3.8%
22	POSTAGE AND FREIGHT	21,703	5,507	5,590	5,673	5,759	22,529	3.8%
23	TAXES	86,810	22,028	22,359	22,694	23,034	90,115	3.8%
24	OTHER	24,415	6,195	6,288	6,383	6,478	25,345	3.8%
25	TOTAL EXPENSE	699,908	179,463	182,155	184,888	187,661	734,167	4.9%

Figure 4-2 A company's financial plan

sheet, column, and row in which the information is placed; for example, Sheet1, column D, row 7. Excel addresses are written with the column reference first, followed by the row. Using this convention, you can write this example address as D7. To add a sheet reference to this address, just place the sheet name and an exclamation point in front of the column and row—for example, Sheet1!D7. A sheet is addressed from A1 for the cell in the upper-left corner to IV65536 for the cell in the lower-right corner.

The information in a cell may be either numbers or text. Numbers, which include formulas that evaluate numbers, can be formatted in many ways, including dollars, percentages, dates, or time. Text can include numbers and can be used as titles, row and column labels, or comments on a sheet. The primary difference between numbers and text is that you can perform arithmetic calculations on numbers but not on text. Think of numbers as arithmetic values and text as everything

else. You can format numbers by entering them with defining features as you enter them. For example, if you enter 3.25, 3.25%, $3.25, 3 2/5, 32.5E-1, or 3,250,325.25, Excel will format the numbers the same way. You can also format numbers with the Format menu.

A *range* identifies one or more cells for use in a formula or in an instruction. A range can be any of the following:

- A single cell address, such as D14.

- A rectangular group of cells identified by the addresses of the top-left and lower-right cells, separated by a colon, such as C5:E12, which is the rectangle extending from C5 in the upper left to E12 in the lower right; such a group may be a column of cells, a row of cells, or a block of several rows and/or columns

- A name or names that refer to one or more cells, such as *Salaries.*

USING AND CHANGING A WORKSHEET

 I know I can drag the intersection between rows and columns to change their size, but what if I want to change the size of several rows or columns to be the same height or width?

Select the rows or columns you want to size by clicking their headings. If you want to change several contiguous rows or columns, press and hold SHIFT while clicking the first and last headings. If you want to change several rows or columns that are not next to each other, press and hold CTRL while clicking each heading. Once the headings are selected, drag the heading intersection of any selected row or column, and all selected rows or columns will be sized to match the one you dragged.

You can size one or several rows or columns more precisely by selecting them as just described and then choosing Row Height or Column Width from the Format menu and entering the width or height you want.

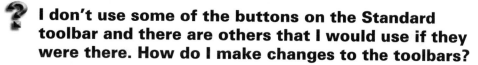

 Tip: *You can automatically size each column to best fit its data by double-clicking on any header border within the selected columns (except the leftmost border).*

 I don't use some of the buttons on the Standard toolbar and there are others that I would use if they were there. How do I make changes to the toolbars?

You can add tools to or remove tools from the toolbar by choosing Customize from the Tools menu and then clicking the Commands tab. To remove a button, simply drag it off the toolbar while the Customize dialog box is open. To add buttons to the toolbar, select the category of the command (to narrow your search), locate the specific command you want the new toolbar button to perform, and then drag that command to the location on the toolbar where you want the button.

 *Note:* *In Excel 2000, you can customize the worksheet menus with the exact same steps used to customize a toolbar. In fact, the worksheet menu is now called the Worksheet menu bar.*

If you remove or change a default toolbar or menu, you can quickly return it to its original settings by clicking the Toolbars tab in the Customize dialog box, choosing the toolbar or menu you want to restore, and clicking Reset. You'll then be asked to confirm that that is what you want to do. Something to remember about using Reset is that you will lose any buttons or options you've added to that toolbar or menu.

Is there a way to enter the date and time in a cell without typing them?

Yes. Press CTRL-; to enter the current date and CTRL-SHIFT-: to enter the current time. These can be placed in the same cell

with a space between them, or in two separate cells. The following table provides the complete list of edit keys.

Key	Function
ALT	Activates the menu bar
ALT-ENTER	Inserts a carriage return into the cell
CTRL-ENTER	Fills the selected cell with the current entry
SHIFT-ENTER	Completes the cell entry and moves up one cell
ALT-BACKSPACE or CTRL-Z	Reverses the previous action
BACKSPACE	Deletes the character to the left of the insertion point
CTRL-LEFT ARROW OR CTRL-RIGHT ARROW	Moves the insertion point one word to the left or right in the entry
CTRL-DELETE	Deletes text from the insertion point to the right end of the current line
CTRL-' (apostrophe)	Inserts the formula from the cell above the active cell at the insertion point
CTRL-' (left quote)	Switches between displaying formulas and displaying values in all cells
CTRL-SHIFT-" (double quotes)	Inserts the value from the cell above into the active cell at the insertion point
CTRL-; (semicolon)	Inserts your computer's current date at the insertion point
CTRL-SHIFT-: (colon)	Inserts your computer's current time at the insertion point
CTRL-K	Inserts a hyperlink
CTRL-D	Fills down
CTRL-R	Fills to the right
DELETE	Deletes the character to the right of the insertion point
END or CTRL-END	Moves the insertion point to the right end of the current line of the entry
ENTER	Completes the cell entry and moves one cell down
ESC	Cancels any changes made during editing, closes the edit area, and returns the original contents to the active cell
F2	Activates the cell and edit area so you can do a character-by-character edit on the active cell

Key	Function
F3	Pastes a defined name into a formula
SHIFT-F3	Pastes a function into a formula
HOME or CTRL-HOME	Moves the insertion point to the left end of the current line of the entry
INSERT	Switches between Insert mode, in which newly typed characters push existing characters to the right, and Overtype mode, in which newly typed characters replace existing characters
LEFT ARROW or RIGHT ARROW	Moves the insertion point one character to the left or right in the entry
UP ARROW or DOWN ARROW	Moves the insertion point between lines in the edit area if the entry occupies more than one line; otherwise, moves the insertion point to the beginning or end of the line
SHIFT-LEFT ARROW or SHIFT-RIGHT ARROW	Selects the previous character or the next character
CTRL-SHIFT-RIGHT ARROW or CTRL-SHIFT-LEFT ARROW	Selects the next or previous word if the insertion point is in a space between words. If the insertion point is in a word, selects to the beginning or the end of the word.
SHIFT-TAB	Completes the cell entry and moves one cell to the left
TAB	Completes the cell entry and moves one cell to the right

How do I find the Contents and Index in the Help system?

First, you must hide the Office Assistant, and then the Index and Contents dialog box will be displayed when you ask for help. Follow these steps:

1. Right-click the Office Assistant and select Options.

2. Clear the Use The Office Assistant selection, and click OK. The Office Assistant will be hidden until you request its presence again.

3. From the Help menu, choose Microsoft Excel Help. The Contents, Index, and Answers Wizard will be available to you.

> *Note:* *To get the Office Assistant back, simply click the Microsoft Excel Help icon or select Show The Office Assistant from the Help menu.*

I can't remember all the keystroke shortcuts. What is a good reference for this?

The keystroke shortcuts can be found under the Keystroke listing in the Index. You can get the index by hiding the Office Assistant, as described in the previous question, and then asking for Microsoft Excel Help. Click the Index tab, enter **keystrokes**, and double-click Keyboard Shortcuts in the topics. A list of the types of keystroke shortcuts will be displayed. As you will see, there are lots of keystroke combinations. If you were to print them, you would have 33 pages of shortcuts. Here are just some of the types of keystroke shortcuts available:

- **Keys for working in a spreadsheet** Keys for moving and scrolling in a worksheet, for moving in a worksheet with End Mode on, and for moving in a worksheet with Scroll Lock on

- **Keys for previewing and printing a document** Keys for seeing your work as it will be printed, and then for actually printing it

- **Keys for working with data** Keys for entering, formatting, editing, and selecting data and cells; for selecting charts and chart items; for use with databases and lists; for outlining data; for use with PivotTable and PivotChart reports; and for use with the OLAP Cube Wizard

- **Keys for working with Microsoft Office** Keys for menus, toolbars, windows, dialog boxes, and edit boxes, and the Office Assistant; and keys for sending e-mail messages and for working with drawing objects, AutoShapes, WordArt, and other objects

The following table lists the function keys. The printed list will be more complete.

Key	Name	Function
F1	Help	Opens the Excel Help window or the Office Assistant
SHIFT-F1	What's This	Displays context-sensitive help
ALT-F1	New Chart	Creates a new chart
ALT-SHIFT-F1	New Sheet	Inserts a new sheet
ALT-CTRL-F1	New Macro	Creates a new Excel 4 macro sheet
F2	Edit	Activates the formula bar for editing
SHIFT-F2	Comments	Allows entering, editing, or deleting a comment that is to be attached to the active cell
ALT-F2	Save As	Opens the File Save As dialog box
ALT-SHIFT-F2	Save	Saves the active document
ALT-CTRL-F2	Open	Opens the Open dialog box
ALT-CTRL-SHIFT-F2	Print	Opens the Print dialog box
F3	Name	Opens the Paste Name dialog box to paste a cell's name into a formula
SHIFT-F3	Function	Opens the Paste Function dialog box
CTRL-F3	Define Name	Opens the Define Name dialog box
CTRL-SHIFT-F3	Create Name	Opens the Create Name dialog box
F4	Absolute	While editing, makes a cell address or range name absolute, mixed, or relative
F4	Repeat Last	When not editing, repeats the last action taken
SHIFT-F4	Find Next	Repeats the last Find command
CTRL-F4	Close	Closes the active document window
ALT-F4	Exit	Closes the application
F5	Go To	Opens the Go To dialog box to move the active cell to a cell address, a range name, or a file that you enter

Key	Name	Function
SHIFT-F5	Find	Opens the Find dialog box
CTRL-F5	Restore	Restores the size of the active document window
F6	Next Pane	Moves the active cell clockwise to the next pane
SHIFT-F6	Last Pane	Moves the active cell counter-clockwise to the previous pane
CTRL-F6	Next Window	Moves the active cell to the next workbook or window
CTRL-SHIFT-F6	Last Window	Moves the active cell to the previous document window
F7	Spelling	Checks spelling
CTRL-F7	Move	Sets up the active document window to be moved with the direction keys
F8	Extend	Toggles the extension of the current selection
SHIFT-F8	Add	Allows the addition of a second selection to the current selection
CTRL-F8	Size	Sets up the active document window to be sized with the direction keys
ALT-F8	Macro	Opens the Macro dialog box
F9	Calculate All	Recalculates all open worksheets
SHIFT-F9	Calculate Current	Recalculates the active sheet
CTRL-F9	Minimize	Minimizes the active workbook
CTRL-ALT-F9	Calculate	Calculate all sheets in the workbook
F10	Menu	Activates the menu bar
SHIFT-F10	Context Menu	Displays the context menu for the active cell
CTRL-F10	Maximize	Maximizes or restores the active workbook
F11	New Chart	Creates a new chart sheet
SHIFT-F11	New Sheet	Creates a new sheet
CTRL-F11	New Macro	Creates a new Excel 4 macro sheet

Key	Name	Function
ALT-F11	VB Editor	Opens the Visual Basic Editor window
F12	Save As	Opens the File Save As dialog box
SHIFT-F12	Save	Saves the active document
CTRL-F12	Open	Opens the Open dialog box
CTRL-SHIFT-F12	Print	Opens the Print dialog box

Are there keystrokes to move from one sheet to another?

Yes. CTRL-PGDN moves down one sheet (from Sheet1 to Sheet2) and CTRL-PGUP moves in the opposite direction. The following table provides the complete list of direction keys.

Key	Moves the Active Cell
LEFT ARROW or RIGHT ARROW	Right or left one column
UP ARROW or DOWN ARROW	Up or down one row
PGUP or PGDN	Up or down one window height
ALT-PGDN or ALT-PGUP	Right or left one screen width
CTRL-UP ARROW or CTRL-DOWN ARROW	Up or down to the first intersection of blank and nonblank cells
CTRL-RIGHT ARROW or CTRL-LEFT ARROW	Right or left to the first intersection of blank and nonblank cells
HOME	Left to column A in the row with the active cell
END	Turns on End mode—when a direction key is pressed next, the active cell moves to the last occupied cell in the direction of the arrow (the END key has the same function as the CTRL-arrow keys, above)
CTRL-HOME	To cell A1
CTRL-END	Down and/or to the right to the lowest and rightmost cell representing the corner formed by the rightmost occupied cell and the lowest occupied cell
END-HOME	Same as CTRL-END
CTRL-PGDN	Down one sheet (from Sheet1 to Sheet2)
CTRL-PGUP	Up one sheet (from Sheet2 to Sheet1)

 How does the Merge And Center button work?

The Merge And Center button makes one cell out of the selected cells, which may contain several rows, and then it centers in that large cell any data that was in the upper-leftmost cell. Excel considers all the merged area to be one cell and *any data in the other selected cells will be lost.* In versions prior to Excel 97, the individual cells remained and the information in the leftmost cell just covered the other cells, which were limited to a single row.

Tip: *To center text across rows without merging the cells and losing their content, choose Cells from the Format menu, click the Alignment tab, select Center Across Selection in the Horizontal drop-down list, and click OK.*

 How can I select multiple cells that are not contiguous, since I can't just drag across them?

Hold down CTRL while clicking individual cells or dragging across two or more independent ranges of cells. For example, all of the highlighted areas shown here were selected by holding down CTRL while dragging across them:

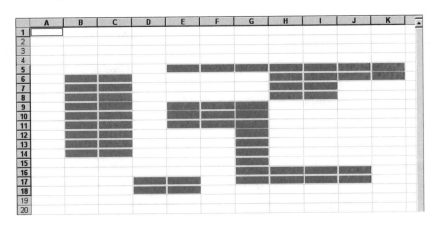

All of the selected areas will be formatted alike if a particular format is chosen while these areas are selected.

My status bar disappeared. Where did it go, and how do I get it back?

Somebody probably turned it off. To get it back, open the Tools menu, choose Options, and make sure the View tab is selected. Then click Status Bar to turn it back on.

I would like to just see the total of a set of numbers without entering a formula to permanently create the sum. How is that done?

Select the set of numbers, and then look in the status bar at the bottom of the window to see the sum:

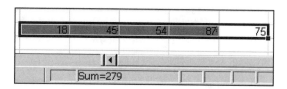

I like having multiple pages or sheets, but I want to see them all at the same time. How do I view multiple pages?

With the multiple-sheet workbook open in Excel, open the Windows menu and choose New Window. Repeat this for each sheet in the workbook. When you have created a window for each sheet, again open the Window menu and choose Arrange | Tiled and click OK. In each window, click a different sheet tab. You should now be able to see a portion of each of your sheets at the same time, as you can see in Figure 4-3.

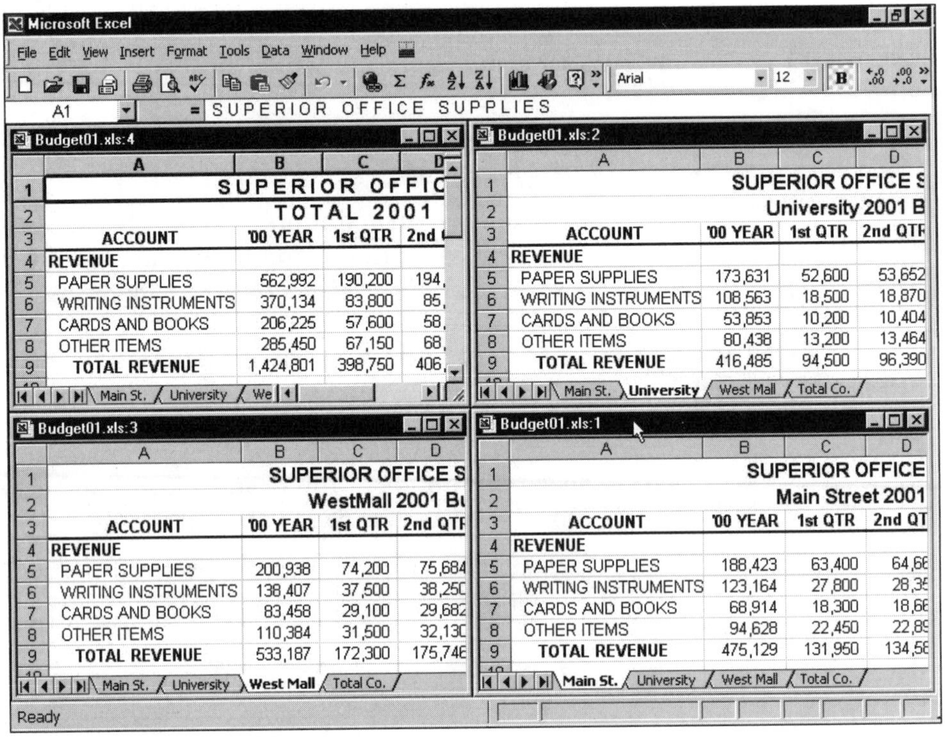

Figure 4-3 Multiple windows displaying different sheets

ENTERING AND CHANGING INFORMATION

When I finish an entry, I press ENTER and go to the cell beneath my entry. What I really want is to go to the cell to the right. How can I change where ENTER takes me?

First, if you press TAB instead of ENTER to complete the entry, you'll go to the cell to the right instead of the cell beneath the entry. Second, you can change what ENTER does by opening the Tools menu, choosing Options, clicking the Edit tab, and selecting Right from the Move Selection After Enter drop-down list, as shown here:

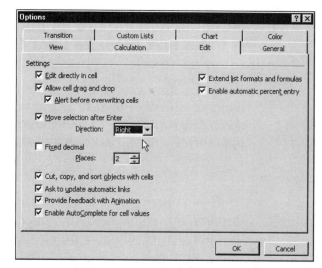

Is there an easy way to delete information in a cell?

If you haven't completed the entry by pressing ENTER, TAB, or an arrow key, or by clicking the Enter button on the formula bar, press ESC, and the information will be removed. If you have completed the entry, select the cell or cells and press DELETE. You can also either click the Undo button or open the Undo drop-down list and undo any of the last 16 actions you have taken, as you can see here:

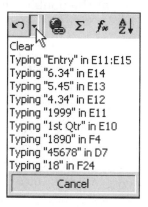

I want some numbers to be numbers and I want some to be text. How do I get Excel to treat some numbers as text?

Based on what you type, Excel determines whether your entry is a number or text. If you type only numbers (0 through 9) or one of the following numeric symbols in the appropriate place, Excel considers your entry a number:

$$+ \quad - \quad (\,) \quad . \quad , \quad : \quad \$ \quad \% \quad / \quad E \quad e$$

If you enter a date or time value in one of Excel's built-in formats, it is considered a number. Finally, a recognizable formula that results in a number is treated as a number. Everything else is text. If you want an entry that would normally be a number to be text, place an apostrophe (') at the left of the entry. (The apostrophe won't be displayed.)

How do I repeat an entry in a number of cells without retyping?

If you want to copy an entry you have typed in one cell into immediately adjacent or contiguous cells, place the mouse pointer over the fill handle in the lower-right corner of the cell, so that the pointer becomes a plus sign (a single-line plus, not the double-line plus). Then drag the cell to the other cells you want filled with the entry, like this:

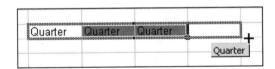

If you want to repeat the entry in widely separated cells, select the original cell, press CTRL-C to copy it, and then right-click each new cell and choose Paste. When you are done, press ESC to turn off the Copy selection.

Is there an easy way to create a series of numbers or words?

Yes. Type the first two entries, select them, and then drag the fill handle (the single-line plus), as shown here:

1st	2nd	3rd	4th
Quarter	Quarter	Quarter	Quarter

This works with any number series, as well as with days of the week, months of the year, and dates. You can also select Fill Series from the Edit menu to open the Series dialog box for other options.

Excel doesn't have an Insert Symbol menu option like Word, so how do I enter special characters?

To enter special characters, follow these steps:

1. Open the Windows Start menu, and choose Programs | Accessories | Character Map. (If you can't find the Character Map—it's not part of a Typical Windows 98 installation—you will need to install it from your Windows 98 CD or disks.)

2. In the Character Map dialog box, select the font you are using, double-click the character you want, click Copy, and then click Close.

3. Return to Excel, right-click the cell in which you want the special character, and choose Paste from the context menu that opens.

If you want the special character in a string of other text, double-click the cell (or select the cell and press F2), move the insertion point to where you want the special character, and then press CTRL-V to paste it in.

Tip: *If you use a special character often, remember the keystroke for that character, which is shown in the lower-right corner of the Character Map dialog box, and then use that keystroke when you need the character. For example, if you use the English pound symbol (£) a lot, you can easily get it by pressing and holding ALT while typing **0163** on the numeric keypad at the right of your keyboard.*

ENTERING AND USING FORMULAS AND FUNCTIONS

 Isn't there an easy way to enter the formula for adding a column of numbers?

Select the cell beneath the column of numbers (or to the right of a row of numbers) and click the AutoSum button in the toolbar. The numbers to be summed will be selected:

	A	B	C	D	E	
	COUNT	▼ X ✓ =	=SUM(C3:C7)		AutoSum	
1						
2		City	January	February	March	April
3		Boston	450	455	459	464
4		NewYork	627	633	640	646
5		Washington	250	253	255	258
6		Atlanta	315	318	321	325
7		Miami	580	586	592	598
8		Total Eastern	=SUM(C3:C7)			
9						

Press ENTER to accept the default selection, or use the mouse to drag over a new selection and then press ENTER.

You can also enter formulas for a range of cells under several columns of numbers, or to the right of several rows of numbers, and click the AutoSum button to automatically create all of the formulas in the range.

 I can never remember the arguments in functions. How can I easily find these?

Use the following steps to see the list of arguments and have them explained as you enter them:

1. Select the cell in which you want the function.

2. Click the equal sign in the formula bar to begin the formula entry process.

3. Open the function drop-down list that appears on the left of the formula bar.

4. Select the function you want to use.

5. Use the following dialog box shown to fill in the arguments that are needed. As you select each of the arguments, you'll see an explanation of it in the lower part of the dialog box, as shown here:

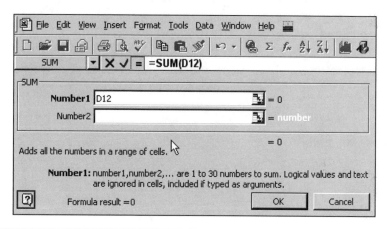

➕ **Tip:** *Open the Paste Function dialog box, by choosing More Functions from the formula bar list, to view all of Excel's functions.*

❓ Excel is calculating one of my formulas incorrectly. The formula is =D1+E1*F1. What's the problem?

You are probably expecting to add D1 and E1 before multiplying by F1. Excel, though, will multiply first and then do the addition. The reason is that Excel has a specific order of calculation, and in that order, multiplication is done before addition (see the sidebar, "Order of Calculation"). You can change the order of calculation with parentheses, so your formula would give you the answer you want if it were written like this: =(D1+E1)*F1. Parentheses must always be added in pairs (left and right) and may be nested more than 25 levels deep.

➕ **Tip:** *Excel has a very handy feature that shows the matching left parenthesis as you enter the right parenthesis. That way you know your parentheses match without having to count them.*

Order of Calculation

Excel calculates or evaluates a formula in a particular order determined by the *precedence number* of the operators being used and the parentheses placed in the formula. The following table describes each operator and gives its precedence number:

Operator	Description	Precedence
:	Range of cell	1
,	Union of cells	2
(a space)	Intersection of cells	3
–	Negation	4
%	Percentage (/100)	5
^	Exponentiation	6
*	Multiplication	7
/	Division	7
+	Addition	8
–	Subtraction	8
&	Concatenation	9
=	Equal to	10
<	Less than	10
>	Greater than	10
<=	Less than or equal to	10
>=	Greater than or equal to	10
<>	Not equal to	10

Operations with lower precedence numbers are performed earlier in the calculation. When two operators in a formula have the same precedence number, Excel evaluates them sequentially from left to right.

 I want to make my formulas more readable. Is there an easy way to do that?

Yes, by entering row and column headings, you can use those headings in formulas to refer to the numbers immediately below or to the right of the headings. You do *not* have to define the rows or columns as named ranges. You can see this here:

	A	B	C	D	E	F	G	H	I	J
SUM ▾ X ✓ = =SUM(Washington)										
1										
2		City	January	February	March	April	May	June	Total	
3		Boston	450	455	459	464	468	473	2768	
4		NewYork	627	633	640	646	652	659	3857	
5		Washington	250	253	251	254	252	255	=SUM(Washington)	
6		Atlanta	315	318	321	325	328	331	1938	
7		Miami	580	586	592	598	604	610	3568	
8		Total Eastern	2,222	2,244	2,267	2,289	2,312	2,335	13,645	
9										

✳ ***Note:*** *If you cannot enter labels into a formula, open the Tools menu, select Options, select the Calculation tab, and make sure that Accept Labels In Formulas is checked.*

How do I freeze an address in a formula so that it does not change when I copy it?

You can make an address absolute, so that both the row and column are fixed, by typing a dollar sign in front of each part of the address or by pressing F4 after typing the address. For example, C3 is an absolute address. You can also have various combinations of fixed and relative addressing called mixed addresses. To get a mixed address, press F4 repeatedly to cycle through all four possible combinations, as follows:

If you	pressing F4 will give you	which is a(n)
C3	C3	Absolute address
C3	C$3	Mixed (fixed row) address
C$3	$C3	Mixed (fixed column) address
$C3	C3	Relative address

✳ ***Note:*** *F4 always cycles through the alternatives in the same order, regardless of which you start with.*

I have a really big worksheet, and every time I make an entry, it takes forever to recalculate the whole sheet. How can I specify manual calculation?

Open the Tools menu, choose Options, select the Calculation tab, and click Manual. Once you have chosen manual

calculation, your worksheet will not be recalculated until
you press F9.

Tip: *If you use manual calculation a lot and want a tool or
menu option for it, choose Customize from the Tools menu;
and in the Commands tab select the Tools category and drag
Calculate Now to either a menu or a toolbar.*

Can I specify a range that is disjointed or not rectangular in a formula or function? If so, how?

Yes. Many formulas or functions that take ranges as
arguments will allow nonrectangular and disjointed ranges
using one of these range operators:

Operator	Name and Meaning
:	Range, a rectangular group of adjacent cells
,	Union, the combination of two ranges
(space)	Intersection, the cells common to two ranges

For example, if you wanted to add two disjointed ranges, you
would do so by summing the union of the two ranges with a
formula such as =SUM(B7:E7,E9:E12). If you wanted the
average of the cells that were common to two ranges, you
would use a function specifying the intersection of the ranges,
as shown here:

SUM	▾	X ✓ =	=AVERAGE(H7:K11 G9:L9)		
G	**H**	**I**	**J**	**K**	**L**
6 =AVERAGE(H7:K11 G9:L9)					
7	35	23	67	83	
8	46	24	38	78	
9 23	78	18	95	45	53
10	93	37	17	12	
11	24	45	73	62	

Tip: *When you enter a function or a formula, do so with
lowercase letters. If Excel properly interprets your formula or
function, it will change all the characters to uppercase, telling
you your entry is OK.*

COPYING AND MOVING INFORMATION

Can I copy a cell to a range of cells?

Yes. There are four copy-to-range methods that work:

- Copy a single cell to another single cell, to a row of cells, to a column of cells, or to a block of cells. The destination (what you select to paste into) is another cell, a row, a column, or a block.

- Copy a single row to a range spanning one or more rows. The destination is a single cell or a part of a column—the leftmost cells of the receiving rows.

- Copy a single column to a range spanning one or more columns. The destination is a single cell or a part of a row—the uppermost cells of the receiving columns.

- Copying a block to a second block. The destination is a single cell—the upper-left cell of the receiving range.

Figure 4-4 shows these four copy range combinations.

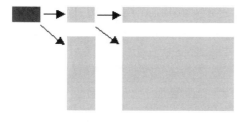

1. A cell can be copied to a cell, a row, a column, or a block.

2. A row can be copied to another row or to a block.

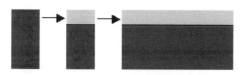

3. A column can be copied to another column or to a block.

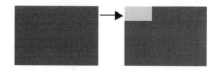

4. A block can be copied to another block.

Figure 4-4 Four copy-to-range options

? I know I can move the contents of a cell by dragging the cell border, but isn't there a way to copy information without using Cut and Paste in the Edit menu?

Yes, there are several ways. The easiest is to hold down CTRL while dragging the cell border; this copies instead of moves the cell contents. You can also select the cell to be copied and press CTRL-C to copy it, select the receiving cell, and press CTRL-V. You can also right-click the source and receiving cells and select Copy and Paste, respectively, from the context or shortcut menu.

? Sometimes when I am copying or moving cells, I want to insert cells above or to the left of existing cells instead of just pasting them over the existing cells. How is that done?

Select the range to be copied or moved. As you begin to drag the border of the range, press and hold CTRL if you want to copy the range, and then additionally press and hold SHIFT to insert the range between other cells. As you continue to drag the range, you'll see a shaded bar appear between cells, showing where the range will be inserted, like this:

When you are happy with the placement of the bar, release the mouse button and only then release SHIFT and CTRL. You can also use Cut or Copy, select the cells below which or to the left of which you want the new cells inserted, and then select Copied Cells from the Insert menu or context menu.

When I move cells containing relative formulas, I find that the formulas still refer to their old locations, as if they had been absolute. How come?

What you want to do is *copy* the cells. Then the formulas will be adjusted relative to their new positions. Excel assumes that when you *move* a formula, you want the formula to keep pointing to the original cells no matter where you move the formula. You'll find this very handy in many situations.

ADDING FORMATTING, PATTERNS, AND BORDERS

How do I format numbers with the new euro symbol?

To have cells display numbers with the euro symbol, use these steps:

1. Right-click the number or range of numbers, and choose Format Cells in the context menu. The Format Cells dialog box will open. Select the Number tab.

2. Select Currency in the Category list.

3. Using the Symbol drop-down list box, choose € Euro (€ 123) as the symbol.

4. Select the number of decimal places and how you want negative numbers to be displayed, as shown next.

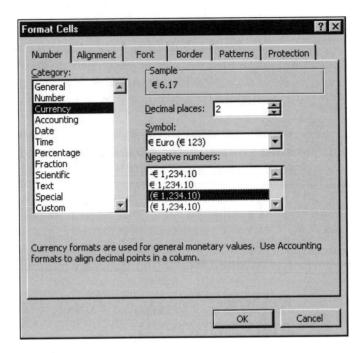

5. When the Format Cells dialog box displays what you want, click OK.

? Why are some of my numbers flush to the right edge of the cell and others are moved to the left one space?

There are several ways to format negative numbers. Most likely, your numbers are inconsistently formatted, some so that when they are negative they have parentheses around them. That means the positive numbers must be moved to the left one space to accommodate the right parenthesis if the number becomes negative. By comparing the first two numbers with the last two, as shown here, you can see how this inconsistency in formatting alters the alignment of numbers:

$3,456.82
$4,139.94
($5,194.23)
$1,324.43
$1,854.56

You can change the way negative numbers appear by reformatting the cells you want changed. Right-click the cells, choose Format Cells from the context menu, and change the negative-number style to either add or remove the parentheses, whichever you want.

I want to apply patterns and fancy formatting to my worksheet in the easiest way possible. What is that way?

You can apply preset formatting to a range of cells by using the AutoFormat option in the Format menu. This opens the AutoFormat dialog box, shown here:

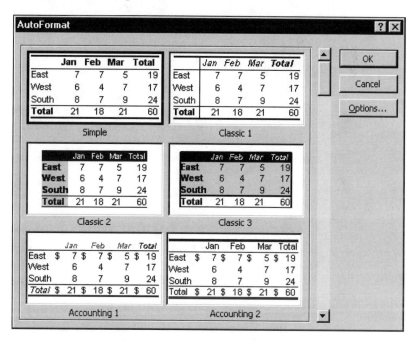

You can apply any of the preset formats to your worksheet by selecting the format you like and clicking OK.

If you were to apply the Classic 2 table format to the Budget2000 worksheet shown previously in Figure 4-2, it would look like it does in Figure 4-5.

	A	B	C	D	E	F	G	H	I	J
1	SUPERIOR OFFICE SUPPLIES									
2	Main Street 2001 Budget									
3	ACCOUNT	'00 YEAR	1st QTR	2nd QTR	3rd QTR	4th QTR	'01 YEAR	% GRTH		
4	REVENUE									
5	PAPER SUPPLIES	188,423	63,400	64,668	65,961	67,281	261,310	38.7%		
6	WRITING INSTRUMENTS	123,164	27,800	28,356	28,923	29,502	114,581	-7.0%		
7	CARDS AND BOOKS	68,914	18,300	18,666	19,039	19,420	75,425	9.4%		
8	OTHER ITEMS	94,628	22,450	22,899	23,357	23,824	92,530	-2.2%		
9	TOTAL REVENUE	475,129	131,950	134,589	137,281	140,026	543,846	14.5%		
10										
11	COST OF SALES	152,041	44,863	47,106	45,303	44,808	182,080	19.8%		
12										
13	GROSS INCOME	323,088	87,087	87,483	91,978	95,218	361,766	12.0%		
14	GROSS MARGIN %	32.0%	34.0%	35.0%	33.0%	32.0%	33.5%			
15										
16	EXPENSE									
17	SALARIES AND WAGES	90,465	23,500	23,853	24,210	24,573	96,136	6.3%		
18	EMPLOYEE BENEFITS	10,856	2,820	2,862	2,905	2,949	11,536	6.3%		
19	FACILITY COSTS	40,709	10,330	10,485	10,642	10,802	42,259	3.8%		
20	UTILITIES	25,330	6,428	6,524	6,622	6,721	26,294	3.8%		
21	SUPPLIES	21,711	5,509	5,592	5,676	5,761	22,538	3.8%		
22	POSTAGE AND FREIGHT	7,237	1,836	1,864	1,892	1,920	7,513	3.8%		
23	TAXES	28,949	7,346	7,456	7,568	7,681	30,051	3.8%		
24	OTHER	8,142	2,066	2,097	2,128	2,160	8,452	3.8%		
25	TOTAL EXPENSE	233,399	59,835	60,732	61,643	62,568	244,779	4.9%		

Main St. / University / West Mall / Total Co.

Figure 4-5 Using AutoFormat on the worksheet in Figure 4-2

I want to reuse a format that I just spent a whole lot of time working on. I'd like to use it in several other locations. Is there a way to do that without having to reapply all the formats one at a time?

Yes, there are two ways to reuse formatting, depending on how much information you want to format. First and most simply, you can use the Format Painter tool in the Standard toolbar. Do that by selecting the cell containing the formatting and clicking the Format Painter button. Then click or drag across the cell or cells in which you want to reuse the formatting.

The second way is to create your own style, like this:

1. Select the cell containing the formatting, and choose Style from the Format menu.

2. Type the name of the new style and turn off or modify any parts of the existing formatting you don't want included. Then click Add, and click OK.

You can now apply the style to selected cells by choosing Style from the Format menu, selecting the style name, and clicking OK. One further step allows you to attach the style to a toolbar button, as described next:

1. Open the Tools menu, choose Macro, and then click Record New Macro. Name the macro after your new style (the name can consist only of letters, numbers, or underscore characters), give it a shortcut key if desired, select Personal Macro Workbook to store the macro in, and click OK.

2. Open the Format menu, choose Style, select your new style in the Style Name drop-down list, click OK, and then click the Stop Recording button in the Stop Recording dialog box.

3. Right-click any toolbar or the menu bar and choose Customize.

4. In the Customize dialog box Commands tab, select Format as the category, choose any command, such as Comma Style (you're going to modify it).

5. Drag the command you choose to where you want it on the toolbar.

6. Click Modify Selection in the Customize dialog box. In the pop-up menu that opens, change the Name as desired, for example, change "&Comma Style" to "&Heading Style." This name is what you see when you place the mouse pointer over the tool. The ampersand (&) specifies that the following letter will be underlined as a keyboard shortcut.

7. Still in the Modify Selection pop-up menu, click Edit Button Image and create the image you want. Click OK when you are done.

8. Again, click Modify Selection in the Customize dialog box, and click Assign Macro.

9. Select your new macro, and click OK.

10. Click Close to close the Customize dialog box.

11. Select a cell or cells that you want to apply your formatting to, and click your new toolbar button.

Can I rotate text in a cell?

Yes. Right-click the cell to be rotated, choose Format Cells, click the Alignment tab, and drag the orientation to the angle you want, like this:

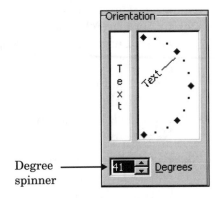

Degree spinner

You can also use the degree spinner to set a more precise position. When you are satisfied, click OK to return to the worksheet and see the results.

Is there any way to split a cell with a diagonal line?

Yes. You can draw it with the drawing tools or, more simply, you can apply a diagonal border, as shown here:

	A	B	C	D	E
12					
13		City / Results	Atlanta	Boston	Chicago
14		Attendance	418	365	847
15		Revenue	188,100	164,250	381,150
16		Expenses	114,950	100,375	232,925
17		Net Receipts	73,150	63,875	148,225

Here's how to add a diagonal border:

1. Type the higher, rightmost text first, press ALT-ENTER, and type the lower, leftmost text. Press ENTER to complete the entry, and the row should automatically resize to fit two lines.

2. Left-align the cell with the new text. In front of the top entry (to its left), enter one less space than the number of characters in the bottom entry. This will right-align the top entry. Then press ENTER.

3. Right-click the cell and select Format Cells from the context menu.

4. In the Format Cells dialog box, click the Border tab, select the line style you want, and click the right-hand diagonal line button, as shown here:

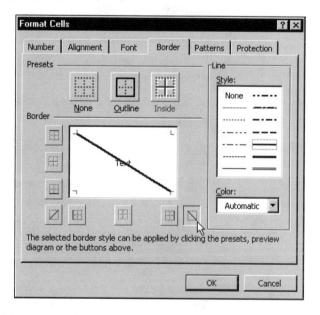

5. Click OK to close the dialog box.

6. You may have to widen the cell or add more spaces to the left of the top entry to make it perfect.

I work a lot with English currency. How do I add a toolbar button for English pound formatting?

Add a toolbar button for English pound formatting with the following steps:

1. Choose Macro from the Tools menu, choose Record New Macro, type **EnglishPound** (with no space) for the macro name, select Personal Macro Workbook to store the macro in, and click OK. A very small Stop Recording dialog box will appear on your screen. All keystrokes and many mouse movements will now be recorded.

2. Open the Format menu and choose Cells. From the Number tab, select Currency, choose £English (United Kingdom) as the symbol, select the number of decimal places and the negative-number format you want, and click OK.

3. Click the small square in the Stop Recording dialog box.

4. Right-click any toolbar or the menu bar, and choose Customize.

5. In the Customize dialog box's Commands tab, select Format as the category.

6. Drag the $ Currency Style command to where you want it on the toolbar.

7. Click Modify Selection, type **&English Pound** for the name, and click Assign Macro.

8. In the Assign Macro dialog box, select PERSONAL.XLS!EnglishPound and click OK.

9. Click Close to close the Customize dialog box.

10. Select a number and click your new toolbar button. The number will be formatted with the English pound symbol.

11. Reopen the Customize dialog box, click your new button on the toolbar, click Modify Selection in the dialog box, and then click Edit Button Image.

12. Click the pixels in the Picture box so that the image on the button is an English pound sign, as shown next.

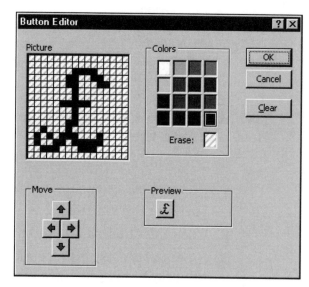

13. When you are satisfied with your image, click OK to close the Button Editor dialog box, and click Close in the Customize dialog box.

CREATING AND FORMATTING CHARTS

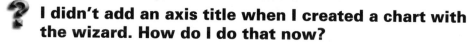

I didn't add an axis title when I created a chart with the wizard. How do I do that now?

You can change and add or delete just about anything on a chart you have previously created. Follow these steps to add an axis title:

1. Right-click the chart, and choose Chart Options. Notice the other options that are available on the Chart Context menu to change the chart type, source data, and location.

2. In the Chart Options dialog box, click the Titles tab and then type the title in the appropriate axis text box. Click OK to close the dialog box.

3. To change the font and alignment of the axis title, right-click the new title and choose Format Axis Title to open the dialog box of that name.

4. Click the Font tab to change the font or the font style or size.

5. Click the Alignment tab and adjust the alignment as desired.

6. When the axis title is the way you want it, click OK.

I want to add a callout with some text to a chart. How can I do that?

You can create a callout by following these steps:

1. Click the Drawing button in the Standard toolbar to open the Drawing toolbar.

2. Click the AutoShapes button.

3. From the context menu, click the Callouts option and then click the callout you prefer.

4. Place the pointer where you want the callout and click and drag the pointer to size the callout. Drag the handles to size it exactly.

5. To place the pointing part of the callout, drag the small yellow square until it points where you want it.

6. Click within the callout to add text. An example is shown in Figure 4-6.

The Chart Wizard automatically assumes what data will be plotted on which axis. How can I change the axis that data is plotted on?

In Step 2 of the Chart Wizard, you can choose whether the series are in Rows or Columns, which are the only choices, even with 3-D charts. If you finish a chart in the Chart Wizard and then want to change the axis assignment, you can do so using the By Row and By Column buttons in the Chart toolbar.

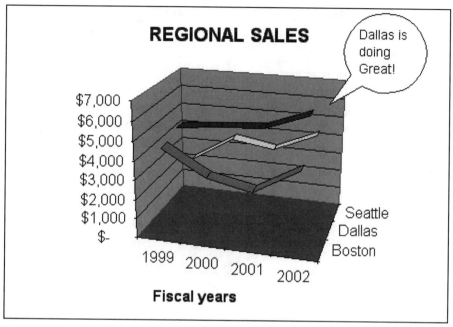

Figure 4-6   Callout created with the drawing tools

What is the best chart type to use with my data?

This is not an easy question to answer, and there are probably several substantially different opinions. For example, the data shown in the chart in Figure 4-7 might be more informative if it were presented in a line chart, as shown in Figure 4-8, but it is not as interesting. The best answer comes from asking yourself whether the chart tells the story you are trying to tell. The "Chart Types" sidebar provides some quick guidelines for the more common chart types.

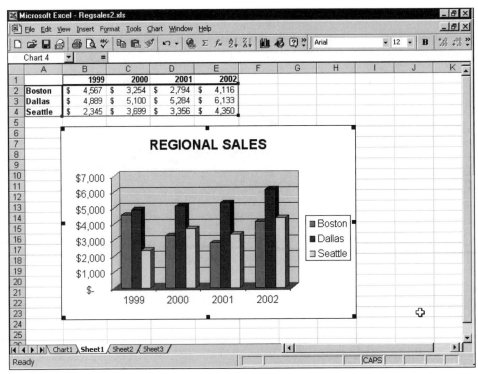

Figure 4-7   An Excel chart and its data range

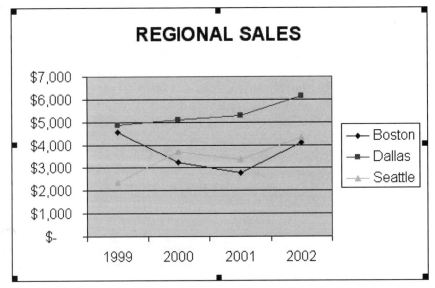

Figure 4-8   The data from Figure 4-7 replotted as a line chart

Chart Types

Excel offers 14 standard chart types, each with a number of variations and combinations. The best way to see how these work with your data is to start up the Chart Wizard, click the different standard and custom chart types, and see how they look in the preview window. Here are some observations about the more common standard chart types:

- *Area charts* show the magnitude of change over time. They are particularly useful when several components are changing and you are interested in the sum of those components. Area charts let you see the change in the individual components, as well as the change in the total.

- *Bar charts* consist of a series of horizontal bars that allow comparison of the relative size of two or more items at one point in time. For example, a bar chart might compare the sales for each of three products in each of five years. Each bar in a bar chart is a single data point or number on the sheet. The set of numbers for a single set of bars is a data series.

- *Column charts* consist of a series of vertical columns that allow comparison of the relative size of two or more items, often over time. For example, a column chart might compare annual sales by presenting a column for each year's sales. Each column in a column chart is a single data point or number on the sheet. The set of numbers for a single set of columns is a data series.

- *Line charts* are used to show trends over time. For example, the line chart in Figure 4-8 shows that Dallas has continuous upward growth while Boston is having a hard time. With line charts, the reader can make a projection into the future (maybe inappropriately). In a line chart, each of the data series is used to produce a line on the chart, with each number in the range producing a data point on the line.

- *High-low-close charts* are line charts with three data series used to display a stock's high, low, and closing prices for a given time period. High-low-close charts also work well for commodity prices, currency exchange rates, and temperature and pressure measurements. The vertical lines are formed by drawing a line between the high and the low data points, while the tick mark is the closing point.

- *Pie charts* are best used for comparing the percentages of a sum that several numbers represent. The full pie is the sum, and each number is represented by a wedge, or slice. An example is a pie chart in which each slice represents the percentage of total sales contributed by different product categories. There is only one data series in a pie chart.

- *Radar charts* show how data changes in relation to a center point and to other data. The value axis of each category radiates from the center point. Data from the same series is connected by lines. You can use a radar chart to plot several interrelated series and easily make visual comparisons. For example, if you have three machines containing the same five parts, you can plot the wear index of each part on each machine on a radar chart.

- *Scatter, or XY, charts* show the relationship between pairs of numbers and the trends they present. For each pair, one of the numbers is plotted on the X axis and the other number is plotted on the Y axis. Where the two meet, a symbol is placed on the chart. When a number of such pairs are plotted, a pattern may emerge. Examples of scatter charts are temperature versus time of day, and years of production experience versus number of parts produced.

❓ What's the difference between data markers and data labels?

A data marker distinguishes one series from another. In Figure 4-7 the data marker is a bar on the chart. It is uniquely colored or patterned for each series.

A data label is a piece of text representing a value plotted on the chart. The sidebar "Elements of an Excel Chart" describes all of the parts of an Excel chart.

Elements of an Excel Chart

Charts have a number of common elements, although there are differences between a 2-D chart and a 3-D one. Most of the chart elements can be changed or created apart from the creation of the chart itself.

Elements of a 2-D Chart

The following illustration shows the elements of a 2-D chart, which are described next:

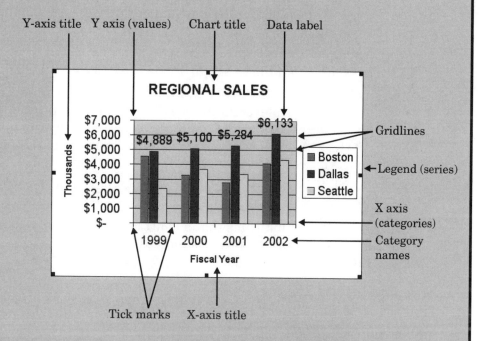

- The *Y axis*, or *value axis*, is normally the vertical axis in a 2-D chart, and it shows the value of the data points that are plotted, such as dollars in the preceding illustration.

- The *X axis*, or *category axis*, is normally the horizontal axis, and shows the categories of the data points that are plotted, such as years in the preceding illustration.

- The *chart title*, which can be taken from a cell on the sheet or added directly to the chart, is the primary descriptive text on the chart.

- The *category names* identify the individual data points. They may be dates, locations, products, and so forth. The category names are taken from the topmost row or the leftmost column, depending on the orientation of the sheet.

- The *legend* is a set of labels that describe each of the data series. These labels are attached to a symbol, a color, or a pattern that is associated with the series and placed on the chart (initially to the right, but you can move it). It is used to distinguish one data series from another. The text for a legend is taken from a text row or column, depending on the orientation of the sheet.

- The *data marker* is used to distinguish one data series from another and has a unique color, symbol, or pattern. It is the bar, line, column, or pie wedge on the chart.

- *Tick marks* are small lines used to divide the two axes and provide the scaling.

- *Gridlines* may be displayed for both axes to help viewers read the value of individual data points. Gridlines are scaled according to the values on the axes and can be changed (only horizontal gridlines are shown in the preceding illustration).

- *Data labels* are sometimes displayed to show the value of single data points.

- The *selected border* indicates that a chart can be sized, moved, or deleted, and it contains nodes or handles for that purpose. The chart in Figure 4-7 has a selected border.

Elements of a 3-D chart

Three-dimensional charts have several additional or changed elements, which are shown here and described next:

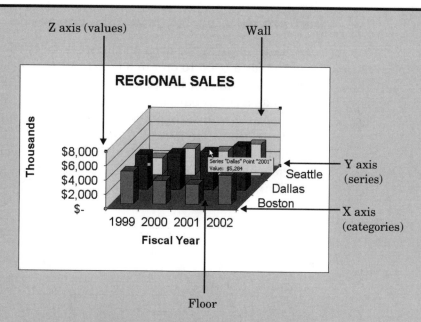

- The *Z axis,* or *value axis,* shows the value of the data points and is normally the vertical axis.

- The *X axis,* or *category axis,* is the same as in 2-D charts and is normally the horizontal axis.

- The *Y axis,* or *series axis,* shows the individual series. It is normally the depth or inward axis.

- The *wall* is the background of the plotted area.

- The *corners,* which are shown with nodes in the preceding illustration, can be rotated to change the view.

- The *floor* is the base upon which the series are plotted.

Each chart element can be accessed and either changed or used to modify the chart in some way.

 ## What are data series and data ranges?

A data range is the area on the worksheet that contains all of the data used to create a chart. A data series is a set of related numbers that produces one element of the chart, such as a set of bars or a line. In Figure 4-7, shown previously, which displays a chart and the data that created it, the data range is A1:E4, and one of the data series is A3:E3—the data for one city, Dallas. In this case, the data series is said to be "by rows." It could just as easily be by columns—the data for one year, as shown here:

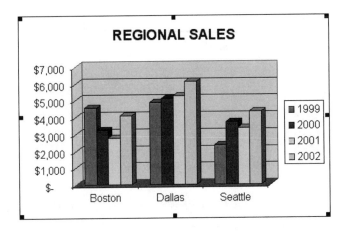

How data will be charted is an important consideration when you create the data. This issue is discussed in the sidebar "Guidelines for Charting Data."

Guidelines for Charting Data

The data that you intend to chart should be prepared with the following guidelines in mind (use the data in Figure 4-7 as an example):

- The data must be in one or more rectangles or ranges (they don't have to be contiguous), with text labels in the topmost row and/or leftmost column. The range may contain numbers and text, but text is interpreted as zeros.

- Excel defines the first *data series*—a range of numbers that is composed of related *data points* to be plotted (points that would form, for example, a single line on a chart)—as beginning with the first cell in the upper-left corner of the highlighted range containing a number not formatted as a date, and continuing across the rows and columns that are highlighted.

- Excel determines whether more rows or more columns are highlighted and, with the assumption that there will be more data points than data series, makes the larger of rows or columns the data points. So, if you highlight six columns and three rows, each column will be a data point (a single number to be plotted) and each row a data series.

- Additional data series can be included in the range by highlighting additional rows or columns, depending on whether you are building a *columnwise* or *rowwise* chart. You can have ten or more data series, but the resulting chart may not be readable.

- If the first column or row of the highlighted range contains labels or date-formatted numbers or the cell in the upper-left corner is blank, the first column or row—depending on whether the data series are down columns (columnwise) or across rows (rowwise)—is used for the X, or *category, axis.*

- The numbers on the Y, or *value, axis* are formatted with the same format that was used with the data points on the sheet.

- The initial default is to produce a column or vertical bar chart. This and other options can be easily changed.

Figure 4-7 contains a range of rowwise data series that fits the guidelines for a standard chart. The first row contains number-formatted dates that are used for the X axis; the next three rows are data series, each containing four numeric data points used to produce the column chart shown in the lower part of the figure. The labels in the legend are taken from the first column.

SORTING, FILTERING, AND SUMMARIZING DATA

 I have a lot of data to enter. What is the easiest way to do it?

First, look at your data and see if there is any repetitive information. If there is, you should split it into several tables so you need only enter the unique information in each record. For example, if you are entering sales information that looks like the data shown at the top of the screen in Figure 4-9, then it should be split into four separate tables, as shown in the lower part of the figure. This way you enter the three small tables only once and enter the minimum information only once.

Excel also provides an automatic data entry form for any database table you create. Simply click any cell in the table, open the Data menu, and choose Form. A dialog box will open, displaying the first record in the table you selected.

```
Microsoft Excel - Newsales.xls                                                    _ 8 X
File  Edit  View  Insert  Format  Tools  Data  Window  Help                        _ 8 X

D  ⸫  ⎘  ⎗  ⎙  ⎘  ABC  ⎘  ⎘  ⬦  ⟳  ·  ⬛  Σ  fx  ⬆⬇  ⬆⬇  ⬛  ⬦  ?  »  Arial       ▼ 10 ▼  B  »

  I10          ▼      =
      A        B        C      D       E        F        G          H          I        J     K    L
 1  Office   Salesman  Rate   Date   Quantity  Product    Price        Sale    Commission
 2  Boston   O'Neal    15%   7-Apr      25   Desktop   $    875  $ 21,875  $    3,281
 3  Denver   Smith     11%   8-Apr      12   Floor     $  1,285  $ 15,420  $    1,696
 4  Boston   Thomas    12%   8-Apr       8   Laptop    $  2,895  $ 23,160  $    2,779
 5  Seattle  Sato      12%   9-Apr       3   Laptop    $  2,895  $  8,685  $    1,042
 6  Boston   O'Neal    15%   9-Apr       7   Floor     $  1,285  $  8,995  $    1,349
 7  Denver   Smith     11%  10-Apr       6   Desktop   $    875  $  5,250  $      578
 8
 9
10  Number   Office          Number  Office  Salesman   Rate
11       1   Boston             101      1   O'Neal     15%
12       2   Denver             102      1   Thomas     12%
13       3   Seattle            201      2   Smith      11%
14                              301      3   Sato       12%
15
16  Number   Product   Price          Date ▼ Salesm ▼ Quanti ▼  Produc ▼    Sale ▼ Commissi ▼
17       1   Desktop     875          7-Apr    101      25          1  $ 21,875  $   3,281
18       2   Floor     1,285          8-Apr    201      12          2  $ 15,420  $   1,696
19       3   Laptop    2,895          8-Apr    102       8          3  $ 23,160  $   2,779
20                                    9-Apr    301       3          3  $  8,685  $   1,042
21                                    9-Apr    101       7          2  $  8,995  $   1,349
22                                   10-Apr    201       6          1  $  5,250  $     578
23
24
25
⎮◀ ◀ ▶ ▶⎮ \ Sales / Sheet2 / Sheet3 /                              ◀
Ready
```

Figure 4-9   Breaking a database into related tables

Click New. A blank form will open, something like the one here (depending on your table):

```
Sales                                        ? X

Office:      [            ]  ▲      New Record

Salesman:    [            ]            New

Rate:        [            ]          Delete

Date:        [            ]          Restore

Quantity:    [            ]

Product:     [            ]         Find Prev

Price:       [            ]         Find Next

Sale:                               Criteria

Commission:                          Close

                           ▼
```

Notice that calculated fields are grayed out. You only have to type entries in blank fields, which speeds up data entry.

How can I import database files into Excel?

The easiest way to get information into Excel is to export the information from its source as a comma- or tab-delimited text file. This means that each record is a single line of text with a carriage return at the end and a comma or a tab character separating each field. If you have a choice, tabs are better than commas, because your data may have commas in it but probably not tabs. Once you have a comma- or tab-delimited text file, start Excel, choose File Open, select Text Files in the Files Of Type drop-down list, identify the folder and file, and click Open. (The Text Import Wizard may open, showing you how the file will be imported and allowing you to make changes. Make any necessary changes, and click OK.) The file will come in as if it were an Excel file, with each record in a separate row and each field in a separate column.

How do I select certain records from my database?

Click any cell in the table, and from the Data menu, choose Filter and then AutoFilter. Drop-down list buttons appear next to each of the field names, like this:

Date ▼	Salesm ▼	Quanti ▼	Produc ▼	Sale ▼	Commissi ▼
7-Apr	101	25	1	$ 21,875	$ 3,281
8-Apr	201	12	2	$ 15,420	$ 1,696
8-Apr	102	8	3	$ 23,160	$ 2,779
9-Apr	301	3	3	$ 8,685	$ 1,042
9-Apr	101	7	2	$ 8,995	$ 1,349
10-Apr	201	6	1	$ 5,250	$ 578

If you open a field name's drop-down list, you will see a list of the unique entries in the column, as well as several special entries. Select the column's entries and the data table will change to show only the records that reflect the chosen entry. For example, if you were to open the Salesmen drop-down list in the previous table and click "101," you would get a new table, as shown next. Chosen entries are called the criteria, and only the records that match that criteria are displayed.

Date ▼	Salesm ▼	Quanti ▼	Produc ▼	Sale ▼	Commissi ▼
7-Apr	101	25	1	$ 21,875	$ 3,281
9-Apr	101	7	2	$ 8,995	$ 1,349

Note: When a criterion is applied, the table only displays the selected records—the rows that don't match the criterion are hidden.

You can return the table to its original view by again opening the drop-down list in which you selected the criteria (displayed in a different color) and choosing All. You can select criteria in several columns and further refine your selection. Also, you can choose Custom in the drop-down list and specify multiple criteria for one column, like this:

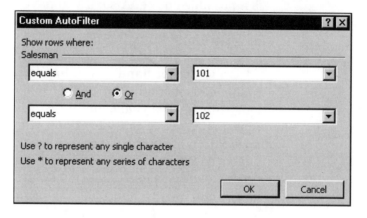

The Custom AutoFilter dialog box allows you to enter criteria other than exact matches, such as "is greater than" or "begins with," and to use the wildcard characters ? and *. The wildcard characters allow matches like 10? to select all numbers from 100 through 109. Look under "Wildcards" in the Help system to find additional information on how to use the comparison criteria and wildcard characters.

 How do I sort on more than three levels? Three is the most the Sort dialog box offers as a choice.

For a four-level sort, you would sort the worksheet twice, sorting the least important fields first, followed by the more important ones. For example, if you were trying to identify

employees by plant location in the order Plant Location, Department, Paygrade, and Employee Name, you would sort first on Employee Name as the Sort By field. Then, in a second sort, you would sort on Plant Location, then by Department, and then by Paygrade.

How do I decide which application to use to store data—Excel or Access or another application?

The principal function of Excel is to analyze data. If you have a database for which analysis is important, and that contains significantly fewer records than Excel's maximum 65,536 rows (each row is a database record, and you normally do not want to build a database you can't add records to), then Excel is a possible choice. Also, if you have a very small database, up to a couple of thousand records, and it will have a short life and limited use, then Excel might be the easiest way to produce and use such a database.

On the other hand, if you have a large database (over a couple of thousand records) that is liable to be around for a long time (over a year), and if fast searching, forms, and reports are major considerations, then Access is the application of choice. Access is also your best choice if you have a complex data set involving, for example, salespeople, products, and sales, and for which three related tables would be the best way to handle the information.

+ ***Tip:*** *If you are creating a database of names and addresses, such as a contacts list, then Outlook may be the best application to use.*

Is there an easy way to create subtotals in a sorted list?

Yes. Open the Data menu, choose Subtotals, and then select the appropriate options from the Subtotal dialog box, shown in the following illustration.

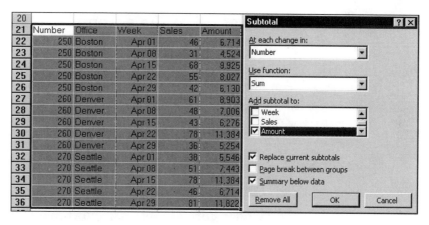

WORKING WITH PIVOTTABLES AND PIVOTCHARTS

 When I create a PivotChart, a data table appears that I have not built. Can I delete it? I want to freeze the PivotChart as it is.

The PivotTable report is a special report that is created at the time you create a PivotChart. If you delete it, changes to the PivotTable will no longer be reflected in the PivotChart, since the PivotTable report supplies the source data to the chart. Here's how you delete it:

1. Click anywhere on the PivotTable report.

2. From the PivotTable toolbar, click PivotTable, click Select, and then click Entire Table.

3. Press DELETE.

 Tip: *If you want to keep the PivotTable for later use, move it to another worksheet. (If you copy it, it will remain linked to the PivotChart.)*

 How do I get rid of the automatic totaling on the rows in my PivotTable? I only want to see columnar totals.

You must reset the PivotTable Options by following these steps:

1. From the PivotTable toolbar, which appears when you are creating a PivotTable, click the PivotTable button down arrow. A context menu will appear.

2. Select Table Options from the menu.

3. Under Format Options, shown here, clear the check mark from the Grand Totals For Rows check box:

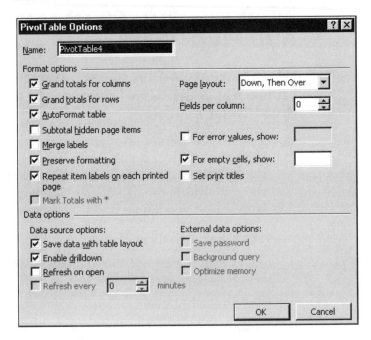

 When I try to reorder the data on the PivotTable, I end up with an unreadable table. How do I keep the fields from interfering with each other?

It sounds like you need to get rid of some of the fields that are getting in your way. If you find that you are having trouble trying to keep your PivotTables clear and easy to read, try deleting some of the data fields, and then reapply them if you find you still need them. Just drag the appropriate data button off the PivotTable to delete that data.

Another possibility is that you have too many data elements showing in the report. By clicking on the down arrow of the data button, you will see a list of all the elements being displayed. Click to clear some of the check marks to show fewer elements, as shown here:

3	Sum of Amount	Office			
4	Week	☑ Boston		e	Grand Total
5	Apr 01	☑ Denver		16.1	21162.75
6	Apr 08	☑ Seattle		3.45	18973.5
7	Apr 15			34.1	27584.55
8	Apr 22			3.7	26125.05
9	Apr 29			.95	23206.05
10	Grand Total			09.3	117051.9
11					
12					
13		OK	Cancel		

I have a worksheet that logs the dollars for each sale of certain products, but I want to show a count of the product sales, not the dollars. How can I change the report to do that?

Very easily. Just click the Field Settings icon on the PivotTable toolbar, and click Count in the Summarize By drop-down list.

How do I find the data fields when they are missing?

You may find that one of these suggestions will bring the fields back to the toolbar.

● The PivotTable toolbar must be floating on the worksheet. If it is docked, drag it onto the worksheet.

● The report must be selected, or the toolbar will not show the appropriate data fields. Click on the report to select it.

● Click the Display Fields button on the toolbar to display the fields.

Chapter 5

Presenting with PowerPoint

Answer Topics!

Presenting with PowerPoint @ a Glance

The topics covered in this chapter are outlined here:

PowerPoint Tools and Features describes the components PowerPoint provides to help you create professional presentations.

Working with PowerPoint and Its Views describes the new tri-pane views, changing a slide's layout, using notes and outlines, and other basic features to get started using the program quickly.

Creating Presentations shows you how you can locate presentations, bypass introductory dialog boxes, use prebuilt presentation templates to create professional presentations, and build your own presentations from scratch.

Using Templates and Masters discusses how to create your own templates, how masters can ensure your presentations have a unified appearance, and how to modify the notes area for expanded usage.

Customizing Presentations offers several ways to enhance presentations, including methods to align objects, using charts, adding voice and music, and providing transitional effects.

 Organizing Presentations shows you how to add comments to slides, copy or move slides from within your current or other presentations, and ways to preview slides in a larger presentation.

 Producing Presentations on Paper and on the Screen shows you how to output a presentation by printing a handout with notes, adjusting the narration time in a slide show, changing a presentation's appearance from color to black and white, and preparing "hidden" slides.

POWERPOINT TOOLS AND FEATURES

PowerPoint provides Office 2000 with tools and features to create stunning presentations. While the other Office products are capable of producing professional-looking reports, letters, spreadsheets, and the like, PowerPoint was created with showmanship as a primary design consideration.

A PowerPoint presentation is a file (with extension .ppt or .htm) that is composed of one or more slides. A slide is a single screen of text, graphics, background, and other objects that illustrate a topic. Like 35-millimeter photographic slides, PowerPoint slides can present information, but they can also do much more: you can print slides to use as handouts, you can attach notes related to each slide for yourself or for distribution to your audience, and you can hide slides in your presentation and jump to them if needed. Slide shows generated from a computer can include sound, video clips, and amazing transitional effects from one slide to the next; in short, you can do just about anything you want in electronic or printed presentations to deliver the impact you're after. The power of the personal computer offers an endless variety of special effects and multimedia features that you can use to enhance your presentation. PowerPoint 2000 also incorporates communication and collaboration technologies, which allow its presentations to be presented through the Web and other remote means.

PowerPoint was designed to allow nonprofessional graphic artists and designers to prepare professional presentations. It does this by providing these tools:

- *Presentation templates,* complete presentations with color schemes, graphics, and dummy text, as shown in Figure 5-1. There are over 20 presentation templates that cover a broad range of corporate needs for printed, electronic (run from a computer through a monitor or projection device), or online use over the Internet or an intranet.

- The *AutoContent Wizard,* which walks you through the process of creating a presentation by getting feedback from you on what specific elements you want in your presentation.

- *Presentation designs,* which provide a single slide with a color scheme and graphics from which to build your presentation. You can start with the design and add your own text or other objects, or you can apply one of the designs to your existing presentation. PowerPoint includes over 40 different designs from which to choose.

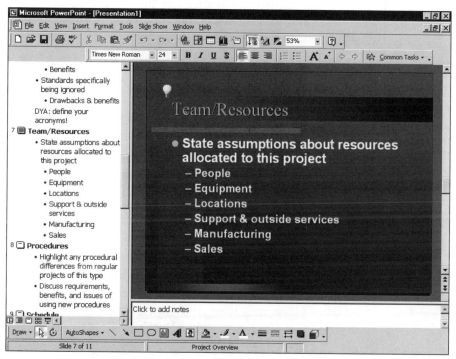

Figure 5-1   Presentation templates provide everything needed for a professional appearance

● *Design assistance* for specific elements, such as the slide layout, color scheme, and background. This method provides the best opportunity for you to use your creative ideas from the start. However, all of these methods allow you to modify the design elements to your liking.

Flexibility in creating a presentation and consistency in delivering it are key aspects of PowerPoint. Many presentations maintain the same "look and feel" throughout their slides by incorporating design elements such as the company logo in the same location on each slide, placing each slide's title and bullets in exactly the same spots, and other consistent formatting techniques. PowerPoint uses masters to ensure that you can lock in those design elements that you want to keep consistent throughout your entire presentation. There are four masters that you can use:

● **Slide Master**   Sets the basic elements of a slide, including placement of the slide title, main text layout and formatting, background, graphics, slide number, date, and other objects

● **Title Master**   Covers the design of the title slide, or first slide, as well as title and subtitle placement and formatting

● **Handout Master**   Sets up the arrangement of multiple slides on a page or the presentation outline for printing audience handouts

● **Notes Master**   Determines the sizing and placement of the slide being described and its corresponding notes area

The true beauty of PowerPoint's ease of use is centered around the six views available for creating, editing, and showing your presentations. Understanding what each view does and how it can be used to accomplish your work will save you much time and effort. The main function of each of the views is described in the following table.

Button	View	Function
	Normal	Combines three views—Slide, Outline, and Notes—into one tri-pane display to provide the most complete overview of your presentation and current slide
	Outline	Condenses slide content to text only for ease in organizing the slides in a presentation, and shows a thumbnail of the slide and notes in a tri-pane display
	Slide	Displays the slide in full view, along with notes and an outline of the presentation in a tri-pane display so that you can incorporate text and graphic elements and modify its appearance
	Slide Sorter	Displays thumbnails of each slide in a presentation to make it easy to rearrange slide order and add transitions
	Slide Show	Previews a full-screen view of the presentation with any transitions or animation, letting you check timing and sequence
	Notes Page	Allows the speaker to include notes that correspond to each slide in the presentation

WORKING WITH POWERPOINT AND ITS VIEWS

 What is the difference between Normal, Slide, and Outline views?

There isn't much difference anymore. In previous versions of PowerPoint, each view had a specific and unique purpose. In PowerPoint 2000, you can see all three views in any one of them, thanks to the tri-pane display. The only real difference is the initial emphasis when you open a view, as seen in the Slide view shown in Figure 5-2. Once the view is displayed, you can drag one of the two pane borders to size each pane to meet your needs.

 Can I easily change the layout of a slide once I've created and saved it?

Sure. In Normal, Slide, Outline, or Slide Sorter view (in Slide Sorter view, select the slide first) choose Slide Layout from the Format menu. In the Slide Layout dialog box, select a new layout and click Reapply, and PowerPoint will try to match it.

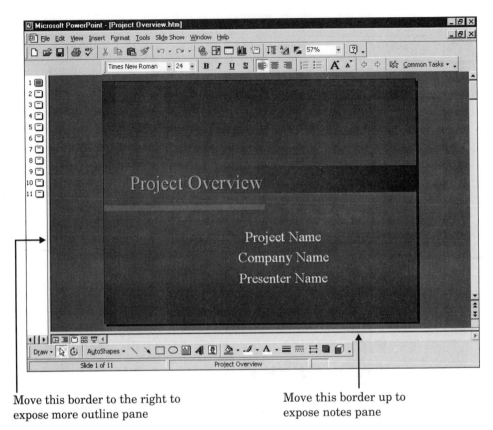

 Move this border to the right to
expose more outline pane

 Move this border up to
expose notes pane

Figure 5-2 Slide view demonstrates the tri-pane display

Can I display a slide and its notes as they will print, and then edit the notes in the same view?

Yes you can, as shown in Figure 5-3. Open the View menu
and choose Notes Page. A preview of the page that will print
is displayed with the slide at the top of the page and the
notes at the bottom. You can directly edit the text of the notes
in this view; but to make changes to the slide, double-click it
to open Slide view.

Tip: *To add a graphic to your notes, you need to be in
Notes Page view; you cannot add a graphic in any of the
tri-pane views.*

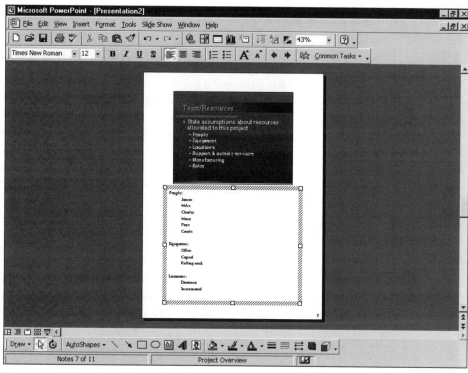

Figure 5-3   Use Notes Page view to see how your slide and notes will print, and edit your notes in the same view

What is the best way to move text in Outline view?

To move a single bullet, position the pointer to the left of the bulleted item until it turns into a four-headed arrow, as shown here:

> ✛ • High-level overview of progress against schedule
> • On-track in what areas

Drag the bullet to another location in the presentation. You can move the text of an entire slide by positioning the pointer over the slide icon to the left of the slide title and then dragging it to its new location; all subordinate text will follow.

 I've e-mailed a copy of a presentation to one of my field reps, but he says he can't open the presentation. What's wrong?

Best guess is either he's using an earlier version of PowerPoint (the PowerPoint 97/2000 file format is not recognizable by previous versions), or he doesn't have PowerPoint installed on his computer. You have a few options:

- Save the presentation as the type corresponding to the version of PowerPoint he's using—PowerPoint 4.0 or 95—and resend the file (some features of your presentation may not display properly, since several new features in PowerPoint 2000 are not supported by earlier versions).

- Save the presentation using Save As Web Page from the File menu. Send any files and folders PowerPoint creates, and your rep can use Microsoft Internet Explorer 4.0 or later to view it.

- Have your rep download the PowerPoint Viewer from the Microsoft web site, http://officeupdate.microsoft.com. He'll be able to view and print the presentation but won't be able to make changes.

- Create a package using the Pack and Go Wizard (Pack And Go on the File menu; you will need your Office 2000 CD1 if you didn't install the wizard initially), which includes all the files and fonts used in the presentation; and, in this case, you could also add PowerPoint Viewer (located on the Microsoft web site or the Office 2000 CD Pfiles\Msoffice\Office\Xlators).

 Note: The PowerPoint Viewer downloaded from Microsoft or included on the Office 2000 CD1 supports PowerPoint 97 file format features. There are a few features available in PowerPoint 2000, such as automatic numbering, that are not supported by the viewer.

CREATING PRESENTATIONS

Whenever I save a presentation, PowerPoint opens the My Documents folder in the Save and Save As dialog boxes. I prefer to save my presentations on a network server. Can I change the default location where my presentations are saved?

Sure. Open the Tools menu and choose Options. Click the Save tab; and in the Default File Location text box, change the path from C:\My Documents to one of your choosing.

Every time I start PowerPoint, the same dialog box appears with choices to open or create presentations. I just want PowerPoint to open so I can use the menu bar and toolbars to get to work. Is there a way to go right to PowerPoint?

Yes and no. The PowerPoint dialog box, shown here, is great for new users to help them get going; but after you acquire more familiarity with the program, you might find it to be just an obstacle between you and your work.

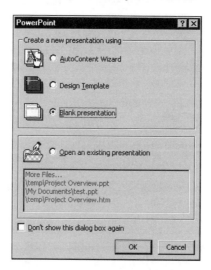

To prevent this dialog box from opening, either select the Don't Show This Dialog Box Again check box or choose

Options from the Tools menu, click the View tab, and click Startup Dialog to clear the check box.

The next time you open PowerPoint, the startup dialog box won't open *but* the New Slide dialog box will appear so that you can select a slide layout. To also prevent this dialog box from opening, select the same Don't Show This Dialog Box Again check box or return to the View tab of the Options dialog box and click New Slide Dialog to clear the check box. Now, when you restart PowerPoint, you will open to a new presentation.

Caution: *If you choose not to have the New Slide dialog box display, whenever you create a new slide you won't be offered the list of AutoLayouts from which to choose. PowerPoint will open a new slide with the default title-box layout.*

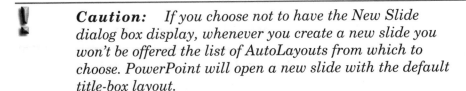

I have many presentations saved on several drives and networked computers. How can I best locate the presentation I need?

Use keywords to uniquely identify each presentation when you create it. Open the Properties dialog box for a presentation by choosing Properties from the File menu. On the Summary tab, type one or more keywords that you'll remember for each presentation, and then click OK.

Tip: *The Properties dialog box also can be opened from the new Office 2000 Open and Save/Save As dialog boxes. Select a presentation in the folder and file text box, open the Tools menu, and choose Properties.*

Use keywords to find a file by following these steps:

1. Click the Open button.
2. Use the Look In box to select the drive on which you think the file is stored.

3. Open the Tools menu and choose Find. In the Find dialog box, open the Property drop-down list box and select Keywords, as shown next.

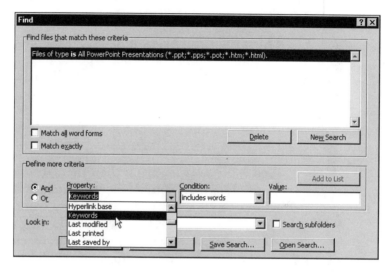

4. Ensure that the Condition box displays Includes Words, and then type the keywords in the Value box.

5. Click Add To List and select the Search Subfolders check box.

6. Click Find Now.

The Find dialog box will close and the Open dialog box will display the filename you were looking for.

Tip: *To remind yourself to add keywords to each presentation, you can automatically display the Properties dialog box when you first save a presentation. Choose Options from the Tools menu, click the Save tab, and then select Prompt For File Properties.*

 I think the built-in presentation templates and designs that PowerPoint provides are great time-savers. Do you know where I can find more templates and designs?

Open the Help menu and choose Office On The Web. You will be connected to the Office Update page on Microsoft's web site. From there you can access all sorts of free downloads and product enhancements such as additional templates.

 Can I open more than one presentation at a time?

Yes. Choose Open from the File menu and navigate to the folder in which your presentations are located. Press CTRL as you click all the presentations you want opened. When you click Open, PowerPoint will display the first presentation and all others can be quickly displayed by choosing them from the Taskbar or by cycling through the list by pressing CTRL-F6.

 Note: *You can concurrently open only as many presentations as your computer's memory (RAM) will allow.*

 I'd like to include a presentation in a web site that I maintain. How can I run the presentation as a slide show on my home page?

PowerPoint 2000 really shines when you want to move your presentations from the desktop to the Web or your intranet. See the following sidebar, "Taking PowerPoint Online," for an in-depth look at how to use PowerPoint online. Also see Chapter 9 for more ways to use Office on the Web.

Taking PowerPoint Online

As a presentation program, PowerPoint is a natural for "strutting its stuff" globally on the Web or locally on your company's intranet. In fact, you can track the parallel advances in multimedia improvements in both PowerPoint and in the HTML world; they really are made for one another. PowerPoint 2000, in concert with the later versions of Microsoft Internet Explorer, makes showing your presentations online as easy as on your local computer. The following procedures take you through a tour of how you can show off your work to the world.

Saving Your Presentation for Online Use

Create your presentation as you usually would; and then, on the File menu, choose Save As Web Page. The Save As dialog box opens, as shown here:

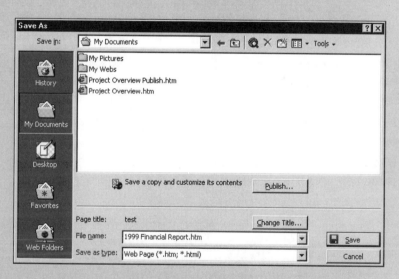

This dialog box has a few features that specifically cater to creating presentations for the Web, as described next.

● Clicking the Web Folders icon on the bar at the left of the dialog box, shown here,

will display your default location for saving Office files: My Documents; or if you have created web sites in other programs such as Microsoft FrontPage 2000 and hosted them on a Web server (for example, Microsoft Personal Web Server, or MSPWS, included with Windows 98), you might see those web folders displayed. (Their location is C:\Inetpub\Wwwroot if you used the default installations for FrontPage and the MSPWS.) You can then open an existing web folder and save the presentation directly into it, or place a hyperlink on the web site's home page to your presentation (which also lets viewers run the presentation from the web site). Of course you can also navigate to any other folder and save your presentation there.

● Clicking Change Title opens the Set Page Title dialog box in which you can type the title you want to appear in the title bar of the browser window when someone views your presentation.

● Clicking Publish provides several options for showing your presentation, as described in the next section.

● The File Name and Save As Type drop-down list boxes default to saving the presentation as .htm pages.

Note: *When you save a presentation as a web page, you are actually splitting the single .ppt file into several files that a browser can interpret. For example, each slide becomes its own .htm page, and graphics are made into individual .gif or .jpg files. For this reason it is advisable to use the Publish feature, described next, whenever you are copying or moving an .htm presentation to another location.*

Publishing Your Content

Publishing is a term that is generally understood to mean packaging up a web page and all its associated files so it can be copied to another location such as a web server for hosting on the Internet or a corporate intranet. Clicking Publish in the web page–specific Save As dialog box does that and also offers several ways to customize how your presentation will be seen in a browser, as shown here:

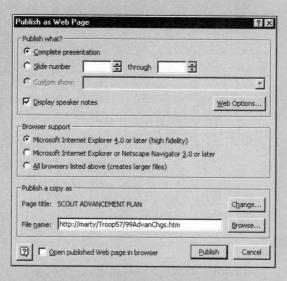

The options available to you include the following:

● Under Publish What? you can select which slides to display, including any custom shows you have within the presentation (see "Customizing Presentations," later in this chapter, for questions on custom shows).

● Clicking Web Options opens the Office-wide dialog box of the same name that provides basic options for any Office files used on the Web, and also some specific options for PowerPoint presentations, as shown next on the General tab.

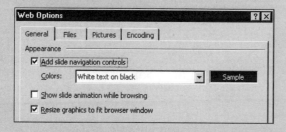

Here you can choose whether to have a set of slide navigation controls on your presentation including its color. These controls

will display notes and outline panes. You can also set graphics to be resized to fit the browser's window and whether slide animations and transition effects will appear in a browser.

● Under Browser Support you can optimize your presentation for the version of Microsoft Internet Explorer you anticipate your audience will be using. This is fine when you are dealing with an environment you can control, such as your corporate intranet; but if you're publishing to the Web, you are better off selecting the third option, All Browsers Listed Above. Note that optimizing for all browsers will increase the file size of your presentation.

● Under Publish A Copy As you can specify where the presentation files should be copied to. Clicking Browse opens the Publish As dialog box, which serves the same purpose as the Web page–specific Save As dialog box.

● Clicking Publish copies files to the location you specified with the options you've selected.

Note: *You can only publish to a web server. If you try to publish to any other folder or drive, you will get an error message.*

Previewing Your Work

After you have saved your online presentation, you will want to preview it in the browsers you expect your audience will be using—the later versions of Internet Explorer and Netscape Navigator should cover almost all of your audience.

● Clicking the Open Published Web Page In Browser check box in the Publish As Web Page dialog box lets you immediately preview the presentation when you publish it.

● After you've saved a presentation for the Web using the Save As dialog box (File | Save As Web Page), you can view it in a browser by first opening the .htm presentation in PowerPoint and then choosing Web Page Preview from the File menu. Your presentation will have an outline on the left listing the title of each slide in the

presentation, the slide itself, any notes you have associated with the page, and slide navigation controls along the bottom, something like this:

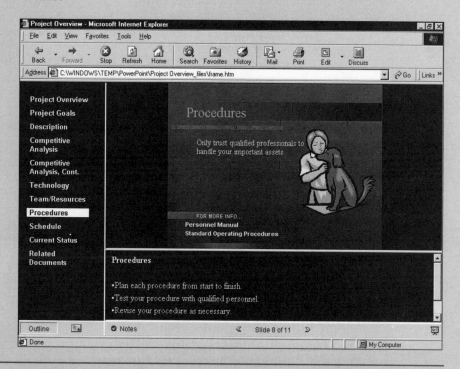

> **Note:** *The ability to open a presentation in PowerPoint 2000 after saving it as an .htm file and to view it as if it were a .ppt file is known as "round-tripping" HTML, a significant advance for those who prepare presentations for Internet or intranet use.*

The navigation controls allow you to change how you want to view the presentation. The following table describes the function of each control.

Button	Function
Outline	Hides or displays the outline pane
	When the outline pane is displayed, lets you view slide titles only or a more expanded outline that includes bulleted items
Notes	Displays the notes pane on slides that have associated notes

Button	Function
⟨ Slide 8 of 11 ⟩	Provides a reference of where you are in the presentation and provides Back and Forward buttons to move from slide to slide
🖥	Displays the presentation slides in full screen view (when in full-screen view, click to advance, or right-click and choose from the context menu)

Note: *After previewing your presentation in a browser, you may want to make changes in your presentation. You can do that directly to the .htm version. However, to view your saved changes, you cannot just click Refresh in your browser; you need to again click Web Page Preview from the File menu. (PowerPoint creates a temporary copy of the presentation for the browser when you click Web Page Preview, which doesn't receive any changes you make until you choose that option again.)*

I need to quickly put together a presentation on the status of a project I'm working on. I need help fast. Can PowerPoint save me?

You bet. When PowerPoint is started, you are presented with a dialog box that offers several "get started" options. Select AutoContent Wizard and click OK. The wizard will walk you through three areas of presentation design, with which you build a presentation to your requirements. These are the three areas:

- *Presentation type,* with which you scan a list of built-in presentation topics to find one that most closely matches your subject

- *Presentation style,* which offers you a choice of output media for the presentation

- *Presentation options,* which allow you to add unique information, such as your title, name, and company

PowerPoint will provide everything for your presentation except the specifics of your project and the coffee and doughnuts. The sidebar "PowerPoint's Presentation

Templates Summary" provides the complete list of available templates for onscreen, printed, or online use.

PowerPoint's Presentation Templates Summary

The following table lists the presentation templates available in PowerPoint:

Presentation Template	Standard Installation	Installed from Office 2000 CD on First Use
Brainstorming Session		✓
Business Plan	✓	
Certificate		✓
Communicating Bad News	✓	
Company Handbook		✓
Company Meeting		✓
Corporate Home Page	✓	
Employee Orientation		✓
Facilitating A Meeting		✓
Financial Overview	✓	
Generic	✓	
Group Home Page	✓	
Introducing A Speaker		✓
Managing Organizational Change		✓
Marketing Plan	✓	
Motivating A Team	✓	
Presenting A Technical Report		✓
Products And Services Overview	✓	
Product Overview	✓	
Project Post-Mortem		✓

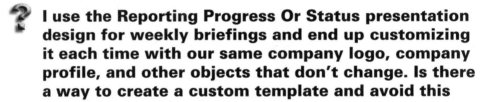

Presentation Template	Standard Installation	Installed from Office 2000 CD on First Use
Recommending A Strategy	✓	
Reporting Progress Or Status	✓	
Selling A Product Or Service	✓	
Selling Your Ideas	✓	
Training		✓

Note: See Chapter 2 for more information on the choices you have for installing components during and after your initial install.

USING TEMPLATES AND MASTERS

 I use the Reporting Progress Or Status presentation design for weekly briefings and end up customizing it each time with our same company logo, company profile, and other objects that don't change. Is there a way to create a custom template and avoid this repetitive work?

Sure. After you have added the text and objects that don't change from one week to another, you can save the Reporting Progress Or Status template as a new template with a name like Weekly Briefing. The Reporting Progress Or Status template will remain intact and you will have created a custom template for your own use. To create a custom template, follow these steps:

1. Click Open on the toolbar, choose the path to your presentation templates (the default is C:\Program Files\Microsoft Office\Templates\1033), select Design Templates (which has the filename extension .pot) in the Files Of Type drop-down list box, and double-click the PowerPoint template you want to start with.

Note: *Although these templates are actually Presentation templates and not Design templates, they are still templates and can be more easily located by selecting Design Template in the Files Of Type drop-down list box.*

2. Make the changes to the template that you want in your new template.

3. Choose Save As from the File menu to display the dialog box of the same name; and in the Save As Type drop-down list box, choose Design Template.

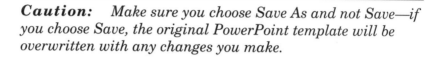

Caution: *Make sure you choose Save As and not Save—if you choose Save, the original PowerPoint template will be overwritten with any changes you make.*

4. Type a name for the new template in the File Name box and use the Save In box to select the folder in which you want to store the template. See the sidebar "Template Folder Locations" for help in storing templates.

5. Click Save.

Template Folder Locations

You can store a template in any folder on your computer or on a network. If you want to store a new template where it will appear with PowerPoint's built-in presentations when you open the File New dialog box, use the folder locations described in the following table:

Presentation Type	Folder Location
Blank presentation	C:\Windows\ShellNew\Pwrpnt9.pot
Presentation designs (schemes that can be applied to your existing material)	C:\Program Files\Microsoft Office\Templates\Presentation Designs
Presentation templates (fully contained presentations with suggested text)	C:\Program Files\Microsoft Office\ Templates\1033

Note: *If you changed these default locations, adjust the listed paths accordingly.*

Most of the speaker notes in my presentation don't fit in the default notes area. I know I can reduce the size of each slide to gain more space for notes, but it seems quite tedious to do this for every slide. Is there an easy way to increase the notes area on speaker notes?

Yes, there is. By using the Notes Master for a particular presentation, you can customize the notes layout for all slides, saving time and ensuring that all slides are sized uniformly. In Normal, Outline, Slide, or Slide Sorter view, choose Master from the View menu and Notes Master from the submenu. Reduce the size of the slide image by clicking it to select it and then pressing SHIFT (to maintain the height-width ratio) while you drag a corner selection handle inward. Enlarge the size of the notes body area by dragging the selection handles in the direction you want the increase to occur, as shown here:

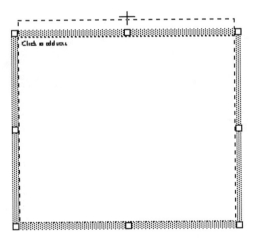

I have a background of our corporate logo in my Slide Master that works well in all but a few slides in my presentation. How do I remove a master background from a slide?

Open the slide whose background you want omitted. From the Format menu, choose Background and select the Omit Background Graphics From Master check box.

Tip: *You can manually override formatting set in the Slide Master for individual slides by changing the formatting in Slide view.*

I don't want to show the page number on my opening slide. How do I remove the page number on the first slide and retain it in the remaining slides?

Follow these steps:

1. Open the Slide Master by opening the View menu, pointing to Master, and choosing Slide Master.

2. Verify that you have a slide Number Area object on the master slide, as shown here:

(If it's not there, you can find out how to add it in the following question.)

3. Choose Header and Footer from the View menu.

4. Select the Slide Number check box to place slide numbers on each slide in the presentation.

5. Select the Don't Show On Title Slide check box to prevent the slide number from appearing on the opening slide.

Note: *You can choose to display or hide the slide number for any slide by displaying the slide in one of the tri-pane views, choosing Header And Footer from the View menu, and selecting or clearing the Slide Number check box.*

I inadvertently deleted the date area from the master slide. How do I restore the date area to the master?

Open the Slide Master by opening the View menu, pointing to Master, and choosing Slide Master, and then right-click an

empty spot on the slide. Choose Master Layout from the context menu, select the Date placeholder, and click OK.

 Tip: *The Master Layout dialog box is a "common task" available from the Formatting toolbar's Common Tasks drop-down list. The Common Tasks list of tasks changes according to what you are working on.*

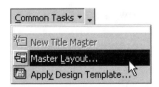

CUSTOMIZING PRESENTATIONS

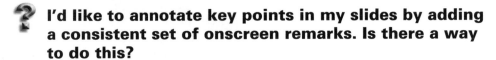

I'd like to annotate key points in my slides by adding a consistent set of onscreen remarks. Is there a way to do this?

Yes. Use callouts to amplify or emphasize elements in your slides. You can manually create callouts by using the Text Box tool (to contain the callout narrative) and the Line tool (to connect the callout with the point of interest); but to achieve fast, consistent results, you can choose from one of several designs PowerPoint provides. On the Drawing toolbar (in one of the three tri-pane views: Normal, Outline, or Slide), click AutoShapes, point to Callouts, and select one of the 20 designs. Click the crosshair pointer where you want the end of the connecting line or shape to begin, and then drag. Figure 5-4 shows an example of a callout.

 Tip: *Customize the size and appearance of AutoShapes by using the Format | AutoShape option.*

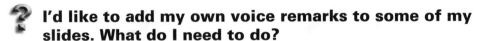

I'd like to add my own voice remarks to some of my slides. What do I need to do?

Foremost, you need to have the required hardware: a sound card and a microphone to record with, and a sound card and

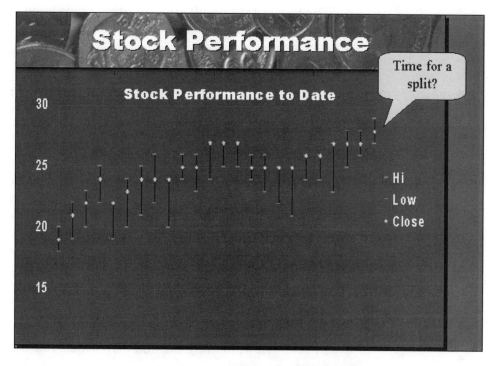

Figure 5-4   Use AutoShapes callouts to emphasize key points in a slide

speakers to play back. Next, you will need to have plenty of hard disk space available. Sound files recorded in PowerPoint can consume disk space at up to 172K per second of recording. Finally, you need to decide if you want to record throughout the presentation or just for a single slide.

Tip: *PowerPoint automatically links sound files if they are greater than a certain preset size. You can adjust the size from the General tab of the Tools Options dialog box.*

To record throughout a presentation, follow these steps:

1. Choose Record Narration from the Slide Show menu.

2. In the dialog box of the same name, adjust recording settings if necessary and click OK.

3. The presentation will start in Slide Show view so you can record narrations on each slide you want.

4. Right-click the screen to navigate through the show and pause narration.

5. End narration by ending the show. (Press ESC, or right-click the screen and choose End Show from the context menu.)

Tip: *For very long narrations you should link the sound file to the presentation; otherwise, the sound is embedded in the presentation file (.ppt), possibly increasing its size dramatically. In the Record Narration dialog box, select the Link Narrations In check box and choose a file location. See Chapter 8 for a complete description of object linking and embedding (OLE).*

An alternative method to record remarks on a single slide is as follows:

1. In Slide view, display the slide for which you want to record remarks.

2. Point to Movies And Sounds on the Insert menu and choose Record Sound.

3. In the Record Sound dialog box, click the Record button to start recording and the Stop button when finished.

4. Give the sound a name and click OK.

Using either method to record sounds will add a sound icon to the slides that contain sound.

Note: *Using Record Sound from the Insert menu will embed the sound in the slide. If you want to link the sound files, you need to record from the Record Narration option on the Slide Show menu.*

 I find it very difficult to align and size boxes and lines in an organization chart for my company. Is there an easy way?

Yes. In PowerPoint, open the slide to which you want to add the chart , open the Insert menu, point to Picture, and then select Organization Chart. (You might need your Office 2000 CD.) This will open Microsoft Organization Chart 2 (described in Chapter 11), a separate program that is included with Office 2000, whose sole purpose is to create and format organization charts. The program opens with the skeleton of a simple chart that you can easily build upon:

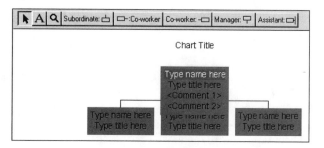

You can save an organization chart as a separate file, copy it to other material you are preparing, or link it to your current presentation. See Chapter 8 for a complete description of linking objects between Office 2000 products.

 How can I quickly align multiple boxes in a column along their centers?

Use PowerPoint's automatic aligning and distributing feature. You can try for hours to get several objects into a uniform position, or, with a few mouse clicks, you can have them all fall into line like good soldiers. Follow these next few steps to achieve perfect positioning:

1. In one of the tri-pane views (Normal, Outline, or Slide), hold SHIFT down while selecting the objects you want to work on.

2. On the Drawing toolbar, click Draw, point to Align Or Distribute, and select Align Center. The objects will align, but their spacing is commonly haphazard.

3. Repeat step 2 but select Distribute Vertically to even the spacing.

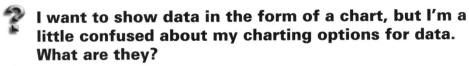 **I want to show data in the form of a chart, but I'm a little confused about my charting options for data. What are they?**

One of the downsides of Office 2000 is that you are often presented with too many choices. PowerPoint 2000 accesses a program called Microsoft Graph 2000 Chart (as do Word and Access) to provide charting functionality. But since you have Office 2000 and not just the stand-alone PowerPoint program, you also have Excel, the charting master, available to you. Which should you use? See the sidebar "PowerPoint Charting" for help.

PowerPoint Charting

Whether you use Microsoft Graph 2000 or Excel 2000 depends mainly on two factors.

- Are you already an experienced Excel user?
- Is the supporting data already in a spreadsheet?

The answers to these questions will help you determine which method is better for you. Microsoft Excel is unquestionably one of the best full-service, data-manipulation and representation programs. If the data you will be displaying in PowerPoint is already charted in Excel or contained in worksheets, why bother creating it twice? Use one of the methods described in Chapter 8 to include the Excel chart in your presentation. If you are presenting data for the first time and don't expect to use it in a spreadsheet, then using PowerPoint's charting capability (Microsoft Graph, covered in Chapter 11) makes sense.

This is not to imply that Microsoft Graph is an inferior charting product. With few exceptions, such as the absence of a Charting Wizard and the ability to perform calculations on data, you will not find many significant functional differences between the two products. Perhaps the main attraction to using PowerPoint's integral charting capabilities is that you avoid any problems with pasting, embedding, or linking files that can arise when using Excel.

I've made several changes to a standard bar chart that I'd like to use in other presentations. Can I somehow save a chart's formatting so I don't have to re-create it every time I want to duplicate the chart's appearance?

Sure. What you're looking to do is create a user-defined chart type that you can select as you would any of the chart types that PowerPoint provides. Create a chart type with these steps:

1. Click Insert Chart on the toolbar, and double-click the chart.

2. Format your chart as you want it to be saved for future use. Right-click the chart element you want to format and choose its Format option on the context menu, or select the element (its name appears on the toolbar) and choose the Format option from the Format menu.

3. Choose Chart Type from the Chart menu.

4. Click the Custom Types tab and choose User-Defined below the list of chart types.

5. Click Add, and in the Add Custom Chart Type dialog box, name and describe the new chart. Click OK twice.

Next time you want to format a chart with these attributes, just select it by name from the Custom Types tab.

Tip: *If you find that the standard bar chart that appears by default every time you create a chart is not useful for most of your work, you can change the default to any other chart type provided by PowerPoint or created by you. Select the new chart type in the Chart Type dialog box, and click Set As Default Chart at the bottom of the dialog box.*

I know there are some neat effects that can be used in the transition between slides in a slide show. Does PowerPoint have any effects for objects in a slide?

Yes. PowerPoint offers a set of effects, called animations, similar to those available for slide transitions for text and

other objects in a slide. For example, you can have the title materialize letter by letter from outside the boundary of the slide as if typed by a typewriter, complete with sound. You can preview the effects with these steps:

1. In one of the tri-pane views (Normal, Outline, or Slide), select the object to which you want to apply the animation.

2. Choose Preset Animation from the Slide Show menu, and select an animation or choose Custom Animation from the same menu to open the dialog box of the same name.

Tip: *You can modify any Preset Animation after you attach it to an object from the Custom Animation dialog box.*

3. On the Effects tab (or Chart Effects tab if your object is a chart), open the Entry Animation And Sound drop-down list boxes and select a sample, as shown here:

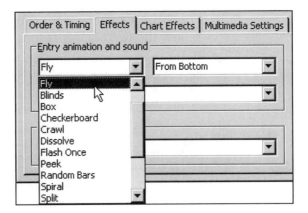

4. Click the Preview button, and the effect you chose will run on the selected object in the preview box.

You can have several animated objects on a slide, change their appearance order, adjust timing, and control a host of other attributes to bring your animation to life.

I've designed a rather complex slide, and I want to lock together several drawing objects so I don't inadvertently change anything. How do I do this?

Use the Grouping feature to make a single object from several component objects. Select all of the objects you want to include as one by holding SHIFT while clicking each of the components, and then right-click any of the selected objects. Point to Grouping in the context menu, and click Group in the submenu. The selection handles that surrounded each object will change to surround the perimeter of all the objects. Now you can move, size, change color, or otherwise change all the objects as one.

Tip: *When selecting multiple objects for a grouping, it may be easier to select all objects on a slide and then deselect those that don't belong in the group. Choose Select All from the Edit menu and then press SHIFT and click those objects you do not want.*

How do I use the Rectangle and Oval drawing tools to create perfect circles and squares?

Press SHIFT as you drag to create the circle or square; the object will be constrained to equal width and height.

Whenever I resize an object, I always seem to stretch it too far in either its height or width. How can I resize an object proportionally?

Avoid trying to resize the object with the selection handles. Instead, right-click the object, choose its format option (for example, Format Picture For Clip Art And Other Pictures or Format AutoShape For Drawing Objects), and click the Size tab. Ensure that the Lock Aspect Ratio check box is selected, as shown next, and then change the object's size by using actual values or percentages.

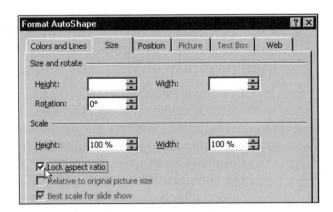

 Tip: *You can also size the image proportionally by dragging one of the corner sizing handles; however, if the Lock Aspect Ratio check box has been cleared, you might alter the ratio.*

I want the same background color in several boxes I've drawn on a slide. What's the fastest way to do this?

First, in one of the tri-pane views (Normal, Outline, or Slide), select all of the objects you want to change as a unit by pressing SHIFT while clicking each object, or by drawing a selection outline around them, as shown here:

Choose Color and Lines from the Format menu, and select a new Fill color from the Color And Lines tab.

 Tip: *New to PowerPoint 2000 is a feature called AutoFit, which expands text placeholders as you add more text. This feature is enabled by default and can be turned off or back on from the Edit tab in the Tools | Options dialog box.*

I'd like to use music on a CD as background sound. Can I do that?

You bet. In a tri-pane view (Normal, Outline, or Slide), point to Movies And Sounds on the Insert menu, and then choose Play CD Audio Track. In the Play Options dialog box, choose the tracks and timing you want and click OK. A CD icon is inserted on the open slide.

Caution: *Using sound from commercial sources can get you involved with copyright infringement. Make sure you have permission to use any multimedia in your presentations if they are used for commercial purposes or, most importantly, put up on the Web.*

The sound file from the CD is not copied to the presentation, so you have to make sure the CD is loaded in your CD-ROM player before you run the presentation. The Office Assistant will prompt you to have the music start either automatically in Slide Show view when the slide with the icon is displayed, or when you click the icon.

Tip: *Make sure your Windows or other CD player program is not open when you try to play the sound track from PowerPoint. If any other CD player is open, the PowerPoint player won't work.*

I want to use some special effects for titles in slides—such as stretching, skewing, and vertical stacking—but I can't figure out how to accomplish these techniques from the standard drawing tools. Am I missing something?

Yes, but you're close. From the Drawing toolbar you can access WordArt, a separate program that ships with Office 2000. It offers the features you want to use, and many others. Click Insert WordArt to open the WordArt Gallery. Choose a special effect, type your title text in the Edit WordArt Text dialog box, and click OK. The text appears on the slide, along with the WordArt toolbar, and you can make further modifications to your title, as shown here:

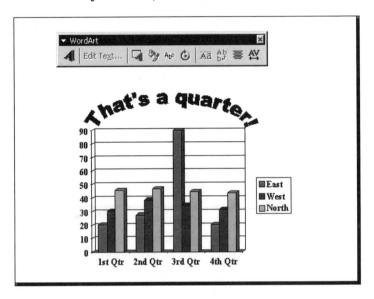

The tools available on the WordArt toolbar are described in the sidebar "The WordArt Toolbar."

The WordArt Toolbar

The following table describes the functions of the WordArt tools.

Button	Tool	Description
	Insert WordArt	Opens the WordArt Gallery and Edit WordArt Text dialog boxes to get you off and running
Edit Te~~x~~t...	Edit Text	Opens the Edit WordArt Text dialog box in which you enter text, change font and font size, and style with bold and italics
	WordArt Gallery	Opens a dialog box in which you can select from several predesigned formats

Button	Tool	Description
	Format WordArt	Opens a dialog box in which you can change color, size, and positioning
	WordArt Shape	Provides several shapes that WordArt can "bend" your text to fit
	Free Rotate	Allows you to rotate your WordArt text around a central axis
	WordArt Same Letter Heights	Changes all letters to the same height
	WordArt Vertical Text	Stacks text in a vertical orientation
	WordArt Alignment	Provides standard alignment tools (left, center, right, and justify) and adds other special effects, such as stretching
	WordArt Character Spacing	Changes the amount of space between characters

I have a self-running presentation and I want to provide viewers the ability to display background data if they want to. Is there an elegant way to do this?

Yes, you can create a button and hyperlink it to, for example, a Word document. When the button is clicked, Word will start and display the document. To implement this, open the slide that will contain the hyperlink, point to Action Buttons from the Slide Show menu, and choose the Document button (third row, second button). Drag the crosshair pointer to create the button and move it to where you want it. In the Action Settings dialog box, choose Hyperlink To, select Other File, and browse to select the file location. Click OK, and run the presentation in Slide Show. The action button in the slide show will look like the one that follows.

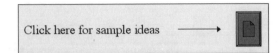

Click here for sample ideas ⟶

I generally work with Snap To Grid turned on, but I can't see the gridlines. How can I view the grid?

Sorry, but the grid is designed to be invisible. If the 12 gridlines per inch were displayed on the screen, the workspace would be cluttered even before you started adding objects.

ORGANIZING PRESENTATIONS

I've created a slide that contains too much information. Besides cutting and pasting data onto new slides, is there a better way to move bulleted items to a new slide?

Yes, but it is not quite as easy as it was in PowerPoint 97 using the Expand Slide feature, which split a slide's data into additional slides for you. In PowerPoint 2000, you need to display the slide in question in one of the tri-pane views (Normal, Outline, or Slide). In the outline pane, place the insertion point after (at the right end of) the bullet where you want to split the slide, and press ENTER. A blank, bulleted line appears. Press Demote on the Formatting toolbar as many times as it takes to have a new slide icon added to the outline, as shown here. Type a new title for the slide, and all bulleted items on the original slide below where you pressed ENTER are moved to the new slide.

4 ▢ **Competitive Analysis**
- Competitors
  - Domestic
  - International

5 ▢⌶
- Strengths
  - Sales force
  - Distribution
- Weaknesses
  - Unique to each competitor

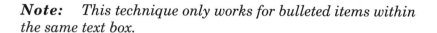

Note: *This technique only works for bulleted items within the same text box.*

Is there an easy way to move two or more slides?

You bet. In Slide Sorter view, select the first slide in the group by clicking it, and then press and hold down SHIFT while clicking any other slides. After all slides are selected, drag any of the selected slides to the position where you want them; and when the vertical line appears indicating where the slides will be moved, release the mouse button. To copy slides, press CTRL while dragging the group.

Note: *When selecting a group of slides for moving or copying, it doesn't matter in what order you select them; they will be arranged in their original numeric order at their new location.*

Does PowerPoint offer any editing resources that can help to improve my presentations?

Yes it does. You can have PowerPoint scan for three key presentation style elements:

- Spelling
- Case and end punctuation
- Visual clarity

Start the review process by choosing Options from the Tools menu and clicking the Spelling And Style tab. Spelling options are provided in several check boxes. Style options can be turned on or off with the Check Style check box. Clicking Style Options opens a dialog box of the same name that lets you choose which elements of style you want checked, as shown in the following illustration.

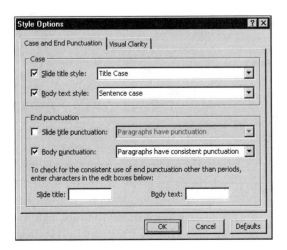

 I've been asked to review a presentation developed by one of my coworkers. Are there revision marks for onscreen edits?

No, there isn't a formal revision-mark feature in PowerPoint. However, you can use onscreen comments to make your annotations a part of the presentation. These can be hidden (click Comments on the View menu to toggle between viewing and hiding comments) so they won't inadvertently appear in a public viewing. To attach onscreen notes, open the slide you want to comment on in a tri-pane view (Normal, Outline, or Slide), choose Insert Comment, and start typing. You can change some of the comment attributes, such as its color, by right-clicking the comment and choosing Format Comment from the context menu. Figure 5-5 shows an example of a comment on a slide in a slide show.

Tip: *When you insert a comment, the Comment toolbar is displayed to offer quick access to comment options and for sending them to other users by e-mail or creating an Outlook task.*

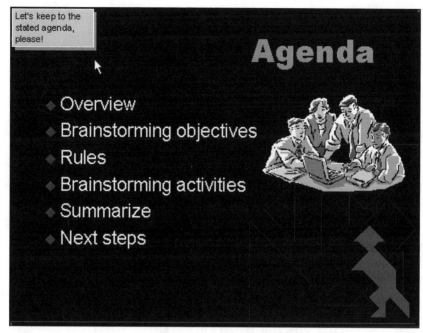

Figure 5-5 Comments are like electronic Post-it notes that can be saved with presentations

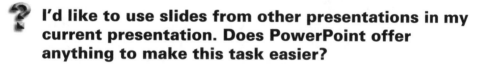

I'd like to use slides from other presentations in my current presentation. Does PowerPoint offer anything to make this task easier?

Yes it does—using a feature called Slide Finder. First, open the presentation in which you want to insert the slides. Select in Slide Sorter view the slide *after* which you want the new slides inserted. Choose Slides From Files on the Insert menu to open the Slide Finder dialog box. Browse to the presentation that contains the slide you want. You can view the slides either as thumbnails—as shown in the following illustration—or in a list, by clicking the buttons in the middle of the dialog box. Select the slides you want (hold down SHIFT to select more than one) and click Insert.

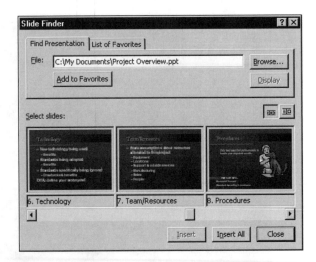

I have a very long presentation and find it difficult to organize my slides in Slide Sorter view because I can only view a handful at a time. How can I view more slides in my presentation?

The number of slides that you can view is determined by several factors, including the video-related components of your computer. Assuming you have the horsepower to display dozens of slides, you can view them all by adjusting the zoom percentage, as shown in Figures 5-6 and 5-7. Choose Zoom from the View menu, and then select a zoom percentage that fits your needs.

Tip: *As you display more slides, the smaller slide titles become difficult or impossible to read. To quickly display a slide's title, press ALT and click a slide. Alternatively, you can click Show Formatting on the toolbar to switch between showing standard slide miniatures and showing only slide titles.*

Figure 5-6 Slide Sorter view at 100% zoom

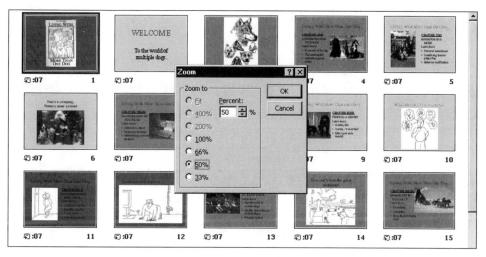

Figure 5-7 Slide Sorter view at 50% zoom

 I have a presentation that I need to modify to use for a couple of different audiences. Is there an easy way to set up this one presentation to be shown to multiple audiences instead of having to create a separate presentation for each audience?

Yes, you can create one or more custom presentations within a presentation, which allows you to organize slides in different sequences and save each as a separate custom show. To create custom shows, do the following:

1. From any view, choose Custom Shows from the Slide Show menu.

2. In the Custom Shows dialog box, click New.

3. In the Define Custom Show dialog box, provide a name for the sub-show and choose from Slides In Presentation the slides that you want by selecting them and clicking Add. You can rearrange the order of the Slides In Custom Show by clicking the up and down arrows to the right of the dialog box.

Run the presentation in Slide Show view, right-click the screen, and point to Go and then Custom Show. Choose which custom show you want to run, as shown here:

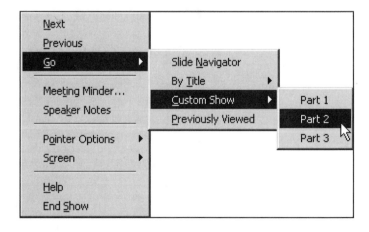

PRODUCING PRESENTATIONS ON PAPER AND ON THE SCREEN

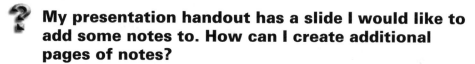

My presentation handout has a slide I would like to add some notes to. How can I create additional pages of notes?

This is a good situation in which to use hidden slides. Create a slide consisting only of notes with these steps:

1. In Slide Sorter view, select the slide that needs the notes and choose Duplicate Slide from the Insert menu.

2. Right-click the new slide and choose Hide Slide. The slide number has a line struck across it.

3. Switch to Notes Page view from the View menu, select the slide image, and press DEL.

4. Type in your notes in the notes area.

You can increase the size of the notes area by dragging one of its top three selection handles upward.

Now, when you print out notes, you will have a second page of notes for this one slide; however, if you choose to run the presentation as a slide show, you won't see the new slide because it's hidden.

When I'm practicing to give a presentation, is there a way for me to set the narration time for slides to the actual time I use when giving the presentation?

Yes. PowerPoint provides a neat feature to do just that. Choose Rehearse Timings from the Slide Show menu, and your presentation will open in Slide Show view. During the running of the slide show, a Rehearsal toolbar is displayed that provides a running counter of the individual slide, as well as a counter for the cumulative amount of time elapsed. You can also advance to the next slide, pause your narration, or repeat the narration of the current slide. When you close

either the toolbar or the show, you will be asked if you want to keep the timings for the next time you run the show.

   Tip: *If a slide is used in one or more custom shows, the timing used last for that slide will be used in all instances in the presentation.*

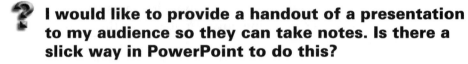

I would like to provide a handout of a presentation to my audience so they can take notes. Is there a slick way in PowerPoint to do this?

Sure. Before you print your presentation, open the Print What drop-down list box in the lower section of the Print dialog box and choose Handouts. Under the Handouts area, choose 3 Slides Per Page, and then print your presentation. To the right of each slide will be space for several lines of note taking, as shown in Figure 5-8.

I want to be prepared to show information on a topic if a question arises, but I don't want my audience to see the slide unless the topic is broached. What is the best way to prepare optional slides?

With a combination of PowerPoint features, you can have a hidden slide waiting in the wings in case it's needed. First, create the slide, and then hide it by choosing Hide Slide from the Slide Show menu. Then place a button on the slide where you think the question might arise; this button will open the hidden slide when clicked. Set up the button with these steps:

1. In Slide view, open the slide that will contain the button, point to Action Buttons on the Slide Show menu, and choose Action Button: Custom.

2. Use the crosshair pointer to click and drag a small button to an inconspicuous place on the slide.

3. In the Mouse Click tab in the Action Settings dialog box, click Hyperlink To, open its drop-down list box, and then click the value that describes the hidden slide. If none of the values matches the slide, choose Slide and find the slide in the list box, as shown here:

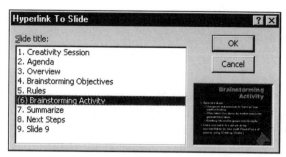

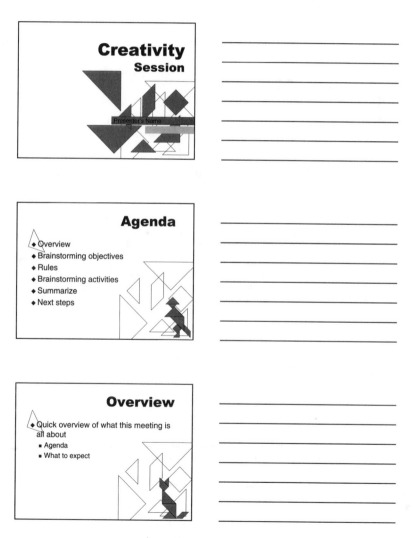

Figure 5-8 Printing three slides per page for audience note taking

Tip: *Hidden files are easily identified in the Hyperlink To Slide dialog box. Look for slide numbers contained within parentheses.*

Now, if a question comes up on the information in the hidden file, simply click the button you created and the hidden slide will appear; otherwise, continue with your presentation and your audience will never see the slide.

Tip: *During a slide show, you can quickly display another slide by right-clicking the screen, choosing Go | By Title, and then clicking the slide you want to display by number or title.*

What is the quickest way to display a particular slide during a slide show?

Press the number key corresponding to the number of the slide and then press ENTER; for example, 5 and ENTER. The sidebar "Slide Show Key Summary" provides the complete list of keys that can be used during a slide show.

Slide Show Key Summary

This table describes the keys that you can use to control a slide show.

Key	Action
B	Toggles between a black screen display and the slide show display
E	Removes any onscreen annotations
H	Advances to the next hidden slide in the show
M	When rehearsing, sets slide advancement to be a mouse click
N	Advances to the next slide or the next animation
O	When rehearsing, uses original timings

Key	Action
P	Returns to the previous slide or the previous animation
T	When rehearsing, sets new timings
S	Stops or restarts an automatic show
W	Toggles between a white screen display and the slide show display
BACKSPACE	Same as the P key
ENTER	Same as the N key
ENTER, when a hyperlink is selected	Follows the hyperlink
Number key, ENTER	Advances to the slide whose number is pressed
ESC	Terminates a slide show
DOWN ARROW	Same as N key
LEFT ARROW	Same as P key
PAGE DOWN	Same as N key
PAGE UP	Same as P key
RIGHT ARROW	Same as N key
SHIFT-TAB	Finds the last or previous hyperlink on a slide
SPACEBAR	Same as the N key
TAB	Finds the first or next hyperlink on a slide
UP ARROW	Same as P key
CTRL-A	Changes the pen to the pointer
CTRL-H	Temporarily hides both the pointer and the Context Menu button
CTRL-L	Always hides both the pointer and the Context Menu button
CTRL-P	Changes the pointer to the pen
CTRL-U	Hides the pointer and onscreen button after 15 seconds
SHIFT-F10	Displays the context menu

Tip: *To return to the beginning of a slide show, press the left and right mouse buttons together and hold for a few seconds.*

I want to use the same presentation for several different purposes. For example, first I'll be delivering it to a live audience, but then I want it to be available for people to look at on their own. How can I quickly switch a presentation from one type to another?

Open the Set Up Show dialog box found on the Slide Show menu. You are presented with several Show Type options that let you control how your slide show will run:

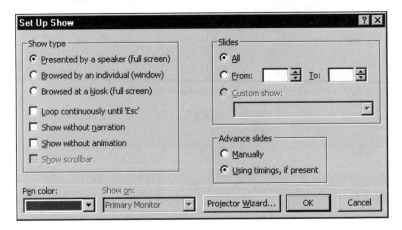

Tip: *If you use your computer to show presentations with an LCD panel or projector, click Projector Wizard in the Set Up Show dialog box to have PowerPoint assist you in setting up the two devices to work together.*

 The built-in presentations provided by PowerPoint look great on the screen in full color, but I print out handouts on a black and white laser printer. Is there a way to view slides without color before printing them?

Yes. PowerPoint has a Black And White view that lets you see what several grayscale and black-and-white schemes look like, and allows you to print in those schemes without affecting the original colored objects and backgrounds. In a tri-pane view (Normal, Outline, or Slide) click Grayscale Preview on the toolbar. To select one of the grayscale or black-and-white options from a context menu, right-click an empty spot to affect the entire presentation, or right-click an individual object to limit the effect to that object, and then choose Black And White from the context menu.

When you print, verify that the Grayscale check box is selected in the Print dialog box. If you don't want any grayscale gradients, select the Pure Black & White check box to print out just black and white.

Tip: *You can see how your entire presentation looks without color by changing to Slide Sorter view before or after switching to Grayscale Preview.*

Chapter 6

Organizing with Access

Answer Topics!

WORKING WITH ACCESS DATABASES 237

? Adding or removing menu items

? Displaying the Database window easily

? Merging data into one master database

? Opening two databases at once

? Reducing a database's size

? Using sample databases

WORKING WITH TABLES 247

? Dividing large tables into smaller ones

? Creating tables quickly and easily

? Printing the Relationships window

? Viewing data that is related to other records

? Rearranging field order permanently

? Adding visual effects in Datasheet view

FINDING DATA 258

? Saving a filter for repeated use

? Building expressions in the Criteria cell

? Changing a current query's type

? Removing all the entries in the grid

? Verifying that there are no blank data fields

CREATING AND MODIFYING FORMS 269

? Changing the layout for forms created by wizards

? Adding data to a table quickly

? Accessing information related to a form

? Changing the order of tabbing

? Transferring formatting between controls

? Applying properties to controls in Form view

PRESENTING INFORMATION WITH REPORTS 278

? Adding text in the Label Wizard

? Aligning controls in report Design view

? Grouping controls

? Removing the dots from the grid

? Understanding types of Headers and Footers

? Speeding up display in Print Preview

Organizing with Access @ a Glance

Access brings a premier data manager to the Office suite. Whether you
are storing a limited quantity of items in a home inventory or cataloging
parts and tracking orders in larger companies, Access provides an
easy-to-use but powerful way to enter, manipulate, and view
information. The sections in this chapter cover the following topics:

The Structure of Access describes the .mdb file format, the
objects—such as tables and forms—that comprise Access, and
using Access with SQL.

Working with Access Databases covers the basic principles
of using an Access database, working with multiple databases
concurrently, using replication so several people can work on a
database at the same time, and modifying how menus appear.

Working with Tables looks at relationships, creating tables,
changing the order of fields, and modifying the appearance of tables.

Finding Data explores the many methods of searching for data,
building expressions, changing the type of a query, saving a filter
for future use, and checking for blank fields.

Creating and Modifying Forms discusses ways of changing
forms that were created by wizards, modifying the tab order
within a form, transferring formatting between controls, and
quickly adding data to a table.

Presenting Information with Reports describes ways of
aligning controls in the design grid, using conditional formatting,
speeding up the display of lengthy reports, addressing mailing
labels, and grouping controls.

 Putting Data Online introduces data access pages and provides information on transferring pages and displaying them quickly in a browser.

 Importing, Exporting, and Linking Data shows how to install converters and how to use data from other programs by importing or linking to Access tables.

THE STRUCTURE OF ACCESS

A database is the container that Access uses to hold its data and supporting objects. Typically, a database file is composed of data for a single table, with any supporting tables stored as separate files in a common folder or directory. Access, however, takes a somewhat different approach in how it structures its database. Access bundles everything that is related to a specific set of data into a single file, which provides a more convenient means for storing or transferring the database. Within the confines of an Access database file (file extension .mdb) are seven objects that handle all the storage, retrieval, display, and manipulation of data. The object types are listed in the Objects bar, shown next, and a list of objects of a specific type can be seen in the Object list to the right by clicking the object type in the Objects bar:

The seven object types are tables, queries, forms, reports, pages, macros, and modules:

- *Tables* provide a matrix consisting of columns of data categories, *fields*; and rows of information, *records*, where each row uniquely defines a set of data. For example, a mailing list contains fields for each individual's name, street address, city, state, and postal code; each record defines a set of data for an individual on the list.

- *Queries* allow you to pose questions and extract just the information you want from one or more tables or from other queries.

- *Forms* provide a graphical means of viewing or entering data, one record at a time.

- *Reports* present data on screen and on paper, formatted to achieve readable, attractive results, in contrast to the row and column appearance of tables and queries.

Pages are new to Access 2000 and provide a direct link between a web page and an Access or Microsoft SQL Server database, using many familiar controls and Office components, such as an Excel spreadsheet, PivotTable, or chart.

Macros provide a quick means of automating relatively simple tasks.

Modules provide the framework for designing sophisticated custom applications using Visual Basic for Applications, a programming language integrated with Office programs.

The Page object file is actually stored outside of the but a shortcut to the file is associated with the object ars in the Database window.

2000 also introduces the concept of a *project* (.adp file extension), which provides the ings for Access to be used as a "front end" the more powerful Microsoft SQL Server ack end." Access and SQL use the ODBC (open nnectivity) standard behind the scenes to provide at ties the two programs together, shielding you re complex tasks of getting the two programs to r. Additionally, Access 2000 offers an enhanced database engine, the Microsoft Data Engine (MSDE), whose format and data are designed to more easily interface with SQL Server. Using MSDE to create projects allows you to test your database on a stand-alone computer in a non-SQL, non-server environment, and then connect to a SQL Server database when you are ready to go live. Within a project, you work with the same display and retrieval database objects as you do in a standard Access database, such as forms, reports, data access pages, and macros. The table object used is actually the data in the SQL database. Two additional objects are provided that support working in a SQL environment: Database Diagrams and Stored Procedures.

Note: *An in-depth discussion of Microsoft Access projects and their connectivity to SQL databases is beyond the scope of this book. This chapter focuses on using Access databases, but makes occasional references to Access projects to illustrate differences between the two formats. An excellent primer on SQL databases is* SQL Server 7 Developer's Guide, *by Michael Otey and Paul Conte (Berkeley, CA: Osborne / McGraw-Hill, 1999). In particular, see the chapter titled "Developing SQL Server Database Applications with Access."*

Databases can be daunting to users who think they are too complicated and too powerful for day-to-day tasks. Microsoft, though, has gone to great lengths to make Access a useful and easy-to-use program for the beginner, as well as for the application developer. Wizards are one powerful tool that make Access easier to use, and they can assist you in performing standard tasks, such as

- Creating a database or project
- Designing professional-looking forms, reports, and data access pages
- Creating charts
- Importing and exporting data from and to non-Access sources, including SQL databases
- Working with SQL Server, including upsizing Access databases and replicating data on MSDE-installed computers

WORKING WITH ACCESS DATABASES

 When I open the Northwind sample database, I get an extra menu item called Show Me. I don't seem to get this in other databases. How do I add or remove menus in my own databases?

Microsoft has created a custom menu bar that includes the Show Me menu and that appears when you open the Northwind database, as shown here:

You can create your own custom menu bar (see Chapter 2 for a description of how to create a custom menu bar) and have it appear when your database opens. After you create the new menu, choose Startup from the Tools menu in the Database window, and select the custom menu bar from the Menu Bar drop-down list, shown here:

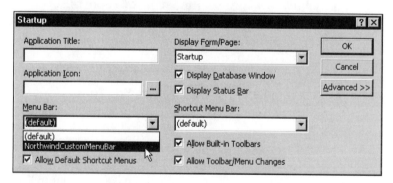

Click OK, and the next time the database is opened, the new menu bar will appear. This is a great way to "hide" certain Access features from those users of your database who like to "tinker." See the sidebar "Startup Options" for a complete rundown on the other attributes you can set at startup.

Startup Options

You can customize how Access presents your database (or application) when first opened. You might consider creating a custom startup to do the following:

- Display an initial form with your corporate logo
- Hide Access features and commands that you don't want available to users
- Display a custom menu bar and toolbars that easily access specific forms and reports
- Accommodate users who are not familiar with the Access user interface by creating one that offers only a limited, but very specific, set of options

Note that the options you choose in the Startup dialog box set global database properties, but they do not override any property settings you may have set for specific forms or reports.

The following table describes the customization options that affect opening a database or starting an application. These options are set by opening the Tools menu and choosing Startup.

Attribute	Allows You To
Application Title	Display your own text in the title bar instead of "Microsoft Access"
Application Icon	Display an icon other than the purple key to the left of the text in the title bar
Menu Bar and Shortcut Menu Bar	Display custom menus in lieu of those provided by Access, and permit or prevent changes to the menu bar
Display Form/Page	Display an opening form or data access page that introduces the user to the database or application
Display Database Window	Display or hide the Database window that shows the contents of each object in the database

Attribute	Allows You To
Display Status Bar	Display or hide the Status bar, located at the bottom of the Access window
Allow Built-In Toolbars and Allow Toolbar/Menu Changes	Permit or deny use of the toolbars and menus provided by Access and any changes made to them
Keys (Advanced option)	Permit or deny use of keys that affect several of the actions described above
ALT-F1 or F11	Display the Database window
CTRL-BREAK	Halt access to records from a server (only in an Access project)
CTRL-F11	Switch display of the Access menu bar and a custom menu bar
CTRL-G	Display the Immediate debug window

 I find that I keep returning to the Database window several times while I'm working in Access. Is there an easier way to display the Database window besides minimizing open windows or forms?

Sure, simply press F11, and the Database window will be brought to the front, as shown here:

I have several field reps that are on the road taking orders. Is there a way for all of them to merge data into one master database and synchronize all their input?

Yes, by using replication you can have as many copies, or replicas, of a database as you want. Then you can combine the data in one location and resolve any possible conflicts.

Replication

The replication process takes an existing database and converts it into a Design Master and one replica (you can easily create more replicas to add to the replica set). The Design Master maintains the structure of the database. Users working with replicas cannot change fields or change the design of any of the database objects; they can only add, modify, or delete data.

! **Caution:** *Replicating a database is a one-way process; once you choose to replicate, you cannot undo the changes made to the database. It's always a good idea to back up the original database when Access prompts you.*

Several changes in Office 2000 accommodate replication, including the following:

● Both Access database files (.mdb) and project files (.adp) can be replicated from their respective Tools | Replication options.

● An improved Conflict Viewer helps resolve problems in synchronizing replica files with the Design Master database file.

● Two additional types of replicas are provided: local and anonymous.

● Developers can use both Data Access objects (DAO) and Jet and Replication objects (JRO) to programmatically replicate and synchronize databases.

● AutoNumber data-type fields are replaced by random numbers to avoid sequencing conflicts.

To replicate an Access database, follow these steps:

1. With the database you want to replicate open, choose Replication from the Tools menu and click Create Replica.

2. Click Yes in the message box that asks whether you want to close the current database, convert it to a Design Master, and create a replica. Also, if asked whether you want to install the feature to start SQL dialogs, click Yes.

3. Click Yes when asked if you want to make a backup copy. In the Location Of New Replica dialog box, a new database is created and named Replica Of *database-name*.

4. Click OK to accept the filename and replica type from the Save As Type drop-down list, or change the location, replica type, and name, and then click OK.

A final message box informs you that the original database has been converted into a Design Master and that the replica has been created.

 Note: *The procedures for replicating an Access project are similar; however, only data is replicated, not the objects contained in the project.*

There are three types, or *visibilities*, of replicas: global, local, and anonymous.

- Global replicas, or *hubs*, are created by default, fully tracked, and you can create other replicas from them. These were the only replica type created in previous versions of Access.

- Local replicas only display data entered on the computer it is installed on; that is, no data from other replicas or the Design Master is displayed.

- Anonymous replicas don't track who's using them, which is especially useful when you are providing replicas to random Internet users.

The Database window identifies each table in the Design Master that is replicable with a double-arrow icon, as shown here:

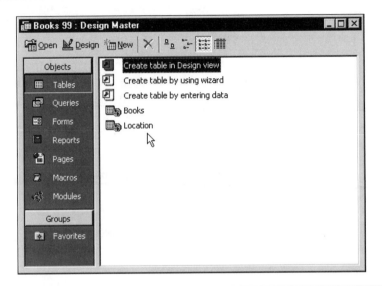

❋ ***Note:***   *If you add subsequent tables to your Design Master, you are given the option of making them replicable along with the original tables in your database when you save them.*

Once replicas have been created and put into use, at some point you have to collect the information that has been entered in the replicas and check for conflicting data. Synchronization compares data between two files in the replica set (which can be two replicas or a replica and the Design Master) and incorporates any new or modified data in each file.

To synchronize files, follow these steps:

1. Open a file—replica or Design Master—in the replica set.

2. Choose Replication from the Tools menu, and click Synchronize Now. The Synchronize Database dialog box opens, as shown next, and you can choose to directly synchronize a replica, or select which synchronizer you want to use.

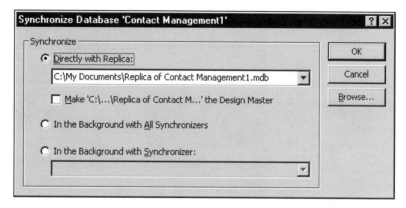

You can choose from three synchronizers: direct, indirect, or Internet. Direct is recommended for LAN environments; indirect and Internet are best for remote situations. To set up either indirect or Internet synchronization you need to use the Replication Manager, contained in the Microsoft Office 2000 Developer kit.

Tip: *If you want to transfer control from the current Design Master to another replica, click the first option and then select the check box below it.*

3. Click OK to start the synchronization process.

4. Click Yes in the completion message box to reopen the database, so you can see if there are any conflicts. Conflicts are resolved in the Microsoft Replication Conflict Viewer dialog box:

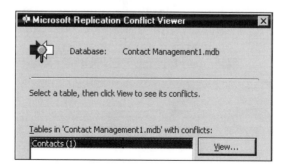

 Tip: *You can also synchronize members of global replicas by using the Briefcase feature included with Windows 98; local and anonymous replicas are not supported in Briefcase.*

I find it annoying that in Access I cannot open two databases at once. Is there a way to work around this limitation?

Yes there is, provided you have the computer resources. Open one database in the currently running copy of Access, and then start a second instance of Access (open the Start menu and click Programs | Microsoft Access) and open the other database. Instead of switching between databases within Access, you'll be switching between the two instances of Access. Use the Taskbar, as shown here, or ALT-TAB to switch back and forth.

I'm working with databases that take up quite a bit of disk space. Is there a way to reduce a database's size?

Sure. The best method to gain more disk space is to compact each database. Deleted tables in a database are notorious for leaving fragmented chunks of unused space throughout a file. Compacting recovers disk space that has been tied up with deleted objects. To compact a database, open it, open the Tools menu, and select Database Utilities | Compact And Repair Database. The new compacted database will replace the original database. You can also automatically have Access compact a database when you close it. Open the Tools menu, choose Options, click the General tab, and then select the Compact On Close check box.

Tip: *Before you compact a database, check its file size by opening the File menu and clicking Database Properties | General tab, as shown here. Repeat after you compact to see how much free disk space you gained.*

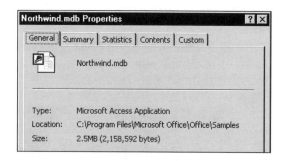

You can also compact a database that isn't open. Follow the same procedure as described for an open database, but when you click Compact Database, the Database To Compact From dialog box opens so that you can select a database. Click Compact, and the Compact Database Into dialog box opens, in which you can select the same file or create a new compacted database with a new filename or location. Click Save.

I just want to create a simple database to track my audio CD collection. Are there sample databases that I can use to get me going?

Yes, there are. Access, like the other Office 2000 products, provides several wizards that assist you in creating databases for common home and business uses. When you first start Access, you are presented with the opportunity to create a database or open an existing one. Select Access Database Wizards, Pages, And Projects, as shown next, and click OK.

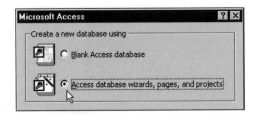

The New dialog box, shown here, opens with the Databases tab displaying the selection of available database wizards.

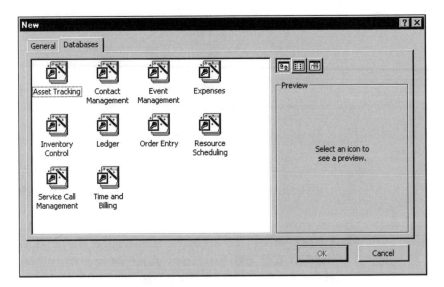

 Tip: *Choosing New from the File menu or clicking the New button on the Database toolbar also opens the New dialog box.*

Double-click the wizard icon that most closely matches your needs. This will open the File New Database dialog box, in which you provide a name and location for the new database-to-be. Click Create to start the wizard. Follow the steps the wizard leads you through, adding or removing suggested fields, including or excluding sample data, choosing a style for forms and reports, and providing a title. Click Finish in the final

wizard dialog box. The database is created, and its startup form displays options for you to start entering data, as shown here:

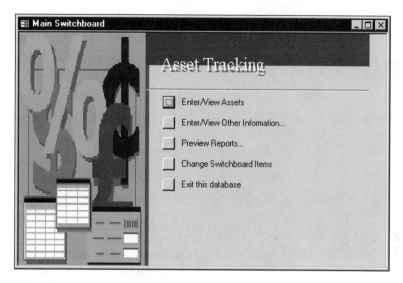

 Tip: *After you create a database, you can use the Table Wizard to set up tables for specific goals. In this example, under the Personal category in the first Table Wizard dialog box, you could pick Recording Artists, Recordings, or Video Collection as a starting point. See the question that begins, "I've come to rely on Office 2000 providing me a template . . ." in the following section.*

WORKING WITH TABLES

 My company's MIS guru told me I should divide tables with a large amount of repeated data into several smaller tables and relate them. Does this make sense?

Yes, it does. This creates a relational database, which is more efficient and easier to use. See the sidebar titled "Relationships," later in this section, for a description of the features and benefits of a relational database scheme.

Table Views

Tables provide the best way to quickly view and navigate through your data, and they often provide the fastest way to enter new information or make changes. There are two views in Access:

- *Datasheet view* displays the common column and row arrangement you find in other data-management programs.

- *Design view* displays and allows modifications to the table's field structure and is where you set properties on fields to control associated attributes.

Datasheet view

While forms let you view and edit data one record at a time, tables in Datasheet view give you access to the full breadth of your information. Datasheet view, shown next, offers the benefit of seeing the whole picture while being able to quickly find just the record or records you want.

		Customer ID	Company Name	Contact Name	Contact Title	
▶	+	ALFKI	Alfreds Futterkiste	Maria Anders	Sales Representative	Ob
	+	ANATR	Ana Trujillo Emparedados y helados	Ana Trujillo	Owner	Av
	+	ANTON	Antonio Moreno Taquería	Antonio Moreno	Owner	Ma
	+	AROUT	Around the Horn	Thomas Hardy	Sales Representative	12L
	+	BERGS	Berglunds snabbköp	Christina Berglund	Order Administrator	Be
	+	BLAUS	Blauer See Delikatessen	Hanna Moos	Sales Representative	Fo
	+	BLONP	Blondel père et fils	Frédérique Citeaux	Marketing Manager	24
	+	BOLID	Bólido Comidas preparadas	Martín Sommer	Owner	C/
	+	BONAP	Bon app'	Laurence Lebihan	Owner	12
	+	BOTTM	Bottom-Dollar Markets	Elizabeth Lincoln	Accounting Manager	23
	+	BSBEV	B's Beverages	Victoria Ashworth	Sales Representative	Fa
	+	CACTU	Cactus Comidas para llevar	Patricio Simpson	Sales Agent	Ce
	+	CENTC	Centro comercial Moctezuma	Francisco Chang	Marketing Manager	Sie
	+	CHOPS	Chop-suey Chinese	Yang Wang	Owner	Ha
	+	COMMI	Comércio Mineiro	Pedro Afonso	Sales Associate	Av
	+	CONSH	Consolidated Holdings	Elizabeth Brown	Sales Representative	Be
	+	DRACD	Drachenblut Delikatessen	Sven Ottlieb	Order Administrator	Wa
	+	DUMON	Du monde entier	Janine Labrune	Owner	67
	+	EASTC	Eastern Connection	Ann Devon	Sales Agent	35
	+	ERNSH	Ernst Handel	Roland Mendel	Sales Manager	Kir
	+	FAMIA	Familia Arquibaldo	Aria Cruz	Marketing Assistant	Ru
	+	FISSA	FISSA Fabrica Inter. Salchichas S.A.	Diego Roel	Accounting Manager	C/

Record: ◄ ◄ 1 ► ►► ►* of 91

If you often find yourself entering or modifying information in Datasheet view, there are several navigation keystrokes that you will find handy. The following table describes the ones you can use.

Keystroke	Function
CTRL-PGDN	Scrolls one screen to the right
CTRL-PGUP	Scrolls one screen to the left
DOWN ARROW	Selects the entry in the current field in the next record
ENTER	Selects the next entry in the field to the right
F5	Selects the record number in the Record box at the bottom of the screen; type a new record number and press ENTER to move to that record
LEFT ARROW	Selects the entry in the previous field
PGDN	Scrolls down one screen
PGUP	Scrolls up one screen
RIGHT ARROW	Same as ENTER
SHIFT-TAB	Same as left arrow
TAB	Same as ENTER
UP ARROW	Selects the entry in the current field in the previous record

A number of keys work to select records in the datasheet. The following table lists these keys.

Keystroke	Function
CTRL-DOWN ARROW	Selects the last record in the current field
CTRL-END	Selects the last record in the last field
CTRL-HOME	Selects the first record in the first field
CTRL-UP ARROW	Selects the first record in the current field
END	Selects the last field in the current record
HOME	Selects the first field in the current record

Design View

The structure of a table is created and maintained in Design view, shown next.

The upper portion of the table Design window contains three columns that are used to set up fields:

- *Field Name* lists current fields in the table and allows you to add new fields by simply typing them in the next blank cell.
- *Data Type* makes available a drop-down list of different field formats that you can assign to fields when you create them.
- *Description* is an optional field in which you can enter an explanation of the field.

Tip: *A field's description appears in the status bar when the field is selected in either a table or a form. If you are working on a shared database, it's best to choose your words carefully.*

Data types are designed for specific uses, and each comes with inherent limitations. Giving some forethought to what you might do with the data in any particular field will help you decide which data type to choose. For example, numbers are allowed in a Text data type, but you cannot perform calculations on them (use the Number data type instead). The data types are described in the following table.

Data Type	Used For
Text	Short text (255-character maximum), numbers that won't be calculated (for example, postal codes), and combinations of text and numbers (for example, street addresses)
Memo	Narrative text (65,535-character maximum)
Number	Nonmonetary numeric data used in calculations
Date/Time	Numbers used in dates and times
Currency	Monetary numeric data
AutoNumber	Automatic assignment of record numbers, either sequentially or randomly
Yes/No	Two-condition data, such as True or False
OLE Object	Objects that are embedded or linked into an Access table (see Chapter 8 for more information on using the Office 2000 products together)
Hyperlink	Links to access World Wide Web sites or HTML documents (see Chapter 9 for more information on hyperlinking)
Lookup Wizard	Assistance in creating a list box from which values can be chosen from a table or a predefined list, eliminating user inputting errors

The lower section of the Design view window lists additional properties that can be set for each field. The selection of properties depends on the data type assigned to the field, as you can see next, where Date/Time properties are listed instead of the Text properties shown in the previous illustration.

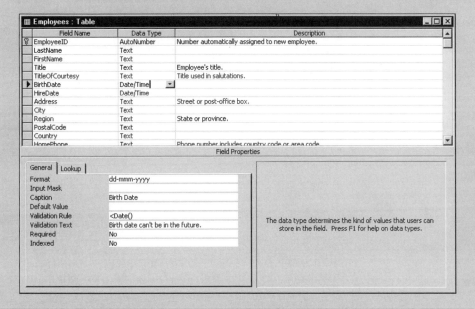

 I've come to rely on Office 2000 providing me a template or other starting point from which I can then make changes to meet my unique needs. Does Access provide a quick and easy way to create tables?

Certainly. There is a very comprehensive wizard that offers suggested table structures. This at least gets you going; in many cases, the wizard requires no further effort on your part to create a complete table. See how Access creates a table for you by following these steps:

1. With an open database, click the Tables tab under Objects in the Database window, and then double-click Create Table By Using Wizard.

2. The first dialog box, shown here, categorizes 45 sample tables as personal or business. Select a category, and then choose the sample that most closely matches your needs.

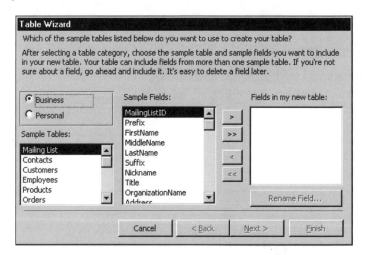

3. Each sample table contains associated fields. It's usually easiest to click the rightward-pointing double-arrow (>>) button to move all of the sample fields to the Fields In My New Table box. Then you can remove the few you don't need with the leftward-pointing single-arrow button. Select and rename fields as needed. Click Next.

4. Name the table and accept the default to have Access assign a primary key for you. You can change it later in Design view if needed. Click Next.

Note: *If you decide to set the primary key yourself, an additional dialog box will let you choose the primary key field and choose between automatic or manual sequencing of records.*

5. The third dialog box provides the opportunity to relate the new table to existing tables in your database. (See the "Relationships" sidebar for a further discussion of relational database structuring.) Click Next.

6. Click Finish in the final dialog box if you are comfortable with the Access-designed table and want to enter data directly in Datasheet view. Otherwise, choose to make changes in the table in Design view or have Access create a simple form for entering data.

Relationships

Relationships are the key element that Access uses to efficiently store and access large volumes of data. In large, or flat-file, tables you often need to add many repetitive fields of information and only a few fields will hold different information. For example, when you take an order from a customer, you need to have his or her name, address, and other personal information, along with the actual contents of what he or she is ordering from you. Every time that same customer places an order, you have to enter the same fields of personal data; because the information is on file elsewhere, it is redundant here. Multiply the amount of redundant data by thousands or even millions of entries and you can see why this might not be the most efficient way to handle large volumes of data. Instead, why not keep all the personal data that doesn't change in one table, and enter the data that does change—the order information—in another table. Tie the two tables

together with a common field, or primary key, such as Customer Number, and you have a relational database.

There are three ways you can define relationships between tables in an Access database:

● *One-to-many* is the most common relationship, where a record in one table (for example, Customers) can have many matching records in another table (for example, Orders). There can be many records in the Orders table that have the same customer, but there is only one record for each customer in the Customer table.

● *One-to-one* relationships match one record in each table. These are not common because they can be easily handled in one table by adding the same fields that would have been created for the second table.

● *Many-to-many* relationships provide for a record in one table to have many matching records in another table, and one record in the second table to also have many matching records in the first table. These relationships employ a third table that contains the primary key from each table, which is essentially the same as using two one-to-many relationships with the third *junction* table.

Relationships are best understood by looking at a visual representation of the associations in the Relationships window, an example of which is shown here.

Junction table for a many-to-many relationship

Selected relationship line

One-to-many relationship

In the Relationships window you can do all of the following:

● *Create relationships* by dragging the related field names from one table to another.

● *Edit relationships* by right-clicking the relationship line between tables and choosing Edit Relationship. The Edit Relationships dialog box offers several options, as shown here:

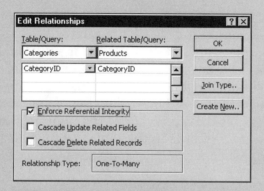

● *Delete relationships* by right-clicking the relationship line between tables and choosing Delete from the context menu.

● *Add additional tables* by clicking the Show Table button on the Relationship toolbar.

● *Save the layout* by closing the Relationships window and answering Yes to save the changes. This doesn't affect the actual relationships; it just saves how you view them.

 To view the relationships for a database, open the Database window and click the Relationships button on the Database toolbar.

I want a co-worker to look over my relational database structure. Can I print the Relationships windows?

Sure. This is a new (and overdue) feature in Access 2000 that creates a report from the Relationships window that you can print, save, or otherwise handle as an Access report. First, open the Relationships window you want (see the "Relationships" sidebar for details on how to open the window), and then choose Print Relationships from the File menu. Right-click the relationships diagram, and choose the option you want from the context menu.

Is there an easy way to view data in a table that is related to other records in the database?

Yes, you can use the new subdatasheets, in which you can view and edit data that is related or joined between tables (or queries, form datasheets, or subforms). Open a table in Datasheet view that is on the one side of a one-to-many relationship, and click the plus (+) in the leftmost column of the row whose related data you want to see. A subdatasheet displays the *many* side of the relationship for each of the *one-side* records in the table. As you can see here, for a unique customer there are several related orders:

	Customer ID	Company Name			Contact Name		Contact Title		
+	CENTC	Centro comercial Moctezuma			Francisco Chang		Marketing Manager		Sier
–	CHOPS	Chop-suey Chinese			Yang Wang		Owner		Hau
		Order ID	Employee	Order Date	Required Date	Shipped Date	Ship Via	Freight	
	+	10254	Buchanan, Steven	11-Jul-1996	08-Aug-1996	23-Jul-1996	United Package	$22.98	
	+	10370	Suyama, Michael	03-Dec-1996	31-Dec-1996	27-Dec-1996	United Package	$1.17	
	+	10519	Suyama, Michael	28-Apr-1997	26-May-1997	01-May-1997	Federal Shipping	$91.76	
	+	10731	King, Robert	06-Nov-1997	04-Dec-1997	14-Nov-1997	Speedy Express	$96.65	
	+	10746	Davolio, Nancy	19-Nov-1997	17-Dec-1997	21-Nov-1997	Federal Shipping	$31.43	
	+	10966	Peacock, Margaret	20-Mar-1998	17-Apr-1998	08-Apr-1998	Speedy Express	$27.19	
	+	11029	Peacock, Margaret	16-Apr-1998	14-May-1998	27-Apr-1998	Speedy Express	$47.84	
	+	11041	Leverling, Janet	22-Apr-1998	20-May-1998	28-Apr-1998	United Package	$48.22	
	*	:oNumber)						$0.00	
+	COMMI	Comércio Mineiro			Pedro Afonso		Sales Associate		Av.
+	CONSH	Consolidated Holdings			Elizabeth Brown		Sales Representative		Berl

Record: ◀◀ ◀ 1 ▶ ▶◀ ▶* of 91

 Tip: *You can display or remove all subdatasheets in a table by opening the table in Datasheet view, clicking Subdatasheet on the Format menu, and choosing Expand All or Remove from the submenu.*

I moved some fields in Datasheet view and saved the layout; but when I ran AutoForm, the order of the fields didn't change. How do I permanently rearrange field order?

You need to rearrange the order of the fields in Design view. Open the table in Design view by selecting it in the Database

 window and clicking Design, or if you are in Datasheet view, click the View button on the toolbar.

In Design view, select a field to move by clicking the field selection button on the left of the Field Name column. A rightward-pointing arrow will appear in the field selection column and the field will be highlighted, as shown here:

Field Name	Data Type	Description	
ShipperID	AutoNumber	Number automatically assigned to new shipper.	
CompanyName	Text	Name of shipping company.	
Phone	Text	Phone number includes country code or area code.	

Shippers : Table

 Note: *To select contiguous fields, click in any column to deselect all rows, and then drag in one continuous motion across the field names you want to select in the field selection column.*

Drag the field indicator button up or down the field list until the heavy border on the top edge of the field is where you want to place the field. Save changes to the table, and the next time you use AutoForm, the field order will be as you changed it.

I would like to add visual effects to the data presented in Datasheet view. For example, can I change the background color of the datasheet?

Yes, and a lot more. While in Datasheet view, choose Datasheet from the Format menu to open the Datasheet Formatting dialog box, shown here:

Datasheet Formatting

Cell Effect
- (•) Flat
- ( ) Raised
- ( ) Sunken

Gridlines Shown
- [✓] Horizontal
- [✓] Vertical

OK
Cancel

Background Color: White
Gridline Color: Silver

Sample:

Border and Line Styles
Datasheet Border   Solid

You have control over displaying gridlines, background and gridline colors, and whether the cells appear flat or have a three-dimensional appearance. The Sample box shows how your changes will look as you make them.

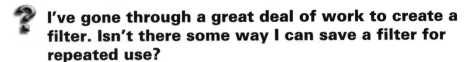

Note: *Cell effects apply to all cells in a table; you cannot change the appearance of an individual cell.*

FINDING DATA

I've gone through a great deal of work to create a filter. Isn't there some way I can save a filter for repeated use?

Yes, there are two ways:

- Access will save the filter for you when you exit the table and choose to save changes. The next time you open the table, you can click the Apply Filter button and the filter will run. However, if you have since created another filter in this table, the original filter is overwritten.

- For a truly permanent save, you need to save the filter as a query. Set up the filter either as Filter By Form or by using the Advanced Filter window. Choose Save As Query from the File menu, and name the query. The next time you want to use the filter, open the new query from the Queries object listing in the Database window, and run it.

Find Methods

Most database programs provide a strong mechanism for adding data; however, the key to a good database program is the ease and speed with which you can extract only the data you want. If the number of records in a table is reasonably small, the only thing you need to do to find particular records is to scroll through the table. However, in tables with hundreds or thousands of records, scrolling is impractical. In this case, you need to rely more on automated features. Access offers several tools to help you find and organize data. The four methods discussed here are searching, sorting, filtering, and querying. The first three methods are on-the-fly techniques that you perform when viewing a table in Datasheet view (filtering can also be applied to forms and subforms).

Searching

The fastest way to search for individual records in a table while the table is open is to click Find in the toolbar and use the Find tab of the Find And Replace dialog box, shown here:

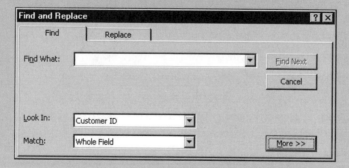

The Find What box is where you type text from a portion of the record you are looking for. As with the Find And Replace dialog boxes in the other Office 2000 products, you don't have to type the entire word or phrase for Access to find the entry. However, the more specific your input, the fewer records you will have to look at. There are a number of parameters you can use to limit the search:

Tip: *Click the More button to display additional search criteria.*

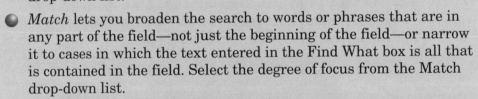

● *Look In* lets you limit the search to the field the insertion point is currently in or the whole table. There is no need to search an entire address table of names, street addresses, cities, and states if you are looking for a ZIP code. Open the table in Datasheet view, position the insertion point anywhere in the field you want to search, and then click the Find button. Select the field name from the Look In drop-down list.

● *Match* lets you broaden the search to words or phrases that are in any part of the field—not just the beginning of the field—or narrow it to cases in which the text entered in the Find What box is all that is contained in the field. Select the degree of focus from the Match drop-down list.

● *Match Case* lets you search by case. Access will only find the words that match the case of the text entered in the Find What box.

● *Search Fields As Formatted* locates text, usually dates, that are formatted differently than they are stored in the table. For example, the fourth of July, 2000, could be entered in the table as 7/4/00, but you could type 04-Jul-00 and still find it.

Tip: *Microsoft recommends formatting dates as four-digit years to minimize any Y2K-related problems—for example, using 2000 instead of 00. You can choose to format the current database or all databases using a four-digit year from the Tools | Options command. Click the General tab and select the appropriate check box under Use Four-Digit Year Formatting.*

Sorting

When sequential listing is an important aspect of trying to find information in a table, sorting provides a very quick way to accomplish that. If you want to sort on a single field, simply right-click the field you want to sort in Datasheet view, and choose an ascending or descending sort from the context menu, as shown here:

 Tip: *You can also sort by using the Ascending and Descending Sort buttons on the toolbar, or by selecting the commands from the Records menu. Before you use either of these methods, make sure the insertion point is in the field to be sorted.*

More detailed sorts can be done on multiple fields. For example, suppose you wanted a quick look at all of your customers named Jones in Seattle. First, you would sort on the City field to focus on Seattle and then on the ContactName field to display all the Joneses. Follow these steps to sort on multiple fields:

1. Open the table to be sorted in Datasheet view.

2. Choose Filter from the Records menu, and then click Advanced Filter/Sort. The Filter window will appear.

    The upper pane of the window displays the table and its field list; the lower pane contains the design grid in which the fields to sort on are assigned. (An example of the Filter window is shown in a few more steps.)

3. In the design grid, click in the leftmost cell in the Field row, if it isn't already selected. Click the down arrow to display the fields in the table and choose the first-level field to sort (the City field in the earlier example).

> *Tip:* *You can also double-click the field name in the upper pane and it will appear in the first blank column in the design grid, or you can drag a field name from the field list to a Field cell in the design grid.*

4. Click in the leftmost cell in the Sort row. Click the down arrow and choose Ascending or Descending.

5. Repeat steps 3 and 4 in the next column to the right for the second-level sort (the ContactName field in our example). Your Filter window should look like this:

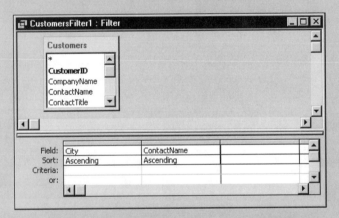

6. Click the Apply Filter button on the toolbar.

> *Tip:* *To return the table to its original unsorted state, click the Apply Filter button again or choose Remove Filter / Sort from the Records menu.*

Filtering

Filtering is a process that creates a subtable of records (called a dynaset) that adhere to criteria that you establish. You can perform

filtering on its own or as part of a query. There are six types of filters you can employ:

● *Filter by selection* is the simplest form of filtering a table and is based on the occurrences of a selected value in a field, one field at a time. Simply click a cell that contains the value you want to filter on, and click the Filter By Selection button on the toolbar. A new table appears with the filtered records. The following example shows all the books in a table that are of the Mystery category.

	BkID	ISBN	Title	Author	PubID	Price	OnHand	Order	Category
▶	1	042511872X	Stolen Blessing	Sanders	6	$4.95	5	2	Mystery
	3	0446360074	Rage of Angels	Sheldon	7	$3.50	4	1	Mystery
	5	0553281798	Trevayne	Ludlum	4	$5.95	4	1	Mystery
	9	0451146425	Lie Down with L	Follett	11	$4.95	2	1	Mystery
	11	0671742760	Dragon	Cussler	14	$5.95	3	1	Mystery
	18	0061000043	A Thief of Time	Hillerman	8	$4.95	1	1	Mystery
*	ıber)				0	$0.00	0	0	

Books : Table

Record: ◄◄ ◄ 1 ► ►► ►* of 6 (Filtered)

● *Filter by form* allows you to choose values in one or more fields or directly enter an expression. In Datasheet view, click the Filter By Form button on the toolbar. The table window shrinks to just the header row and one blank row. Click the blank cell in the field you want to filter first, and choose a value from the list of values for that field or enter an expression. To filter on more than one field, the procedure varies depending on the criteria you want the records to satisfy:

● **Both criteria (And operator)** Select or enter a value in a different field.

● **Either criteria (Or operator)** Click the Or tab in the lower-left corner of the window, and enter or select a second value. Each time you select an Or value, another Or tab is added, so you can string together as many values as you want.

Click the Filter button on the toolbar to filter the data; click it a second time to remove the filter.

● *Filter by input* doesn't offer a selection option, but it provides a fast gateway into the filtering process. In Datasheet view, right-click the field you want to filter; type the field value or expression in the Filter For box, as shown here; and press ENTER.

Click the Apply Filter button to remove the filter.

> *Note:*   *For complex criteria involving more than one field in an expression, you can right-click anywhere on the datasheet and enter the expression in the Filter For text box. For example, to find records that have a ratio of On order fields to On hand fields greater than 50 percent, you would enter* **[On order]/[On hand]>.5** *(assuming there are no records with zero On hand fields).*

- *Advanced filtering* uses the same filter window as sorting; however, you can establish criteria in addition to sorting. This method provides the most flexibility in setting up complex filters. Choose the fields to filter on by either double-clicking in the field list in the upper pane or selecting from the Field drop-down lists in the design grid. Then enter a field value or an expression in the Criteria row. You can filter using the Or and And operators on one or more fields. Click the Apply Filter button to perform the filtering.

Queries

There are several queries available in Access to achieve similar, yet different, results. A sampling of what you can do with queries includes the following:

- *Action queries* perform tasks on data, such as removing a group of records.

- *Append queries* add records to a table or another query.

- *AutoLookup queries* automatically add data to a record.

- *Crosstab queries* summarize data in a spreadsheet format.

- *Make-table queries* create tables using criteria against either the current or another database.

- *Pass-through queries* send commands to an ODBC-compliant database.

- *Select queries* find data in one or more tables or other queries, using criteria you establish, and then display the data in a logical order. Select queries are the most commonly used type of query.

Queries are Access objects, which means they can be named, saved, and called by VBA modules in custom applications, just like tables, forms, and reports. In fact, the output from a query (called a dynaset) resembles a table, as shown here:

Title	January	February	March	April
A Brief History			$15.26	$30.52
Dragon				$9.52
Hackers			$16.16	
Hard Drive				$20.66
Making of Micro			$11.66	
Patriot Games			$4.21	$8.92
The Power of W				$44.92
Whirlwind				$20.66

Sales by Book per month - 1999 : Crosstab Query — Record: 1 of 8

The dynaset appears to be a table, but any modifications to data performed in the dynaset are ultimately stored in the underlying table.

Designing a query from scratch can be a large undertaking, but Access relieves most of the effort by providing wizards to walk you through the steps. Use the Simple Query Wizard to create a basic select query with the following steps:

1. In the Database window, click Queries under Objects and then click the New button. The New Query dialog box appears, as shown in the following illustration.

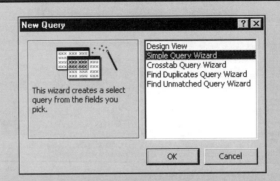

2. Double-click Simple Query Wizard to start the wizard.

3. In the first query wizard dialog box, choose the fields from the tables or queries in the database that are pertinent to extracting the data you want. You can add fields from multiple objects. Click Next.

4. Provide a name for the query and click Finish to view the query. You can easily switch to Design view after the query opens (click the View button on the Query Datasheet toolbar) to add criteria, add and remove fields, and rearrange the order of the fields in the dynaset.

I'm trying to build an expression in the Criteria cell of a query, but I'm having trouble putting it together. Can Access help me out?

Sure. Access provides a feature called the Expression Builder to help users build expressions in several objects, including query Design view. To open the Expression Builder, shown in Figure 6-1, right-click the Criteria cell where you want the expression, and choose Build from the context menu. You can type directly in the Expression box, or you can paste operators from the row of buttons and expression elements from the three list boxes.

Expression box   Operator buttons

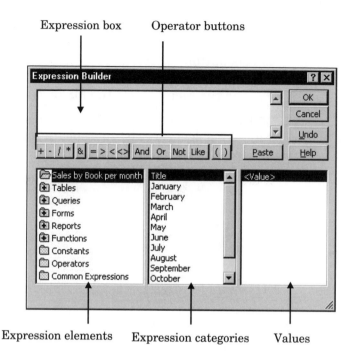

Expression elements   Expression categories   Values

Figure 6-1   Expression Builder

 Tip: *The operator button bar contains several of the most commonly used operators. For a complete list of operators, double-click the Operators folder in the leftmost list box.*

The leftmost list box contains folders of expression elements. Double-clicking a folder displays its contents by categories of expression elements in the middle list box; values for each category are displayed in the rightmost list box.

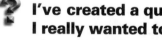 **I've created a query using the Simple Query Wizard, but I really wanted to create a new table with its results by changing the current select query into a make-table query. Can I change a current query's type?**

Yes. To do this, follow the steps listed next.

1. Open the query you've created in Design view, and choose Make-Table Query from either the Query menu or the Query Type button drop-down list (the appearance of this button reflects the last query built and may look different from what is shown here; you may have to fully expand the menu to see the Make-Table Query).

2. In the Make Table dialog box, shown next, name the new table (or select an existing table to replace), choose the database in which to locate the table, and click OK.

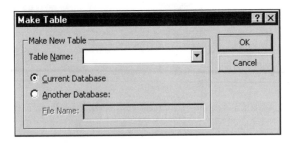

3. Modify the fields that appear in the Design view grid and their criteria as necessary.

4. Switch to Datasheet view to preview the new table. When satisfied, return to Design view and click the Run button on the toolbar.

5. Click Yes in the message box that tells you that you are about to paste new rows into a new table.

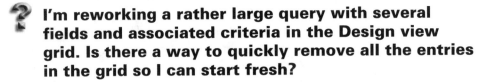

I'm reworking a rather large query with several fields and associated criteria in the Design view grid. Is there a way to quickly remove all the entries in the grid so I can start fresh?

Sure. Choose Clear Grid from the Edit menu when in query Design view.

Tip: *The query Design view grid is also called the "query by example" (QBE) grid.*

 How can I verify that there are no blank fields after data entry?

Simple. Create a query based on the table that contains the field you want to check. Drag the field from the field list to the grid, and type **Null** in its Criteria cell. Access will change the cell entry to Is Null when you move out of the cell. Run the query by clicking the Run button and Access will display any records that are blank in the chosen field.

 Tip: *The opposite of Is Null is Is Not Null, which returns records in which there is a value in the chosen field.*

CREATING AND MODIFYING FORMS

I like using the AutoForm Wizards to create quick data-entry forms, but I'm getting a little tired of the same background that appears for every form I create. Is there an easy way to change the layout for forms created by the AutoForm Wizards?

Yes, there is. The layout you are currently using is actually one of ten AutoFormats that are available. The layout that appears in the AutoForm Wizard is the default layout or the last AutoFormat chosen. To select one of the other nine layouts for AutoForm, follow these steps:

1. Open a form created by AutoForm, click the View button down arrow on the Form View toolbar, and click Design View (or you can simply click the View button directly if the Design View icon is displayed).

2. Choose AutoFormat from the Format menu to open the AutoFormat dialog box.

3. Click each of the Form AutoFormats and see how they appear in the sample box. There are two buttons that offer other features:

   ● *Options* adds three check boxes that allow you to control the format's attributes.

● *Customize* opens the Customize AutoFormat dialog box, in which you can create a new AutoFormat based on the current form, modify an existing AutoFormat, or delete one.

 Tip: *In Design view, you can further modify the form and save these changes to be incorporated in the new AutoFormat.*

4. Select an AutoFormat that you want to use for future AutoForm Wizards, and click OK.

5. Click the View button to return to Form view, and close the form. You don't have to save the form to change the future layout.

Form Design View

AutoForm and the Form Wizard are great for putting together simple forms, but sooner or later you will need to venture beyond their capabilities. Form Design view offers complete flexibility for what controls are placed on a form, how they are arranged, and how the form's overall appearance can be enhanced. Shown next is a form in Design view.

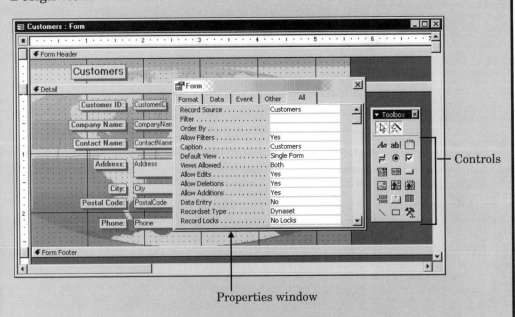

Properties window

Controls

Controls (objects in the Toolbox) are placed in the three main sections of a form to provide labeling and gateways to the underlying data. The Header and Footer controls provide consistency from record to record, such as the form title or special instructions to the user of the form.

> *Tip:* *If you don't see the Header and Footer sections, choose Form Header/Footer from the fully expanded View menu.*

The Detail section takes up the bulk of the form, with controls that show the field data in the underlying table or query, one record at a time.

Controls can be placed in any section by dragging them from the Toolbox to the location on the grid where you want them placed. Move and size the controls as needed, and use the horizontal and vertical rulers to assist you in organizing the layout.

There are two types of controls:

- *Unbound controls* provide visual information, but no data is directly displayed or edited from an underlying data source. Examples are labels, line separators, command buttons, and images such as logos.

- *Bound controls* are directly linked with the data in the underlying table or query. They display data and allow it to be edited. Examples are combo boxes, list boxes, and option buttons.

Many controls have wizards associated with them that start when you place the control on the grid. This is what the Combo Box Wizard looks like:

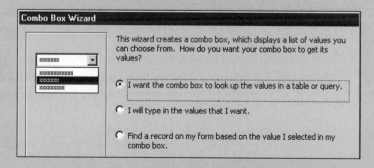

Properties

Each control in Access has several attributes, or *properties*, that can be modified to change its appearance, how it interacts with the data, and what actions occur on user input. To see the properties for any control, right-click the control and choose Properties from the context menu.

> ***Tip:*** *Any time in the design process you want to see how the form will look in "real life," switch to Form view by choosing Form View from the View menu.*

I've been entering data in a table using Datasheet view, but I think I'd like to try using a form to guide me through the fields. Do I have to design and create a full-blown form to quickly add data to a table?

 No. If all you're looking for is a simple data-entry form without any customization, such as special formatting or added controls, you can have Access make one for you. Select the table or query that the form will be based on in the Database window, and click the New Object/AutoForm button in the Database toolbar. If only the New Object button is available, click the down arrow to open it, and click AutoForm. If the AutoForm button is not visible, open the table or query, and you should see it.

 Tip: *You can also choose AutoForm from the Insert menu when either the Tables or Queries objects are displayed.*

A data-entry form that includes an entry box for each field will be created. Enter data for one record at a time. Start a new record by pressing TAB in the last field, clicking

 the New Record button on the status bar, or clicking the New Record button on the Form View toolbar. Close the form when you're through, and provide a name to save it with.

The next time you want to add records in this table, choose the form name from Forms in the Database window. See the "AutoForm Wizards" sidebar for other uses of AutoForm.

AutoForm Wizards

Creating a form by selecting a table or query in the Tables or Queries tab of the Database window is the simplest way to create a form, but the result is pretty spartan. Without much more effort, you can have a form with a layout that is closer to what you want and with a more appealing background. To create a form with AutoForm, select Forms in the Database window and click New. The New Form dialog box displays the three AutoForm options:

- *Columnar*, a formatted form with all fields shown in a single column and only one record shown at a time
- *Tabular*, a formatted form with all fields laid out horizontally across the window, showing multiple records
- *Datasheet*, a form that looks just like a table in Datasheet view, showing multiple records with no special formatting

Select an AutoForm, and choose a data source by typing the name of a table or query, or by choosing one from the drop-down list box. Click OK to create the form. When you close the form, you can choose to save it so it will be available in the Forms object list for future use.

I find myself constantly having to look up other ordering information from an Orders Detail table when I'm entering data in the Orders form. Is there a better way for me to access supplemental information related to the data in a form?

You bet. This is a perfect application for a subform, which is essentially a form within a form, as shown in Figure 6-2. Through the subform, you can see data in a second, related table. (See the sidebar on "Relationships" in the "Working with Tables" section of this chapter for more information on related tables.)

To create a subform, follow these steps:

1. Open the form that will contain the subform in Design view.

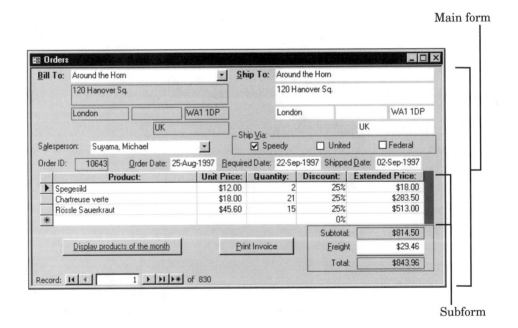

Figure 6-2 A subform is a form within a form

2. Open the Toolbox, if it isn't open, click the Subform/
Subreport button, and drag it to size on the grid. The
Subform/Subreport Wizard opens, as shown here:

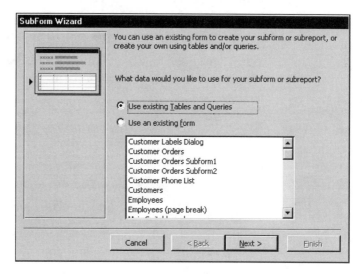

3. You can select whether to base the subform on existing
tables and queries, or on a form. Accept the default
option to build the subform from a table or query, and
click Next.

4. Select the fields from tables and queries that you want to
appear in the subform. Click Next.

5. Select or define your own links between the main form
and the subform. Click Next.

Note: *It is not necessary to link a field between the
main form and subform; however, you may get more
accurate information if they are linked than if you retype
the information.*

6. Provide a name for the subform, and click Finish.

7. The subform doesn't look particularly impressive in
Design view, so switch to Form view to see the complete
subform and the data from the fields you chose.

After I rearranged the controls on my form, I found that in Form view when I press TAB to move from control to control, the focus doesn't move in sequential order. How can I change the order of tabbing so it follows the logical pattern of the form?

What you need to do is change the tab order for the form. When you initially create a form, the tab order is set in one of three ways:

- *AutoForm* and the *AutoForm wizards* set the tab order the same as the field order in the data source.

- *Form Wizard* sets the tab order according to the order of the fields you choose for the form.

- *Design view* sets the tab order according to the order in which the controls are created.

To change the tab order, open the form in Design view, and choose Tab Order from the fully expanded View menu. Select the section of the form you want to change the tab order for, click the selection box next to a control name to select it, and then drag the selection box up or down the list into a new position, as shown here:

Tip: *To move a single control, first click the selection box to select it, and then drag it. To move contiguous control names, drag across their selection boxes to select them, and then drag a second time to move the selection.*

Click OK, and then switch to Form view to verify your
expectations.

 Tip: *In the Tab Order dialog box, click the AutoOrder
button if your form has a typical left-to-right and
top-to-bottom logic to its controls. Access automatically
changes the tab order to reflect that layout. Depending
on your layout, you may have to make minor manual
adjustments.*

I've changed the formatting of a label that I want to apply to all the labels in my form. Is there a way I can transfer formatting from one control to another?

 Sure, use the Format Painter to apply formatting from one
control to one or several others. Select the control that has
the formatting to be copied and *double-click* the Format
Painter button on the Form Design toolbar. (To display the
Form Design toolbar, choose it from the View menu's
Toolbars option.) The mouse pointer changes to an arrow and
paint brush and you can click several other labels to replicate
the original formatting. Click the Format Painter button
again to turn this feature off.

 Tip: *If you are applying formatting to only one other
control, click the Format Painter button once (instead of
double-clicking). The Format Painter will turn off after you
apply it.*

I get a little annoyed by having to repeatedly switch to Form view to see the effects of properties I've set in Design view. Is there a workaround for a more WYSIWYG way of applying properties to forms?

Yes, there is. By default, Access only lets you make property-
based design changes in Design view; however, you can
change the Allow Design Changes property for a form and
make changes in Form view. Do so with the following steps.

1. Open the form in Design view, and double-click the form selector to open the form's property sheet.

Form selector ➤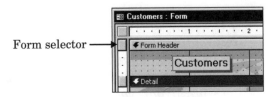

2. Click the All tab, scroll to the bottom of the properties list, and click the box to the right of the Allow Design Changes property.

3. Click the down arrow, select All Views from the drop-down list, and click outside the box.

The next time you switch to Form view for this form, you can right-click a control and choose Properties to display its property sheet.

PRESENTING INFORMATION WITH REPORTS

 In the mailing labels I'm creating, I need to include the abbreviation for "care of" before the company name, but I don't see any options in the Label Wizard's Available Fields list for commonly used address terms. How do I add text that isn't offered in the Available Fields list?

Although it isn't particularly evident how to do this, it's actually very easy. Many users that haven't upgraded since the earlier versions of Access are also taken aback by the lack of punctuation buttons. To add free text or punctuation marks, simply type them in the Prototype Label box in the Label Wizard, as shown here:

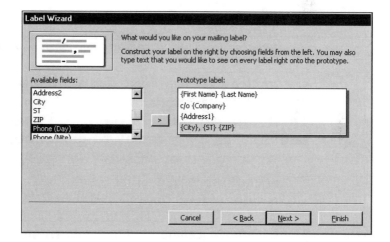

To do this, move the First Name field to the box, press SPACEBAR, and then move the Last Name field to complete the first line. Press ENTER to begin a new line, type **c/o**, press SPACEBAR, and move the Company field over to complete the second line. Use the same procedure to set up the address lines with spaces and commas.

Is there a better way to align controls in report Design view than by trying to drag them into position with the mouse?

Yes, there are a number of ways Access can provide assistance with placement of controls; however, the first thing you need to do is select the controls that you want to change. Once the controls are selected, right-click one of them and choose Align from the context menu. You can align the objects on any edge (left, right, top, or bottom) of any of the selected controls. Choose the side on which to align them from the submenu to have Access reposition the controls. You also can have Access align a control or controls to the grid by choosing Align, as above, and then selecting To Grid in the submenu.

 Tip: *For the Align feature to work as designed, select only controls that are in the same column or row.*

 I read the previous question on selecting controls in order to align them, but what I really want to do is "permanently" select them so I can move them as one unit. Is there a way to group controls?

New to Access 2000 is a grouping feature similar to what you might have used in other programs. Grouping allows you to position several controls and then "lock" them together so they act as one object to be moved or sized. This is especially useful when combining multiple graphics to produce a complex logo, for example.

To group controls, select them by dragging a selection rectangle around them if they are contiguous, or select the first control by clicking it, and press and hold SHIFT and click the other controls to be grouped. Then, on the Format menu, click Group. A selection border with sizing handles encloses the controls, as shown next. To separate, or ungroup, them, select the grouped controls and choose Ungroup from the Format menu.

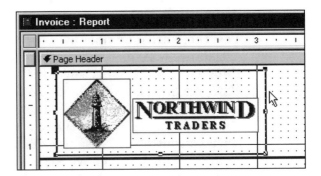

 Tip: *You can only group controls within the same section of a report (or form). You cannot, for example, group a control from the Header section with one from the Detail section.*

 I like to use the grid to help me position controls, but I find the dots distracting. Is there a way to remove the dots from the grid?

Sure. Open a report in Design view; right-click the report selector in the upper-left corner, as shown next; and choose Properties from the context menu.

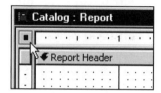

In the Report property sheet, click the Format tab and change the Grid X and Grid Y dot values to be greater than 24 dots per inch. This will make them impossible for your monitor to display.

 Tip: *If you are using centimeters as your measurement scale, change the Grid X and Grid Y values to be greater than 9 dots per centimeter to make the dots invisible.*

 I'm a little confused by the different types of headers and footers in a report. What's the difference between the Report Header (and Footer) and the Page Header/Footer?

The Report Header and Footer define the beginning and end of a report. The Report Header displays and prints at the top of the report's first page; the Report Footer displays and prints at the bottom of the report's last page.

The Page Header/Footer appear on every page and are useful for page numbering and report identification.

 My report takes what seems to be an inordinately long time to display in Print Preview. Can I do something to speed up display in Print Preview?

Probably. In reports that have to process a large amount of data, you can get an idea of how it looks by using Layout Preview instead of Print Preview. You compromise viewing all your data, since only a sampling is used to display the layout; but for purposes of checking the layout, that's all you need.

 Note: *Do not rely on, or be alarmed by, the data presented in Layout Preview, as it is commonly incorrect.*

To view your report in Layout Preview, open the report in Design view and choose Layout Preview from the fully extended View button drop-down list.

 I've gone to a great deal of work to create a good-looking form that would also make a fine report. Is there any way to use a form layout to create a report?

You bet. You can save the form as a report, but first you have to make available the toolbar button that executes the save. Add a new button to a toolbar with these steps:

1. Open a form in Design view that you want to save as a report, as shown in Figure 6-3.

2. Choose Toolbars from the View menu, and click Customize. The Customize dialog box opens.

3. In the Commands tab, select the Form/Report Design category. Scroll down the Commands list (if necessary) until Save As Report is visible, and then drag the command to a convenient location on the Form Design toolbar, as shown here:

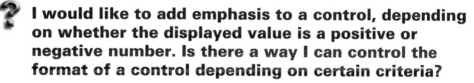

Figure 6-3 A form to be saved as a report

4. Close the Customize dialog box, click the Save As Report button, and provide a name for the report.

5. In the Database window, open Reports on the Object bar, and double-click the new report name. Compare Figure 6-3 with Figure 6-4 to see how a typical transformation appears.

I would like to add emphasis to a control, depending on whether the displayed value is a positive or negative number. Is there a way I can control the format of a control depending on certain criteria?

Yes, you can, by applying a conditional format to the control. You can choose a unique set of formatting styles, such as bold and italic text, and fill and text color, that will be applied to the control according to the value in the field; whether an expression is True or False; or when the control has the focus. Additionally, you can set up to three conditions for each control. Apply a conditional format with these steps:

1. Open the report (or form) in Design view, and select the control.

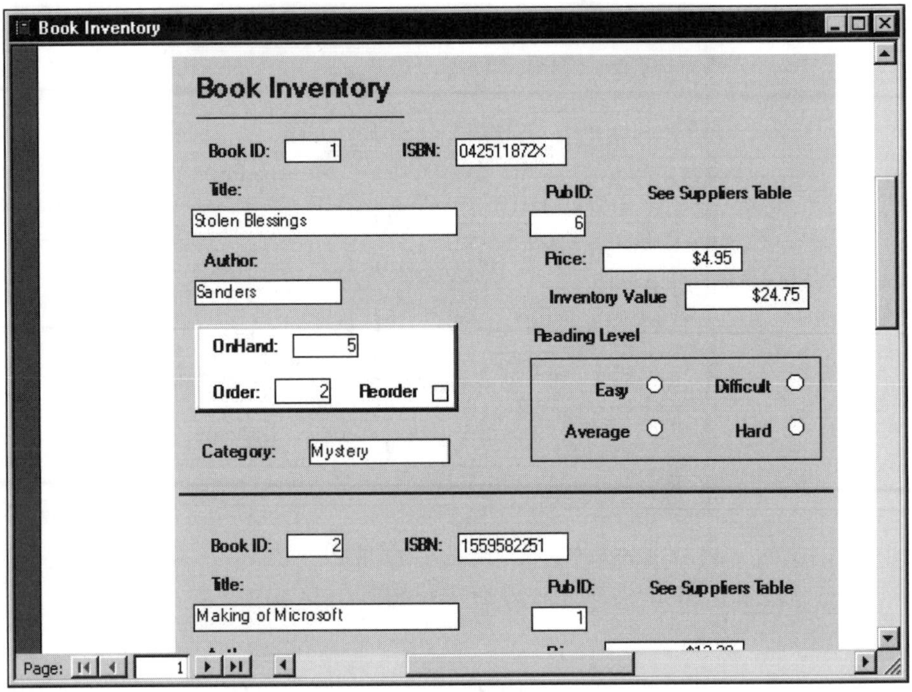

Figure 6-4 A report created from the form in Figure 6-3

2. Choose Conditional Formatting from the Format menu, and open the first Condition 1 drop-down list box. Depending on the element you choose from the drop-down list, you may have to set criteria for the value in the control or enter an expression.

You can also choose to display alternative formatting for the control when the conditions of the element you selected are satisfied. The condition shown next would change the control's default formatting to bold italic with a red fill if the field value is negative.

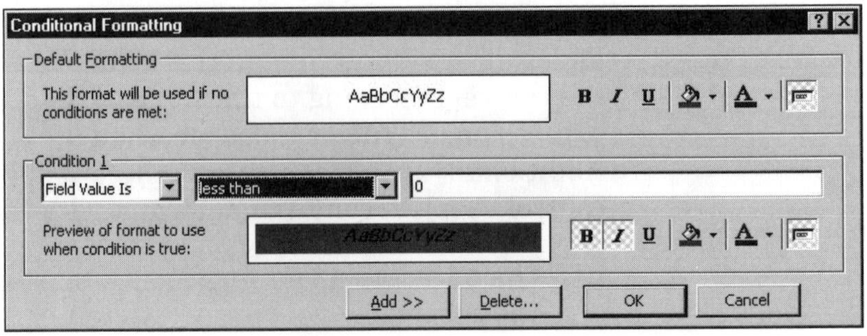

3. Click the Add button to assign additional conditions. Click OK when you are done.

PUTTING DATA ONLINE

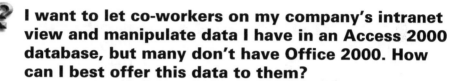

I want to let co-workers on my company's intranet view and manipulate data I have in an Access 2000 database, but many don't have Office 2000. How can I best offer this data to them?

Thanks to Internet Explorer 5 (and later versions of this browser), you can use a new object in Access 2000 to easily create web pages that resemble traditional Access forms and reports and that are connected to an Access (or SQL) database. These data access pages, or *pages*, are actually copied to the user's local computer so that any viewing manipulations they do in Internet Explorer, such as filtering, sorting, or adjusting a PivotTable, do not affect the underlying database. On the other hand, you can create a page that allows the user to input data that is saved to the database.

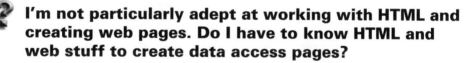

I'm not particularly adept at working with HTML and creating web pages. Do I have to know HTML and web stuff to create data access pages?

No. If you are familiar with using the Access tools for designing forms and reports, you're in good shape.

Note: *Once you create the pages, you will need to be comfortable with publishing the pages to a web site for use on a corporate intranet or the Internet. Microsoft FrontPage, included with Office 2000 Premium edition, provides full-service web site creation and administration— see Chapter 10.*

Figure 6-5 shows the design grid, Toolbox, and floating toolbar for a page designed to allow users to manipulate a PivotTable and see the results in a chart. Both the PivotTable and chart are available as tools from the Toolbox. The

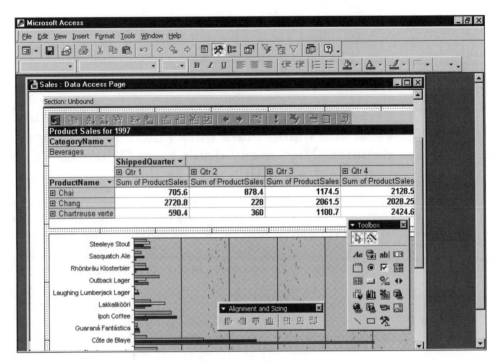

Figure 6-5 A data access page is designed using many familiar tools

simplest way to create a page is by using the Page Wizard or an existing web page. Both methods are available from the Pages object in the Database window.

I want to e-mail a data access page to someone to review for me. What do I have to do for that person to not only view the page, but also access the data?

Data access pages are handled a little differently by Access than other objects within the database. All objects except pages are contained within the .mdb database file; however, pages are stored as separate .htm files in the same folder location as the parent database file. The icons and filenames you see in the Database windows are actually shortcuts to the files themselves. In order for someone to view both pages and the underlying data you need to transfer both the .mdb file and the page .htm files.

+ ***Tip:*** *To quickly find out the filename and path to a data access page, point to the page in the Database window. A ScreenTip will display that information.*

After I make design changes to a data access page, how can I quickly see how those changes will look in Internet Explorer?

That's an easy one. In either Page view or Design view, choose Web Page Preview from an expanded File menu. The page will open in Internet Explorer.

IMPORTING, EXPORTING, AND LINKING DATA

I want to save a database I created in Access 2000 to a dBASE 5 file; but when I open the Save As dialog box, I don't have that option. What's the story?

You cannot save an Access database to another file format; you can only export an object such as a table or form to another file format. To export an object, either select the object in the Database window, or open the object and choose Export from the File menu. Open the Save As Type drop-down list to see which formats are available for export for that particular object. Click Save to create the file.

I'd like the users of my database to be able to quickly jump to amplifying information that's stored in Word documents. Can I use hyperlinks from Access to Word?

Yes, you can; but if I told you how in this chapter, we would have written Chapter 9 for nothing. See Chapter 9 for the answer to this question and others on hyperlinking.

I have data in a Paradox 4 file that I want to add to an existing Access 2000 table. Can I import data from other programs to a table?

No, sorry; you can't do it in one easy step. Only data in Access tables, text files, and spreadsheet files can be directly added

(or appended) to an existing Access table. The first thing you'll need to do in this situation is import the Paradox file into a new table with these steps:

1. Choose Get External Data from the File menu, and click Import.

2. In the Import dialog box, select Paradox (*.db) from the Files Of Type drop-down list box, and locate your data file, as shown next. Click Import.

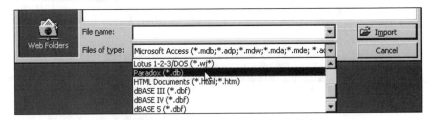

3. Click OK in the message box that indicates a successful import, and close the Import dialog box.

The new table is displayed with its original filename in the Database window, along with your existing tables.

The second part of the procedure appends the data in the new table to an existing table. For this, you need to create an Append query. Use the Simple Query Wizard to create the query with the pertinent fields from the new table, and then in query Design view, choose Append Query from the Query menu. You will be asked to name the table that is to be appended. Back in Design view, be sure the fields to be appended in the new table have the same field names as in the table you're appending into. When you are satisfied with your design, run the query to add the new data.

 Our inventory control department maintains their records in a dBASE IV database, but there are occasions when I'd like to view and possibly add data to the master inventory. Can I view and edit another program's data from within Access?

Yes, you can. By creating a link to the dBASE file, you can view and edit data; create your own forms, queries, and

reports in Access; and still allow the inventory control department full use through their dBASE program. The major limitation to using linked tables is that you cannot change the structure of the linked file; for example, you can't delete fields or change data types.

 Note: *Linking, as described here (to link tables), is not the same as the linking used in object linking and embedding (OLE). See Chapter 8 for questions and answers that deal with OLE.*

To link data, follow these steps:

1. Choose Get External Data from an expanded File menu, and click Link Tables.

2. In the Link dialog box, select dBASE IV (*.dbf) in the Files Of Type drop-down list, and locate the file to link to. Click Link.

3. If the Select Index Files dialog box appears, select the associated index file and click Select. If there is no index file, click Cancel.

Note: *Depending on the file type you are linking to, you may or may not see the Select Index Files dialog box.*

4. Click OK in the message box that informs you the table was successfully linked, and close the Link dialog box.

The linked table appears in the database window Tables object list with an arrow and "dB" to the left of the table name, as shown here:

Note: *You can also link to a table in another Access database.*

Chapter 7

Communicating with Outlook

Answer Topics!

Communicating with Outlook @ a Glance

Outlook 2000 adds the messaging, scheduling, and task-organizing functions within Outlook. In this chapter, you will find the following topics:

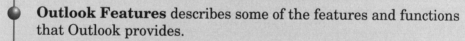

Outlook Features describes some of the features and functions that Outlook provides.

Creating and Sending E-mail answers questions related to producing, sending, and receiving e-mail, including filtering incoming mail, handling contact addresses, and attaching objects.

Using the Calendar addresses the way in which you work with the calendar to schedule meetings, coordinate meetings with others, import other calendar data, and enter data more efficiently, among other topics.

Entering and Maintaining Contacts provides answers to questions on entering and changing contact information and on using the contact file in a mail merge operation.

Establishing and Using Task Lists discusses how to create tasks, coordinate tasks with the calendar, and assign or receive tasks to and from others, among other topics.

Keeping a Journal and Making Notes shows you how to create journal entries automatically, view journal entries for a contact, and create and use notes.

OUTLOOK FEATURES

Outlook belongs to a new class of information management programs that combine information from

- Electronic mail sources, such as Internet mail, Microsoft Mail, the Microsoft Exchange, cc-Mail, CompuServe mail, and other sources
- Personal information, such as scheduling, contact lists, task lists, journals, and notes
- Group information, including meetings, events, group contacts, task assignments, and the sharing of journals and notes
- Traditional computer information contained in disk files and folders, both personal and public

Outlook provides a fully integrated and easily used means of locating, controlling, using, and storing all of this information. To do this, Outlook replaces the following applications:

- Your mail client, including the Windows 97 Exchange client (the Inbox) or any other mail program you might be using
- Microsoft Schedule+ or any other personal or group scheduling program
- Personal information management programs (PIMs) such as ECCO, ACT!, SideKick, and Lotus Organizer

Microsoft Outlook includes seven components that perform the following functions:

- *Inbox* and the *Mail Group* for all e-mail–related functions
- *Calendar* for personal and group scheduling
- *Contacts* for maintaining business and personal contact information, including e-mail and Web page addresses
- *Tasks* for maintaining personal and group to-do lists or assignments

- *Journal* for recording or automatically collecting information tied to a time line

- *Notes* for creating, collecting, and categorizing extraneous information

- *Other* for accessing, viewing, and sharing all other disk files

When you open Microsoft Outlook for the first time after installing it, you will see a window similar to the one shown in Figure 7-1. In addition to the normal menu bar, toolbar, and status bar, the Outlook window has two major areas:

- The Outlook bar, on the left, contains shortcuts that open corresponding folders. The shortcuts in the Outlook bar are divided into groups that, in Figure 7-1, include the Outlook Shortcuts, My Shortcuts, and Other Shortcuts. (The last two folders are provided by default and can be renamed by you. Your shortcut groups may vary, because any custom folders are retained from previous versions.) You can create additional groups, add and remove shortcuts, and change where and how the shortcuts appear.

- The information pane on the right displays the information selected in the Outlook bar. In it, you can select one of several views; add and delete columns; and group, sort, or filter the information being displayed.

An optional area that is not initially displayed in the Outlook window is the folder list, shown here:

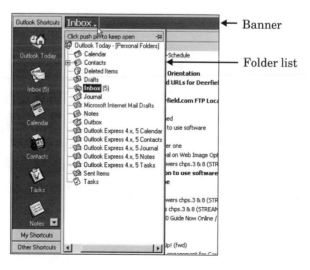

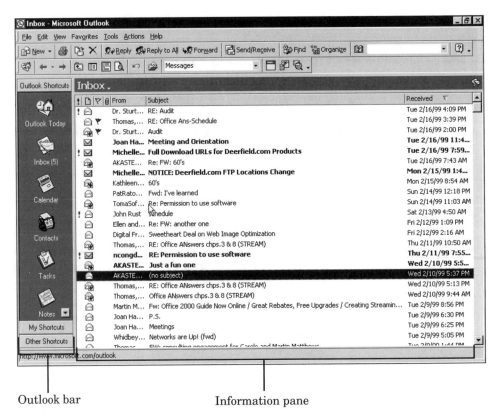

Outlook bar   Information pane

Figure 7-1   The Microsoft Outlook window

 The folder list shows the folders that are available in the selected Outlook group. You can display the folder list by clicking the left end of the banner above the information pane, clicking the Folder List button in the toolbar, or by choosing Folder List in the View menu. The number of unread items in a folder is shown in parentheses next to the folder.

The Outlook bar is the primary way of selecting the Outlook component or folder that you want displayed in the information pane. Whatever is displayed takes control of the Outlook window, determines some of the menu options and toolbar buttons, and is said to be "active."

CREATING AND SENDING E-MAIL

Can I attach or include other items in my e-mail message? If so, how?

There are a number of items you can include in e-mail messages, such as files, other e-mail messages, bitmapped images, audio clips, and hyperlinks to intranet and Internet web sites. The following points describe how to do this:

● **Files** To attach an ordinary file, such as a Word file, position the insertion point in the body of the message and select Insert | File. The Insert File dialog box opens. Select a file (which will enable the Insert button) and then, in the lower-right corner, click the down arrow next to the Insert button and choose Insert as Attachment. The icon for the file appears in your message below the text, as shown here:

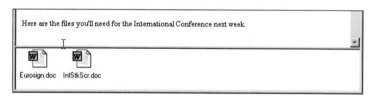

When using Plain Text or HTML formats, the attachments are added to the end of the message in a separate area. With Rich Text, they are added inline with the text.

 Tip: *If some of the items on the Insert menu are unavailable, it is probably because you are using Plain Text format. To enable more options, select Format | HTML or Rich Text.*

● **E-mail messages** Attach another e-mail message to your message by choosing Insert | Item and selecting the item from the Insert Item dialog box that opens. Make sure Insert as Attachment is selected, and click OK. The icon appears below your message (with Plain Text or HTML format; otherwise, in the message text), as shown here:

RE: Audit

● **Hyperlinks** Add a hyperlink or link to your message by simply typing or pasting a URL (Uniform Resource Locator, or World Wide Web address) in the message. Outlook automatically changes the color of the hyperlink in the text (blue is the default), and underlines it. If you click Insert | Hyperlink after having enabled the hyperlink option in the Insert menu (by choosing HTML from the Format menu), a Hyperlink dialog box will be displayed to help you type the URL. If you click a link, your default browser will open and display the linked Web page (assuming that you are connected to the Internet or an intranet through which you can reach the URL).

● **Other items** Attach other items in the same way. For instance, insert graphics with Insert | Picture, a straight line with Insert | Horizontal Line, and a unique signature (perhaps with your logo) with Insert | Signature.

 Note: *The items available on the Insert menu depend on the text format you are using.*

I understand that Outlook has some way to automatically process incoming mail, but I can't find anything like that. What am I missing?

Microsoft has a very powerful tool for use with Outlook that automatically processes your mail so it is easier for you to handle. This tool, the Rules Wizard, uses rules you set up to automatically organize your messages. You access it by selecting Tools | Rules Wizard, as described in the sidebar titled "The Rules Wizard" in this section.

Outlook Mail Window

The Outlook mail window contains a list of mail you have sent (Sent Items) or mail you have received (Inbox). There are several ways to view the list of mail, but the most common is the table-like list of messages shown here:

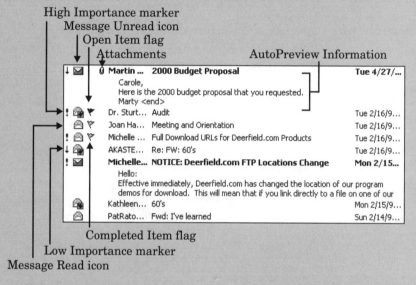

If the added space used does not bother you, then AutoPreview is a handy way to see a bit of a message's contents to determine whether it will be worth reading the rest of the message. From the View menu, click AutoPreview to see the first three lines of all messages, or, if you have the Advanced Toolbar displayed, you can select Messages With AutoPreview as the current view to see the first three lines of unread messages only. That view and others are also available from View | Current View or the Current View drop-down list on the toolbar. The other views in the Current View drop-down list, shown next, allow you to focus on one element of the message, such as the sender or the subject.

The views are further described in the following table.

View	Description of Default Features
Messages	A list of messages in date and time order that displays the sender, the subject, and the date/time received fields
Messages With AutoPreview	A list of messages as in Messages view, with the first three lines of the message displayed if the message is unread
By Follow-Up Flag	A list of messages as in Messages view, with the messages grouped by type of message flag (Open Item or Completed Item) and showing the follow-up due date
Last Seven Days	A list of messages as in Messages view, but displaying only those received in the last seven days
Flagged For Next Seven Days	A list of messages whose follow-up due dates fall within the next seven days, in ascending order of due dates (earliest first) and including sender, subject, message flag, and due by fields
By Conversation Topic	A list of messages as in Messages view, with the messages grouped by conversation topic (the default is by subject)
By Sender	A list of messages grouped by sender and displaying the subject and the date and time received
Unread Messages	A list of messages as in Messages view, but displaying only those that are unread

View	Description of Default Features
Sent To	A list of messages in order of date and time sent and showing the recipient, the subject, and the date and time sent
Message Timeline	Messages shown as icons along a daily time line based on the time they were sent

In the Message Timeline view, messages are represented by icons along a daily time line, as shown here. Any of the views can be changed, and new views can be added.

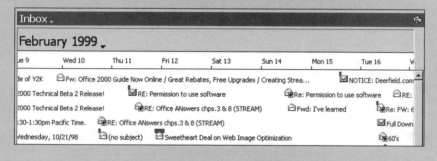

The Rules Wizard

The Rules Wizard walks you through the construction of rules that, when they are applied, will select messages that fit your criteria and then handle the selected messages in the way that you specify. A rule has two components: selection criteria and actions to be performed on selected messages. For example, if you want to search your incoming mail for a particular sender and a particular subject, you would establish a rule that all mail from that sender with that particular subject would automatically be moved to a separate folder after it is read (the action). Some things you can do with the Rules Wizard include the following:

● Assign categories to messages

● Move selected messages to a folder

- Delete selected messages
- Flag selected messages
- Forward selected messages or redirect an e-mail message to a person or distribution list
- Mark the sensitivity of selected messages
- Perform a custom action when selected records arrive
- Perform alternative conditions when receiving e-mail
- Produce a special sound or message when selected messages arrive
- Reply to selected messages using a template
- Print a message
- Start a program

After you have acquired and installed the Rules Wizard, you can create a rule that selects mail with a particular sender and subject and places that mail in a separate folder by following these steps:

1. With the Inbox open in the Outlook window, select Tools | Rules Wizard. The blank Rules Wizard dialog box will open. Click New to start a new rule. The Rules Wizard dialog box opens, as you can see here:

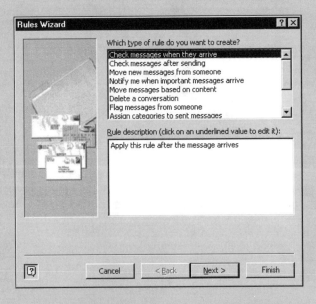

2. In the Which Type Of Rule Do You Want To Create? list box, select the rule that you want to create.

3. In the Rule Description box, click any underlined words and complete the dialog box that will be displayed.

4. Click Next, and complete the dialog box. Continue responding to the questions and conditions that each rule requires.

> *Tip:* *If you want a rule to apply to several people, create a distribution list containing those people, as described in the question about creating a mailing list—"I frequently send e-mail to the same group of people . . ."—later in this chapter.*

5. In the last dialog box, type the name of the rule you have just created. If you want this rule to apply to the messages you already have, click Run This Rule Now On Messages Already In "Inbox." Make sure the Turn On This Rule check box is checked, and click Finish. You are returned to the original Rules Wizard dialog box, in which your new rule now appears. This dialog box allows you to turn on or off specific rules and perform other rule-management functions. For now, click OK. When you next bring up the dialog box, your new rule will appear.

The Rules Wizard is an extremely powerful tool for managing your e-mail.

? I know I can just type it in, but is there an easier way to capture an e-mail address on a message I received?

You bet! Simply drag the From field to the Contact shortcut in the Outlook Shortcut bar. The Contact window, shown in Figure 7-2, will be displayed with the information filled in for you. Check that the information is correct, and then click Save and Close.

Another way to display the Contact window is to right-click the name in the From field, and choose Move To Folder from the context menu. A Move Items dialog box allows you to choose the folder, which in this case is Contacts. When you select the folder and click OK, the Contact window will be

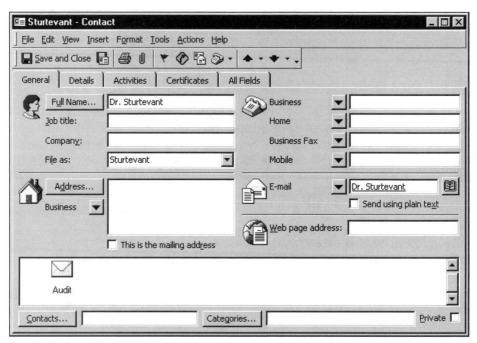

Figure 7-2   Drag an e-mail's From field to the Contacts shortcut to create
a new Contact record

displayed; then the e-mail address will automatically be
added to your address book.

    Tip: *When you add a new contact in this way, the e-mail*
address appears to be the same as the display name. You can
verify the e-mail address by right-clicking the name in the
E-mail field and choosing Properties.

I would like to categorize my mail so I can sort it into topics that can be more easily dealt with as a group. How is that done?

The easiest way to add categories to an Inbox message is
to right-click the message and select Categories from the
context menu. This opens up the Categories dialog box, from
which you can choose one or more categories.

If you want additional categories, or if you want to add
your own categories, click the Master Category List button in

the Categories dialog box. The Master Category List opens, in which you can type a new category name in the text box at the top and click Add, or you can select one of the additional categories in the list. Click OK to close the Master Category List. To add the new or additional category to your message, you'll need to select it in the Categories dialog box. For more information, see the sidebar "Handling Incoming Mail."

Handling Incoming Mail

Handling your incoming mail may or may not be a problem. If you only get a few pieces of mail a day, it is easy to handle. If you get hundreds of pieces a day, you have a real task ahead of you. Outlook provides a large number of features and tools to help you work through the task, however large it is. The following table describes those tools.

Feature or Tool	Description
AutoPreview	Lets you see the first three lines of either unread messages (using the Messages With AutoPreview view) or all messages (with the AutoPreview toolbar button)
Message icons and bolded/unbolded subject text	Identifies whether a message is read or unread
Message flag	Indicates that a flag has been set or cleared on a message
Importance markers	Indicates that a message is of high or low importance, using the Importance setting in View | Options of the message window, buttons on the toolbar, or in the Properties dialog box opened from File | Properties
Categorizing	Allows you to add categories to messages so they can be grouped or filtered using the Edit | Categories dialog box or the context menu opened when you right-click a message

Feature or Tool	Description
Replying and forwarding	Allows you to quickly reply to or forward a message, using the Reply, Reply To All, and Forward toolbar buttons
Sorting	Allows you to sort on any field in either ascending or descending order by clicking the field name in the Information pane or by choosing View	Current View	Customize Current View	Sort
Searching	Allows you to search your message files in many different ways using Tools	Find or the toolbar button.
Grouping	Allows you to group all messages that have the same contents in a given field by using View	Current View	Customize Current View	Group By, or by clicking the Group By Box toolbar button and dragging the column heading by which you wish to group to the Group By box
Filtering	Allows you to select a set of messages based on complex criteria using View	Current View	Customize Current View	Filter
Adding reply annotation if not using Microsoft Word	Allows you to identify changes you've made to a message using an e-mail editor other than Microsoft Word by opening Tools	Options	Preferences tab	E-mail Options, and then clicking Mark My Comments With
Dragging and dropping	Allows you to drag information from one part of Outlook to another, to the desktop, or to other applications or folders (you can't drag onto your desktop if you're using Windows NT earlier than version 4)
Adding folders	Allows you to store messages in subfolders under the Inbox or, Sent Items, or even under Personal Folders, to more quickly find what you are looking for
Organizing	Provides shortcuts for using folders, colors, views, and the junk mail/adult content filter by selecting Tools	Organize or clicking the Organize button.
Setting rules	Allows you to describe how the messages you receive should be handled

 An associate has a different-looking window for creating and reading mail messages. How can I change the message window?

In addition to the slight differences between Plain Text and Rich formatted messages, you can create a greater change in the message window by using Microsoft Word as an editor. Outlook creates two similar but different e-mail message windows: the normal message window, shown in Figure 7-3, and the WordMail window, shown in Figure 7-4, which uses Microsoft Word for e-mail.

If you want to change your message window, select Tools | Options, click the Mail Format tab in the Options dialog box, and check or uncheck Use Microsoft Word To Edit E-mail Messages.

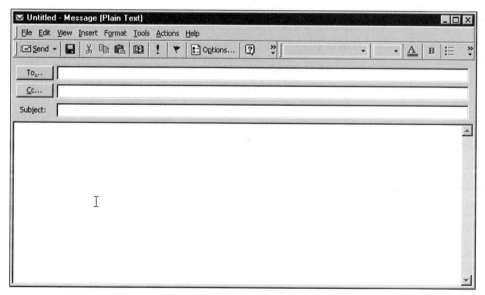

Figure 7-3 Outlook normally uses an editor that is more limited, but is faster and easier to use

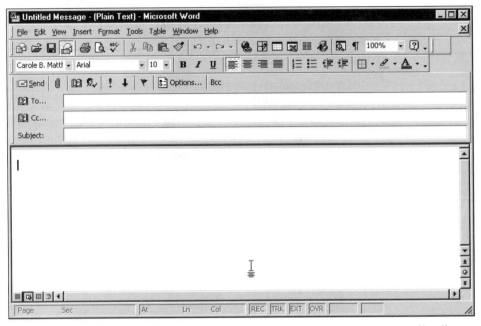

Figure 7-4 You can choose to use Microsoft Word as your e-mail editor for more options

I frequently send e-mail to the same group of people. Is there a way to create a mailing list so I don't have to re-enter or select all these names each time?

Sure—you can create a distribution list containing the names of the people in your group, and then you only have to enter the distribution list name when you address a message. Use these steps to create a distribution list:

Address Book

1. Click the Address Book button in the toolbar, or select Tools | Address Book from either the Outlook or message window to open your address book.

2. Click the New button in the Address Book dialog box. A drop-down menu will be displayed with two options, as shown here:

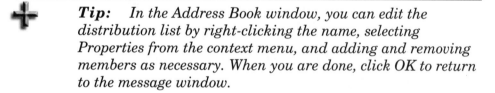

3. Select New Group from the menu. A Properties dialog box will be displayed.

4. Enter the Group Name you want to use to identify this particular distribution list (this is the name you'll type in the To and Cc boxes).

5. Click Select Members, and double-click as many names in your address book as you want on the list, or enter new names by clicking New Contact.

6. If you want to enter additional information, such as a mailing address or web site name, select the Group Details tab and fill it in.

7. When all the members have been added, click OK to return to the message or Outlook window. In the message address box, only the distribution list name appears (in bold), but the message will be sent to all the names on the list.

Tip: *In the Address Book window, you can edit the distribution list by right-clicking the name, selecting Properties from the context menu, and adding and removing members as necessary. When you are done, click OK to return to the message window.*

I have built up several hundred mail messages and am having a hard time finding particular messages. What are the best ways to find messages?

There are two approaches that you can use: finding and filtering. Finding and filtering vary in degree—you can find something using a quick and easy format, or you can create a sophisticated and complex filter. There are advantages to both.

Filtering Messages

To filter, use the following steps:

1. With the Inbox open (or you could use Sent Items, if you wish), open View | Current View | Customize Current View | Filter. The Filter dialog box opens, as shown next.

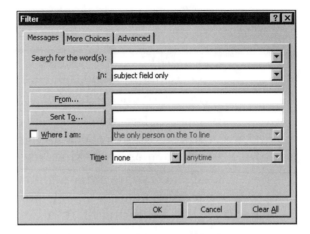

2. In the Search For The Word(s) text box, enter the word or words that you want to search for. Choose whether you want to search in the subject field only, in the subject field and message body, or in frequently used text fields to search the majority of the text fields in the message. You can also specify from whom and to whom the messages were sent, if you know. At the bottom of the Messages tab, you can select one of several different time fields in which to look for a time span.

3. In the More Choices tab, note the Categories option, which is one of the principal ways that categories can be used. Here you can also specify whether you want to filter messages with attachments, important codes, or read or unread statuses. You can also filter for a range of size and for matching case.

4. The Advanced tab allows you to build more complex, free-form criteria to search on; you can create conditions that specific fields must match.

5. When you have established the filter criteria you want to use, click OK. Click OK again in the View Summary dialog box. The Outlook window reappears with the Inbox (or Sent Items, if that's what you started with) displayed, and the words *(Filter Applied)* are shown in the Inbox banner above the information pane. Only those messages that satisfy the filter criteria will be shown.

6. After you have looked at your filtered messages, you can remove the filter by opening View | Current View | Customize Current View | Filter, clicking the Clear All button to remove the filter, and then clicking OK and then OK again. When you return to the Inbox, you'll see that the filter has been removed.

Finding Messages

If you wish to use Find instead of Filter, select Tools | Find to open the Find pane, shown next. Notice that it is quite simple compared to the Filter command.

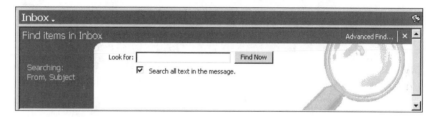

1. Enter the text for which you want to search. If you want to search only the Subject field, remove the check mark by Search All Text In The Message.

2. Click Find Now. The found items will be displayed in the window. You will also see additional options in the Find pane. You can click Advanced Find in the upper-right corner of the Find pane if your quick-and-easy approach has not been successful. Clicking it will display a dialog box very similar to the Filter dialog box. You can also click Clear Search and start over with new criteria.

3. When you have finished with the Search, click the Close icon (the ×) in the upper-right corner of the Find pane to remove it.

How many names can be in the To or Cc box of the message window?

You can have a large number (over 300) names in the To and Cc address blocks. If you type in more than one name, put a comma between them. Then, as they are checked against the address book, a semicolon will automatically replace the

comma between the names. You can, of course, also select the names from the Address Book to start with, rather than type them.

I send out almost the same message frequently. I tried storing it in Word and copying and pasting it into my e-mail, but that is a pain. Is there a better way to repeatedly send the same message?

You bet. Outlook allows you to create and use both custom forms and templates for this purpose. The default message window is an existing form that you can customize. A template is a standard blank message form with custom text in the body of the message. A custom form differs from a template in that the field structure (such as To, Cc, and Subject) can be changed from a normal message. There may be more or fewer fields and they may be in a different order or position, or the fields may have different labels or sizes. You can also add validation criteria to check what is entered into a field, add a calculation to a field, and even include some Visual Basic for Applications programming to determine how fields, and the form in general, behave. An example of a custom form is the While You Were Out message shown here:

Creating a Template

You can create a template by opening the standard Outlook blank message, adding the text you want to repeat, and then saving it as a template. Do that with the following steps:

1. From the Outlook window, with the Inbox open, click the New Mail Message toolbar button to open a new message window.

2. Leave the To and Cc fields blank, type what you want for the Subject, and enter the message text. An example of a saved template is shown here:

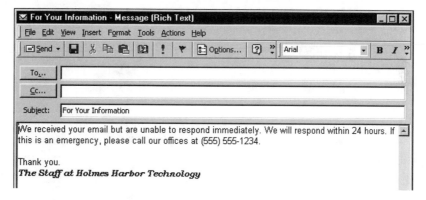

3. Save your template by opening the File menu and choosing Save As. Under Save As Type, select Outlook Template (*.oft) and click Save. The new template will be saved in C:\Windows\Application Data\Microsoft\ Templates (assuming that you use the default folder scheme). The new template will be saved under the name you used for the subject.

4. Close your message window (by clicking the × in the upper-right corner of the window) and answer No when asked if you want to save the file (this is asking if you want to save it in your Inbox, which you don't—you've already saved it as a template).

5. To use your template, click the arrow to the right of the New Mail Message toolbar button, and then select Choose Form from the New Message menu. The Choose Form dialog box will open. Click the down arrow for Look In, and select User Templates In File System. Your .oft file should be visible to you.

6. Double-click your file, and it will open as a new message window with the subject and body filled in as you left them. All you need to do is fill in the To information and click Send.

Tip: *Any of the built-in templates can be customized and then saved under either the existing template name or a new one.*

Using Custom Forms

If you want a custom form that simply repeats the text in the subject and body of a message, you can use a template rather than creating a custom form. However, if you want to change the field structure of a message to add or delete fields or to rearrange fields, then you need to create a custom form and use that form to apply the new structure to your messages. Forms, of course, can also have special text in the subject and body of the message.

Note: *Many of the best features of using a form rather than a template, such as adding fields, changing field positions or labels, and resizing or deleting fields, are transmitted to the message recipient only if you are using a Microsoft Exchange server on a LAN. If you transmit a message with those features over the Internet, an intranet, or while using a different mail server over a LAN, you'll lose the features and the message will revert to a standard e-mail format and field set. A customized form may still help you create the message and be worthwhile for that reason, but don't expect your Internet recipient to see your fancy formatting.*

Outlook has three features that are used to work with forms:

● To create a form, use Design A Form in the message window's Tools | Forms menu.

● To save a form, use Save As in the message window's File menu or on the design toolbar, and specify the File Type.

● To find a form, use Tools | Forms | Choose A Form from the Outlook window.

Look at the Design view of the message window by opening a new message. Then, choose Tools | Forms | Design This Form. The message window changes to Design view and the Field Chooser opens, as you can see here.

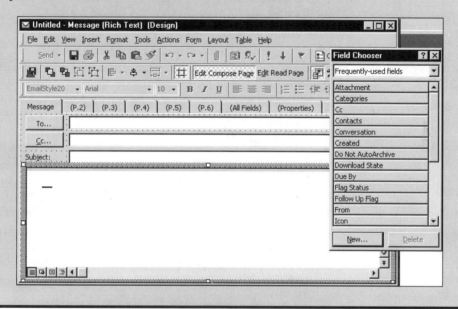

Some of my e-mail correspondents use the same signature block on all their messages. Is there an automatic way of doing that?

Yes, you can automatically add a closing and signature with Outlook's AutoSignature feature. Follow these steps to create one:

1. Select Tools | Options, and click the Mail Format tab.
2. Click Signature Picker, shown next.

3. In the Signature Picker dialog box, click New.

4. In the Create New Signature dialog box, enter a name that you will use to identify the signature. Choose whether you want to Start With A Blank Signature and create the signature from scratch, or select another signature to use as a template (if there are any), or use another file as a template. You will have to enter a path or click Browse if you are using another file to get started with. Click Next.

5. In the Signature Text box, type (or paste) the text you want to be included in your signature. This can be anything you want: a signature alone, a closing and a signature, or a statement of some type. To give your signature some further uniqueness, you can use the Font and Paragraph buttons to set the font and font size, color, style, and so on. You can also click Advanced Edit to load FrontPage and create a more artistic signature.

6. When you are done, click Finish. The signature will be listed in the Signature Picker dialog box, an example of which is shown here:

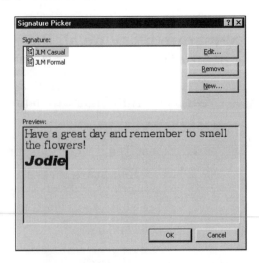

7. Click OK when you have your signature the way you want it. In the Mail Format tab, click Use This Signature By Default to have it placed on all new messages. Decide if you also want the signature placed on replies and forwarded messages. If you do want it on those documents, remove the check mark next to Don't Use When Replying Or Forwarding. When you next open a new message window, you'll see your selected signature automatically placed on the message.

Tip: *If you are using Microsoft Word as your e-mail editor, you use a slightly different technique. If you want to create, turn off, or change a signature while you are creating a message, choose Tools | Options; and, on the General tab, select E-mail Options. However, to remove the signature on a single message, it's easier just to select it in the message and press DELETE.*

What's the meaning of the underline in the To and Cc boxes of the message window?

When a name in the address box is underlined, it indicates that it has been checked against and is in agreement with the address book.

How can I get automatically numbered lists in the e-mail messages I create?

If you want additional formatting, such as AutoCorrect, bullets and numbered lists, tables, more exotic paragraph styles, or (my favorite) spell checking as you type, you can create your e-mail using Microsoft Word as your editor. You can change to Microsoft Word as your e-mail message creator and reader with the following steps.

Note: *Many of Microsoft Word's formatting features are not observable by recipients of a message unless they are using Microsoft Word 97 or 2000 as their e-mail editor.*

1. From the Outlook window with the Inbox open, select Tools | Options, and click the Mail Format tab.

2. Place a check mark in the Use Microsoft Word To Edit E-mail Messages check box. Click OK to close the Options dialog box.

3. Click the New Mail Message toolbar button, opening a new message window. It is hard to see the difference between this window that uses Microsoft Word as its editor, and the normal message window. Notice the Table menu and the additional buttons on the toolbars. If you open the menus, you'll see additional differences; for example, if you open the Help menu, you will see Microsoft Word Help in addition to Outlook Help.

 Note: *The Microsoft Word editor takes longer to load the first time it's used in a session; but, if you use it again, it appears instantly, and you will not have the added load time.*

4. Use the To, Cc, Subject, and message fields as you would in the normal message window. While typing the body of the message, try special formatting, see the Spelling and Grammar Checker operate as you type, and use AutoText and other Word features to enhance the template.

USING THE CALENDAR

 How can I accept meeting requests automatically if they don't conflict with other things in my schedule?

To set up automatic acceptance of meeting requests that do not conflict with other items on the Calendar, follow these steps:

1. Open Tools | Options, and select the Preferences tab.

2. Click Calendar Options, and then click Resource Scheduling. The Resource Scheduling dialog box will be displayed. In this

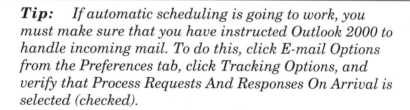

dialog box, the first three check boxes control the automatic response to meeting requests, as follows:

● **Automatically Accept Meeting Requests And Process Cancellations** All meeting requests and cancellations are automatically accepted, unless you have checked either of the other two check boxes.

● **Automatically Decline Conflicting Meeting Requests** All meeting requests that conflict with currently scheduled activities are automatically declined.

● **Automatically Decline Recurring Meeting Requests** All meeting requests that are recurring are automatically declined.

3. Click OK when you are done.

Tip: *If automatic scheduling is going to work, you must make sure that you have instructed Outlook 2000 to handle incoming mail. To do this, click E-mail Options from the Preferences tab, click Tracking Options, and verify that Process Requests And Responses On Arrival is selected (checked).*

With the first two boxes checked, all requests that don't conflict with scheduled activities will be automatically accepted and will appear on your Calendar. This can save you considerable time responding to requests, and all the meetings appear on your Calendar, where you will be reminded of them.

What is the difference between appointments, meetings, and events?

In the Outlook Calendar, you can enter three types of activities:

● *Appointments,* which take time on your Calendar, are less than 24 hours in length, and do not require inviting

others to attend. Examples include a sales call, lunch with a buyer, and time you want to set aside to write a report.

● *Meetings,* which are appointments that require that others be invited or that resources be reserved. Meetings are set up using the Plan A Meeting dialog box to identify participants, send meeting requests to them, and track the responses.

● *Events,* which are 24 hours or more in length and do not occupy time on your Calendar. Each event appears as a banner on that day's schedule. Examples include birthdays, anniversaries, trade shows, and your vacation.

I work in a small office in which all of our computer files are completely shared. In that environment, is there any way I can directly change an associate's Calendar?

If you have been given permission by the person, you can literally open his or her Calendar and make an appointment. To do so, follow these steps:

1. Open File | Open | Personal Folders File or Other User's Folder.

2. If you choose to open a Personal Folder, you will immediately go to the Open Personal Folders dialog box in which you can indicate where your folders are to be found.

3. The Connect To dialog box may appear, where you select the path and .pst file in which you want to make an appointment (this may be C:\Exchange\Mailbox.pst or C:\Windows\Local Settings\Application Data\Microsoft\Outlook\Outlook.pst). The selected Outlook.pst file will be copied as an additional set of folders into the list of Outlook folders on your computer.

4. Click the Folder List button in the toolbar to open the folder list. You will now see two complete folder lists—one for you and one for your associate (you may have to open them). For example, you would see two sets of personal folders (the names of your parent folders will be different, but the Calendar, Contacts, Inbox, and so on will be the same).

Note: *If you open an Exchange Server folder, you will see the Other User's Folder dialog box. There, you can enter the name of the owner (you can use the Exchange Global Address List by clicking the Name button) and, in the Folder drop-down list, you can choose the folder you want to go to. Upon clicking OK, you'll go straight to the folder you chose. (To open someone's folder in the Exchange Server, you must have been given permission, which the owner can do by selecting Tools | Options and clicking the Delegates tab.)*

Open the two Calendars in two different windows to see them side by side and to prove that they are different, as shown in Figure 7-5.

5. Given that you have already set up the meeting in your Calendar, right-click and drag it to the other Calendar, and click Copy in the context menu that appears.

Note: *You can also directly enter, move, or delete appointments, events, or meetings in an associate's Calendar; you can do anything you can do in your own Calendar, as long as your associate has shared the folder, parent folder, or drive containing the file.*

6. When you are done working with your associate's Calendar, right-click on the parent folder (Personal Folders), choose Close Personal Folder from the context menu, and the folder will disappear.

The Outlook Calendar

The Outlook Calendar is the successor to Schedule+. The Calendar provides both individual and group scheduling and allows you to enter and maintain tasks that are kept in Outlook Tasks. The Calendar lets you do the following:

- Schedule appointments and meetings and track events and holidays
- Look at what you've scheduled for one day, one week, or one month, in two time zones
- Quickly move from one date to another, both for observation and to reschedule an activity
- Plan meetings by looking at times when others can attend; send out meeting requests, and look at the list of attendees who have responded
- Schedule meetings online with video, audio, or chat capabilities
- Establish activities that recur every day, week, month, or year for a fixed or open-ended time
- Publish your free/busy schedule, be alerted when you receive a meeting request, be notified when you have an overlap, and automatically display meetings that you are requested to attend
- Show national and religious holidays, and control the work hours in a day, what days are work days, and when the year starts
- Save your calendar in HTML format so that others can see what your time commitments are; with their permission, view the calendars of others so you can see what their free/busy time is

The default Outlook Calendar pane, shown in the following illustration, has three major areas:

- The daily schedule on the left, with the times listed
- The Date Navigator in the upper right
- The TaskPad in the lower right

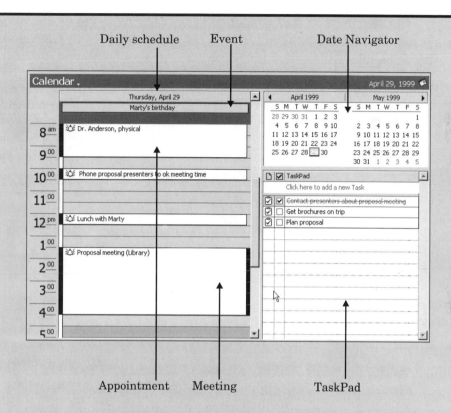

Daily schedule　　Event　　Date Navigator

Appointment　　Meeting　　TaskPad

The default view is the Day/Week/Month view, which shows the current day, one day at a time. The daily schedule shows events like birthdays and holidays at the top and appointments, meetings, and other activities in minimum half-hour increments down the schedule. The Date Navigator gives you one to six months (depending on the width of the daily schedule and the length of the Date Navigator) in which you can open any date by clicking it. The TaskPad lists current open, late, and past-due tasks of your own or that someone else has given or owes you. Outlook provides many alternatives to this view.

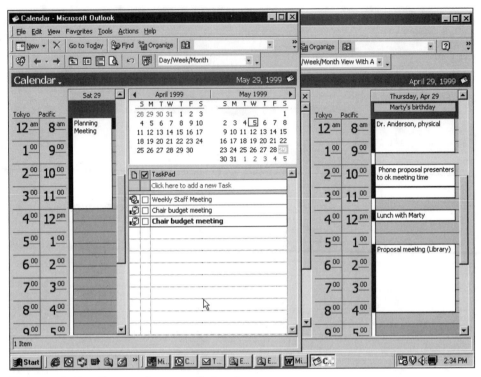

Figure 7-5 Comparing two Calendars

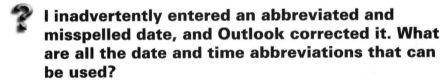

I inadvertently entered an abbreviated and misspelled date, and Outlook corrected it. What are all the date and time abbreviations that can be used?

The Outlook Calendar has a feature called AutoDate, which allows you to enter dates and times as text and convert that text to numeric dates and times. For example, you can enter **next tue** and be given next Tuesday's date, or you can enter **sep ninth** and see that date. You can enter this in any date or time field in Outlook, such as the Go To Date dialog box reached from the View | Go To menu, or the Start and End date and time fields in the appointment and event forms and the Actions | Plan A Meeting dialog box. Following are some of the things you can do:

- Abbreviate months and days (for example, *Dec* or *fri*).

- Ignore capitalization and other punctuation (for example, *wednesday*, *april*, and *lincolns birthday*).

- Use words that indicate dates and times (for example, *tomorrow*, *yesterday*, *today*, *now*, *next week*, *last month*, *five days ago*, *in three months*, *this Saturday*, and *two weeks from now*). Words you can use include *after*, *ago*, *before*, *beforehand*, *beginning*, *end*, *ending*, *following*, *for*, *from*, *last*, *next*, *now*, *previous*, *start*, *that*, *this*, *through*, *till*, *tomorrow*, and *until*.

- Spell out specific dates and times (for example, *August ninth*, *first of December*, *April 19th*, *midnight*, *noon*, *two twenty pm*, and *five o'clock a.m.*).

- Indicate holidays that fall on the same date every year (for example, *New Year's Eve*, *New Year's Day*, *Lincoln's Birthday*, *Valentine's Day*, *Washington's Birthday*, *St. Patrick's Day*, *Cinco de Mayo*, *Independence Day*, *Halloween*, *Veterans Day*, *Christmas Eve*, *Christmas Day*, and *Boxing Day*).

My Calendar doesn't display holidays. Do I have to manually add them?

You don't have to type each holiday into your Calendar, but you do have to select which holidays you want and tell Outlook to add them.

Note: *When you start Outlook for the first time, the Office Assistant's Welcome To MS Outlook "helper" dialog box has an option to Add Holidays To Your Calendar.*

If you have already run Outlook, then set up the holidays you want displayed with the following steps:

1. From the Outlook window, select Tools | Options; and, on the Preferences tab, click Calendar Options. The Calendar Options dialog box will open.

2. Click Add Holidays; select your country; if desired, select one of the religious sets of holidays (Christian, Jewish, or Islamic); and then click OK. You'll see a message that the holidays are being imported.

3. Click OK to close the Calendar Options dialog box and OK again to close the Options dialog box. Open your Calendar and you'll see that the holidays you chose have been added to your Calendar as events.

Note: *Once you have added holidays to your Calendar, they can be edited, moved, and deleted like any other event.*

When I am entering appointments directly in the Calendar instead of in an appointment form, it seems like sometimes I can enter text and sometimes drag the appointment, but I am not sure when. How does this work?

When directly working on the Calendar, you can either work "inside" the time slot to enter and edit the description directly, or you can work "outside" the time slot to change the time span and the start time, move the activity by dragging, or change some of the options through the context menu. When you click a time slot, you are able to enter and edit data directly. To move "outside" the time slot, you must press ENTER or click another time slot. To size or move an appointment (or meeting or event), drag the time slot or its border without first clicking the time slot.

I am currently using ACT! as my personal information manager. I would like to import ACT! data into Outlook but can't find a way to do that. Is there a way?

Yes, there is. Some personal information manager (PIM) import/export options include Schedule+ 1.0 and 7.0, Tab and Comma Separated values (DOS and Windows), dBASE,

FoxPro, Access, Excel, ACT!, ECCO, Lotus Organizer, SideKick, and Personal Address Book. To import the items using the CD-ROM, follow these steps:

1. Choose File | Import And Export.

2. Select Import From Another Program Or File from the list of options on the Import And Export Wizard dialog box. Click Next

3. Click the ACT! version you want to import in the Import A File dialog box. Click Next.

4. If you do not have the Import/Export programs installed, you will be asked if you want to install them now. If some of the programs are not available on your hard disk, you will be instructed to insert your Office 2000 CD. When you do this, click OK.

5. Follow the rest of the instructions presented by the Import And Export Wizard to install and convert the file.

Tip: *From ACT! (or other PIMs) you can export a comma- or tab-separated values file that can be read into Outlook without the CD.*

 I like using the Outlook Calendar, but I am used to carrying a Day-Timer for reference and making notes. Is there a way to print the Calendar in a pocket format?

Yes. Outlook includes a number of printed formats that fit the various sizes of binders made by several companies for such a purpose. Look at the printing options with the following steps:

1. With the Outlook Calendar open, select the day, week, or month that you want to print. (You don't have to do this first, since you can select the period in the Print dialog box, but selecting it prior to printing allows you to see on screen what will print.)

2. Open the File menu and choose Print. The Print dialog box opens.

3. The first decision is choosing which print style you want to use in the Print Style area, shown here:

Click the one you want (but try the others to see what they are like).

4. Click Page Setup to open the dialog box for the style you chose. Click Print Preview to see the default of all the options. Click the Page Setup button to return to Page Setup.

5. Make the changes that you want in the Options and Fonts areas and then click the Paper tab. This tab, as you can see in Figure 7-6, allows you to select the type of paper or form you are using in your printer, as well as the size and type of the page you want printed on the paper.

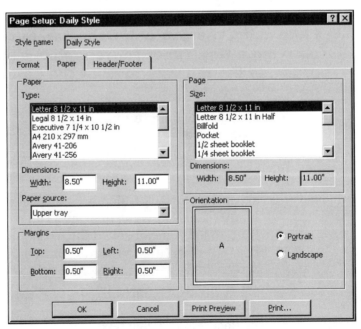

Figure 7-6   The Paper tab in the Page Setup dialog box

6. Make the choices that are correct for you, and then click the Header/Footer tab to see its defaults. Make any necessary changes.

7. Click Print Preview to see your results. If they are acceptable, click Print to return to the Print dialog box, and click OK to print.

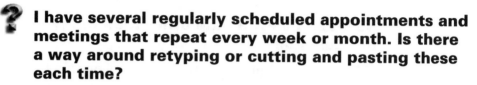

I have several regularly scheduled appointments and meetings that repeat every week or month. Is there a way around retyping or cutting and pasting these each time?

 You bet. You can define any appointment, meeting, or event to be recurring either when you create the Calendar item or when you edit it by clicking the Recurrence toolbar button or by choosing Recurrence in the Actions menu. This opens the Recurrence dialog box, which you can see in Figure 7-7. Here you can set the recurrence pattern and when the recurrence should end.

Note: *Setting up appointments and events as recurring can save you a lot of time re-entering activities, but it can also generate a lot of entries, which may unnecessarily fill your Calendar.*

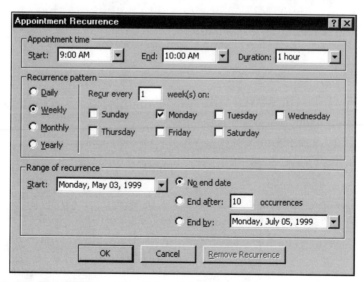

Figure 7-7   The Recurrence dialog box

❓ I know about recurring appointments, but how can I repeat an appointment just a few times?

You can copy an activity by right-clicking and dragging it to where you want the copy, and then selecting Copy from the context menu that appears when you release the right mouse button.

❓ How can I view a date other than today's in the Calendar?

This is the function of the Date Navigator in the upper-right section of the Outlook Calendar. You can click a date to see that date, you can click a week to see it, or you can drag across several days to see them. There are also ways to scroll the months in the Date Navigator to display different ones. See the sidebar "Using the Date Navigator" for the details.

Using the Date Navigator

The Date Navigator, in the upper-right corner of the Calendar window (and shown next), allows you to pick any date from April 1, 1601, to August 31, 4500 (Microsoft wanted to make sure that Outlook had staying power!). To cover this span of over 2,800 years, Outlook provides a number of tools with the Date Navigator to perform the following functions:

- Show details for a day in one of the months displayed in the Date Navigator, by clicking the day.

- Show details for a day with activity in one of the months displayed in the Date Navigator, by clicking a day that appears in boldface.

- Show details for several days in the months displayed in the Date Navigator, by holding down CTRL while clicking the days, or by dragging across the days if they are contiguous.

- Show details for a week in one of the months displayed in the Date Navigator, by clicking to the left of the first day of the week.

● Show details for several weeks in the months displayed in the Date Navigator, by holding down CTRL while clicking the weeks to highlight them, as shown next, or by dragging across the weeks if they are contiguous.

◄	April 1999							May 1999					►
S	M	T	W	T	F	S	S	M	T	W	T	F	S
28	29	30	31	1	2	3							1
4	5	6	7	8	9	10	2	3	4	5	6	7	8
11	12	13	14	15	16	17	9	10	11	12	13	14	15
18	19	20	21	22	23	24	16	17	18	19	20	21	22
25	26	27	28	29	30		23	24	25	26	27	28	29
							30	31	1	2	3	4	5

● Show details for one of the months displayed in the Date Navigator, by dragging across all the weeks of the month.

● Move an activity currently displayed to another date, by dragging the activity to that date in the Date Navigator.

● Make a small change to which months are displayed in the Date Navigator, by clicking the left and right arrows in the month bar.

● Make a large change to which months are displayed in the Date Navigator, by first clicking a month's name (or bar), as shown here, and then dragging up or down the list:

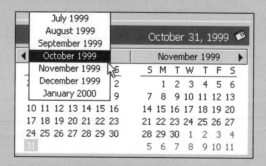

If you drag the mouse either above or below the list, the list will scroll.

● Make direct and possibly large changes in the date displayed, by choosing View | Go To Date or by pressing CTRL-G.

 I do a lot of business in Japan and would like to see their time zone, as well. Is there a way to view different time zones?

Sure. To look at two times zones at the same time, use the following steps:

1. Select Outlook Tools | Options; and, on the Preferences tab, click Calendar Options.

2. Click Time Zone. The Time Zone dialog box will open.

3. Select and label both your time zone and the additional one, as shown next.

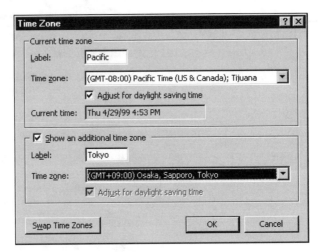

4. Click OK three times to close the Time Zone and both Options dialog boxes. The two time zones will appear in your daily schedule:

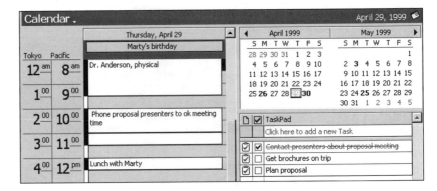

ENTERING AND MAINTAINING CONTACTS

Outlook Address Book versus Contacts—what's the difference? Aren't they one and the same?

If you open the Outlook Address Book, you'll see the message No Entries In This Address Book. The reason is that the Outlook Address Book is a parent folder for Contacts, so Contacts is where you have to look for the addresses in the Outlook Address Book. This allows you to get addresses from additional folders of contacts, if you wish to divide your contacts into several folders to make them easier to find. In the illustration in the preceding sidebar, you can see how several folders are used within the Contacts folders.

I know I can look up an e-mail address in my Contacts address book, but isn't there a more direct way to address e-mail from Contacts?

Yes, you can use the New Message button in the toolbar by following these steps:

1. With the Contacts folder showing, select the contact by clicking the name.

2. Right-click the name, and select New Message To Contact or click the New Message To Contact button in the toolbar. A new message window opens with your contact's e-mail address in the To text box.

3. Fill in the remainder of the message form, and click Send.

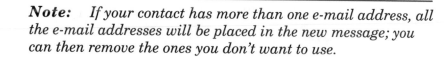

Note: *If your contact has more than one e-mail address, all the e-mail addresses will be placed in the new message; you can then remove the ones you don't want to use.*

Many of the Contacts fields are not displayed in a Contact form. How can I see and edit all the fields in a Contacts record?

The Contact window, displayed when you are viewing a contact's data, can display all the fields. Select the All Fields tab and then select All Contact Fields from the Select From drop-down list.

Outlook Contacts

Outlook Contacts provides an easy way to enter, access, and maintain a comprehensive list of names, addresses, and phone numbers. It also provides many other features. With Contacts you can accomplish the following:

- Create an e-mail distribution list consisting of contacts from several folders
- Track all activities connected to a contact, such as e-mail, tasks, journal entries, documents, and appointments
- Enter a full name and have Outlook divide or parse it into first name, middle name, and last name
- Enter a full address and have Outlook parse it into street, city, state, postal code, and country
- Enter a phone number and have Outlook format it into area code, phone number, and extension (in the United States) or other formats (for other countries)
- File contacts under name, company name, or separate entries that make them easy to find
- Find and open a contact quickly anywhere in Outlook
- Maintain 15 or more phone numbers and up to three mailing addresses and three e-mail addresses for each contact
- Quickly dial a contact's phone number, send a letter to a contact's address, or view a contact's web site
- View a map of a contact's address anywhere in the United States
- Send e-mail to, set up an appointment with, assign a task to, or maintain a journal of activities with a contact
- Use your contact list as your e-mail address book, and create a mailing list that can be filtered for mail merges
- Make use of vCards, allowing you to create and send them with your e-mail messages, and to import and store vCards from others
- Create a custom form to gather your own contact information
- Print your contact list in many different formats that can fit the binders of different time management systems

The initial Contacts view is one of address "cards," as shown in here, similar to what you might see if you spread out business cards on a table:

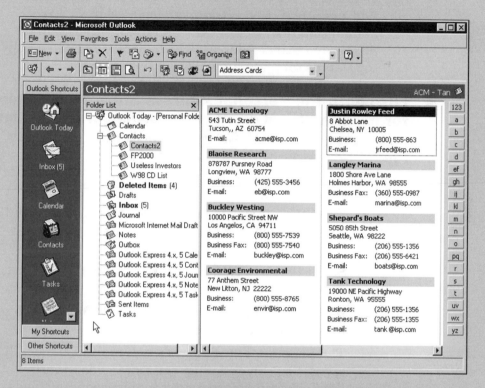

Each card contains a single address, the business and home phone numbers, fax numbers, and e-mail addresses. On the right side of the window is a set of alphabetical buttons; if you click one, you'll be shown the part of the contact list starting with the letter you clicked. You can scroll through the list by using the horizontal scroll bar at the bottom of the window. You can directly edit the information being displayed by double-clicking an entry (this opens the more detailed Contact form). You can also directly use an entry to make a phone call, send e-mail or regular mail, set up meetings, and assign tasks.

> ***Tip:*** *Take particular care in making entries to the File As field. In the built-in views, it is the basis of how the cards are arranged (the sort field). It also allows you to identify an entry any way that makes sense to you, not just by name or company.*

You will see all the Contacts fields. You can enter and edit all but the following fields: Attachment, Modified, Outlook Internal Version, Outlook Version, Read, and Size (which are all automatically set); and Business Address, Business Address Street, Home Address, Home Address Street, Mailing Address, Notes, Other Address, Other Address Street, and Street Address (which are set and edited only in the Details tab).

I use both the Personal Address Book and Contacts for my e-mail and don't see any reason for it. Can I import my Personal Address Book into Contacts, so I need only one address book?

Yes, you can. Here's how:

1. From the Outlook window, select File | Import And Export. Accept the default Import From Another Program Or File, and click Next.

2. Select Personal Address Book from the file-type list, and click Next.

3. Identify the file to be imported, and use Browse to search for it, if needed. Click Next.

4. The Import A File dialog box will indicate what will occur. You can click Map Custom Fields to verify that the fields will be exported into corresponding fields. Click Change Destination to change to a destination other than the Contacts folder. The folder must exist already.

5. Confirm that the action to be taken is to import your Personal Address Book to Contacts, and click Finish. You will see a message showing the import progress. When it is completed, you'll see your Personal Address Book entries in your Contacts folder.

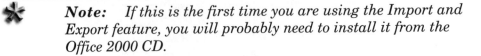

Note: If this is the first time you are using the Import and Export feature, you will probably need to install it from the Office 2000 CD.

 How can I use names in Contacts in a Word mail merge?

Most likely you will not want to create a mail merge of all your contacts, only a selected group of them. To create this subset and begin the Outlook part of the mail merge, follow these steps:

1. With the Contacts folder open, create a view of those contacts to be included in the mail merge. Choose the easiest way to create the view you want. You can use Filter, Group By, Sort from View | Current View | Customize Current View, and you can select the By Category option from the Current View drop-down list box on the toolbar.

2. If you want only certain members of the contacts displayed (for example, only officers in a club or company), have some way that you can identify them during the merge in Word—a special code that Word can use to filter, for example. You can also highlight contacts by clicking them in the Current View while pressing CTRL for a noncontiguous selection. After getting the Current View and the contacts the way you want them, you are ready to begin the mail merge.

3. Select Tools | Mail Merge, and the Mail Merge Contacts dialog box will appear, as shown here:

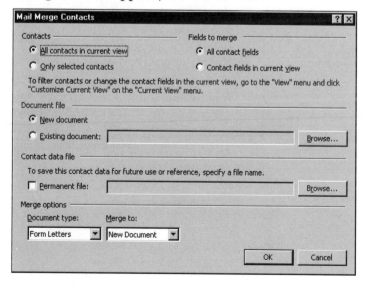

4. Complete the dialog box by making the following choices:

- **Contacts** Include all contacts in the view, or select only some of them. If you have selected some of the current view contacts, only those will be included in the selection. You will also have a chance within Word to filter by some other criteria—which is more appropriate for larger databases.

- **Fields to Merge** Merge all contact fields or only those visible in the view (which helps to reduce the time and space required for transferring all the Contacts fields). If you choose Contact Fields In Current View, make sure that the fields you want to include are displayed in the current view.

- **Document File** Create a new document or use an existing one.

- **Contact Data File** Save the contact merge file to a permanent file so it can be used for another mail merge.

- **Merge Options** Merge to one of several document types or merge to a new document, printer, or e-mail.

5. Click OK to continue. Microsoft Word will be started up and the Mail Merge Helper will appear.

6. At this point, your options on what to do next will vary depending on what documents you have previously prepared. You may have to insert merge fields into a document, or reset requirements, for labels, for example. You may have to create a main document and edit it. Perhaps you will have to get data and edit it, if that has not been done by Outlook. Much of this will be done for you. Refer to Word Help if you have questions on the specific tasks. At some point, your Mail Merge Helper will look like the following and be ready for the actual merge.

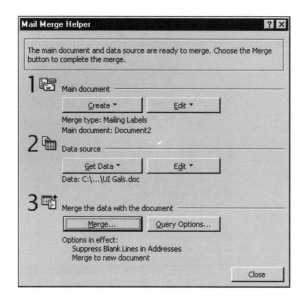

7. Click Merge. A Merge dialog box will appear, in which you can designate whether you want to merge to a new document or an existing one, and specify which records to merge.

8. Click Merge again and the action will take place.

ESTABLISHING AND USING TASKS LISTS

 Can I add a field to Tasks and sort on it?

Yes, here are the steps to create a new field called Order:

1. In the Task window, select View I Current View I Define Views.

2. In the Define Views For "Tasks" dialog box that opens, click Modify, and then click Fields in the View Summary dialog box.

3. Click New Field, type **Order**, and click OK three times; then click Close to create the new field.

4. Type numbers into the new Order field to represent the priority in which you want your tasks arranged. When you are done, click the column heading to arrange tasks in your priority order, as shown here:

		Subject	Due Date	Order
		Click here to add a new Task		
☑	☐	Get pricing for Thompson	Thu 5/20/99	6
☑	☐	Prepare budget for 2000	Wed 6/16/99	5
☑	☐	Get brochures on trip	None	5
☑	☐	Prepare for staff meeting	Mon 5/3/99	4
☑	☐	Plan Fall meeting	Thu 9/23/99	3
☑	☐	Find out about billing error from Enterprise Printing	None	3
☑	☐	Plan proposal	Fri 5/28/99	2
☑	■	Work up numbers for Master Craft	Mon 5/10/99	1
☑	☑	~~Contact presenters about proposal meeting~~	~~Thu 1/29/99~~	~~1~~

Tasks

 Note: *When you add a new field, it is by definition a text field and is sorted and handled as text unless you change the Type of the field. When you put numbers in a text field, the numbers 10 and 11 will sort after 1 instead of after 9. Therefore, you must decide if you want more than nine numbers; and, if so, you must consistently use two-digit numbers (01, 02, and so on).*

Outlook Tasks

Outlook Tasks allows you to create and maintain to-do lists to accomplish the following:

● Establish and track one-time and recurring tasks for yourself

● Send task requests to other individuals and to groups, and track their progress

● Reorder and reassign tasks

● Categorize and prioritize tasks

● Schedule tasks and look at them in the Calendar

● Track percent complete and prepare status reports

The default view of Tasks, and the view that you saw in the Calendar's TaskPad in the preceding question, is the Simple List. It shows you one column for icons, a second for the check box, a subject, and a due date. The first column shows you the type of task; these are described further in the following table:

Button	Description
	Your own normal task
	Your own recurring task
	A task you've assigned to someone else
	A task you've assigned that's been accepted
	A task you've assigned that's been declined
	A task someone has assigned to you

The second column has a completion box to show if the task has been completed or not (a check mark indicates completion). The subject is displayed in one of four styles:

● *Normal type* indicates current tasks with a future due date.
● *Bold type* indicates tasks about which you have unread messages.
● *Colored type* (typically red) indicates past-due tasks.
● *Strike-through type* indicates tasks that are completed.

You can arrange or sort the task list by clicking a field in the heading, clicking once to sort the field one way (descending for dates and times; ascending for all other fields), and clicking again to sort the same field in the opposite direction. You can directly edit the information displayed in the list and you can open the more detailed Task form by double-clicking an entry. You can also prioritize and categorize this list and use it with the Calendar.

It's handy having my task list on the screen with my Calendar, but is there an easy way to create appointments with tasks or create blocks of time to work on the task?

You bet; you can do that by simply dragging a task to the Calendar. This causes an Appointment form to open, allowing you to identify some time you can spend on the task. Also, if you need a meeting to accomplish a task, you can set one up by dragging a task to the Calendar; and, after the Appointment form opens, use the Plan A Meeting dialog box, available from Actions | Plan A Meeting, to schedule a meeting and invite those you want to come.

My boss is in another office, so I often get assignments via e-mail. How can I create tasks directly from e-mail?

You simply drag the e-mail message to the Tasks icon in the Outlook bar. When you do that, a task is created that contains the e-mail message and uses the subject of the message as the task subject. For example, say you get this message:

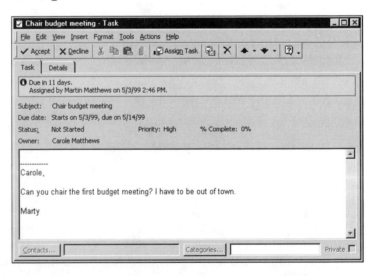

If you close the message and then drag the Inbox entry to the Tasks icon in the Outlook bar, you'll get a Task form automatically created and saved that looks like Figure 7-8. The original e-mail message is copied to the notes part of the

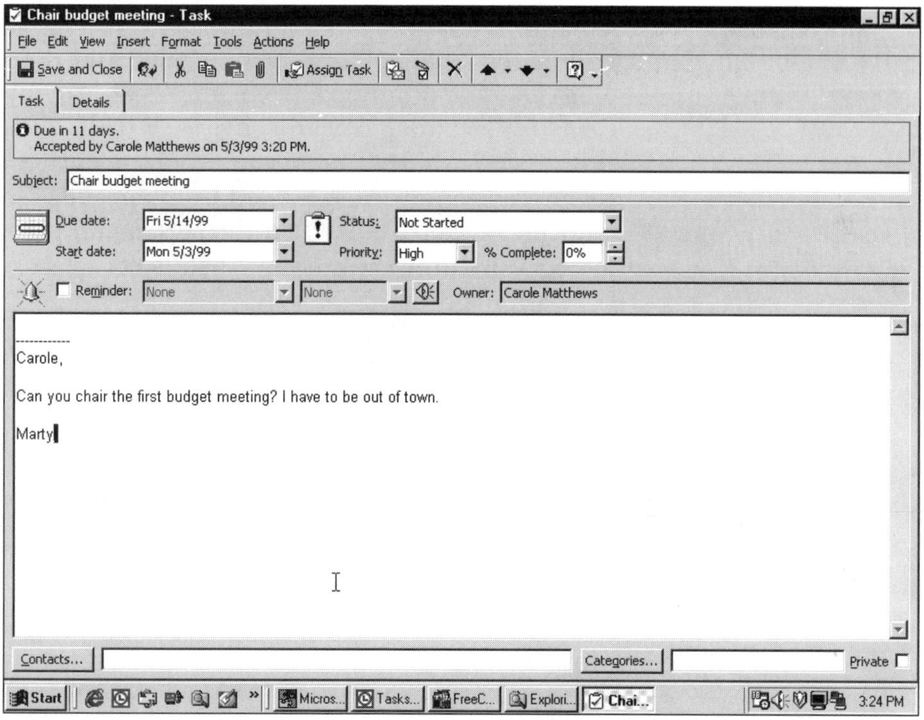

Figure 7-8   Task created from e-mail

task, and the subject is copied to the task subject. The due
date, if not specified, can now be set, as can all the other
parts of a detailed task. When you save and close the Task
form, you'll have a normal entry in your task list tied to the
original e-mail message.

I have several tasks that I have to do every week. How can I make a task a recurring one?

Outlook has an option to make any task you enter a recurring
task on either a periodic basis or upon the completion of the
previous task. In either case, the new task appears when the
previous one is complete. If the recurrence is set for a periodic
basis, after the last occurrence, the new task appears on the
specified day of the week, month, or year. If the recurrence is
based on completion, then after completion of one occurrence,
the new task appears a fixed number of days in the future.
Here's how this works:

1. In the Simple List view of a task list, double-click a task
   you want to recur to open its form.

 Recurrence...

2. Click the Recurrence button in the toolbar. The Task Recurrence dialog box opens, as you can see in Figure 7-9. Note the difference from the Appointment Recurrence dialog box you saw with the Calendar (Figure 7-7). With Tasks, you have the option to regenerate a new task a fixed number of days, weeks, months, or years (based on the setting on the left of the dialog box) after the current task is complete.

● Select the Recurrence Pattern you want: what time period (Daily, Weekly, Monthly, Yearly), when the pattern is to be calculated (Every *x* Week(s) on a selected weekday, or Regenerate New Task *x* Week(s) After Each Task Is Completed).

Tip: *You can enter the dates in words, such as "Two weeks before" or "Next Thursday," rather than a specific date.*

● Select the Range Of Recurrence: when to start and when to end (No End Date, End After *x* Occurrences, or End By *Date*).

3. Click OK.

 Note: *If the task is overdue (the Due Date is prior to today's date), the task will be listed in another color (typically red) in the Task window to highlight the fact that the task is late.*

4. Click Save And Close in the toolbar. Back in the Tasks list, notice that the new task has a different icon.

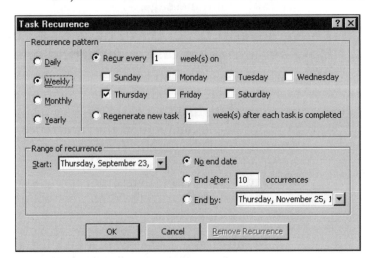

Figure 7-9 The Task Recurrence dialog box

Tip: *If you want to stop a task from recurring, double-click the task to open its form, click the Recurrence button, and click Remove Recurrence.*

I want to send a task to someone else. How can I do that?

Outlook has included the capability to send a task to someone, allow him or her to accept or reject it, and keep a copy of it to track, all within Tasks. Follow these steps:

1. From the open Tasks folder, double-click the task you want to transfer to open it in the Task form. Click the Assign Task toolbar button, and the Task form will change to a combination task form and e-mail form, as you can see in Figure 7-10.

2. Click the To button to open your Address Book, and select the contact you want to send the task to. Make any other appropriate changes, such as the status, the

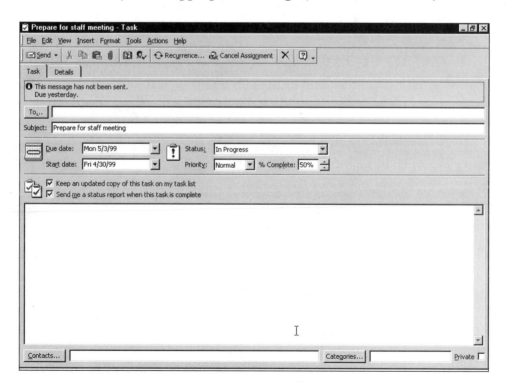

Figure 7-10 Sending a task to someone else

priority, or a note. Click one or both of the two check boxes if appropriate: one keeps the task visible to you in your list, and the other automatically sends you a status report on completion.

Note: *You can set the default for keeping the task visible and automatically sending status reports by selecting Tools | Options | Other tab | Advanced Options | Advanced Tasks.*

3. Click in the text area, and write a note to the recipient, if needed to clarify the task.

4. When you are ready, click Send.

The recipient of the task request will see a message in his or her Inbox that makes it very clear that a task request has been received, as you can see here:

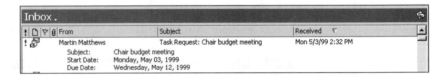

Also, upon receipt of a message request, a task is automatically added to the recipient's task list, even if the message has not been opened. When either the Inbox message or the task is opened, a form like this is displayed:

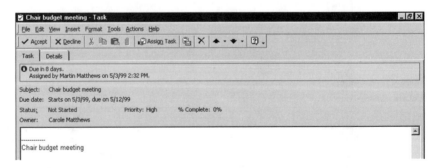

Notice that the toolbar has Accept and Decline buttons. When one is clicked, a message of the decision is automatically sent back to the original sender of the task, a notice that the message is being returned is also sent to the recipient of the

task, and the recipient is given the chance to add a note. Here are examples of such messages:

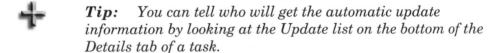

If the task-requesting message is accepted, the ownership of the task goes from the sender to the recipient, and the task becomes a permanent part of the recipient's task list. If the task is declined, the ownership stays with the sender and it is removed from the recipient's task list. Once the recipient has accepted a task, he or she can then change any of the settings, such as the due date and status. When such a change is made (for example, completing the task) and the Send Me A Status Report When This Task Is Complete option has been checked, the originator will be notified of the change with a Task Update message, like this:

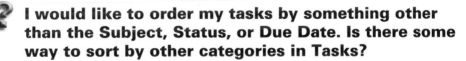

Tip: *You can tell who will get the automatic update information by looking at the Update list on the bottom of the Details tab of a task.*

I would like to order my tasks by something other than the Subject, Status, or Due Date. Is there some way to sort by other categories in Tasks?

Yes, if you select the Detailed List view of Tasks, you can put any information you want in the Categories field, and then use that information to arrange your tasks.

 Note: *You cannot sort by the Categories field, but you can group on Categories, which gives you almost the same results.*

Add categories to your tasks by following these steps:

1. To create new categories in the Category list, right-click a field of a task, choose Categories from the context menu, and click Master Category List. Type the name of the category in the text box at the top and click Add. Add as many categories as you want and click OK.

2. In the Categories dialog box, click a category you want for the current task and click OK. Repeat this last step for each of the tasks in your task list.

3. Select By Category from the Current View drop-down list (if you get a message asking if you want to save the current view settings, answer No), and click the plus button to open each group and see your tasks grouped by category.

Tip: *You can have the groups all expanded (opened) or collapsed (closed) by default by selecting View | Current View | Customize Current View | Group By, and then opening Expand/Collapse Defaults and selecting All Expanded or All Collapsed.*

4. Click the Due Date heading to sort by date within each category, and your categories will each be sorted separately by the dates within the category.

Note: *To manually arrange your tasks, you must first clear all sorting and grouping parameters by clicking Clear All in the Sort and Group By dialog boxes opened from View | Current View | Customize Current View.*

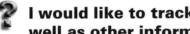**I would like to track the time spent on a task, as well as other information. Is there a way to do that?**

Yes. First, though, you might want to reset the default for the number of hours to use in calculating days and weeks by selecting Tools | Options, clicking the Other tab, and then selecting Advanced Options. Fill in the default for Task Working Hours Per Day (default set as 8) and Task Working Hours Per Week (default set as 40) if it is different than what is currently being used as the default.

After the default is set, you can enter the actual information. The Details tab of the Task form allows you to enter billing, mileage, and contact information, as you can see here:

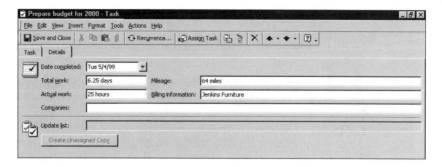

With this information recorded, you can create a custom view to see it for all your tasks, or you can export it to Excel, where it can be summarized.

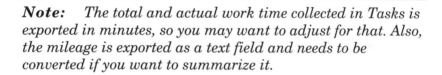

Note: *The total and actual work time collected in Tasks is exported in minutes, so you may want to adjust for that. Also, the mileage is exported as a text field and needs to be converted if you want to summarize it.*

While I'm entering due dates for tasks, I sometimes need to double-check a date. Is there some way to view a calendar while entering due dates for tasks?

Yes, the date can be entered using the AutoDate feature described earlier in the "I inadvertently entered an abbreviated and misspelled date . . ." question in the "Using the Calendar" section of this chapter. For example, you can type **next tue** to get the date for next Tuesday, or you can type **10/23** or **oct 23** for that date. Also, you can click a date field and click its drop-down arrow to open the Date Navigator, which gives you a calendar to look at:

KEEPING A JOURNAL AND MAKING NOTES

 ### In the Journal time line, what does the bar over an activity represent?

The bar above the icon in the Journal window, as shown here, represents the duration or length of time taken by the activity. In other words, it increases in length the longer the activity takes.

 ### How can I control what activities are journalized?

For the most part, Journal entries are created automatically: by sending an e-mail message; by creating an Office document; or by setting up a meeting, making a phone call, or creating a task in Outlook. You can control which activities automatically create Journal entries in two ways: by selecting the type of activities or by selecting the contacts they relate to. Follow these steps:

1. From the Journal window, select Tools | Options and click Journal Options. This opens the Journal Options dialog box, as you can see here:

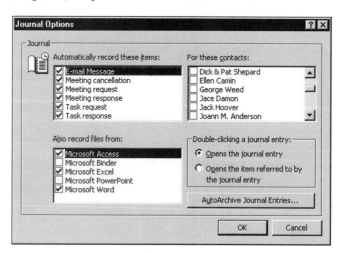

2. In the Automatically Record These Items section, select the Outlook activities that you want Journalized for the contacts that you indicate in the next step.

3. In the For These Contacts section, select the people in your contact list for whom you want to Journalize selected Outlook activities.

4. In the Also Record Files From section, select the Office 2000 documents whose creation and modification you want Journalized.

5. In the Double-Clicking A Journal Entry section, you have two choices: when you double-click a Journal icon (or when you select Open from the File or context menus), either the Journal Entry form or the original document that caused the creation of the Journal entry will open. Select one of these two options. When you are done, click OK twice to close the Journal Options and Options dialog boxes.

Note: *If you choose to open the original document when you double-click a Journal entry icon, you will have no way to open the Journal Entry form for that document. On the other hand, if you choose to open the Journal Entry form for the item, you'll see an icon for a shortcut to the item that will immediately take you to it.*

I like the idea of using Outlook Notes instead of sticking the little yellow paper ones all around my screen; but usually, when I want to write myself a note, Outlook is not running and it is easier to just write myself a paper note. Is there a way to create a note quickly without starting Outlook?

Yes, if you have another note on your screen, you can create a note any time, without having either Outlook or its Notes component open. If you have a note on your screen, just click the icon in the upper-left corner, and choose New Note.

 I had heard that I could drag Journal entries from one category to another to change the category, but this doesn't work. Did I just hear wrong?

No, but you can't do it in the By Category view of Journal entries. You must use the Entry List view and then group by categories. Follow these steps:

1. From the Journal window, open the Current View drop-down list box and choose Entry List. This view shows all of your Journal entries as a list.

2. Add categories to all the Journal entries that you want to categorize by either directly entering the category (double-click the Categories cell in the entry in which you want to add it and type the category name in the Categories text box of the entry Journal form) or by right-clicking the entry, choosing Categories from the context menu, and then selecting a category from a list.

3. When you have finished entering the categories you want, you can quickly look at the activities in each category by clicking the Group By toolbar button and then dragging the Categories column header to the Group By box. Your result should look something like Figure 7-11.

With your Outlook window configured like the one in Figure 7-11, you can quickly add categories to entries by dragging them from the None group to the particular category group you want the entries to have, or you can change categories by dragging entries from one category to another.

 Tip: *You can also group by category by right-clicking the Categories column heading and selecting Group By This Field from the context menu.*

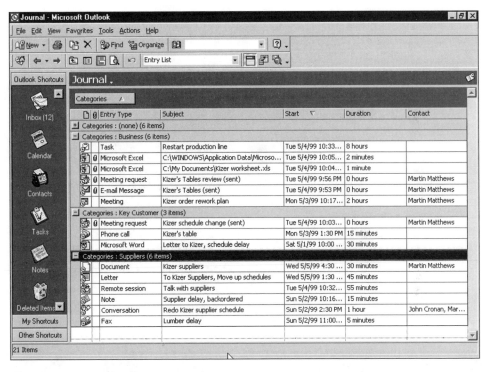

Figure 7-11   List of Journal entries grouped by categories

 I can't seem to sort my Journal entries by contact, and yet I want to view all the Journal entries related to a contact. How can I do that?

You are correct that you cannot sort on Contact or Categories using either the column headers or the Sort dialog box. However, you can use the By Contact or By Category Journal views to group your Journal entries by either Contact or Category. Also, the Contact form includes an Activities tab, in which all the Journal entries for a particular contact are displayed. This window, shown here, not only displays Journal entries

but also allows you to control what is displayed, to sort the display, and to add and delete Journal entries (from the Actions menu).

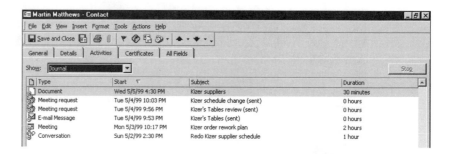

 Note: *If you select Create New Journal Entry When Starting New Call from the New Call dialog box (which is accessed from the AutoDialer button or Actions | Call Contact | New Call), you can time your call and keep notes about it.*

Outlook Notes and Journal

Outlook Notes, a small but useful feature, is a computer version of 3M's Post-it Notes. You can use a note to quickly and briefly capture an idea, a name, a phone number, driving directions, a question, or any other brief note. You can keep several Notes on your screen and look at them as either a listing or as icons in Outlook. You can use Notes of different colors and attach categories to them for easy sorting and grouping

The Outlook Journal is the central collection point for status information, not just within Outlook but for all of Microsoft Office 2000 (see the next illustration). The Journal automatically collects information on a time line about the messages, phone calls, and documents you are handling. In particular, the Journal can be set to automatically collect information about the following:

- E-mail messages sent from or received by Outlook, to or from individuals selected in your contact list

- Meeting requests, responses, and cancellations sent in Outlook to and from selected individuals in your contact list

- Task requests and responses to and from selected individuals in your contact list
- Documents created or revised with Microsoft Access, Excel, Office Binder, PowerPoint, Word, and other compatible programs
- Phone calls, faxes, letters, and other Office 2000 documents sent to and, if electronic, received from, selected individuals in your contact list

You can also manually create Journal entries for conversations or any of the above interactions with others, electronic or otherwise, or just to make a note. The Contact form has a page that displays all of the Journal entries for a particular contact—which can easily be all of the activities with that contact. Additionally, the Journal allows you to accomplish the following:

- Categorize your entries so that they can be grouped on some basis other than those built into Outlook
- Track the time spent on Journal activities, such as writing a report, making or taking a phone call, and holding a meeting
- Look up a document in the Journal based on its creation or revision date when you don't know its filename or subject

The default view of the Outlook Journal window is a time line view of activities by type, as shown here:

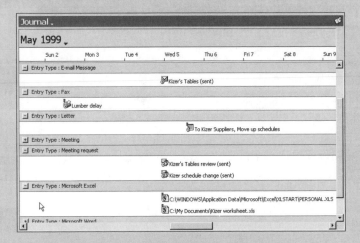

In this view, you have the familiar choice of seeing a day, a week, or a month, similar to your options with the Calendar. The types of activities that can be included in the Journal, their icons, and how they can get there are shown in the following table:

Icon	Activity	How Journalized
	Conversation	Manually entered
	Document	Manually entered
	E-mail	By sending or receiving a message to or from Outlook, or manually entered
	Fax	Manually entered
	Letter	Manually entered
	Meeting	By sending or responding to a meeting request or canceling a meeting, or manually entered
	Note	Manually entered
	Office 2000 application	By opening and closing a file in any Office 2000 application, or entering manually
	Phone call	By placing a call with the AutoDialer, or manually entered
	Remote session	By initiating a remote session from Outlook, or manually entered
	Task	By sending or responding to a task request, or manually entered

Chapter 8

Integrating Office Documents

Answer Topics!

Integrating Office Documents @ a Glance

Office 2000 provides a number of ways in which you can easily combine files created in the various applications. These are detailed in the following sections:

Ways in Which to Integrate Office 2000 Documents explains the ways in which you can integrate Office 2000 documents.

Sharing Files and Folders discusses how to transfer information from one Office application and use it in another.

Pasting, Embedding, and Linking Between Applications shows how to transfer information and maintain a link back to the original application.

Using Binders explains how binders can be used to group information from several applications.

Adding and Modifying Documents Within a Binder describes how to work with documents within a binder.

Working with the Binder File looks at how binders as files themselves are handled.

Sharing Binders covers how to use binders in a group.

WAYS IN WHICH TO INTEGRATE OFFICE 2000 DOCUMENTS

Among the more powerful ways you can integrate Office 2000 documents are

● The merge function between Word and Access, which provides a way to combine an Access database with a Word mail-merge main document to produce large mailings, including printing envelopes and labels.

● A PowerPoint presentation file, which can contain files that have been created in Word and Excel. It can also contain information from Access; however, this information must first be embedded in a Word or Excel document, and then inserted in PowerPoint.

● The cut and paste functions, which can be used to combine information from an Excel worksheet with text and graphics that were created in a Word document in order to produce various documents, such as company reports and newsletters.

● Object Linking and Embedding (OLE), which is used to insert information from a file in one application into a file in a different application. When the information is embedded, the functions of the embedded application can be used to edit it in the destination document. If the embedded data is linked, changes in the original document are automatically updated when displayed in the linked document.

● The Binder application, which is used to combine documents from several applications into one document, such as a large report or a book. These documents can be rearranged or modified within the binder file, and page numbering and common headers and footers can be added.

SHARING FILES AND FOLDERS

 I don't see how to insert an Access report in a PowerPoint presentation. Is there a way to do this?

The best way to display an Access report in PowerPoint is to first send the report to Word. Then import the Word file into PowerPoint. To send the report to Word, do the following:

1. In Access, open the database and preview the report that you want to send to Word.

2. Choose Office Links from the Tools menu.

3. Click Publish It With MS Word. The report is then displayed in a Word document window and is saved as an RTF file in your My Documents folder.

   To insert the report in a PowerPoint presentation, follow these steps:

1. Create or open the PowerPoint file into which you want to insert the report.

2. Choose Object from the Insert menu.

3. Click Create From File.

4. Click Browse and then click My Documents on the Shortcut bar to the left of the Browse dialog box. If the Word document containing the report is in a different folder, locate this folder.

5. Select the filename. Be sure the file you select has a Word file icon in front of it.

6. Click OK to return to the Insert Object dialog box, shown here:

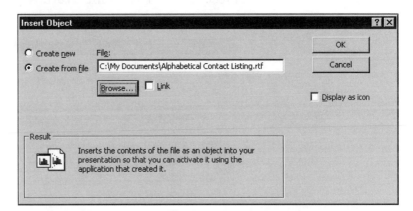

7. If you want any edits that are made in Word to change the display in PowerPoint, click the Link check box to select it. See the question "What are the differences between pasting, linking, and embedding?," later in this chapter.

 Tip: *If you select Display As Icon, an icon will be inserted. In the presentation, you can double-click the icon and the file will be opened in Word.*

8. Click OK to insert the object in PowerPoint, and save the PowerPoint file.

 Note: *You can insert the database file from Access into PowerPoint; however, it will only be displayed as an icon. Then you can double-click the icon to go to Access and preview the report.*

I know how to produce a mail merge output in Word using an Access database, but I work primarily in Access. Is it possible to merge from Access?

Yes, you can do the following to start a mail merge from Access.

1. Open the table in Access from which you want to start the merge. You cannot start this procedure from Form view or Design view.

2. Choose Office Links from the Tools menu.

3. Select Merge It With MS Word to go to the Mail Merge Wizard shown here:

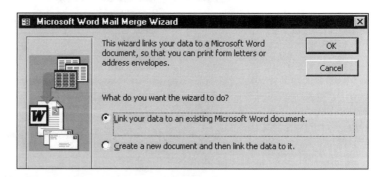

4. Select one of the following and then click OK.

● **Link Your Data To An Existing Microsoft Word Document** If you select this option, choose the existing main document from the Select Microsoft Word Document dialog box. The field names must match in both documents. Skip the following steps and perform the merge from Word in the usual way. See Chapter 3 for more specific information about this.

● **Create A New Document And Then Link The Data To It** This will open a new Word mail merge document. If you select this option, continue with the rest of the steps.

5. Click Insert Merge Field on the Mail Merge toolbar, and select the fields to be inserted at specific locations, as shown here. Type text and insert graphics as appropriate.

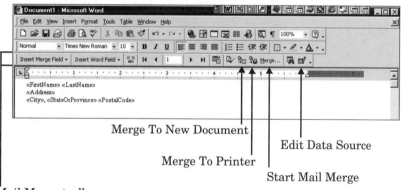

Merge To New Document

Merge To Printer

Edit Data Source

Start Mail Merge

Mail Merge toolbar

6. Save the main document and perform the merge. You can choose from the following on the Mail Merge toolbar:

● **Merge To New Document** Display the output in a new document window.

● **Merge To Printer** Send the output directly to the printer.

● **Start Mail Merge** Select only specific records to merge or sort the records to be merged.

 Note: *To go to the database, click Edit Data Source on the Word main document Mail Merge toolbar. To return to the main document in Word, click the Word filename in the Taskbar. If you open this main document again and click Edit Data Source, the database table name will be displayed in the Taskbar where you can click it to display the table.*

 I have an existing main document in Word, and I want to use an Access database with it in a merge, but the field names are different in each application. Can I merge when the field names are different in Access and Word?

Yes, but the field names in the main document should be changed to match those in the database, and that can easily be done. Open the main document and attach the database table using the Mail Merge Helper in Word. Then click the View Merged Data button and make the necessary changes. To do this, follow these steps:

1. Open the existing main document.

2. From the Tools menu, choose Mail Merge and click Get Data.

3. Select Open Data Source. The Open Data Source dialog box is displayed.

4. Select MS Access Databases in the Files Of Type box to display the filenames of the databases, as shown in Figure 8-1.

5. Select the database containing the table you want.

6. Click Open to see the Microsoft Access dialog box.

7. Select the table and click OK.

 8. Click Close in the Mail Merge Helper dialog box, and click the View Merged Data button. The Invalid Merge Field dialog box will be displayed. See Figure 8-2.

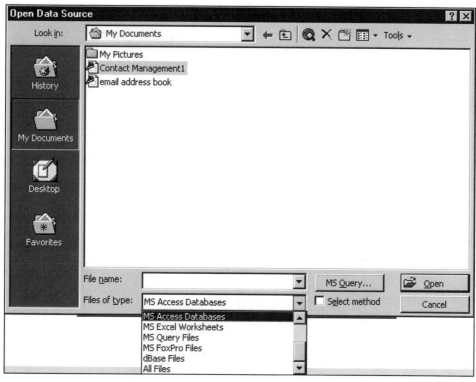

Figure 8-1   The Open Data Source dialog box

9. Click the down arrow in the list box containing the field names in the database, and select the appropriate name to replace the invalid name in the main document. Your other option is to remove the invalid field from the main document by clicking Remove Field.

10. Click OK, and repeat step 9 as needed. Then perform the merge.

This procedure will change the fields in the main word document, so when you try to merge it with the original Word data file, you will have to use this same procedure to perform the merge. It probably would be a good idea to save the updated main document (with the merge fields from the database table) with a different name than the original main document.

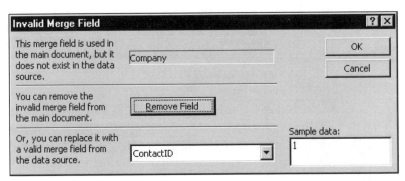

Figure 8-2 Invalid Merge Field dialog box

 Note: Other types of files that can be opened and used in a Word Mail Merge are address books containing Internet mail addresses such as Outlook Contacts, files saved in Rich Text format, or Text format, MS Excel worksheets, MS Query files, dBASE files, and MS FoxPro files.

See Chapter 3 for more specific information about performing a mail merge in Word.

PASTING, EMBEDDING, AND LINKING BETWEEN APPLICATIONS

 What are the differences between pasting, linking, and embedding?

Pasting, linking, and embedding are three ways in which you can transfer information from one application to another. Also, they are related in that you begin in the originating application by copying or cutting the information to be transferred. They differ only in how the information is handled in the receiving application.

Pasting inserts a copy of the information into another location in the same document, into another document in the same application, or into another document in another application. In any of these cases, a copy of the information becomes an integral part of the new document and it is edited in the receiving application. Pasting is accomplished by selecting the information, cutting or copying it (depending on whether you want to move or copy it) to the Clipboard, and pasting it into its destination. For example, if you paste a range of Excel cells into Word, the data is inserted as a Word table and is edited using the Word table functions.

Linking creates a link to information created in one location from another location in the same document, from another document in the same application, or from another document in another application. In any of these cases, the information stays a part of its original document and is edited in the original application. Any change made to either the original document or the link is reflected in both areas. There are two ways to create a link:

● After copying the information to the Clipboard, select Paste Special in the receiving document's Edit menu, and check the Paste Link option in the Paste Special dialog box, as shown in Figure 8-3.

● Without originally copying the information, select Object in the receiving document's Insert menu, select the Create From File tab, enter the filename or browse to find it, and check the Link To File option in the Object dialog box (see Figure 8-4).

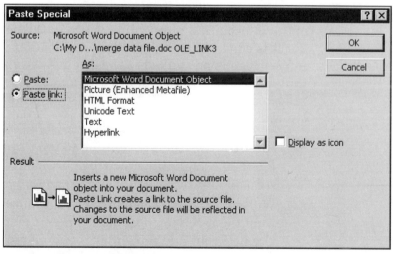

Figure 8-3 The Paste Special dialog box

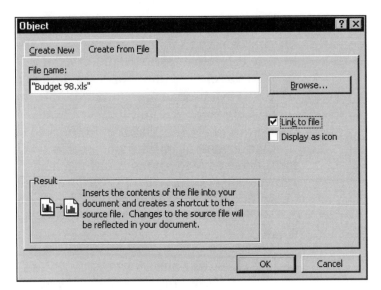

Figure 8-4 The Object dialog box

 Tip: *If the Paste Special option is not showing, click the down arrows in the Edit menu to show additional options or double-click the menu heading.*

Embedding places a copy of information created in one location into another location in the same document, in another document in the same application, or in another document in another application. In any of these cases, a copy of the information physically resides in the new document, but it is edited in the originating application. Also, the information is not linked to the original document, meaning that any changes made in the original document will not be reflected in the embedded object. As with linking, there are two ways to do this:

- After copying the information to the Clipboard, select Paste Special in the receiving document's Edit menu without checking the Paste Link option.

- Without originally copying the information, select Object from the receiving document's Insert menu, select the Create From File tab, enter the filename or browse to find it, and don't check Link To File.

What are the advantages of using embedding rather than linking?

Use embedding without linking if it is not essential that the current data in the original document be available when you work on the embedded information. This allows the document containing the embedded object to be moved to another computer, where edits can be made if that computer has the same application that was used to create the original object. Embedding without linking is useful if you frequently want to take a document home to work on it or to give it to another person to edit or use in some way.

When I selected and copied an item and then clicked the Paste button on the toolbar, I saw a small window labeled Clipboard that showed the item I had copied. I clicked the item and closed the window, but I didn't see the window again. What happened, and how can I display the icons for items in the Clipboard again?

You actually displayed the Clipboard toolbar, which is a new feature in Office 2000. To see it again, right-click any toolbar in Word, Access, Excel, or PowerPoint, and select Clipboard. Or you can choose Toolbars from the View menu and select Clipboard.

The Clipboard toolbar, as shown here, displays icons of the most recent items that have been cut or copied. Up to 12 objects can be placed on the Clipboard and pasted from there.

 It seems fairly easy to link objects in Excel or Word, but I am unable to use these steps to embed tables or text in Access. How do I do this?

You first have to format a field in an Access table as an OLE Object field. Then you can choose Object from the Insert menu in Access to link to an Excel or Word document. An example of this is when a company logo created in Word is used in an Access form or report. If changes are made to the original logo in Word, they are reflected in the Access form or report.

 Note: *Also refer to Chapter 6 for information about exporting and importing Access files.*

To format a field in Access as an OLE object field so that you can insert a linked object into that field, follow these steps:

1. Open the Access table to which you want to link an Excel or Word object in Design view. To do this, open the table, click the View button on the toolbar, and select Design view (or create a new table in Design view).

2. Move to the field that you want to format as an OLE object field. Type a field name and press TAB to go to the Data Type column. Click the down arrow to display the list of choices, and select OLE Object, as shown in Figure 8-5.

3. Close Design view; name and save the table, if necessary; and open the table in Datasheet view.

4. Move to the field that has been formatted as an OLE Object field, and choose Object from the Insert menu to display the Insert Object dialog box.

5. Select Create From File, type or browse for the filename, and select the Link option:

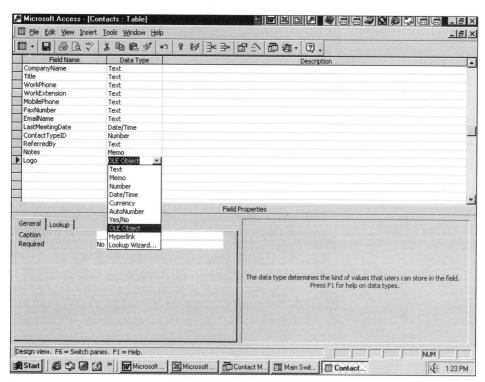

You may also select Display As Icon, if you wish.
Click OK.

Figure 8-5   Design view in an Access table

 Note: *If you choose Display As Icon, this will display an icon rather than the actual text or table when viewed in Form view. If you don't select it, the actual text, table, or other object will be displayed when you are in Form view. When you are in Datasheet view, only the name of the type of file being embedded will be displayed.*

 I selected and copied a range of cells in Excel and pasted it into a Word document; however, the information was inserted as a Word table, not as an Excel worksheet. Isn't it possible to actually paste an Excel worksheet into Word that is not formatted as a Word table?

Yes. If you choose Paste Special from the Edit menu (rather than just Paste) and select Microsoft Excel Worksheet Object, the data will be inserted in the Word document as an Excel object. You can then double-click it to display the Excel toolbars and work on the data in Word using the Excel functions.

To copy data from an Excel worksheet to a Word document using Paste Special, do the following:

1. Open the worksheet in Excel, select the range of cells to be copied, and click the Copy button on the toolbar or choose Copy from the Edit menu to copy the range to the Clipboard.

2. Open the Word document.

3. Move the insertion point to the place where you want to insert the data.

4. Choose Paste Special from the Edit menu. The Paste Special dialog box is displayed, as shown next:

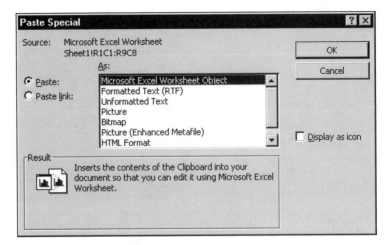

5. Select the Paste radio button, then be sure to select Microsoft Excel Worksheet Object, and click OK. The worksheet will be inserted in the Word document. When you click the object, handles will be displayed and you can work with it as you might work with other objects, such as pictures, WordArt, or AutoShapes.

 Note: *If you select HTML format, the selection that is inserted is in a Word format only, and you will not be able to double-click it to edit it in Excel.*

6. To use Excel to edit the embedded object, double-click it. The Excel toolbars are displayed, as you can see here, giving you all the capabilities you would have in Excel itself. If you chose to link the embedded object when using Paste Special, you will open the worksheet in Excel. However, if you did not link the object, the worksheet will remain in Word, but the Excel toolbars will be available to use when you edit it.

Excel menus

Excel toolbars

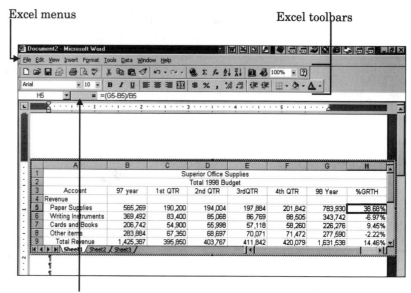

Excel formula bar

7. When you have finished editing the Excel object, click anywhere outside the table to close the Excel menus and toolbars and return to Word.

When you use Paste Special, the embedded object is not necessarily linked to the original Excel worksheet (although it can be). If the Paste Link option is not selected, changes made to the worksheet in Excel will not be reflected in the worksheet in Word.

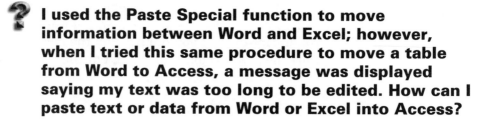

I used the Paste Special function to move information between Word and Excel; however, when I tried this same procedure to move a table from Word to Access, a message was displayed saying my text was too long to be edited. How can I paste text or data from Word or Excel into Access?

Use Paste Append in Access rather than Paste Special. The following steps show how to do this.

1. In either Word or Excel, select the text or table, and click the Copy button on the toolbar or choose Copy from the Edit menu to copy the selection to the Clipboard.

2. Open the Access table and move the insertion point to where you want to insert the selected block.

3. Choose Paste Append, rather than Paste Special, from the Edit menu in Access. When you do this, a message will be displayed telling you that you are about to paste a number of records and asking if you are sure you want to do it. Click Yes. The selected text will be inserted.

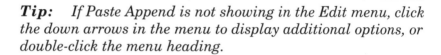

Tip: *If Paste Append is not showing in the Edit menu, click the down arrows in the menu to display additional options, or double-click the menu heading.*

This text is not linked to the original text in either Word or Excel; therefore, any edits will not be automatically applied to the text copied to an Access table. For information about linking text in Access, see the earlier question in this section that begins "It seems fairly easy to link objects in Excel or Word, but I am unable to use these steps to embed tables or test in Access . . ."

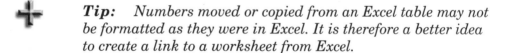

Tip: *Numbers moved or copied from an Excel table may not be formatted as they were in Excel. It is therefore a better idea to create a link to a worksheet from Excel.*

Can I resize or crop an object?

Yes, you can do both. Resizing changes the overall size of the object without changing the amount of data, text, or image contained in it. Cropping actually cuts some of the data, text, or image from what is displayed.

- To resize an object, select the object to display the sizing handles, and then point to any of the handles and drag it to a different size. To resize the object more precisely, right-click the object and choose Format Object from the context menu. Click the Size tab and change its Height and Width, or Scaling values.

● To crop the object, select the object and display the Picture toolbar. To do this, right-click any toolbar and select Picture, or choose Toolbars from the View menu and select Picture. Then click Crop, as shown next, and position the Crop mark on any of the handles to drag it to a different position.

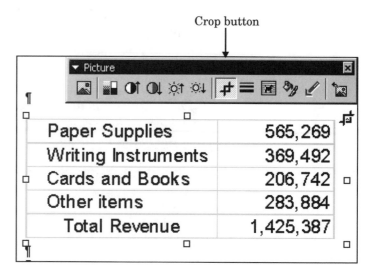

Crop button

Paper Supplies	565,269
Writing Instruments	369,492
Cards and Books	206,742
Other items	283,884
Total Revenue	1,425,387

There are times when I do not want Excel data that is linked in a Word document to be changed, even though I have changed the data in Excel. Can I update linked data in Word if I need to do this later?

Yes, the default setting for linked data is to automatically update the information; however, you can change this so that you can control when the data is updated. To turn off the automatic update option, do the following:

1. In Word, select the linked object and choose Links from the Edit menu to display the Links dialog box shown in Figure 8-6.

2. Select Manual for the type of update, and click OK. Now any changes made in the original document will not be displayed in the linked object unless you manually update it.

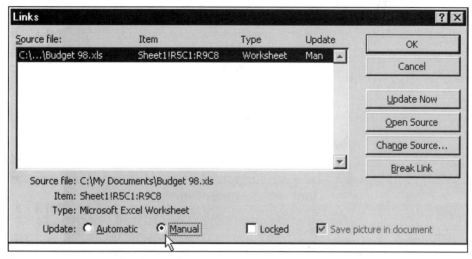

Figure 8-6 The Links dialog box

To manually update the object, select it in the destination document, choose Links from the Edit menu, and click the Update Now button in the Links dialog box. Any changes that have been made in the original document will now be reflected in the linked object.

 Tip: *The Break Link button in the Links dialog box will remove the link from the object. If you want to reestablish the link, delete the object and reinsert it.*

USING BINDERS

I know that either the Binder or the Briefcase can store files from various Office applications. Why should I create a binder when I can store all the files I want to work with in the Briefcase?

A binder is used to combine files that you want to group together, such as a company report or a project. The following features make it easy to combine files in the Binder.

- The files—each in a separate section—can be arranged in the order in which you want to present them, and the page numbering will be consecutive throughout the binder when it is printed. The page numbering that is used in the binder does not change the original page numbering in each individual document when it is opened in its own application.

- You can create headers and footers that apply to the entire binder and will be printed on each page in every section. Or you can have different headers and footers for each document in the binder.

- You can rearrange the order of the files by simply dragging the icon that represents each section or file to a different position. See Figure 8-7.

- These documents can be opened and edited; however, they are usually inserted in a binder after they are completed in their own application.

 I want to change a Binder template, but I don't see how I can open the template. How do I do this?

You need to know where the Binder templates are located in order to open one. To do this, right-click the Office Shortcut bar, select Customize, and click the Settings tab, as shown here:

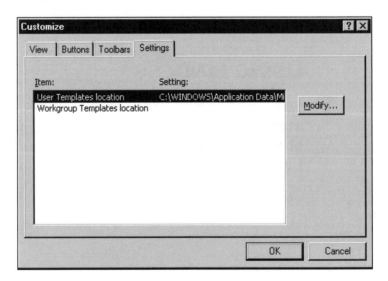

Section icon

Show/Hide Left Pane button

	A	B	C	D	E	F	G	H
1				Superior Office Supplies				
2				Total 1998 Budget				
3	Account	97 year	1st QTR	2nd QTR	3rdQTR	4th QTR	98 Year	%GRTH
4	Revenue							
5	Paper Supplies	565,269	190,200	194,004	197,884	201,842	783,930	38.68%
6	Writing Instruments	369,492	83,400	85,068	86,769	88,505	343,742	-6.97%
7	Cards and Books	206,742	54,900	55,998	57,118	58,260	226,276	9.45%
8	Other items	283,884	67,350	68,697	70,071	71,472	277,590	-2.22%
9	Total Revenue	1,425,387	395,850	403,767	411,842	420,079	1,631,538	14.46%

Left pane

Figure 8-7   A Binder window

Tip: To display the Office Shortcut bar, click Start on
the Taskbar, choose Programs | Microsoft Office Tools |
Microsoft, and click Office Shortcut Bar.

Usually, the Binder templates will be in C:\Windows\
Application Data\Microsoft\Templates; however, they
may be in a username folder, if you have one.

 Note: You will not see the Blank Binder template in the Templates folder. The Blank Binder is a template, but it is called an NFT file (non-file-based template). There is not a physical .obt file for it and it exists within the Binder itself. If you want to change the Blank Binder, you will have to create a new binder template and name it Blank Binder. Then move it to the templates folder where it will be used as the default Blank Binder template.

Once you know where the templates are located, do the following to open and edit:

1. Start the Binder application by clicking Start on the Taskbar and choosing Programs | Microsoft Office Tools | Microsoft Binder, and then choosing Open Binder from the File menu.

2. In the Open Binder dialog box, click the down arrow in the Look In box and locate the folder containing your template, as shown here:

 Tip: If your template is not displayed, make sure that Binder Templates is shown in the Files Of Type box.

3. Double-click the folder in which your template is located.

4. Double-click the template you want to edit.

5. Make the changes and then save the template. Make sure when saving that Binder Templates is showing in the Save As Type box.

I don't see an option in any of the Office applications that allows me to create a binder. How do I do this?

The Binder is a separate application. In Office 2000, it is located in the Microsoft Office Tools submenu. (If you do not find the Binder, you may have to install it. See the sidebar, "Installing the Binder," for instructions.) When you start the Binder, a new blank binder is opened and you can save it and then add files. Follow these steps:

1. Click Start on the Windows Taskbar.

2. Select Programs, select Microsoft Office Tools, and click Microsoft Binder. The blank Binder window is opened, as you can see here:

 Tip: *You can also click the Office Tools button on the Office Shortcut bar to open the Office Tools window. Then click Microsoft Binder to open it.*

3. Choose Save Binder from the File menu, type a name, and click Save. The Binder is stored in the default My Documents folder unless you choose a different drive or folder. In the Save As Type box, it is saved as a binder file.

You can now create files within the binder by choosing Add on the Section menu, or you can add existing files to the binder by choosing Add From File in the Section menu. See the next section, "Adding and Modifying Documents Within a Binder," for more specific information about this.

 Note: *To open a saved binder, open Microsoft Binder, choose Open Binder from the File menu, and select the binder you want.*

Installing the Binder

If Microsoft Binder is not on your Microsoft Office Tools menu, it has not been installed. The Binder is an "install on first use" program, which means that if you did not have it installed in an earlier version, it will not be installed in your typical Office upgrade installation. To install the Binder application, do the following:

1. Open Control Panel and click Add/Remove Programs.

2. Select Microsoft Office 2000 Premium, as shown here, and click Add/Remove to start the installation process.

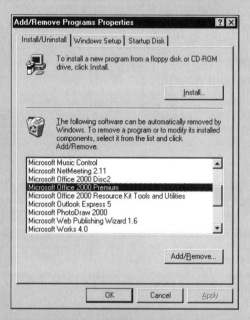

3. Click Add or Remove Features in the Setup dialog box, as shown next.

4. Click the plus sign to the left of Office Tools, select Microsoft Binder, as shown here, and click Update Now. You may be prompted to insert the Office 2000 CD.

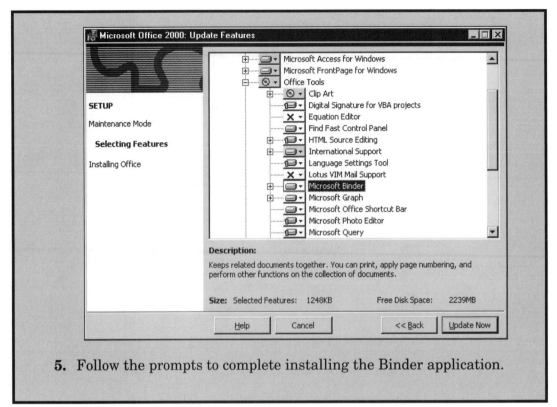

5. Follow the prompts to complete installing the Binder application.

I saw only one supplied template in the Binder tab. Are there more, or can I create a custom binder template?

There is one supplied template, Blank Binder, that can be used for a binder; however, you can create your own template fairly easily by adding new documents or adding documents from a file to a new binder. Then save the binder as a template. The following steps outline the details of doing this:

1. Open the Binder application and choose New Binder from the File menu.

2. In the General tab, select Blank Binder and click OK.

3. Add documents or templates from various applications. Create new documents, if you like. See the next section,

"Adding and Modifying Documents Within a Binder," for specific steps for doing this.

4. To save the binder file as a template, choose Save Binder As from the File menu, type a filename, click the down arrow in the Save As Type list box and select Binder Templates, click Save, and close the binder.

To use the new template, choose New Binder from the File menu. The icon representing the new template and its filename are displayed in the General tab. Binder Templates are files with the extension .obt and they are located in the C:\Windows\Application Data\Microsoft\Templates folder.

Note: You will not see the Blank Binder template in this folder. The Blank Binder is a template, but it is called an NFT file (non-file-based template). There is not a physical .obt file for it and it exists within the Binder itself. If you want to change the Blank Binder, you will have to create a new binder template and name it Blank Binder. Then move it to the templates folder where it will be used as the default Blank Binder template.

What happens to the headers and footers that are created with the original documents if I use a common header or footer in a binder, and how do I do that?

They are not changed when the document is opened in the original application, just as the original page numbering remains unchanged in the original documents. However, the headers or footers in the binder replace original ones when the document is printed as part of the binder. To create a common header and footer in a binder, follow these steps:

1. Open the binder file in which you want to add a header or footer.

2. Select Binder Page Setup from the File menu, and click the Header/Footer tab if it isn't already open, as shown in Figure 8-8.

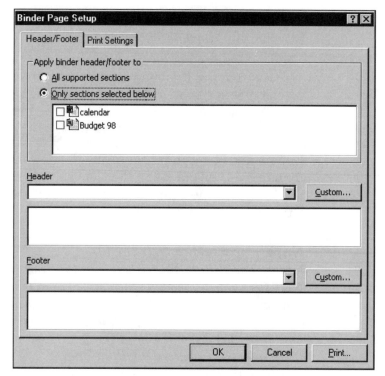

Figure 8-8 The Binder Header/Footer tab

3. Click either Only Sections Selected Below or All Supported Sections. If you selected Only Sections Selected Below, click the sections you want to have show the header and footer.

4. Choose one of the default headers or footers from the drop-down list, or create a custom header or footer by clicking one of the Custom buttons to open the Custom Header or Custom Footer dialog box shown next. Then type text or insert what you want in each of the three sections.

Once you have entered text, you can format it by clicking the Font button and choosing the font name, style, and size that you want. You can also insert a number of other items in the section boxes by clicking the appropriate buttons, as listed here:

Button	Function
A	Opens the Font dialog box
	Inserts the page number
	Inserts the section number
	Inserts the number of sections
	Inserts the section name
	Inserts the binder name
	Inserts the current date
	Inserts the current time

I want to start page numbering at a number other than one. How do I do that?

To start page numbering at a number other than one, do the following:

1. Choose Binder Page Setup from the File menu of a binder, and select the Print Settings tab.

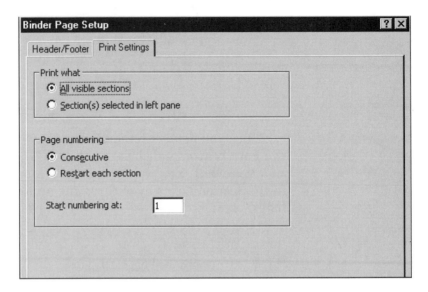

2. In the Page Numbering section, choose either Consecutive or Restart Each Section, and then enter the page number that you want to use in the Start Numbering At box.

3. Click OK when you're done.

ADDING AND MODIFYING DOCUMENTS WITHIN A BINDER

 How can I add Access files to a binder?

Access files cannot be copied directly to a binder; however, you can embed an Access table in a Word document or in an Excel worksheet and then add those files to a binder. To do this, follow these steps:

1. Open the database table in Access that you want to be in the binder. If you like, select the records you want to copy to Word or to Excel, or select the entire table.

2. Choose Copy from the Edit menu.

3. Switch to either Word or Excel, and choose Paste from the Edit menu.

4. Save the table in the application to which you copied it.

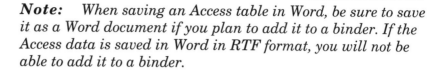
Note: When saving an Access table in Word, be sure to save it as a Word document if you plan to add it to a binder. If the Access data is saved in Word in RTF format, you will not be able to add it to a binder.

5. Open the binder you want, and choose Add From File in the Section menu.

6. Select the file that contains the Access table—you may have to select All Files in the Files Of Type box—and click Add.

In the Binder Section menu, how should I decide whether to choose Add or Add From File?

Choose Add to create a new document from within the binder. Choose Add From File to insert a document that already exists in Excel, PowerPoint, or Word.

Adding a New Document

To add a new document to a binder, follow these steps:

1. Choose Add from the Section menu to display the various templates, as shown next:

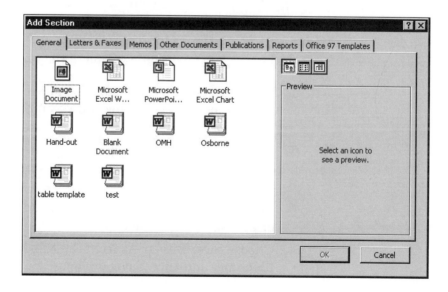

The General tab displays Word Document, Excel Worksheet and Chart, PowerPoint Presentation templates, and others. You also can use an Image Document template that allows you to insert a scanned image. Click the other tabs to see additional templates.

2. Select the type of template you want to use for the document in the current section.

3. Click OK. The Binder window changes to the application used to create the document in this section.

4. Create the document.

5. Repeat steps 1 through 4 for additional documents that you want to create in the binder. You can also add documents that have already been created (see the next section for details).

6. When you're done, choose Save Binder As from the File menu, type a name, and click Save; or choose Save Binder if you have already named the file.

 Tip: *Each section can also be saved as a separate document. To do this, select it, choose Save As File from the Section menu, type a filename, choose the Save In location, confirm that the Save As Type is correct, and click Save.*

Adding an Existing Document from a File

To add an existing document from a file, follow these steps:

1. In the Binder window, choose Add From File in the Section menu to open the Add From File dialog box, shown in Figure 8-9.

2. Select the file you want, and click Add. The document is shown in the window, and the appropriate toolbars for the application used to create the file are displayed.

3. Repeat steps 1 and 2 for inserting additional documents, or add (create) new documents in the binder.

4. Choose Save Binder As from the File menu, type a filename, and click Save; or choose Save Binder if you have already named the file.

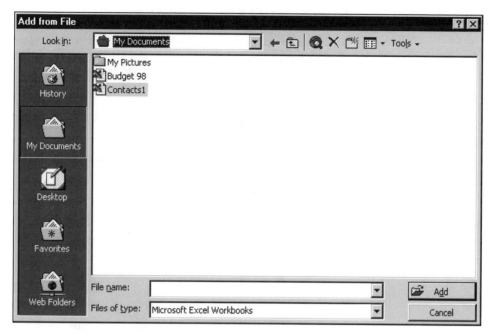

Figure 8-9 The Add From File dialog box

 Tip: *You can also drag a document to the left pane in the binder from Windows Explorer, My Computer, or the desktop.*

 If I edit documents in a binder, will this change the original file in the application in which it was created?

No, the documents are not linked when you choose Add From File in the Section menu, although you can link them if you wish, by choosing Add in the Section menu rather than Add From File.

 Note: *Excel worksheets in the binder can be edited there; however, these changes will not be reflected in the original document in Excel.*

To link a document in the binder with a document in the original application, do the following:

1. Choose Add in the Section menu.

2. Select a template from the application that was used to create the document to be linked, and click OK. The application (Word, Excel, PowerPoint) associated with the template is opened in the Binder.

3. Insert the document by choosing Object from the Insert menu and selecting the file.

4. Click the Create From File tab and enter the path and filename, or click Browse to locate the file.

5. Double-click the file to return to the Object dialog box.

6. Click Link To File, and then click OK. The menu bar, standard toolbar, and formatting toolbar from the application used to create that document will be displayed; and, except for an Excel document, you can double-click on the inserted object to edit it in its original application. Changes in the original document will be reflected in the linked document in the binder.

I inserted an Excel worksheet that had an extra blank page in a binder. I tried to use the Page Break Preview option in the View menu to remove the extra page in the binder, but it was dimmed. How can I use the Excel Page Break Preview option in a binder?

You will have to delete the file from the binder, and then edit the worksheet in Excel and add it to the binder again. To do this:

1. In Binder, right-click the file's icon to display the list of options, as shown here:

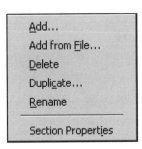

2. Choose Delete from the context menu and click OK when prompted.

Note: *Be sure you inserted the file originally rather than created it in the binder. If you delete a file that is created in the binder, it is gone and cannot be reinserted.*

3. Open the worksheet in Excel, choose Page Break Preview from the View menu, and drag the right edge of the extra page to the left to remove it.

4. Save the file, return to the binder, and choose Add From File in the Section menu to reinsert the file.

WORKING WITH THE BINDER FILE

I inserted a Word document in a binder, but when I opened the binder the next time, I didn't see the document. How can I display an unseen document in the binder?

The document has been hidden. To display the document again, do the following:

1. Choose Unhide Section from the Section menu to display the Unhide Sections dialog box, which lists the sections in the binder:

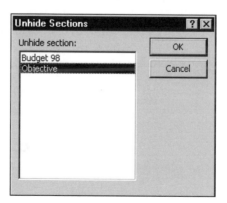

2. Select the name of the section you want to see, and click OK.

Tip: *To hide a section, select the section and choose Hide*
from the Section menu.

I tried to drag an icon in the left pane to a different
position in the binder, but I was unable to do this.
How do you move a section from one position to
another in a binder?

There are two ways to do this. Either drag an icon to a
different position in the left pane using a modified drag
procedure, or choose Rearrange from the Section menu. To
drag the icon to a different position, use these steps:

1. Click the icon for the document that you want to move to
   make it active. This is essential. The document cannot be
   moved unless it is active.

2. Point to the icon, hold down the mouse button—a page
   pointer will be displayed—and drag it to the position
   you want.

Tip: *If all icons are selected, you will not be able to drag*
just one of them. To remove the selection, choose Unselect All
from the Section menu. Then you can select the file you want
to move, and drag it to a different position.

To move a section by using the Rearrange option, follow
these steps:

1. Select any section and choose Rearrange from the
   Section menu. The Rearrange Sections dialog box will
   be displayed, as shown here:

2. Select the section you want to move, and click either Move Up or Move Down to move it to the place where you want it in the binder. Click OK when you are done.

I decided I wanted to move a file to a different binder, so I chose Delete from the Section menu. I then opened the other binder and chose Add From File from the Section menu to insert it. Is there an easier way to move files from one binder to another?

Yes, you can drag the file icon from one binder to another. Use the following steps to do this:

1. Open both binder windows, displaying the left pane in each window. Reduce the size of one of the windows, and rearrange them so that you can see both.

2. Drag the file icon from one binder's left pane to the left pane of the other, as shown in Figure 8-10. To do this, click the icon for the document that you want to move to make it active. This is essential. The document cannot be moved unless it is active. Then point to the icon, hold down the mouse button—a page pointer will be displayed—and drag it to the position you want.

3. Make sure you save the changes.

When I opened a binder we had been using in our office, I noticed that the pane showing the icons had disappeared from the left of the Binder window. What happened?

Show/Hide Left Pane has been turned off. To display the left pane, which contains the icons, click Show/Hide Left Pane again. This button is located in the menu bar to the left of File.

If the Show/Hide Left Pane button is not showing in the menu bar, choose Binder Options from the File menu, click

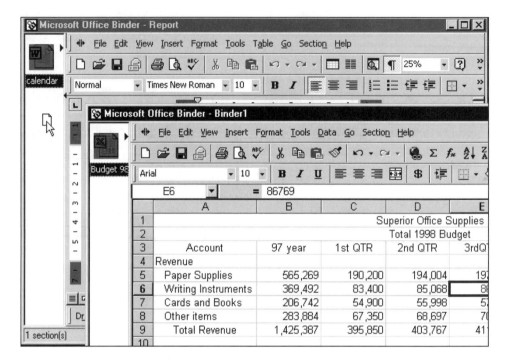

Figure 8-10   Dragging a section between Binder windows

the Show Left Pane And Left Pane Button check box, shown next, and click OK.

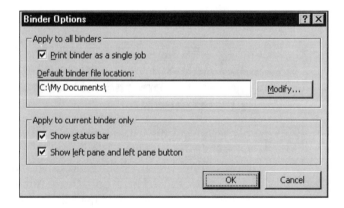

When I was in Binder Print Preview, I wanted to print the entire binder, but I was not able to print the Excel worksheets from there. I exited from Binder Print Preview and clicked the Print button, but then only the current section was printed. How do I print an entire binder?

Exit from Binder Print Preview and choose Print Binder from the File menu to open the Print Binder dialog box, as shown in Figure 8-11. The All Visible Sections option is the default for printing, and it prints all sections (including the Excel worksheets) *except those that are hidden.* If you want to print only several selected sections, choose the Section(s) Selected In Left Pane option. This will print only the sections that you have selected. Then click OK to print.

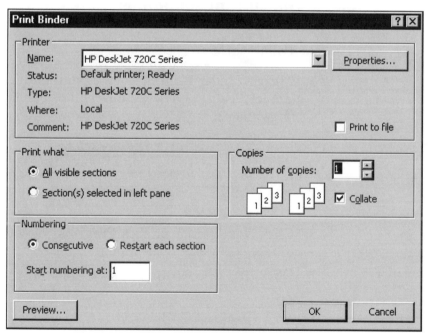

Figure 8-11   The Print Binder dialog box

Tip: *If you are not sure whether there are any hidden sections, click Sections on the menu bar to display the options. If Unhide Section is dimmed, then all sections in the binder are displayed. If Unhide Section is active, click it to display the Unhide Sections dialog box. Select the name of the section(s) you want to display, and click OK.*

To select more than one section, do either of the following:

● To select *nonadjacent* section icons in the left pane, hold down the CTRL key and click each of the sections.

● To select *adjacent* section icons, click the first icon that you want to select, hold down the SHIFT key, and click the last icon that you want to select.

I clicked the Print Preview button when I was in a binder, but the only document I could view was the one in the current section. Is there a way to view all the pages in a binder in Print Preview?

Yes. Follow these steps:

1. Choose Binder Print Preview from the File menu. A Binder Print Preview window will be displayed, as shown here:

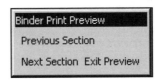

2. Click Next Section or click Previous Section to display other documents in the binder.

3. Click Exit Preview to leave the Preview window.

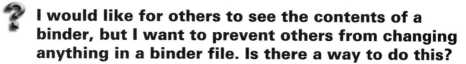

SHARING BINDERS

I would like for others to see the contents of a binder, but I want to prevent others from changing anything in a binder file. Is there a way to do this?

Yes, you can save the binder with the Read-Only attribute for the entire file turned on. To do this, use the following steps:

1. Open Windows Explorer, navigate to the folder where your binder file (.obd file extension) is located, and right-click the filename of the binder.

2. Choose Properties. In the General tab (shown in Figure 8-12), select Read-Only and click OK.

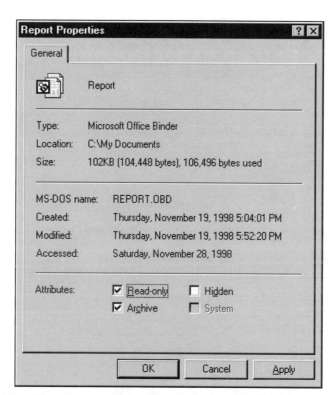

Figure 8-12 The General Tab in the Report Properties dialog box

Note: *If a binder is saved with the Read-Only attribute turned on, it can be opened and saved with another name without the Read-Only attribute applied to it. Edits can then be made to this new binder.*

Is there a way to prevent others from changing the contents of a section in a binder?

You can turn on Protect Document and enter a password that is required in order for the document in that section to be opened and edited. The procedure that is used to do this depends upon the type of file to which you want to apply the password. See the following sidebars, "Protecting an Excel Document" and "Protecting a Word Document," for specific information about each.

Protecting an Excel Document

Use the following steps to protect an Excel document in a binder:

1. In the binder, select the Excel document, choose Protection in the Tools menu, and select Protect Sheet. A Protect Sheet dialog box is displayed, as shown here:

2. Select the options you want—Contents, Objects, or Scenarios— type a password, and click OK. Another password dialog box will be displayed.

Tip: *Although the password is optional, requiring a password prevents others who do not know the password from removing the worksheet protection.*

3. Type the password again and click OK.

To remove the password protection in the Excel file, follow these steps:

1. Select the Excel document and choose Protection from the Tools menu.

2. Click Unprotect Sheet, type the password, and click OK.

Protecting a Word Document

You can protect a Word document in a binder with these steps:

1. In the binder, select the Word document and choose Protect Document in the Tools menu. The Protect Document dialog box, shown next, is displayed.

2. Select the options you want—Tracked Changes, Comments, or Forms.

- **Tracked Changes** Allows you to make edits in the Word document; however, they will be marked either as deleted text or added text, and you cannot change this. The marks can be neither accepted nor rejected, as they are in an unprotected Word document with Track Changes turned on.

- **Comments** Allows a reviewer to insert comments but not change the contents of the document.

- **Forms** Allows no changes to be made to the document except in form fields or in unprotected sections. To turn protection on or off for a section, click Sections in the Protect Documents dialog box, and then select the section number that you want to be protected.

3. Type a password and click OK. Another password dialog box will be displayed.

> *Tip:* *Although the password is optional, requiring a password prevents others who do not know the password from removing the document protection.*

4. Type the password again and click OK.

To remove the password protection in Word, do the following:

1. Select the Word document and choose Unprotect Document from the Tools menu.

2. Type the password and click OK. Edits can now be made without being marked as tracked changes.

> *Note:* *You can also use the steps just given for protecting Excel and Word documents when they are created in their own applications, before adding them to the binder.*

Chapter 9

Using Office with the Internet and Intranets

Answer Topics!

Using Office with the Internet and Intranets @ a Glance

Office 2000 provides many new and useful features, but none as apparent as the tools that enhance integration of desktop computing with the online world of the Internet and local intranets. From within the Office 2000 programs you can cross the desktop/online boundary.

 The Online Capabilities of Office 2000 Programs provides an overview of the features provided by each program in the Office 2000 suite that allow you to create online documents.

 Creating Internet and Intranet Documents looks at saving documents directly in the Web's HTML format, using web themes or templates to give a document predefined elements and colors, and adding web graphics and formatting.

 Adding Hyperlinks to Office Documents covers jumping from one Office document to another, to objects within documents, or to Internet and intranet sites.

 Accessing the Web and Intranets with Office 2000 discusses using search pages and other ways of finding sites, previewing HTML documents, and transferring files across the Internet and intranets.

 Using and Publishing Web Pages with Office 2000 shows how to include Access databases in a web page, and how to use Internet Explorer and Web Find Fast.

 Using Word with Your E-mail explores ways of accessing Word's features with your e-mail even if your correspondent doesn't have Word, as well as how to add a signature to your e-mail.

THE ONLINE CAPABILITIES OF OFFICE 2000 PROGRAMS

The Office 2000 programs simplify the process of creating online documents across the suite in many ways, such as allowing you to insert hyperlinks, as shown here:

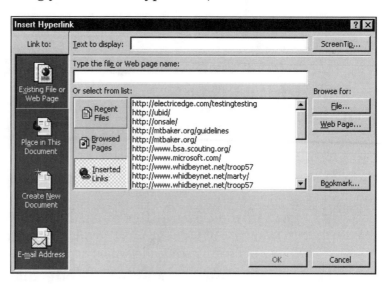

However, due to the different objective of each program in the suite, there are unique capabilities provided in each program that expand upon the standard online capabilities. For example, after inserting a hyperlink into a PowerPoint slide, you can determine what mouse action, a click or a simple point, activates the hyperlink jump in a slide show. Following are some other examples of inherent online capabilities found in the individual Office 2000 programs:

- *Word* provides an easy way to create individual web pages. Using many standard word processing features, you can quickly create quality online documents without knowing HTML. Additionally, using Word as your e-mail editor provides the full range of its features to your communication channels.

- *PowerPoint* easily transfers its powerful presentation features to HTML, providing ready-to-run online

presentations that only require you to edit some sample text.

● *Access* offers interactive access to a live database, as well as dedicated hyperlink fields you can specify to jump to Internet addresses, such as vendor home pages.

● *Excel* seamlessly converts ranges of data from worksheets to graphic tables in HTML documents. As with Access, you can create forms that receive user information and store that data in a convenient format for tabulation.

● *Outlook* stores the online particulars of contacts so you can effortlessly send e-mail or view any web pages or other HTML documents associated with that person or organization.

● *FrontPage* provides a full-featured web site authoring and managing program.

● *Publisher* allows you to do web publishing, but without many of the features of FrontPage.

● *PhotoDraw* allows you to create pictures that you can use in web pages or send in e-mail.

CREATING INTERNET AND INTRANET DOCUMENTS

 I've created several HTML documents in Word and saved them in a cryptic filename convention that I've been using for years. I posted these files on my web site and heard from others that my filename was appearing as the title for these pages when viewed in their browsers. Is there a way I can change the title of an HTML document, but not the filename?

Yes. Choose Properties from the File menu to open the Properties dialog box shown in Figure 9-1. Enter a more descriptive name for your document in the Title box, and click

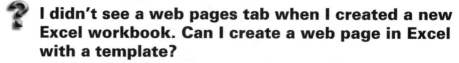

Figure 9-1   The Properties dialog box

OK. The new name you chose for a title will now appear in the title bars of web browsers when the document is opened, but it will not appear in the title bar of Word.

  Tip: *The title has special significance since it is used when searching for a document.*

I didn't see a web pages tab when I created a new Excel workbook. Can I create a web page in Excel with a template?

There is not a web page–related template that you can choose when you create a new workbook; however, you can save an

existing workbook, or selected parts of a workbook, as an HTML file. Do the following:

1. Open an Excel worksheet that you want to publish.

2. Choose Save As Web Page from the File menu to display the Save As dialog box shown in Figure 9-2 (you can also choose Save As from the File menu, and then select Web Page as the Save As Type with the same result).

3. Choose to save either Entire Workbook or Selection. If nothing is selected, the current selection is the current sheet that is displayed. If you have a chart and want to save it, select it before choosing Save As Web Page and it will be the current selection.

 Tip: *If you choose Selection, you can also choose Add Interactivity and allow your web page viewers to change your worksheet or chart and see the results even if they do not have Excel.*

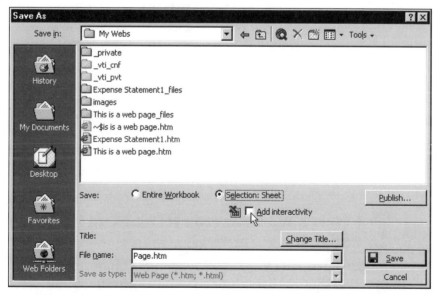

Figure 9-2 The Excel Save As dialog box

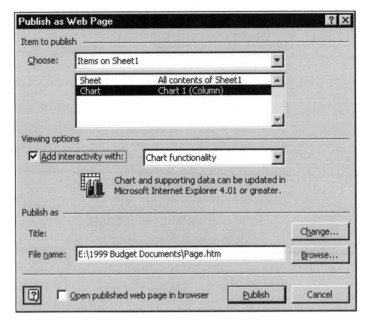

Figure 9-3 The Excel Publish As Web Page dialog box

4. Select either Save, which simply saves the worksheet or chart as an HTML file, or Publish, which opens the Publish As Web Page dialog box shown in Figure 9-3. Here you can choose the items to publish and the type of interactivity.

 Note: *Refer to the section "Using and Publishing Web Pages with Office 2000," later in this chapter, and your network manager or your Internet service provider for procedures on publishing HTML files.*

I have a worksheet in HTML. Can I get it back to the native Excel format?

Yes, all Office 2000 files in HTML format can be returned to their native format. Simply open the HTML file in its native application, and then save it in its native format. All of its original formatting and properties will be preserved.

I want to use the drawing tools in Word to create a graphic, but the Drawing toolbar doesn't offer the standard selection of tools. How can I create graphics for Word HTML documents?

You can still use the drawing tools you are familiar with. Open the HTML document in Word, choose Picture from the Insert menu, wait a moment for the full submenu to open, and then select New Drawing. A picture boundary box appears with the standard Drawing toolbar, as shown in Figure 9-4.

You can reposition the graphic by using the alignment buttons on the Formatting toolbar or by dragging the graphic to a new paragraph location. Once you have completed your drawing and gone on to other areas of your web page, you can come back and change the drawing using the full drawing tools by double-clicking the drawing.

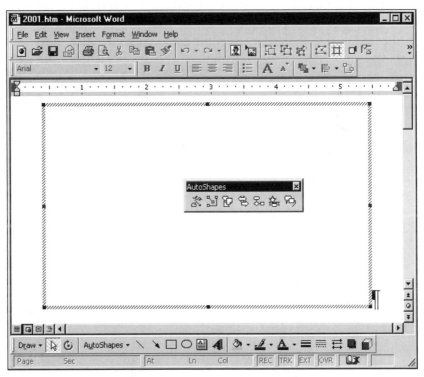

Figure 9-4   A new drawing being added to a web page

 Tip: *You can choose how text flows around a picture by right-clicking the graphic, choosing Format Object from the context menu, and clicking the Layout tab.*

 Tip: *Always preview your HTML documents in a browser to see how they will appear to other users before you post them for public viewing. Displaying a file in more than one browser, such as Microsoft Internet Explorer and Netscape Navigator, will let you know if there are any features you've added that aren't supported by the more popular browsers.*

Are there special templates or wizards for creating PowerPoint web pages?

No, there are no prebuilt presentation templates available for web pages. You can use the AutoContent Wizard to create your own presentations, or you can use any of the existing templates and, when you are done, use Save As Web Page on the File menu. This opens the Save As dialog box shown in Figure 9-5. You can also convert any standard

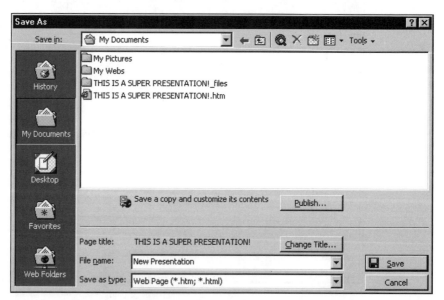

Figure 9-5 You can save any presentation as a web page

presentation for use on the Internet or an intranet by using Save As Web Page.

 Note: *Uploading a file to a server is often more involved than just copying a file from one computer to another, and it depends upon the procedures used in your particular situation. Contact your network manager or your Internet service provider for specific information about how to publish your web pages, and review the section "Using and Publishing Web Pages with Office 2000," later in this chapter.*

 ### Can I convert existing Office documents to web pages to display on the Internet?

Yes, you can create web pages from Word, Excel, and PowerPoint documents. Simply open one of these types of documents in the program in which it was created, and then resave the file using Save As Web Page from the File menu, enter the filename, and click Save.

Are there any templates or wizards for creating web pages in Office? If so, where are they?

Yes there are, but only in Word. To create a web page using a template or wizard in Word, do the following:

1. Choose New from the File menu. In the General tab, there is a Web Page template for creating a blank web page.

2. Select the Web Pages tab, and select the template or wizard you want. Figure 9-6 shows the Web Pages tab in Word.

3. Create the document, and when you're done, choose Save As from the File menu. Notice that the file type is an HTML document. If you like, you can also save the file as a Word document.

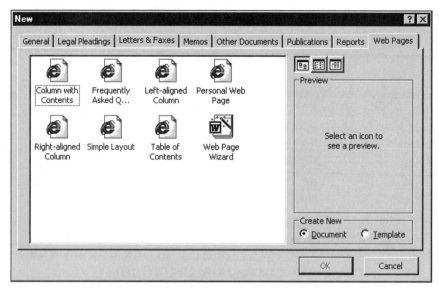

Figure 9-6 The Web Pages tab in Word

In Access 97 there was an option to Save To HTML, which opened the Publish To The Web Wizard. Both of these are now gone. How do I create database-related web pages in Access 2000?

Access 2000 allows you to create three types of web pages, all of which are stored separately from the database in which they originated:

- *Data access pages* allow the viewer to interactively change, add to, and manipulate data in an Access, SQL Server, or Excel database. The data can be in tables or queries.

- *Server-generated HTML,* or *Active Server Pages (ASP),* dynamically create a web page from a user request based on an Access table, query, or form. The viewer can only look at the data and cannot change, add to, or manipulate it.

- *Static HTML pages* are snapshots of database tables, reports, queries, or forms. These allow the web viewer to see how a database object looked at the time they were created.

Note: In the case of both data access pages and server-generated HTML, the database must be available to the web server.

Creating Data Access Pages

You can create a new data access page using AutoPage, using a wizard, using an existing web page, or on your own. To use any of these techniques, follow these steps:

1. Open the database in Access so that the Database window is visible.

2. In the Database window, under Objects, click Pages and then click New in the toolbar.

3. The New Data Access Page dialog box will open, as shown here:

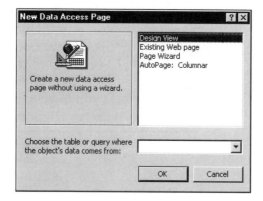

Here you have the following choices:

- **Design View**   Create your own data access page from scratch.

- **Existing Web Page**   Use an existing web page as a model for a new data access page.

- **Page Wizard**   A wizard will lead you through the creation of a data access page.

- **AutoPage Columnar**   A columnar data access page will automatically be created.

4. When you have completed creating your page and you try to close it, you will be asked to save the page, and the type will automatically be changed to Web Page.

 Note: *If you have established a default theme for your web pages, AutoPage will automatically apply that theme to the new page. Otherwise, the Straight Edge theme will be used.*

Creating Server-Generated HTML Pages

You can create server-generated pages by exporting a database table, query, or form as either an active server page (ASP) or as IDC/HTX files by opening the table, query, or form, and choosing Export from the File menu. IDC/HTX represent a pair of files that together generate the HTML page upon request using an older Internet Information Server (IIS), while ASP is a single file that does the same thing with IIS 3.0 and above. The IDC (Internet database connector) contains query information to retrieve the desired data, as well as information on how to connect to the data source, which can be either an Access or SQL database. The HTX (HTML extension file) contains the formatting tags and data placeholders that are replaced with data from the query in the IDC. The ASP file contains all of this information in a single file.

When you have selected the type of file and clicked Save, you will see a dialog box appear, similar to the one shown next, that allows you to specify several pieces of information, including the data source name and the server URL.

Microsoft Active Server Pages Output Options	? ☒
HTML Template:	Browse...
Data Source Information	
Data Source Name:	Northwind.mdb
User to Connect As:	
Password for User:	
Microsoft Active Server Pages Output	
Server URL:	http://marty/
Session timeout (min):	
	OK Cancel

After publishing either an ASP file or a set of IDC/HTX files (see "Using and Publishing Web Pages with Office 2000," later in this chapter), when the server receives a request for the page from a browser, it connects to the database, gets the

current information, places the information correctly formatted in the pages, and sends it to the user.

Creating Static HTML Pages

You can create a static HTML page by exporting a database table, query, form, or report as an HTML document (.htm or .html). This saves the current snapshot of the table, query, form, or report in a separate file that can be published to and viewed over the Internet or an intranet. Use these steps for that purpose:

1. Open the database that contains the information you want to display.

2. In the Database window, under Objects, select Tables, Queries, Forms, or Reports, and then choose the specific table, query, form, or report.

3. Open the File menu and choose Export. The Export dialog box will open. Select the folder; enter the name; choose HTML Documents as the Save As Type, as shown in Figure 9-7; and click Save.

Figure 9-7   Saving a database object as an HTML document saves a static page

 Note: *Once you have created any of the above types of database-related pages, you will need to publish those pages on a web server. That process is described in the question on putting an Access database on a web site in the "Using and Publishing Web Pages with Office 2000" section, later in this chapter.*

ADDING HYPERLINKS TO OFFICE DOCUMENTS

I want to create a hyperlink to text in another Word document. What is the easiest way to do this?

To insert a hyperlink to a block of text in a document, do the following:

1. Open both Word documents and choose Arrange All from the Window menu to display both.

2. Select the block of text that you want the hyperlink to go to.

3. Drag the selected text with the right mouse button to the location in the other document where you want the hyperlink to appear.

4. Release the right mouse button and choose Create Hyperlink Here from the context menu, like this:

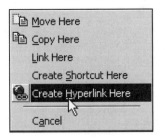

5. Some or all of the words from the selected text will appear as a hyperlink. Use SHIFT and the left and right arrow keys to select the hyperlink text, and type in

words that are more meaningful. The hyperlink will end with the first space you type.

Tip: *You can also copy the selected text to the Clipboard and use Paste As Hyperlink (expand the Edit menu to see this option) to insert the text in the other document. This same technique can be used to insert graphics (from PowerPoint and other Word documents), ranges in an Excel worksheet, and Access objects into a Word document.*

What's the difference between hyperlinks and linked documents?

A *hyperlink* will take you immediately to a block of text, an Office 2000 object, a document file, or a web site.

The primary purpose of *linking* is to allow editing in an original file to be automatically reflected in the linked data that is pasted into other files. See Chapter 8 for more information on linking.

What are some reasons for using hyperlinks in Access?

Creating hyperlinks to web sites can be especially useful in an Access database. For example, if your company buys products from a number of different manufacturers, you can create a database table that contains company names, addresses, and names of sales reps for each supplier, and create a hyperlink field that contains the address (the Uniform Resource Locator, or URL) of each manufacturer's web site (if they have one). This would allow the user to go directly to that web site to see the latest product updates and information. An educator can create a table with a hyperlink field to publishers' web pages, where the latest textbooks that are available from each company are listed.

A hyperlink to a file on a network also provides an easy way for users to share information without duplicating files. See the related questions on Access in this section, for information on creating hyperlinks in Access.

 How do I insert a hyperlink in an Access database?

This requires two basic steps:

1. Select the table in which you want the hyperlink, go to Design view, insert a new field in the table, and choose Hyperlink as the data type.

 2. Go to that field in the table, choose Hyperlink from the Insert menu or click Insert Hyperlink on the toolbar, and insert the URL if you are linking to a web site on the Internet, a UNC (Uniform Naming Convention) address or path for intranet documents, or a path and filename if you are creating a hyperlink to another file on your local drive. See the "Addressing" sidebar, later in this chapter, for a further description of addressing formats.

 Tip: *You can also insert a hyperlink field when you open the table in Datasheet view. To do that, move the insertion point to the place where you want to insert a new field. Choose Hyperlink Column from the Insert menu. Then you can choose Rename Column from the Format menu to give the field an appropriate name. The sidebar "Inserting a Hyperlink in an Access Table" gives specific steps for doing this.*

Inserting a Hyperlink in an Access Table

To add a hyperlink field to a database table, do the following:

1. Open the database, select the table that you want to contain the hyperlink field in the Database window, and click Design to go to Design view.

2. Move to the first vacant cell in the Field Name column, and type a field name.

3. Press TAB to move to the Data Type column and click the down arrow to display the list of field-type choices shown here:

4. Select Hyperlink, and then type a description as shown here:

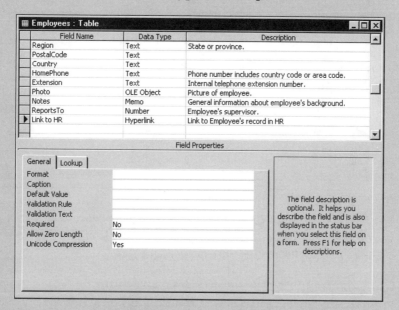

5. Close Design view and return to the Database window.

To add a hyperlink to the table, use the next set of steps.

1. Open the table in Datasheet (table) view, and move to the first cell in which you want to enter a hyperlink.

2. Do either of the following:

- If you know the name, type in the hyperlink: a URL, a UNC address, or a path and filename. See the "Addressing" sidebar, later in this chapter, for a further description of addressing formats.

- Choose Hyperlink from the Insert menu to go to the Insert Hyperlink dialog box, shown here:

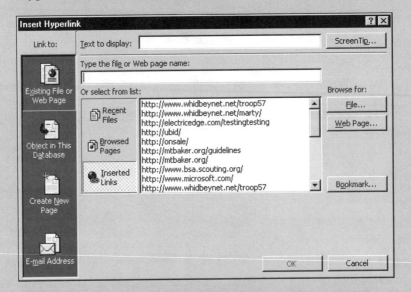

> *Tip:* *You can also click the Insert Hyperlink button to go to the Insert Hyperlink dialog box. This button is active only when the insertion point is in a hyperlink field.*

3. Click the Link To object on the left, and enter or select one of the options presented (the sites listed depend on what you have been working with). Or click the File or Web Page buttons under Browse For to locate the file or web site that you want. If you are linking to a specific bookmark within a file or web, click the Bookmark button to find it. When you are done, click OK to insert the hyperlink in the cell.

4. Save the table. To go to the site or file, just click the hyperlink name.

 ## How do you use hyperlinks in Access forms or reports?

The procedure for inserting a hyperlink in either a form or a report is basically the same.

 Note: *Hyperlinks created in reports don't work when viewed in Access; however, they will work if the report is exported to Excel, Word, or HTML.*

There are two types of hyperlinks you can use:

● Hyperlinks that are stored in the table that the form or report is based upon

● Hyperlinks that are attached to labels or pictures in forms and reports, or to command buttons in forms

To use a hyperlink field in a form or report, be sure you have added a field with a hyperlink data type to the table on which your form or report is based. (Refer to the sidebar "Inserting a Hyperlink in an Access Table" and to the "How do I insert a hyperlink in an Access database?" question, both earlier in the chapter, for specific steps for doing this.) Then follow these steps:

1. Create the form or report the same way you usually do, or open in Design view an existing form or report based on a table that contains a hyperlink field. Refer to Chapter 6 for specific information about creating forms and reports.

2. If the list of field names is not displayed, choose Field List from the View menu.

  Tip: *You can also click the Field List button to display the list of field names.*

3. Select the hyperlink field name from the list, and drag it to the desired position in the form or report.

4. Save and close the form or report design. Then you can open the form or report, click the hypertext name, and be transferred directly to the file or web site to which it is linked.

To add a hyperlink to a label, follow these steps:

1. In Design view, select the label and click the Insert Hyperlink button.

2. Enter a URL, UNC address, or path in the Type The File Or Web Page Name text box. If you are hyperlinking to a location or object within an Office 2000 file, browse to specify its location.

3. Click OK. The URL or path will appear on the form or report as a label in the default hyperlink color. Move the label into position, and change the text and background color to what you want the user to see in Form view.

4. Switch to Form view to test the hyperlink.

 To attach hyperlinks to a picture or command button, insert the picture or command button and open its Properties sheet. In the Hyperlink Address property box, click the Build button on the right to open the Insert Hyperlink dialog box, and navigate to the URL or file you want to open when the picture or command button is selected.

I don't see how to insert a hyperlink in an Excel worksheet. The Hyperlink option in the Insert menu is dimmed, as is the Insert Hyperlink button. Is there a way to do this? If so, how?

If the Excel worksheet is a shared worksheet, the Hyperlink option in the Insert menu is dimmed, and you will have to remove the Shared attribute before inserting a hyperlink. See the sidebar "Removing a Shared Attribute from a Worksheet in Excel" for instructions for doing that.

Removing a Shared Attribute from a Worksheet in Excel

You cannot insert a hyperlink in an Excel workbook that is shared. Clear the Shared attribute with these steps:

1. Open the worksheet, and choose Share Workbook from the Tools menu to display the Share Workbook dialog box.

2. On the Editing tab, clear the Allow Changes By More Than One User At The Same Time check box, and notify any users who may have the workbook open to close it before you remove the workbook from shared use.

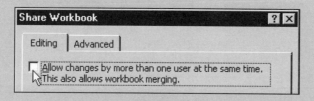

3. Click OK, and when prompted, click Yes to remove the workbook from shared use.

 How do I insert a hyperlink in PowerPoint?

Use the familiar Insert Hyperlink button or choose Hyperlink from the Insert menu to open the Insert Hyperlink dialog box to link to another file, Internet, intranet, or document location. Note that in PowerPoint, if you are in any view besides Slide Show view when you click the hyperlink, you will not jump to the linked file or object. To activate the hyperlink, click the Slide Show button, shown on the left, or choose Slide Show from the View menu, and then click the hyperlink.

Using Action Settings to Create a Hyperlink in PowerPoint

Normally, you initiate a hyperlink by clicking text or an object when the mouse pointer changes into the "pointing" hand.

In PowerPoint, you can also initiate a hyperlink by just moving the mouse pointer over the hyperlinked text or object. Use these steps:

1. Select the text or object that is to be the hyperlink in the PowerPoint presentation.

2. Choose Action Settings from the Slide Show menu (you may need to fully open the menu).

3. Select Hyperlink To in the Mouse Click or Mouse Over tab, depending on how you want the user to be able to activate the hyperlink.

4. Click the down arrow in the Hyperlink To box to display a list of choices, as shown here:

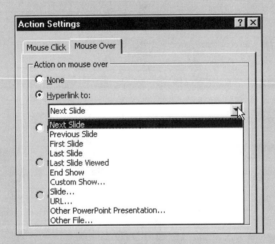

5. Select the option you want, and supply location information as prompted.

6. Click OK in the Action Settings dialog box to insert the hyperlink in the presentation.

To see the link, go to Slide Show view and click or pass the mouse pointer over the hyperlink text.

Refer to other questions in this section for more specific steps for creating a hyperlink to a web site or to another document. Also, see the preceding sidebar "Using Action Settings to Create a Hyperlink in PowerPoint."

I know I can insert a hyperlink in Word that can be used to go immediately to a web site, but are there any other uses for hyperlinks?

Yes, a common use of hyperlinks is to go to a web site on the Internet or an intranet, but you can also insert a hyperlink to another document on a network. The following steps show you how to do either of these.

1. Open the document that is to contain the hyperlink, and select the text that will be formatted so that you can jump to the referenced document or URL.

2. Choose Hyperlink from the Insert menu or click Insert Hyperlink on the toolbar. The Insert Hyperlink dialog box is displayed.

3. As you have seen in other Office components, you can select a Link To destination on the left and a specific URL or file and possibly a bookmark on the right. Select one of these, or click File or Web Page to browse to locate a document from a folder or a particular web site.

4. When you're done, click OK to leave the Insert Hyperlink dialog box.

Now, when you move the mouse pointer over the text or item, a ToolTip will display the hyperlink. Also, when you or other readers open this document, you or they can click the hyperlink to go immediately to the referenced document or URL.

ACCESSING THE WEB AND INTRANETS WITH OFFICE 2000

 I'd like to access the Web from Office 2000 in much the same manner that I use Internet Explorer. What is the best way to go online from within an Office 2000 application?

Display the Web toolbar by clicking View | Toolbars | Web in Access, Excel, Outlook, PowerPoint, or Word. (If you do this a lot, you can add the Web Toolbar button from the Web category in the Customize dialog box, which is opened by right-clicking a toolbar.) The Web toolbar buttons are essentially the same as those on the Internet Explorer toolbar. The following sidebar, "The Web Toolbar," describes what each button does.

✛ ***Tip:*** *Besides using the Web toolbar to open a web document, you can enter the document's address in the File Name box of the File Open dialog box, and click Open. See the sidebar "Addressing," later in the chapter, for information on proper addressing syntax for the Internet and intranets.*

The Web Toolbar

A gateway to the World Wide Web and corporate intranets is through the buttons on the Web toolbar, shown here:

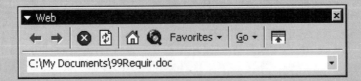

The Web toolbar is available in Word, Excel, Access, Outlook, and PowerPoint. Display the toolbar by opening the View menu, choosing Toolbars, and clicking Web. The buttons in the Web toolbar are described in the following table.

	Button Name	Description
←	Back	Allows you to move backward through previously opened web pages or hyperlinks, once a page or document has been opened
→	Forward	Allows you to move forward through previously opened web pages or hyperlinks, once a page or document has been opened
⊗	Stop Current Jump	Ceases the process of finding and displaying a web page or hyperlink document
▣	Refresh Current Page	Updates the display of the current document
⌂	Start Page	Displays and allows you to modify the web page or document that is first located
◙	Search The Web	Opens Internet Explorer and connects to a Microsoft Network (MSN) search palette, where you can type in a keyword and choose a search engine
Favorites ▾	Favorites	Allows you to quickly access or add frequently visited sites to a list
Go ▾	Go	Provides a drop-down list of the buttons on the Web toolbar; a good one-stop button if you're trying to reduce the number of buttons on a toolbar
▤	Show Only Web Toolbar	Hides other toolbars to gain maximum viewing area
C:\My Documents\99Requir.doc	Address Box	Provides a means to type a web-page address or an intranet or local computer document address; pressing ENTER takes you to the specified location

Note: There are many terms used to describe what you access when going online, such as web page, web site, online document, spreadsheet, presentation, table, and so forth, as well as other variations for local items. Generally, the HTML files found on the World Wide Web are referred to as web pages; those items found on an intranet or on a local computer are called HTML documents.

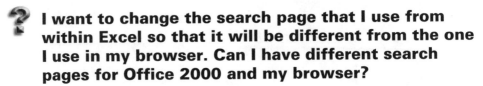

I want to change the search page that I use from within Excel so that it will be different from the one I use in my browser. Can I have different search pages for Office 2000 and my browser?

No. "One for all" is the motto in this instance. (This is also true for the Start page.) Several of the web features that are a part of Office 2000 programs are shared components with your browser (assuming your browser is compatible with Office 2000). Therefore, whichever search engine and start page you have chosen in your browser is what will come up in your Office 2000 applications. You can, of course, then switch to any other search engine.

I'm trying to find an HTML-format marketing analysis spreadsheet on one of our servers, but I don't know what the URL is. Can I open an HTML document without knowing its URL?

Sure. Actually, you don't need to use URLs to open HTML documents stored on a network. You can just navigate normally (using the Open dialog box in Excel or Windows Explorer, or the Find feature in Windows 95/98) to find the file's location and double-click its filename. The spreadsheet should open in Excel as it would appear in a browser, as shown in Figure 9-8. For a review of addressing conventions used for online documents, see the sidebar "Addressing."

I understand I should view my HTML documents in a browser to see how they will look to users on the Web. How can I quickly preview HTML documents in a browser from Office 2000 programs?

Word, Excel, PowerPoint, and Access all offer a way to preview HTML files. When an HTML document is opened in any of these applications, you can choose Web Page Preview from the File menu to open the document in your default browser. See the related questions in this section that discuss accessing the Web.

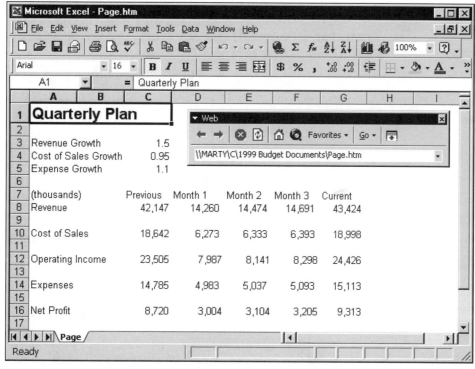

Figure 9-8 An HTML document opened in Excel

Addressing

Different addressing conventions are used, depending on where you're searching for an online item:

● To open a web page, type its address, or URL (Uniform Resource Locator), in the Web toolbar Address box. A URL takes the form of *protocol://domain/path*; for example, http://www.microsoft.com/office.

● To open a document on a LAN-based intranet or on a local drive, type the UNC (Uniform Naming Convention) or a standard *drive:\path* designation. A UNC takes the form of *computername*\ *drive**path*; for example, \\marty\c\1999 Budget Documents\Page.htm.

Using either convention, press ENTER after typing in the address.

 I need to transfer a file to a client using FTP (File Transfer Protocol). Can I transfer files and access FTP sites from Office 2000 applications?

Yes, you can. However, before you begin the file transfer process, you have to provide the Office application with the necessary information to connect to the FTP site. Add a site to your FTP Locations list with these steps:

1. Open the document you want to transfer, and then open the Save As dialog box from the File menu Save As option.

2. Click the down arrow next to the Save In list box, and click Add/Modify FTP Locations. The Add/Modify FTP Locations dialog box opens, as shown in Figure 9-9.

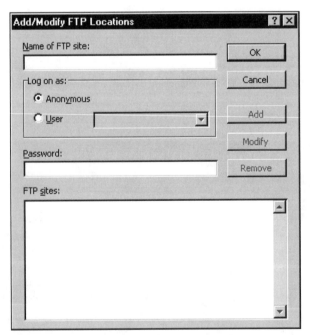

Figure 9-9 The Add/Modify FTP Locations dialog box

3. Type in the FTP site name; choose to log on either as Anonymous or, if you have a username, choose User and enter the name; and type in the applicable password (*guest* is a common password for Anonymous logons).

4. Click the Add button and then click OK.

The FTP site will now be listed in the Save As (or Open) dialog box, as you can see in Figure 9-10.

To transfer a file to an FTP site, follow these steps:

1. Log on to your Internet service provider (ISP).

2. Open the Save As dialog box, if it's not already displayed.

3. Open the Save In list box and select the site name, and you will connect with the FTP site.

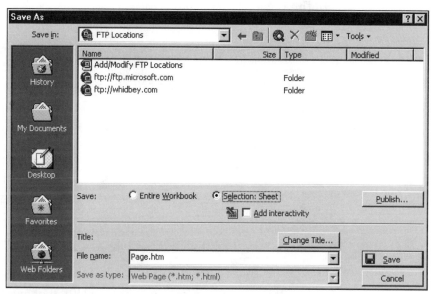

Figure 9-10 Transferring a file to an FTP site

4. Navigate to the folder in which you want to transfer your document, and click Save.

✳ ***Note:***   *To transfer a document from an FTP site to your local computer, use similar steps, except operate from the Open dialog box instead of the Save As dialog box.*

 Besides Outlook's Web toolbar, are there other ways I can access the Web?

Yes, using Outlook's Contacts folder you can open a contact window that has an associated web page, as shown in Figure 9-11, and then click the web page address. Your browser will open and display the contact's web page. From the browser, you will then have access to other web pages and HTML documents.

Also, in any messages you receive in Outlook that have hyperlinked text (usually identified by the color blue) to web pages, you can click the text to open your browser and jump to the page.

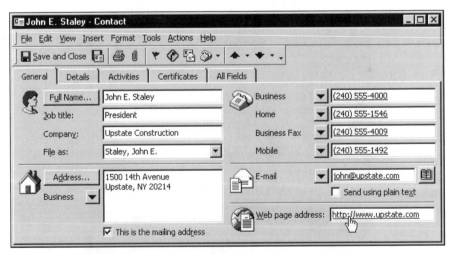

Figure 9-11   Outlook's contacts can contain a URL that can be clicked to open the related page

USING AND PUBLISHING WEB PAGES WITH OFFICE 2000

 I want to be able to send my web documents to my Internet service provider so I can publish them on the Web. Does Office 2000 provide any tools or features that can assist me in publishing web documents?

Yes, there are publishing wizards available to guide you through the process of assembling and copying the necessary files to display your documents on the Web.

Once you've created HTML documents in Office 2000, you'll want to get them out to the rest of the world, whether that's really the rest of the world via the Web, or a subset of the world on an intranet. In either case, Office 2000 can help you out, and with a little help from some free Microsoft software, you can even create your own intranet on your personal computer.

To be able to publish web documents beyond your own hard drive, you need Internet server software to handle the communication from one computer to another and across the Web. Internet service providers, such as America Online, and large corporate intranets rely on server programs such as Microsoft Internet Information Services (IIS) running on a Windows NT server that can handle the heavy volume of activity they experience. For the rest of us using Windows 95/98, there is a way to have use of a server to handle most of the operations that a small networked workgroup or individual user will need. Microsoft offers the Personal Web Server, packaged in Windows 98 and several of their Internet products (for example, FrontPage 98). It supports many advanced features used in web pages, such as data collection and access, and is used in developing, testing, and staging web applications. The Personal Web Manager dialog box is shown in Figure 9-12.

In order to get your HTML documents and associated files to a server for publishing, you can use the FTP capability

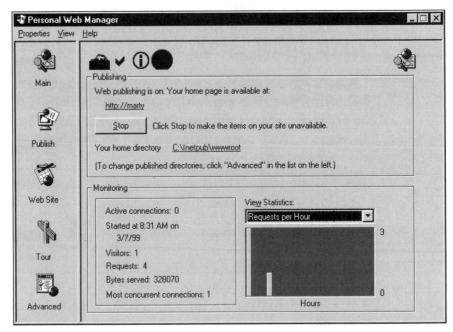

Figure 9-12   The Personal Web Server properties dialog box

described in the "I need to transfer a file to a client using FTP . . ." question in the "Accessing the Web and Intranets with Office 2000" section of this chapter. Additionally, there is a Web Publishing Wizard on the Windows 98 CD (you may need to run Add/Remove Programs from the Control Panel, open Internet Tools, and select Web Publishing Wizard). Once installed, the wizard, which is started from Start | Programs | Internet Explorer | Web Publishing Wizard, will walk you through the process of copying all the necessary files to the Internet or intranet server, as shown in Figure 9-13.

Note: *Although Word, Excel, Access, and PowerPoint offer many features to make creating and publishing online documents easy, they cannot do the job of a dedicated web-authoring program, such as Microsoft FrontPage. For more information on creating your own web pages and web sites, read Chapter 10 of this book; and, if you want more, read* FrontPage 2000: The Complete Reference, *by Martin S. Matthews and Erik B. Poulsen (Berkeley, CA: Osborne/McGraw-Hill, 1999).*

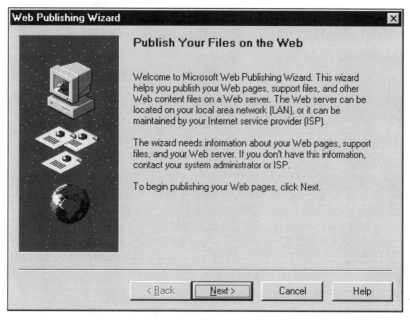

Figure 9-13   The Web Publishing Wizard dialog box

Can I put an Access database on a web site?

Yes. First, in the "Creating Internet and Intranet Documents" section of this chapter, see the question "In Access 97 there was an option to Save To HTML . . .," and create your choice of data access pages, server-generated HTML pages, or static HTML pages. When you have completed your new pages, you need to publish them to a web server. "Publish," in this case, simply means to copy your pages to a specific folder on the computer that is acting as the web server. This may mean different things depending on where you are publishing. Your publishing destinations may include the following:

- Your computer, using Microsoft Personal Web Server (MSPWS), giving access to a small group over a LAN

- A corporate server on your network, giving access to your company over an intranet

- An Internet service provider's (ISP's) server, giving access to the world over the Internet

In the second and third alternatives, there are a number of options, most importantly the path to and name of the folder (or directory, which is the same thing) in which you are going to publish your database. The only way to determine what is right for you is to ask your network administrator or Internet service provider's representative how and where to publish your database. You may be told, especially in the case of an ISP, that you need to FTP your files to the server (meaning that you need to copy your files to the server using the File Transfer Protocol). If so, see the "I need to transfer a file to a client using FTP . . ." question in the "Accessiong the Web and Internets with Office 2000" section of this chapter.

If you are using MSPWS on your computer, you need to create a new folder under C:\Inetpub\Wwwroot\ if you are using the version of MSPWS that came with Windows 98. If you have an older version of MSPWS, you need to create a new folder under C:\Webshare\Wwwroot. Once you have created this new folder, you need to copy your pages to it either by saving the pages there from Access, or by using the Windows Explorer to copy them.

Copying and Accessing the Database

If you are publishing either data access pages or server-generated HTML pages, your pages must have access to your database. If you are publishing data access pages on your computer using MSPWS, this is not a problem; the database is already on your computer and the pages are correctly bound to that data, so even if you have copied the pages to a different directory, the correct link to the database should still be there. If you are publishing server-generated HTML pages on your computer with MSPWS, you do not have to copy the database, but you do have to set up a system data-source name (explained further on in this answer).

In all other cases, you are going to have to copy your database to the server. When you do that, you will probably have to modify the HTML behind the page to point to the new database location. Use these steps to do that:

1. Open your page in a browser, such as Internet Explorer.
2. Open the View menu and choose Source.

3. In a section that begins "<OBJECT" (without the quotation marks) look for a statement that begins "Data Source=" like this:

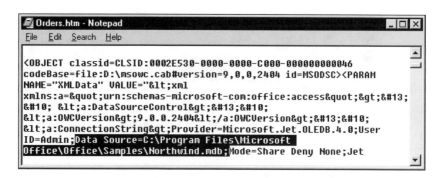

4. Change the path that follows "Data Source=" so that it correctly points to where your database resides. If it is in the same folder with your page(s), you can just remove the path, leaving only the database name.

5. Save your page where you originally opened it.

Setting Up a System Data-Source Name

If you are working with server-generated HTML pages, you will have to set up a system data-source name (DSN). If you are publishing to a corporate intranet server or an ISP, you will have to ask your network administrator or ISP to do this for you. If you are using the MSPWS on your own computer, you can use these steps:

1. Open the Start menu and choose Settings | Control Panel. In the Control Panel, double-click ODBC Data Sources. The ODBC (open database connectivity) Data Source Administrator dialog box will open, as you can see in Figure 9-14.

2. Click the System DSN tab and click Add. The Create New Data Source dialog box will open, displaying a list of ODBC drivers.

3. Double-click Microsoft Access Driver to open the ODBC Microsoft Access Setup dialog box.

4. Enter a name for your data source (probably the name of your database), and click Select. The Select Database dialog box will open.

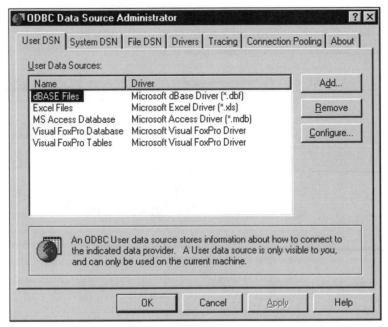

Figure 9-14 Establishing a data source name for server-generated HTML pages

5. Locate the folder and select the file that is your database, as shown next, and then click OK three times. You will now have both a data source and database driver set up for publishing server-generated HTML pages.

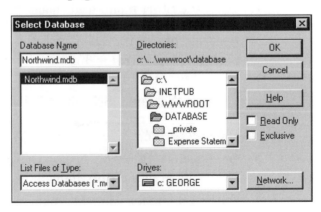

I've created a web document in Word that I want to view in Internet Explorer to see how it will look on our company's intranet. After I open Internet Explorer, I always find it cumbersome to have to type the path to an HTML document on my hard drive in the Address box. Is there a better way to access local HTML documents from Internet Explorer?

Yes. As in other Windows programs, Internet Explorer has an Open option on the File menu. Choosing this option displays the Open dialog box, shown here, which has a different appearance than most Open dialog boxes:

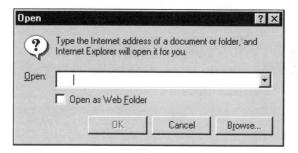

You have three methods to locate an HTML document:

- Type in the address/path in the Open box.
- Click the down arrow in the Open box, and select an address or path that has been used previously.
- Click the Browse button to display the more familiar Open dialog box, in which you can navigate to the file.

You can also choose Web Page Preview from the File menu of whatever Office application created the document, or you can locate the file in the Windows Explorer and double-click it.

USING WORD WITH YOUR E-MAIL

 What is "WordMail" and how do I enable it?

If you are using Outlook (not Outlook Express) as your e-mail handler, you may use Microsoft Word to create, read, and edit

e-mail messages. This is called "WordMail." You can turn on WordMail from Outlook by opening the Tools menu, choosing Options, clicking the Mail Format tab, and selecting Use Microsoft Word To Edit E-mail Messages, like this:

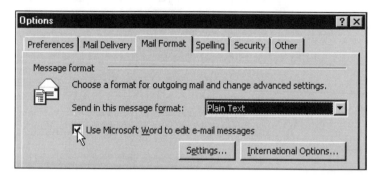

 What is the advantage of using Word to create e-mail when basically all I want to do is type the message?

If all you want to do is type a message, and you are not going to edit a shared document or you are not particularly concerned about formatting, then you probably do not need the Word functions. However, using Word as your e-mail editor makes more Word functions available than are available in Outlook's default editor. See the sidebar "WordMail Functions" for specific uses of Word in e-mail messages.

WordMail Functions

The following is a sampling of Word functions you can use in the e-mail message window:

Use the Edit options to

● Paste As Hyperlink.

● Find, Replace, and Go To text in the message. Without Word, only the Find and Find Next options are available.

Use the View options to

- Display the message in Normal, Web Layout, Print Layout, or Outline view.
- Display any and all of the Word toolbars. If you are not using Word, only the Standard, Formatting, and Clipboard toolbars are available.
- Use the Document Map feature.

Use the Insert options to

- Insert page, column, and section breaks.
- Insert date and time, fields, symbols, comments, footnotes, captions, cross-references, objects, and bookmarks.
- Add a table of contents or an index, if you like.

Use the Format options to

- Format text in newspaper-type columns.
- Format text with bullets or numbers, borders, or shading.
- Set new tab stops. If you are not using Word, default tabs are set every half-inch, but you are not able to set new tab stops.
- Use styles. The choices here are limited and are not the same as those available in Word.
- Use AutoFormat. The choices here are to automatically format the message as e-mail, as a letter, or as a general document.
- Format the background with colors.
- Apply a theme.

Use the Tools options to

- Check spelling and grammar as you type.
- Use a grammar checker, select a language, use the Thesaurus, or use word count.
- Use automatic features, such as AutoSummarize, AutoCorrect, and AutoSignature.
- Track changes.
- Create, run, and edit macros.

- Use templates and add-ins.
- Use the Table function to create and edit tables.

Note: *Many of the special formatting and other features that WordMail can add to e-mail are not observable by recipients over the Internet. If you are on a network with an Exchange server, then the additional formatting will be transferred to the e-mail recipient within the network. Otherwise, it will be stripped out.*

 Can I create a signature that will be added automatically to my e-mail messages, and can I have more than one?

Yes, you can create one or more signatures in Word, name them, and choose a default for both new messages and replies. If you do this, either in Word or in an Outlook WordMail message window, the new signature will be displayed automatically in your message window whenever you open it. If you open the message window without using Word as your e-mail editor, the signature will not be displayed automatically. Create a new signature with the following steps:

1. Open a new WordMail message window.

2. Type and format the text for the signature, add a picture if you want, and then select all of it.

3. Open the Tools menu, choose Options, select the General tab, and click E-mail Options. The E-mail Options dialog box will appear.

4. Type a name or title for that particular signature, and click Add. If you have more than one signature, you will be asked if you want to make the current signature the one to use for all messages. Click Yes or No.

5. If you have more than one signature, you can choose which to use for new messages, and which to use for replies.

Figure 9-15   Choosing which signature to use for particular messages

6. Click OK twice. The signatures are saved as AutoText entries in the Normal template under the names you gave them.

When you create a new message, the default signature that you specified will automatically be added to the message. If you want a different signature, and have more than one, right-click the signature and a context menu will pop up, allowing you to make another choice, like this:

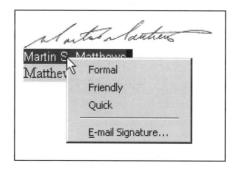

> *Tip:* *If you do not want to use WordMail for writing your e-mail messages in Outlook, you can turn that option off by opening the Tools menu, choosing Options, clicking the Mail Format tab, and clearing the Use Microsoft Word To Edit E-mail Messages check box. You can still have a plain text signature added by default, and you can choose from among several signatures.*

I have been told that reading e-mail in Word is easier. I don't see much difference except for changes in formatting. Are there other differences?

No, there are no significant differences.

If I send a Word e-mail message to someone who doesn't have Word, what happens to the text?

The message will be displayed as text only, without any of the formatting that may have been applied if Word were used to create the message. For example, symbols that may have been inserted will not be displayed as symbols; if you have entered a table, the text in the table will be displayed as tab-delimited text, not in a table format; and text in newspaper-type columns will no longer be formatted in columns.

Chapter 10

Creating Web Pages with FrontPage

Answer Topics!

Creating Web Pages with FrontPage @ a Glance

FrontPage allows you to create web pages in a WYSIWYG (what you see is what you get) environment. It allows you to easily add text with a wide range of formatting, pictures, and links, called *hyperlinks*, to other pages and files. FrontPage provides the means to manage sets of pages called *web sites*, and to publish these sites on the Internet or an intranet. FrontPage also provides a number of tools to facilitate web page creation, such as tools to easily make tables, forms, frames, and tables of contents; as well as interactive components, such as search forms, hover buttons, and hit counters. The eight sections in this chapter will cover FrontPage web creation, from exploring the Internet and intranets to advanced FrontPage techniques:

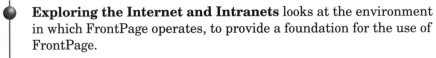

- **Exploring the Internet and Intranets** looks at the environment in which FrontPage operates, to provide a foundation for the use of FrontPage.

- **Automatic Web Page Creation** discusses the automated techniques for creating web pages with FrontPage.

- **Directly Creating and Formatting Web Pages** describes the manual methods of creating and formatting web pages with FrontPage.

- **Adding Pictures and Hyperlinks to Web Pages** shows you how to add pictures and links to your web pages. The hyperlinks allow the user to jump to different places on the same page, to other pages in the same web site, and to other web sites.

- **Using Tables and Frames** explains how to use cell-oriented tables, similar to a spreadsheet, and frames that give you independent sections of a window, to improve the layout of a web page.

- **Working with Forms** covers the creation and use of forms, including their layout, the verification of data, and handling the information returned from a form.

- **Applying FrontPage Components** explores the many components that you can add to a FrontPage web page to create such elements as a table of contents, a search form, a recurring header or footer, a hover button, or a hit counter.

- **Using Advanced Techniques** addresses the ways you can enhance your web pages with the advanced features in FrontPage, such as customizing themes, using style sheets, and dynamic HTML.

EXPLORING THE INTERNET AND INTRANETS

What is the difference between an intranet and the Internet?

The Internet is a worldwide public network (a wide area network or WAN) that provides a number of services, including the World Wide Web (the Web), which is a graphical means of exchanging multimedia information. An intranet is a graphical means of exchanging multimedia information over a private, local area network, or LAN. In other words, an intranet is equivalent to the Web, and the principal difference is that the Web uses a WAN (the Internet) for its transmission, while an intranet uses a LAN.

What is an extranet?

An extranet is the extending of an intranet to selected external users over the Internet. For example, a company may allow suppliers or customers to use the Internet to access a selected subset of the company's intranet data.

What is a web page?

A *web page* is a text file containing Hypertext Markup Language (HTML) formatting tags and links to graphics files and other web pages. The text file, which in its raw text form looks like Figure 10-1, is stored on a *web server* and can be accessed by other computers connected to the server via the Internet or a LAN. The file can be accessed by the use of *web browsers*—programs that download the file to your computer, interpret the HTML tags and links, and display the results on your monitor. When the text file in Figure 10-1 is displayed in a browser it looks like Figure 10-2.

Web pages are interactive, and they can use multimedia. The term *multimedia* is used to describe text, audio, animation, and video files that are combined to present information; for example, in an interactive encyclopedia or a game. You also hear the term *hypermedia* to describe multimedia in web pages. Web pages are made interactive to allow the reader or user to send information or commands back to the web site that hosts the web application. For

```
www.msn[1] - Notepad
File Edit Search Help

<HTML>
<HEAD>
<script language=javascript>
function mOvr(src,clrOver) { if (!src.contains(event.fromElement)) {
src.style.cursor = 'hand'; src.bgColor = clrOver; }}function mOut(src,clrIn) { if
(!src.contains(event.toElement)) { src.style.cursor = 'default'; src.bgColor =
clrIn; }} function mClk(src) {
if(event.srcElement.tagName=='TD'){src.children.tags('A')[0].click();} }
</script>
<META HTTP-EQUIV=Content-Type content="text/html; charset=iso-8859-1">

<META http-equiv=PICS-Label content='(PICS-1.1
"http://www.rsac.org/ratingsv01.html" l comment "RSACi North America Server" by
"inet@microsoft.com" r (n 0 s 0 v 0 l 0))'>
<title>MSN.COM</title>
<LINK REL=STYLESHEET TYPE="text/css" HREF="/global/start_IE4_new.css">
<!-- 4/13/99 10:51:09 AM 18511 //-->
<script language="Javascript">
var userEng         = true;
var CookieAUTOREF   = "";
var qurls = new
Array();qurls["sALTA"]="http://jump.altavista.digital.com/ie3.go?q=";qurls["sAOLN"]
="http://netfind.aol.com/search.gw?c=web&lk=excite_netfind_us&src=1&search=";qurls[
"sEXCI"]="http://www.excite.com/search.gw?trace=a&search=";qurls["sHOTB"]="http://w
ww.hotbot.com/?SW=web&SM=MC&DC=10&DE=2&RG=NA&_v=2&act.search.x=89&act.search.y=7&MT
=";qurls["sINFO"]="http://www.infoseek.com/Titles?col=WW&sv=M8&lk=noframes&nh=10&qt
=";qurls["sLYCO"]="http://www.lycos.com/cgi-bin/pursuit?cat=lycos&mtemp=ms1&etemp=m
s1error&part=MICROSOFT&query=";qurls["sYAHO"]="http://search.yahoo.com/bin/search?h
c=0&hs=0&p=";qurls["sMSN"]="http://search.msn.com/results.asp?RS=CHECKED&UN=doc&CO=
20&Form=MSNH&MT=";qurls["sMSNI"]="http://search.msn.com/results.asp?RS=CHECKED&UN=d
oc&CO=20&Form=MSNH&TK=1&MT=";qurls["sSNAP"]="http://hmc.snap.com/search/directory/r
```

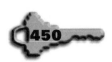

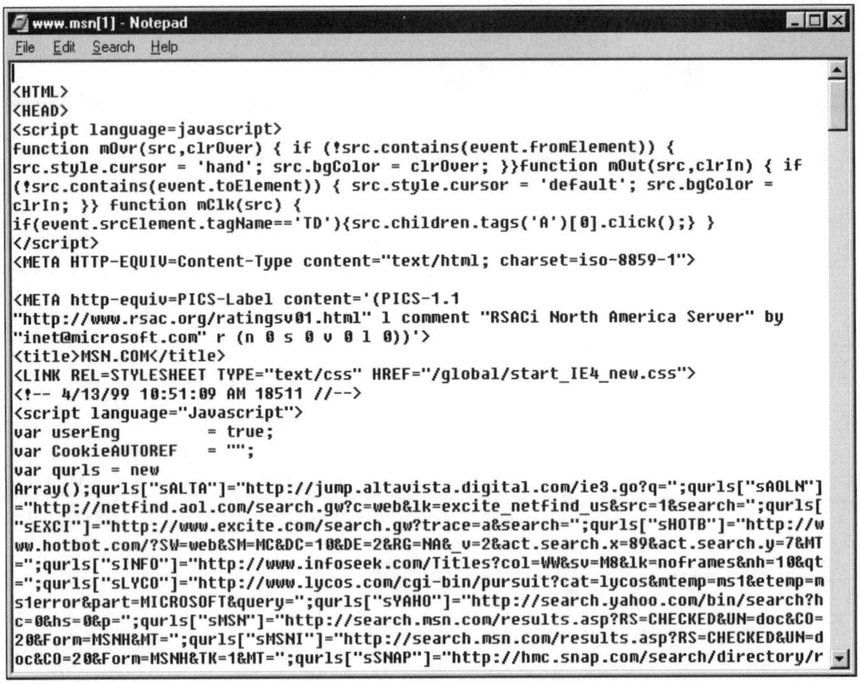

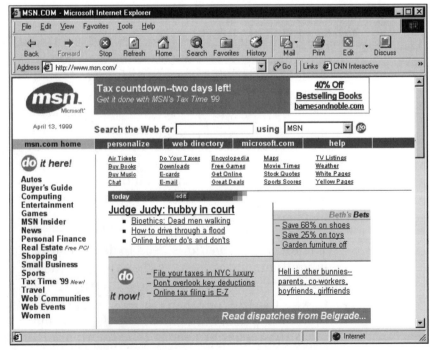

Figure 10-1 The HTML text file behind MSN's home page

Figure 10-2 A browser displaying the HTML text in Figure 10-1

example, Figure 10-2 shows a box for the user to enter search criteria and send it back to the server.

Each web page has an address, called the *uniform resource locator* (URL). The URL for the MSN home page is http://www.msn.com. The URL is displayed in the Address box at the top of the browser window (below the toolbar). A URL is the path on the Internet to a specific web page. It is used in the same way you use a path name to locate files on your computer. In this case, the URL tells you that the web page is located on a web server with the domain name *msn.com* connected to the World Wide Web ("www"). A *domain* is one or more networked computers; the domain name provides a single address through which browsers can access the network from the Internet. The network's domain server routes the request to the correct place within the network. The actual filename of the *home page* (the top-level page of the web, which usually serves as a table of contents for the web) is usually either Default.htm or Index.htm; it is implied by being unstated. The default web page filename is set on the web server. This is the page that will be displayed if no web page filename is specified.

What does the alphabet soup (TCP/IP, HTTP, and HTML) associated with the Internet mean?

The Internet operates worldwide with many different computers, many different communications systems, and many different languages, and this is managed through a set of standards or *protocols* that everybody uses. The "alphabet soup" refers to these Internet protocols.

TCP/IP (Transmission Control Protocol/Internet Protocol) controls how information is packaged to be transferred between computers connected through the Internet. The IP defines how computers on either end of the transmission are addressed, while the TCP defines the addressing of the "envelopes" that contain the information being transmitted.

HTTP (Hypertext Transfer Protocol) is the language used to exchange information on the World Wide Web. Requests for information are composed in HTTP by a browser, such as Internet Explorer or Netscape Navigator, and then sent using TCP/IP to a designated server. The server then composes a responding message containing web pages in HTTP and returns it to the browser using TCP/IP.

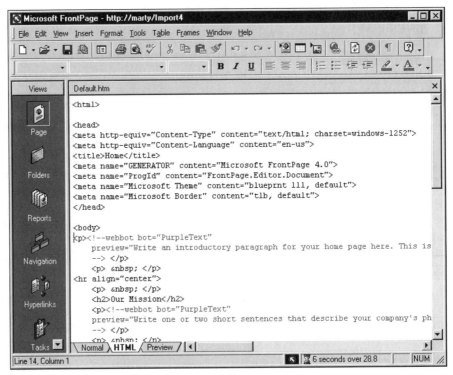

Figure 10-3 FrontPage Page view's HTML tab

HTML (Hypertext Markup Language) is the language used to create the web pages that are distributed on the Web. FrontPage takes the pages you create, translates them into HTML, and provides the means to look at and directly edit the HTML in the Page view HTML tab, shown in Figure 10-3. A browser uses HTML to properly format and display the information sent to it.

 ### When I browse a page on the Internet or an intranet, is it actually stored on my machine?

Yes. Web browsers download the web pages and pictures and store them in temporary files in a *cache*, on the users' hard disk. This speeds up subsequent loading of the pages. The browser checks to see if the file on the web server is newer than the files in the cache. If the pages are the same, the cached page is read from the hard disk rather than downloading the file from the Internet. If the version on the web server is newer, it is downloaded.

In Netscape Navigator 4, users can control the cache in the Preferences dialog box, opened by choosing Preferences from the Edit menu. The cache can be cleared anytime, and a time limit for saving cached files can be set. In Internet Explorer, the cache ("Temporary Internet Files") is controlled from the General tab of the Internet Options dialog box, opened by choosing Internet Options from the View menu in Internet Explorer 4 or the Tools menu in Internet Explorer 5.

In describing web pages, I've heard people talk about "CGI" and "Perl." What do these terms mean?

A CGI script is a Common Gateway Interface script. Gateways are programs that handle information requests and return a document or create a document on the fly. Form requests are the most common use of gateways. The Common Gateway Interface is a convention on how gateway scripts and programs are to be used on the web server. Gateway programs, or scripts, are external executable programs that can run on a variety of servers. These programs can be written in any language that produces an executable file, including C or C++, Perl (see the next paragraph), Python, TCL, Visual Basic, shells, and many others. It doesn't matter what language the program is written in, as long as the resources to run it are on your server. There are many sources of free CGI scripts on the web.

Perl, which stands for Practical Extraction and Report Language, is an interpreted computer language similar to C and was developed at NASA's Jet Propulsion Laboratory. Perl runs under UNIX and is used for system administration tasks, such as extracting information from text files or assembling a text string into a command that can be sent to the operating system.

 I've been told I can use the Microsoft Personal Web Server and the FrontPage server extensions to create a small intranet. What are these and is this correct?

The Microsoft Personal Web Server (MSPWS) allows you to publish a web site on your computer rather than on some other Internet or intranet server. MSPWS simply sits in the background on your computer as a task, and is included in the Windows 98 package. MSPWS is a scaled down version of Microsoft's Internet Information Services (IIS); IIS is included with Windows NT 4 and Windows 2000 Server and is all the web server you need to run a large intranet or a full World Wide Web site.

Release 4 of MSPWS is in Windows 98 and Release 3 was included in the FrontPage 98 package. If you do not have either of those, you can download MSPWS Release 4 from Microsoft (http://www.microsoft.com/ie/pws/).

FrontPage server extensions add the functionality needed to implement the interactive parts of a FrontPage web site. If you want to use all of the components of FrontPage, especially the interactive components, you need to have the FrontPage server extensions installed on the web server you are using to deliver your web site. This web server might be MSPWS, the company intranet server, or an Internet web presence provider (WPP). If your intranet server or web presence provider is not using the FrontPage server extensions, you should suggest that they do so. The server extensions are available from Microsoft (http://www. microsoft.com/ frontpage/wpp/) for virtually every popular Windows NT- and UNIX-based server. Microsoft maintains a rapidly growing list of WPPs that do have the FrontPage server extensions installed (http://microsoft.com/frontpage/wpp/list/).

The Microsoft Personal Web Server with the FrontPage server extensions are all you need to set up a small intranet. By default, MSPWS is configured to start automatically upon startup of Windows. You can tell it's running by the icon that appears in the notification area on the right end of the Taskbar. If you want to stop it, double-click the icon and click Stop in the Personal Web Manager dialog box that appears.

What is the difference between an Internet service provider and a web presence provider?

Though the terms Internet service provider (ISP) and web presence provider (WPP) are sometimes used interchangeably, there is a difference. An ISP provides access to the Internet, usually through a dial-up (modem) connection. A WPP hosts web sites. That is, a WPP stores web files on a server that is accessible over the Internet. Often your ISP and your WPP will be the same company. In this book the terms "presence provider" and "web host" refer to a WPP.

When do you use each of the FrontPage views?

FrontPage allows you to look at and work with a web site in six different views. These views and their uses are as follows:

- **Page view**   Allows you to create and edit a web page by adding and laying out formatted text, pictures, sounds, video, frames, tables, forms, hyperlinks, and other interactive elements. Page view provides a WYSIWYG (what you see is what you get) editing environment where you can edit existing web pages, including those created elsewhere on the Web, as well as create new web pages. In Page view you can use page wizards, templates, and themes; apply FrontPage components for interactive functions; create forms and tables; add image maps with clickable hot spots; and convert popular image formats into GIF and JPEG formats used on the Web.

- **Folders view**   Allows you to look at and manage an entire web site at its files and folders level.

- **Reports view**   Allows you to look for errors or potential problems with your web site in any one of over ten reports on such subjects as Unlinked Files, Slow Pages, Broken Links, and Component Errors.

- **Navigation view**   Allows you to check and change the way a user gets from one page to another and then back to the home page.

● **Hyperlinks view** Allows you to check and organize the hyperlinks in a web site in a drag-and-drop environment.

● **Tasks view** Displays the Tasks list and allows you to track the tasks required to produce a web site, identifying who is responsible for them, their priority, and their status.

Tip: *Right-click an empty area of the right pane of Navigation view and choose Zoom | Size To Fit to see all the pages if they are out of the window.*

Can more than one person edit a web site?

Yes, but you would need to give the others permission to do it. How that permission is given differs depending on where the web site is stored. If it is on your computer, they would simply need permission to edit a file on your hard disk. If it is on a server, either locally or remote, they would need user IDs and passwords to access the file. Also, if someone other than you has permission to edit a web site you are about to work on, you should copy the current version from the server and then edit it, rather than trusting the copy on your local machine. This avoids the "Twilight Zone effect," where changes that you made are overwritten by someone else's changes. Microsoft has a product called Microsoft Visual SourceSafe, which prevents this effect on intranets.

Tip: *It is important to keep your web pages updated. First, it provides a reason for people to come back and look at them. Second, it prevents information on the page from getting out of date.*

AUTOMATIC WEB PAGE CREATION

What is the difference between a wizard and a template?

In Page view, wizards and templates allow you to automatically create a new page with many features on it.

Wizards and templates differ only in the amount of interaction between you and the computer during the creation process. *Templates* create a ready-made page without any interaction on your part. *Wizards* use one or more dialog boxes to ask you a series of questions during creation. Based on your answers to these questions, a customized page is created. Whether you use a template or a wizard, you can customize the resultant web pages and elements in Page view.

The General tab of the New dialog box (opened from the File menu) in Page view provides a number of *page* wizards and templates (as distinct from the *web* wizards and templates available when you create a new web site) to help you create many specialized pages. These are shown in Figure 10-4.

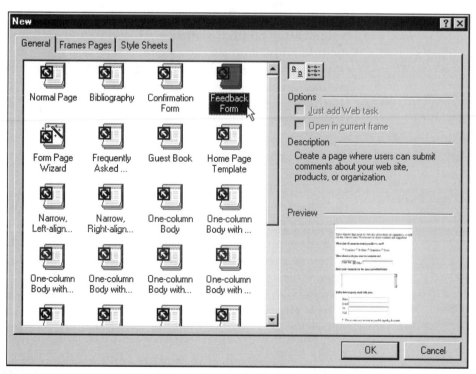

Figure 10-4   Some of the page wizards and templates that are available when creating a new web page

 Note: *The New Page button on the toolbar gives you a new page using the Normal Page template—it does not open the New dialog box and provide access to the list of templates and wizards.*

How do templates differ from actual web sites or web pages?

Templates are model or prototype web sites or web pages, identical in every detail to an actual web site or web page. The only thing that distinguishes them is that they are in a special folder. You can view a template in a browser and use it like any other web site or web page. In fact, a template is just a web site or web page that has been set aside to serve as a model for other web sites or web pages.

Because they are stored in different folders, think of web site templates and web page templates as two distinct types of templates, although there are many similarities. *Page* templates generally create a single page that becomes part of a separately created web site, although a page template can include additional linked pages. A *web site* template creates a full FrontPage web site with one or more interconnected pages. This means that it includes all of the folder structure that is a part of FrontPage. In both cases, though, you create the web site or the web page in the same way that you would create any other web site or page.

When the web site or page is the way you want it, you then place it in a special folder set up for templates with the extension TEM. For example, Test.tem is a folder containing the files for a template named "Test." The files within the template folder are just the normal .htm extension HTML web files, plus an .inf template information file and a .dib file, which is a thumbnail image of the template that appears in Page view's New dialog box Preview section.

What are themes, and how do I use them?

Themes are a group of features that can be assigned to a single web page, as well as to an entire FrontPage web site, that specify how the page or site will look. Themes control the

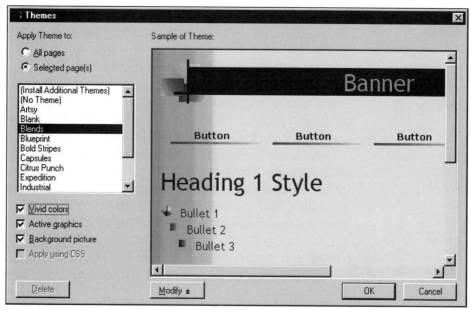

Figure 10-5 A theme can be applied to one or more pages or to an entire web site

fonts used; the colors of text, background, and other objects; and the repetitive graphic elements used, such as buttons and banners. You assign themes to pages by opening the pages in Page view; selecting Theme from the Format menu; and then choosing Selected Pages in the Themes dialog box, as shown in Figure 10-5. When you do that, you affect only the selected web page. If you want to apply a theme to an entire web site, you would choose All Pages. Overall, the purpose of a theme is to provide a cohesive, unifying look and feel to your entire web site. Therefore, themes are usually applied to entire sites.

You can view or remove themes in the HTML tab of Page view (click HTML in the bottom left of the Page view window). The HTML code

```
<meta name="Microsoft Theme" content="capsules 110, default">
```

indicates that the Capsules theme has been applied to a page. You can remove a theme by selecting this line of HTML code in the HTML tab and pressing the DEL key.

Along with applying a new theme to an open web page, you can also edit many of the page format elements using page formatting. For example, you can change font color, font size, and paragraph alignment. However, other formatting options cannot be changed after applying a theme, such as the background and the default text and hyperlink colors. If you open the Themes dialog box from a page with an existing theme, the Modify button lets you change the colors, graphics, and styles used in a theme and then save it as a new theme or a replacement for an existing theme.

Is it really a good idea to use the Under Construction icon proposed in several wizards?

Using the Under Construction icon is generally not a good idea. If at all possible, finish the web site before putting it on the server for public consumption.

What does the "CSS" mean in the Theme dialog box?

CSS in the check box in the lower-left of the Theme dialog box (opened from the Format menu, Theme option) or the Choose Theme dialog box (opened from a web wizard) stands for "cascading style sheets," which are used to apply consistent styles in a web site.

What are shared borders, and how are they applied?

Shared borders are sections of a web page set aside for content that will appear on each page of your web site. Shared borders are *borders* because they are at the top, bottom, left, or (rarely) right side of a page. They are *shared* because they include content that is shared by every page in a web site that isn't specifically excluded (you can turn off the shared borders for a given page).

Shared borders are applied to an open web site in any view by choosing Shared Borders from the Format menu to open the Shared Borders dialog box shown in Figure 10-6.

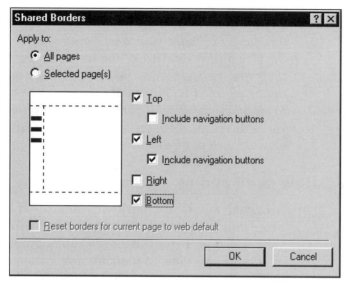

Figure 10-6 Shared borders can be placed on any of the four sides of a page

Here you can choose to apply the borders to all or just selected pages, select which of the four borders you want to use, and specify whether you want to include navigation buttons in the border. If you want different shared borders on a given page, open that page in Page view, select Shared Borders from the Format menu, make sure Current Page is selected, and then turn on or off the borders you want.

Shared borders often include navigation bars. All the FrontPage web sites generated by wizards or templates include navigation bars in the shared borders. Here are some examples of other useful shared borders:

- A top shared border with page titles
- A bottom shared border with copyright information, site contact information, and other text or images you want to appear on the bottom of every page in your site
- A left shared border with general information you want to place in every page in your site, such as links

Tip: *Shared borders are rarely placed on the right side of web pages because your users may not see them. Depending on the size and resolution of the user's screen, and the size of their browser window, the right side of your web pages may not be visible to them unless they use the horizontal scroll bar to see it. Since shared borders often include navigation bars, you will normally want the shared border to be visible as soon as your web page downloads.*

How can I add navigation bars to my web pages?

Navigation bars (navbars) are generated automatically in FrontPage. They include hyperlinks to other pages within your web site. FrontPage uses the page relationships shown in Navigation view to identify navigation buttons. The hierarchy you assign when you create a web site and that is shown in Navigation view determines the options available to you for navigation bars.

To assign navigation bars to shared borders, you must choose the Include Navigation Buttons check box in the Shared Borders dialog box described in the previous question. If you created your FrontPage web site using a wizard or template, or independently chose the Include Navigation Buttons, navigation bars are created automatically. The actual page-to-page relationships that are utilized by the navigation bars are best viewed and changed in Navigation view. In that view, if you right-click a page, you will see an option to include or exclude that page in a navigation bar. In Page view, right-click the navbar or its note placeholder, and choose Navigation Bar Properties to open the dialog box of that name shown in Figure 10-7. Here you can determine the hierarchical structure of the navbar, as well as its orientation and appearance.

 Note: *In the Orientation And Appearance section of the Navigation Bar Properties dialog box, you can choose to have the hyperlinks displayed as either graphical buttons or text. For the buttons to be displayed as graphics, you must apply a theme to the web site. Otherwise, the links will be displayed as text, even if Buttons is selected.*

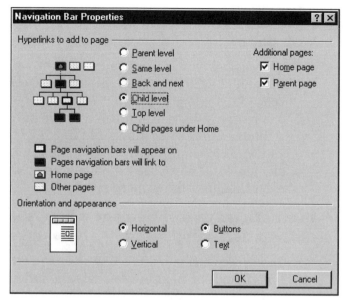

Figure 10-7 FrontPage will automatically generate navbars with several hierarchical orientations

DIRECTLY CREATING AND FORMATTING WEB PAGES

 What is the fastest way to create a web site?

Probably the fastest way is to use existing or legacy files already in computer form. For example, Microsoft Word files that have consistently formatted headings using heading styles will give you web pages with automatically created links to each of the headings in the document. Another way to speed up the process is to scan printed documents that you want incorporated (like travel brochures for the details of a travel offering) and then use optical character recognition (OCR) software to convert them to word processing files. Be sure to carefully edit any OCR-generated text (the process is less than perfect), and make sure you have written permission to reproduce other people's copyrighted material.

How can I reduce the space between lines on my web page?

The easiest way is to use SHIFT-ENTER in place of ENTER at the end of each line. This will take out over half of the line space. A single paragraph, though, cannot have more than one paragraph style, nor can a single paragraph contain more than one bulleted or numbered line. For that reason, when you want to change style or have another bullet or list element, you must use ENTER placed at the end of each line, even though it takes more space.

I've noticed that if I indent a line, the next line is automatically indented. Is there a way around this?

Yes there is. If you press ENTER at the end of an indented typed line, the next line will also be indented; however, if you press the DOWN ARROW key, the second line will be left aligned without the indents.

I don't understand how "Normal" is used in regard to font size. What does it mean?

"Normal" font size is not a particular size, but rather allows the default size of the current paragraph style to take precedence.

Is there an easy way to make the background the same on several pages?

Yes. To make the background the same on several web pages, get the first page the way you want it. Then open the second page, right-click it, and choose Page Properties to open the Page Properties dialog box, click the Background tab, click Get Background Information From Another Page, and select the first page. Click OK.

Note: *There is no Background tab on a page with a theme.*

What do the wavy red lines mean in my text?

The wavy red lines under words are the spelling checker telling you that these words are not in the spelling dictionary and may be misspelled. You can right-click these words to get a list of alternative correctly spelled words, as well as commands to ignore the suspected misspelling or add the word to the dictionary. You can also permanently turn off these lines by opening the Tools menu, choosing Page Options, and then clicking Hide Spelling Errors In All Documents in the General tab of the Page Options dialog box.

When I save my web pages, I'm always asked if I want to save my pictures on those pages. These pictures are already on my hard disk, so do I have to save them again?

Yes. Always save your images with your web files, so that when you copy the web site to a server, FrontPage can copy them all together for you.

Is there an easy way to add horizontal lines to my web page?

Yes. FrontPage provides easy ways to add such lines through the Horizontal Line option in the Insert menu. Also, in the Insert menu, you can choose Picture | Clip Art, select the Web Dividers category, and pick from 60 options.

How can I tell if my web pages have been saved since I changed them?

You can tell if a page has been saved since it was last changed by looking in the Window menu. If the page has an asterisk (*) beside it, it needs to be saved.

How can I hide pages in my web site from a search?

You can hide pages, such as style pages or pages that you are using only to include in other pages, from the Search Form by placing the pages in the special web folder *webname*_private. The Search Form does not search this folder.

I'm told by users that pages that I thought look really great do not look good on their screens. How can I prevent this?

It is probably because they are looking at your pages with either a different browser, or at a different resolution, or

both. Be sure to check how both Netscape Navigator and Microsoft Internet Explorer display your web pages at several resolutions (640×480, 800×600, and 1024×768). You may be surprised at the differences, but better you be surprised than your users.

You can change the resolution on most systems by right-clicking a blank area of the desktop and choosing Properties. In the Display Properties dialog box, open the Settings tab, drag the Screen Area slider to a different resolution, as shown in Figure 10-8, and click OK. You will be told that your desktop will be resized and that you have 15 seconds to accept it or your original resolution will be restored. Click OK, and if you want to keep the new resolution, click Yes.

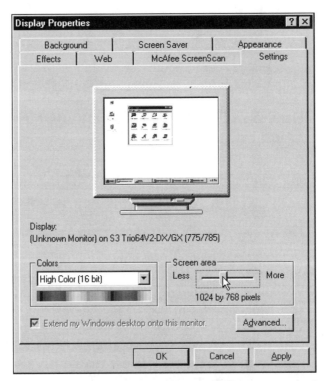

Figure 10-8 Looking at your web pages at different resolutions allows you to see how others will see them

ADDING PICTURES AND HYPERLINKS TO WEB PAGES

 What are hyperlinks, and how do you use them?

Hyperlinks (or *links*) allow the user of a web site to quickly jump from one page to another, or to a particular element on the same or another page (called a *bookmark*), or to a different web site. You can make either text or a picture be the element the user clicks to make the link, and you can map different areas of a single picture to different links (the different areas are called *hot spots*).

 You create a link by first selecting the object that you want the user to click, and then clicking the Hyperlink button in the toolbar, or by choosing Hyperlink from the Insert menu. In either case, the Create Hyperlink dialog box will open, as shown in Figure 10-9. Here, you can choose an

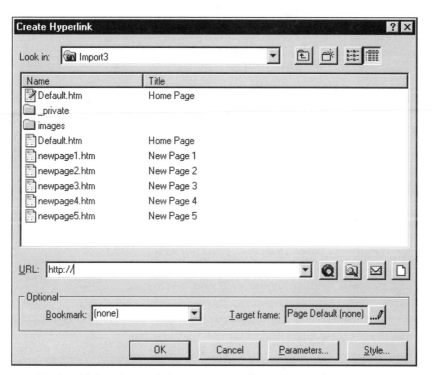

Figure 10-9 Using hyperlinks, you can allow your web page user to jump to other pages in your web site or to a different web site

existing page as the link, enter a URL, use your web browser to find a link, make a hyperlink to a file on your disk or to an e-mail address, or create a new page and link to it.

 The hyperlinks within my web site seem to take me to different places each time they are used. What causes this, and how can I fix it?

When you choose a page as a link, you are not taken to any particular part of the page. The page is just opened. If you are opening the page for the first time in a session, you'll be taken to the top of the page. If you have previously opened the page in the current session and scrolled down it, then when you return, you'll be taken to wherever you scrolled. This may or may not be what you want. You can control where you go on a page through bookmarks. *Bookmarks* are objects (text or graphics) that have been selected as destinations for a link. To establish a bookmark, select the object, open the Insert menu, choose Bookmark, and click OK.

Tip: *You must identify the bookmark before you establish the link, unless you want to go back and edit the link after it is established.*

 How can I create an e-mail link on my web page?

A link to an e-mail address uses the *mailto* capability found in most browsers. This allows the user to click the link to open a new message in the user's e-mail program. FrontPage will create a mailto link when you enter text that looks like an e-mail address (two text strings, without spaces, separated by the @ character), for example, webmaster@myweb.com. Alternatively, you can select the text and choose the Make A Hyperlink That Sends E-mail button in the Create Hyperlink dialog box.

 Is there an easy way to see where a hyperlink will take you?

Yes. Position the mouse pointer over the link, and, in the left end of the status bar, you will see the URL for the link.

 Tip: *Each page in your web site, regardless of the level, should have a direct link back to the home page. This allows users to quickly get back to the starting point in one click.*

I don't like the way my hyperlinks look. Is there a way to change that?

Hyperlinks do not have to be underlined, although they should be displayed in a different color than the body text. With Netscape Navigator (and Communicator) 4.03 and later, you can use the Preferences option in the Edit menu; and with Microsoft Internet Explorer 4.0 and later, you can use the Internet Options option in the View menu (Internet Explorer 4) or Tools menu (Internet Explorer 5) to control whether hyperlinks will be underlined, and you can also set the color they will be displayed in.

I am constantly making mistakes when I type URLs. Is there an easier way to get URLs into the various places they're used?

Sometimes there is no alternative to typing them, and it is very easy to make mistakes in doing that. There are at least two tricks that can save you having to type URLs:

- If you click the Use Your Web Browser. . . button in the Create Hyperlink dialog box, locate the Web site you want to link to, and then return to the Create Hyperlink dialog box, the URL will be automatically copied to the URL text box in the Create Hyperlink dialog box.

- You can drag across the URL in the FrontPage Page Properties dialog box, press CTRL-C to copy it to the Clipboard, open a browser, click the Address box, and press CTRL-V to paste the URL there.

I'm constantly being told I have broken hyperlinks in web pages. How can I better manage these?

FrontPage provides some excellent tools for managing hyperlinks. The Hyperlinks view provides a comprehensive visual reference, as you can see in Figure 10-10. Besides the

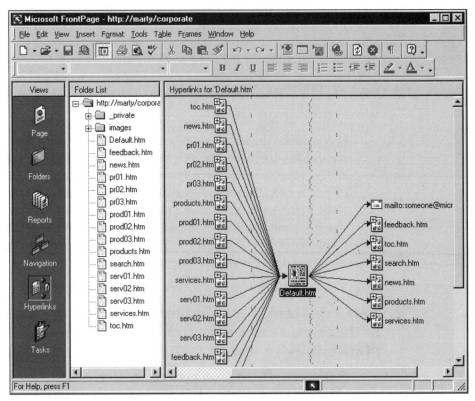

Figure 10-10 Hyperlinks view provides the foundation for managing hyperlinks

obvious visual checking that you can do in Hyperlinks view, it has the ability to verify that links are valid through the Verify Hyperlink button on the Reporting toolbar. FrontPage also has a command in the Tools menu that helps you with link management: Recalculate Hyperlinks updates the display of all links, as well as the server databases used by the Include and Search components.

Note: *When you have broken a link, the icon for the linked page is broken in the Hyperlinks view of FrontPage.*

How can I locate pictures for my web site?

There are at least three sources of pictures: pictures unique to your site that you or someone else took, either with a digital camera or regular photographs that are scanned into your computer; unique pictures that you or someone else drew with a graphics program; and public or private clip art, which are stock photos and drawings in a library. To locate any of these files, open the Insert menu, choose Picture, and select either Clip Art or From File. From File opens the Picture dialog box, which gives you several methods of locating a picture file. To get an image from the Internet, click the Use Your Web Browser. . . button (upper button at left); to get images from a file, click the Select A File. . . button (lower button at left). Also, you can type or select a URL in its box, or use the list box to get them from your current web site.

When should I use GIF format and when should I use JPEG format for the pictures that I include in a web site?

GIF (Graphics Interchange Format) and JPEG (Joint Photographic Experts Group) are the two most common formats used for pictures in web pages. As a general rule, if you have a simple line drawing without many colors, you should use GIF; when you have a color photograph, you should use JPEG because for complex colored pictures JPEG will often produce smaller files. If you have pictures in other formats, FrontPage will convert those with up to 256 colors to GIF files and those with more than 256 colors to JPEG files.

How can I align pictures on a web page?

There are three ways. First, you can left-, center-, or right-align a picture by selecting it and clicking the Align Left, Center, or Align Right buttons, shown next, in the toolbar normally used to align text.

The second way is to select the picture, open the Format menu, and choose Position to open the dialog box shown in Figure 10-11. In the Position dialog box, you can position

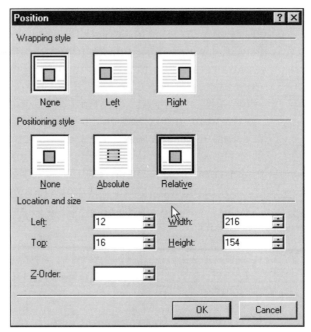

Figure 10-11 The Position dialog box allows you to very precisely position objects on a page

either pictures or other objects exactly where you want them with Absolute positioning or at a specific point in the text flow with Relative Positioning. The Position dialog box also allows you to determine how text will wrap around objects.

A third way to align pictures is to right-click, choose Picture Properties, click the Appearance tab, and choose an alignment from the drop-down list.

 Note: *Positioning with the Position dialog box only works in the newer web browsers such as Internet Explorer 4 and Netscape Navigator 4.*

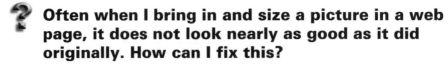 **Often when I bring in and size a picture in a web page, it does not look nearly as good as it did originally. How can I fix this?**

Before exporting a graphic from a graphics program to a web page, it's best to size the graphic as desired. Even though you can resize the graphic in FrontPage, you cannot add more

pixels. Enlarging a graphic will make it appear jagged. Also, choose a moderate number of colors, or even grayscale, to reduce the file size and therefore the download time.

How can I make my own textured background?

Most textured backgrounds are made by tiling a small graphic. You can make your own with any small image, optimally 96 × 96 pixels. If the image has a repeatable pattern, it is possible to get it to be reasonably seamless, as FrontPage has done in its samples.

A color that looked fine in FrontPage looks terrible in my browser. How can I choose a color that looks good in a browser?

You have probably created a custom color that ends up being dithered in the browser. What you want is a "browser-safe" color. FrontPage provides a palette of 127 such colors, plus 6 shades of gray, as shown here:

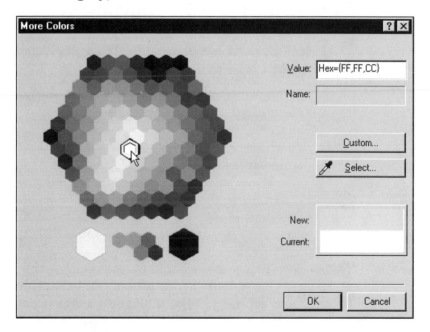

To open this palette, right-click the object you want to color (background, text, line, hyperlink, or table), click Font,

open the Color drop-down list to display the basic set of 16 browser-safe colors, and click More Colors. As a final check, look at how both Netscape Navigator and Microsoft Internet Explorer display any custom color you use.

 ### How can I make the background on a picture the same as the background on my page?

 This is done with the Set Transparent Color tool in the Pictures toolbar that is normally displayed when a picture is selected. This tool allows you to click any color in the picture and make it transparent, allowing the page background to show through.

Note: *Transparent backgrounds only work with GIF 89a files. If you try using a transparent background with a JPEG, you will get a dialog box that says the JPEG will be converted to a GIF.*

USING TABLES AND FRAMES

 ### I don't want a spreadsheet in my web page, so why should I use tables?

Web tables provide a means of dividing some or all of a page into rows and columns. Tables can be used to display tabular data as well as to simply position objects and text on a page, perhaps with a border around it. Say you have two pictures and three blocks of text. If you create a two-column by three-row table, you can easily lay out your page. One example is shown in Figure 10-12. You can turn off the borders so they cannot be seen. Many web pages are created with tables and have nothing to do with spreadsheets; they simply use the table to facilitate layout.

 Tables are created by using either the Insert Table button in the toolbar (which allows you to set the number of rows and columns in the table) or the Insert option on the Table menu, which opens the Insert Table dialog box, shown next:

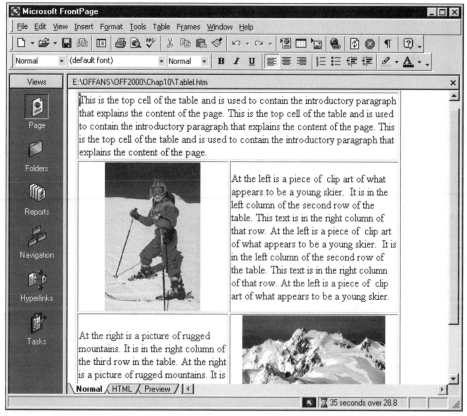

Figure 10-12   Example of a page created with a table in FrontPage

Option	Description
Rows	Specifies the number of rows in the table.
Columns	Specifies the number of columns in the table.
Alignment	Aligns the table on the left, center, or right of the page. Default alignment is the same as left alignment.
Border Size	Sets the number of pixels in the border. A 0-pixel border will not appear in a browser, but you'll see a dotted line in FrontPage. The default is 1.
Cell Padding	Sets the number of pixels between the inside edges of a cell and the cell contents on all four sides. The default is 1.
Cell Spacing	Sets the number of pixels between adjacent cells. The default is 2.
Specify Width	Sets the width to be a fixed number of pixels or a percentage of the window size, if Specify Width is selected. Otherwise, the table is the sum of the cells, which are individually sized to contain their contents within the size of the window. If the percentage method is selected, each cell is given an equal percentage of the table.
Style	Opens the Modify Style dialog box in which you identify the styles and their formats to be used in the table.

Table 10-1 Table Properties

The Insert Table dialog box allows you to specify the size, layout, and width of the table you are creating, as detailed in Table 10-1. Once a table is created, you can modify it through the table's context menu, which appears when you right-click the table. From the menu, you can choose Table Properties to change the overall properties of the table, or Cell Properties to change the properties of a single cell.

 Is there a way to create a table larger than the Insert Table drop-down list's five rows by four columns, without using the Insert menu?

Yes, you can create a table with more rows or columns than shown in the Insert Table drop-down list by dragging past the edge of the initial 5 × 4 grid. The box will expand to display the number of rows and columns you select.

+ ***Tip:*** *Pressing TAB in the last cell of a table will insert a new row at the bottom of the table.*

I've been having trouble with cells not lining up in a table. How can I prevent this?

You have probably changed the width of individual cells. This only works if you make the cells a multiple of the columns beneath and above the row you are changing. Otherwise, you should change the width of an entire column, and you should make sure that the sum of the cell widths in a row does not exceed 100 percent, or you will get unpredictable results.

My tables often don't come out the way I want them to. Is there a way to correct this?

You are probably creating a table based on a percentage of the screen, with columns as a percentage of the table, so that it will fit any size of screen. There are often problems getting the table to display the way you want it to when you do this, because the browser will resize the table as it sees fit. If you use fixed pixel widths based on the minimum 640 × 480 screen size (you probably shouldn't use more than 600 pixels for the width), you'll be able to create a more consistent look.

Why is it that when I change the alignment in a cell, nothing happens?

Cell padding and spacing may prevent much movement, especially vertically, in a cell when you change the alignment. Right-click the cell, choose Table Properties, and adjust the values for cell padding and spacing.

How can I select an entire row or column?

To select either a row or a column, move the mouse pointer to the outer edge of the table—the left edge for a row, the top edge for a column—until the mouse pointer changes to a heavy arrow (shown at left), and click. If you drag the heavy arrow, you can select multiple rows or columns.

 ## How do frames differ from tables, and how do I create them?

While both frames and tables divide a page into sections, they do so in very different ways with very different results. *Tables* are typically a smaller section of a page that has been divided, while *frames* are actually several pages that have been tiled and each allocated a section of the viewing window. Frames provide a way of organizing a web page by combining several pages on one page, each in a tile or *frame*. Each frame is its own page that can be scrolled and changed without affecting any of the other frames.

In FrontPage, frames are built by using frames-page templates. Frames-page templates establish a structure of blank pages, and the HTML to view them in frames within a single window. This structure of pages, along with the HTML, is called a *frames page*. (In previous versions of FrontPage, the frames page was known as a *frameset*.) You use the Frames Pages tab of the New dialog box to create the several pages necessary for a given layout. In the Frames Pages tab, you can choose one of several templates, as explained in Table 10-2, or you can create a custom layout

Template	What Is Created on a New Frame Page
Banner and Contents	Creates three frames: a banner across the top, a contents frame on the left, and a main frame
Contents	Creates two frames: a contents frame on the left and a main frame
Footer	Creates a main frame with a narrow footer frame across the bottom
Footnotes	Creates a main frame with a footnote frame across the bottom
Header	Creates a main frame with a narrow header frame across the top
Header, Footer, and Contents	Creates four frames: a header frame across the top, a contents frame on the left side, a main frame, and a footer frame across the bottom

Table 10-2 Frame Templates Available in Page View

Template	What Is Created on a New Frame Page
Horizontal Split	Creates two frames, split horizontally
Nested Hierarchy	Creates a full-height contents frame on the left, a header frame, and a main frame. The header frame changes according to the link chosen on the left frame to give more links that will then appear in the main frame.
Top-Down Hierarchy	Creates three frames, split horizontally. The "middle" header frame acts like the header frame in the Nested Hierarchy.
Vertical Split	Creates two frames, split vertically

Table 10-2 Frame Templates Available in Page View *(continued)*

with the rows, columns, and dimensions that you want. After creating the layout you want, you are shown the layout and asked how you want to determine the page contents, as shown in Figure 10-13.

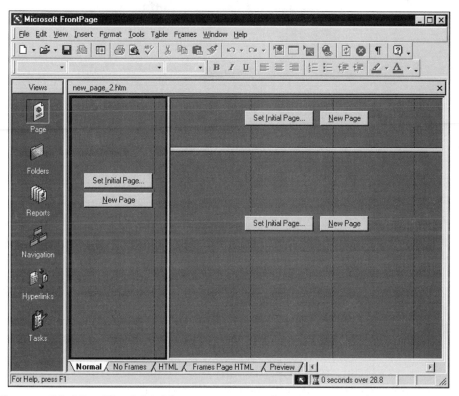

Figure 10-13 The initial frames page ready to accept each page

 I want to use frames, but there are still people with browsers that can't handle them. How do I work around this?

This is handled by creating a No Frames page. If the user's browser does not support frames, the No Frames page is displayed instead. FrontPage will automatically create a No Frames page when a frames page is created, as you can see by clicking the No Frames tab at the bottom of Page view when a frames page is open. Here you see the default No Frames page:

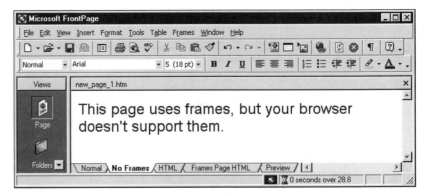

You can use this page either to direct the user to download a browser that supports frames, by creating hyperlinks to Microsoft's or Netscape's browser-download web pages, or to re-create your frames pages without frames. This is a case in which you could possibly use a table to replace the frames.

WORKING WITH FORMS

 Why would I want to use forms on my web page?

Forms are the mechanism for collecting user input—for getting information back from a user of your web page. The other web elements you have learned about facilitate your communication with the user. Forms have classically (meaning "last year," in the context of the Web) required either programming or the use of canned programs on a web

server. FrontPage has instead provided its server extensions and components, which save you from any programming. FrontPage then goes further by giving you powerful tools to incorporate these functions in a WYSIWYG environment. FrontPage provides a comprehensive Form Page Wizard to lead you through the development of a form. In addition, FrontPage has a complete set of tools both in the toolbar and in the Insert menu to allow you to create any form you can dream up.

Forms in a web page are very similar to those on paper. You are given boxes to fill in, options to select, and choices to make. The advantages of computer forms over paper forms are that computer forms can be easily modified; you don't have to decipher someone's handwriting; and the data starts out in computer form, so it does not have to be retyped into a computer. As with paper forms, though, the design of a form is very important if you want the user to fill it out willingly and properly. The three cardinal rules of forms are keep it simple, keep it short, and make it very clear what the user is supposed to do.

 Is there a simple way to get form information back to me?

To save information directly into a database, choose Send To Database in the Form Properties dialog box, and then set the necessary parameters in the Options For Saving Results To Database dialog box. To transfer the results of a web form to a spreadsheet or other applications, use a text file to collect the information. You can choose a comma-, tab-, or space-delimited file (the tab-delimited file probably being the best choice), all of which are fairly easy to import into most program formats. After you have created a form, right-click inside the form boundary and choose Form Properties. In the Form Properties dialog box that opens, either accept the default folder and name or enter your own, and click Options. In the Options For Saving Results Of Form dialog box, you can choose the file format you want returned with the results, as shown in Figure 10-14.

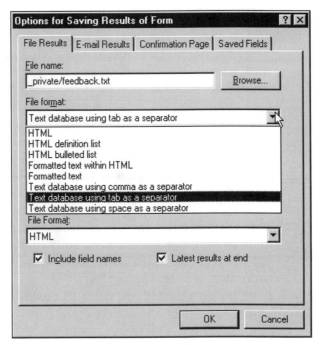

Figure 10-14 Although there are a number of file formats you can use to collect form results, a tab-delimited text file is probably the easiest to use

Note: *The reason the default folder for storing form results is /_private/ is that a search of the web site by a FrontPage Search Form will skip this folder and not display any of the contents in the search results.*

More than once I've lost all of my spacing used to lay out a form. Why, and how can I prevent it?

If you use the Formatted style, and you change the paragraph style on any of the form fields from Formatted to any other style, you'll lose all the leading spaces that produced the original field alignment. This can easily happen if you backspace up to the first paragraph. If this happens to you, click Undo to quickly recover. The only real way to prevent this is to use a table for your layout instead of the Formatted style.

 Note: *The Formatted style is the only HTML style that allows more than one contiguous space.*

I've changed the width of a text box, but that doesn't seem to limit the number of characters I can enter. How can I do this?

Changing the width of a text box does not affect the maximum number of characters the field can contain. To do that, use the Form Field Validation dialog box. Right-click a form field, and select Form Field Validation (not all form fields support validation). For a text field, the Text Box Validation dialog box, shown in Figure 10-15, is displayed. The Max Length text box displays the maximum number of characters the field will accept, regardless of the width of the field. If the maximum length is greater than the width, the text will scroll in the text box until the maximum length is reached.

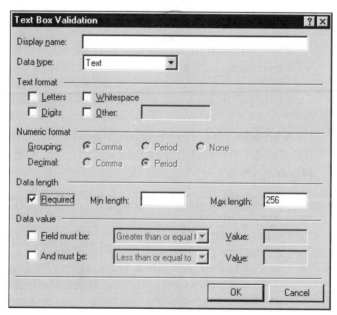

Figure 10-15 You can limit the number of characters in a form field in the Validation dialog box

 Whenever I create a table, my fields are widely spaced vertically. How can I get them closer together?

If you put form fields in the same form block (the area created by choosing Form | Form from the Insert menu and enclosed by a dashed line, as shown next) and use SHIFT-ENTER to create a new line, you can stack the fields closer together, and they will all have the same form properties.

 I'm having problems aligning the labels in my form. How can I do that?

If you format form fields with the Formatted paragraph style, you can often align the labels and text boxes using multiple spaces. However, it's not always possible to get all the form elements to line up exactly that way. This is because a space in a form text box is not the same width as a character space. The surest way to align form elements is to create a table and use a separate cell for each label and each field.

 I've made the field width and maximum length the same, but I still must scroll the field to see it all. How come?

Even if you set the field width and maximum length to the same number, all the text might not fit in the text box without scrolling. This is because the width of a character, as determined by the HTML, is not always the same as a character displayed on the screen. Test your form fields in a browser by entering the maximum number of characters and setting the width accordingly.

 How can I limit what is entered in a form field?

Field input in a form often needs to be limited to specific types of information, such as allowing only numbers (no letters), or requiring that a field not be left blank. Form validation has traditionally been done on web servers by the form handler (*server-side* validation). This has the disadvantage of requiring the form to be sent to the server, validated, and then sent back to the user if the validation fails. Besides the time involved, server-side validation places a greater demand on the web server's resources. If your web site is receiving a large number of hits each day, this can slow down the server. Validating a form before it's sent (*client-side* validation) has the advantages of speeding up the process and placing less demand on the web server.

Client-side validation is performed by the web browser. FrontPage generates a JavaScript or VBScript script that is run by the browser to validate the form. JavaScript (the default) is supported by both Netscape and Microsoft, while VBScript is supported mainly by Microsoft. Some browsers do not support either scripting language. If the browser being used does not support the scripting language used, the client-side validation is ignored.

To set the validation criteria, right-click a form field and select Form Field Validation. You can validate all the fields in a form except check boxes and push buttons in this way. Validation criteria for one-line and scrolling text boxes are set in the Text Box Validation dialog box that you saw previously in Figure 10-15.

APPLYING FRONTPAGE COMPONENTS

 What are FrontPage Components?

FrontPage components (WebBots, in earlier versions of FrontPage) provide automation in a web page—the ability to do more than just provide text and pictures on a page. For example, components return information to you that has been entered on a form, or they can enable users to participate in a discussion group. Most of FrontPage's components, though, just make creating and maintaining a web site easier. In other web-authoring packages, this same capability requires various levels of programming. In FrontPage, you simply have to set up and enable a component.

Some components are buried in other features, such as the form-handling components, while others are stand-alone tools that you can use directly. The stand-alone components are shown in the following illustration of the Insert menu Component flyout:

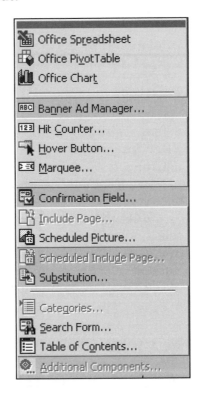

In addition, there are four additional components you can use that are opened from the Insert menu, rather than from the Component flyout. These are the Date and Time component, opened with the Date And Time option; the

Comment component, opened with the Comment option; the Navigation Bar component, opened with the Navigation Bar option; and the Page Banner component, opened with the Page Banner option.

Is a hit counter all that accurate?

Hit counters were popular in the past, but most are actually useless for compiling any real information about traffic on a web site. What they record is *page views*—the number of times a particular web page has been loaded by a browser. Advertisers are generally more interested in *visits,* the actual number of people who access a site. One visit will have a number of page views. If the visitor reloads a page, the hit counter will record it as a separate hit, which is what limits the hit counter's usefulness. Hit counters can be fun to have on a page though, especially if you don't take them seriously.

Note: *For an excellent explanation of web site statistics, see Web Site Stats, by Rick Stout (Osborne/McGraw-Hill, 1997). The included CD-ROM contains versions of popular web-tracking software, which are much more useful than the hit counter. If you intend to have advertising on your site, you will need to provide better statistics than the hit counter can provide. These statistics come from analyzing the web server logs, as is explained in Stout's book.*

What is the difference between Shared Borders and the Include Page component? Don't they both give you the same objects on several pages, such as a constant header and footer?

Yes, there are several similarities between Shared Borders and Include Page. Shared Borders is a newer way to handle this situation. The Include Page component allows you to include one web page on another.

For example, if you wanted a section with identical contents on every page, you could put the contents on a web page and then include that page on all others in the web site.

Future changes to the contents of that page would then automatically appear on all the pages that include the page. Shared Borders lets you specify that a header, footer, far left, or far right column are the same on all pages in a web site that don't specifically exclude them.

The difference between the two is the flexibility of Include Page (you can have as many of them as you like, but only one set of shared borders) versus the simplicity of Shared Borders (you just have to turn them on and type, whereas you have to create and specifically include the included pages).

When I added the Table of Contents component to a page, I did not get a table of contents. How come, and how do I fix it?

When you add the Table of Contents component to a page, you do not see the full table of contents. It is only when you open the page in a browser that the full table is displayed.

I've added a Search Form component to my web, but I would like to have some information kept out of the search. How do I do that?

If you want a page not to be found by the Search Form component (such as style pages and included pages), place the pages in the _private folder of the current web site—that folder is not searched. If you're using FrontPage's default folder structure and Myweb, the full path to the private folder for that web site would be C:\Inetpub\Wwwroot\Myweb_private.

USING ADVANCED TECHNIQUES

After looking at the existing themes, I still can't find one I like. Are others available?

Yes. If you cannot find a theme you like, you can choose Install Additional Themes from the top of the themes list (accessed from Format | Theme) to have more themes to choose from (you need to have your Office 2000 CD in its drive).

I have looked at all the existing themes and think that I would like to create one of my own. How do I do that?

As this book is being written (Spring 1999) there is no way to create your own theme from scratch, but you can do almost the same thing by modifying an existing theme. Supposedly, later this year, Microsoft will release a FrontPage 2000 Software Development Kit (SDK) that will have that capability, but this kit was not available to the authors.

You can customize one of the existing themes to add your own logo or change the styles, colors, and graphics used, and then save the theme with your name. Do this by opening the Format menu, choosing Theme, selecting a theme and the options (such as Vivid Colors) that are closest to what you want, and clicking Modify. This adds three more buttons that you can use to modify the colors, graphics, and text styles in the theme, as shown here:

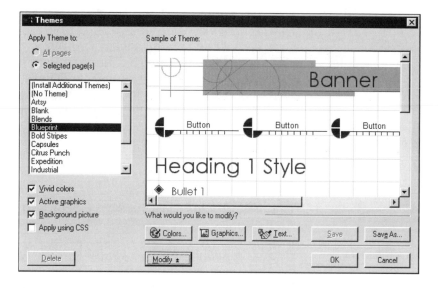

What are style sheets and how are they used?

Style sheets, which are also called cascading style sheets (CSS), allow you to predefine a number of styles and then consistently apply those styles throughout a web site. This not only gives a consistent look to your web site, but it saves you time, and it also allows you to change the entire site by simply changing the style sheet. You can use style sheets with themes, but you can also define your own style sheets and use them to control the web sites you create.

There are two types of style sheets: *embedded style sheets* apply only to the page on which they reside, and *external style sheets* are linked to and used in a number of pages. How these two types of style sheets are created is different, although their use is the same.

Note: *Early web browsers, before Internet Explorer 3 and Netscape Navigator 4, cannot use style sheets, and pages that are formatted with them probably will not look as they are intended. There are two style sheet standards: CSS 1.0, which covered formatting, and CSS 2.0, which covered the positioning and layering of page elements. Internet Explorer 3 supports CSS 1.0, and Internet Explorer 4 and later and Netscape Navigator 4 and later support both CSS 1.0 and 2.0.*

An embedded style sheet is created in the page in which it will be used by opening that page in Page view. Then open the Format menu and choose Style. The Style dialog box, similar to the one shown in Figure 10-16, will open. Here you can either modify an existing style or create a new one.

Note: *If the Style option is dim (not available) in the Format menu, it has been disabled. It can be enabled by opening the Tools menu, choosing Page Options, clicking the Compatibility tab, and clicking CSS 1.0 and CSS 2.0 under the Technologies section.*

An external style sheet gives you the benefit of being able to apply a set of styles to a number of pages, a whole web site, or even several web sites. Then, with a single change in the style sheet, you can change all of the pages to which it is linked. External style sheets provide a very powerful means of maintaining a consistent look for all pages in a site.

To create an external style sheet, open the FrontPage File menu and choose New | Page. Click the Style Sheets tab.

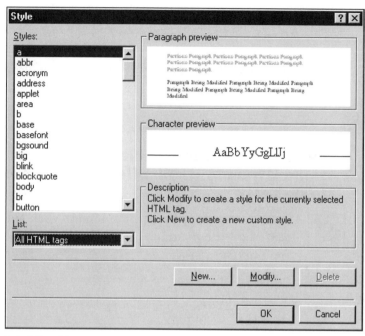

Figure 10-16   You can create new styles or modify existing ones in the
Style dialog box

This tab allows you either to create a style sheet from scratch
(the Normal Style Sheet) or to start with one of 12 ready-
made style sheets, which are also used in the themes. The
description will give you an idea of the style sheet. In any
case, you can add to and modify the style sheet you
start with.

 **I've heard the Dynamic HTML is really cool. How do I
use it?**

Dynamic HTML allows you to animate or give motion to most
of the elements on a page. For example, you can have a
paragraph fly in when a page is loaded, or a button move or
change when the mouse pointer hovers over it or clicks it.
FrontPage 2000 allows you to easily apply Dynamic HTML
by selecting the object that you want to animate, opening the
Format menu, and choosing Dynamic HTML Effects. A
floating toolbar will appear and ask you to choose an event to

trigger the effect. You then choose the effect and any attributes it needs, as shown here:

 I've got a number of objects that I want to apply the same Dynamic HTML effect to. Is there an easy way to do that?

Yes, you can copy animation effects with the Format Painter, located on the Standard toolbar.

Chapter 11

Working with the Rest of Office

Answer Topics!

Working with the Rest of Office @ a Glance

Office 2000 includes several applets, or subapplications, that add considerably to the power of Office 2000. In the five sections of this chapter, the primary ones are described.

- **Drawing** covers the Drawing applet, which is available in Word, Excel, and PowerPoint, and supplies a group of tools for drawing and formatting shapes, such as standard shapes (rectangles, squares, circles, and so on), lines, arcs, freeform drawing lines, and automatically drawn shapes of all types. The drawings can be modified with color, line style, shadow, 3-D effects, and more.

- **Microsoft Graph** describes Graph, which is a charting tool used in Word, PowerPoint, and Access (Excel has its own graphing feature that is separate from this one).

- **Clip Gallery** discusses Clip Gallery, which contains clip art, pictures, sounds, and video clips that can be inserted into your Word, Excel, Access, PowerPoint, and FrontPage documents and presentations.

- **Equation Editor** explores Equation Editor, which allows you to create complex mathematical expressions in Word, Excel, Access, and PowerPoint.

- **Building Organization Charts** looks at the Organization Chart applet, which provides the tools to create organization charts in Word, Excel, Access, and PowerPoint.

> *Note:*   *Graph, Clip Gallery, Equation Editor, and Organization mini-applications are not part of the default installation and will probably have to be installed with the Add/Remove control panel. Also, if you are in an Office application while you install one of the mini-applications through the Add/Remove control panel, you will have to close and reopen the Office application to have the mini-application appear in the Object listing.*

DRAWING

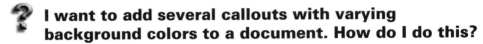 **I want to add several callouts with varying background colors to a document. How do I do this?**

Follow these steps to draw and then add text and color to callouts:

1. In Excel and Word, display the Drawing toolbar by right-clicking a toolbar and selecting Drawing. In PowerPoint, the Drawing toolbar is displayed at the bottom of the screen by default.

2. Click the AutoShapes button, select Callouts as shown here, and then select the shape of callout you want. The mouse pointer will become a crossbar.

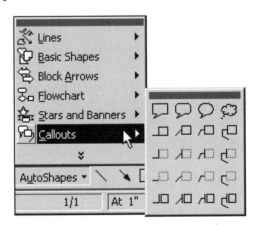

3. Place the pointer on the document where you want the callout, and drag it to about the size you want.

 Note: *You must first select the callout before you can size, move, or otherwise change its appearance.*

● To alter the size of the callout, place the pointer on one of the callout's eight control handles. When a

two-arrow pointer appears, as shown next, drag it to
the size you want. You can also use the Format |
AutoShape dialog box, if dragging seems difficult.

- To change the placement of the callout, place the
  pointer on the border of the callout but not on a
  control handle. When a four-arrow pointer appears,
  as shown here, drag the callout where you want it.

- To change the position of the callout leader, place the
  pointer just above its tip until the pointer becomes a
  yellow, diamond-shaped icon, as shown next. Then
  drag the tip to a new location.

4. Select all the callouts that you want to have the same
   color. Do this by either surrounding them with a
   selection rectangle or by clicking each one while pressing
   SHIFT. Figure 11-1 shows three callouts selected at once.

Tip: *Click the Select Objects button on the Drawing toolbar
to select objects with a selection rectangle.*

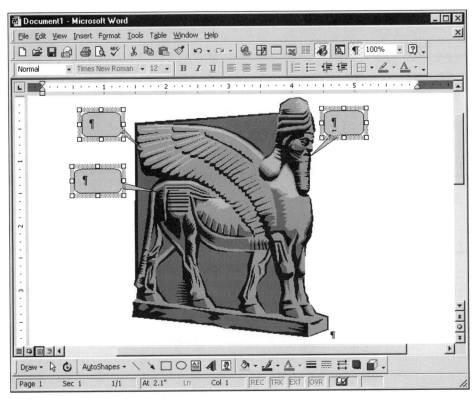

Figure 11-1 Simultaneously selected callouts

 5. From the Drawing toolbar, click the down arrow next to the Fill Color button, shown at left, and select a color.

How can I draw a circle quickly?

While you are dragging the Oval tool, press SHIFT for a perfect circle. To draw a perfect square, drag the Rectangle tool while pressing SHIFT.

 Tip: *To draw images from the center out, press CTRL while dragging the Rectangle or Oval tool. To draw a perfect circle or rectangle from the center out, press both CTRL and SHIFT while dragging the Rectangle or Oval tool.*

How can I manipulate the shapes of letters in a title?

You can use WordArt on the Drawing toolbar (found in Word, Excel, and PowerPoint). Follow these steps to create and then manipulate a title:

 1. Click the Insert WordArt button, shown at left, and a menu of styles is displayed, as shown here:

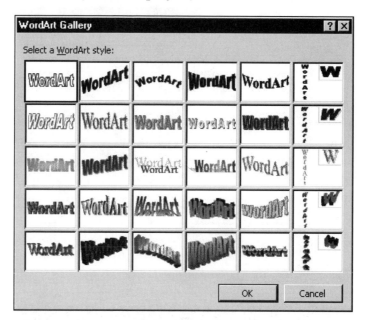

2. Select a style and click OK. A text box is displayed, in which you can type your text, as shown here:

3. Type your title and click OK. The WordArt is inserted into your document.

4. You will now have a graphic that can be manipulated using the WordArt toolbar. In addition to using the buttons in the toolbar, you can stretch and skew the letters by pulling on the control handles of the selected object. Here is an example of a title manipulated with WordArt:

Note: *In the illustration, the mouse pointer is dragging a ninth control handle that will skew the letters to increase or decrease their tilt.*

The Drawing Toolbar

The same Drawing tools are found in Word, Excel, PowerPoint, and Publisher, and they can be accessed from the Drawing toolbar. The Line, Arrow, Rectangle, Oval, Text Box, and AutoShapes tools enable you to draw lines and shapes. When you click one of these tools, the pointer changes to a crosshair pointer that you drag to form the line or shape. Except for the WordArt tool, the remaining tools, which alter shapes or lines, require that you select an object before clicking the tool. The functions of the Drawing tools are described in the following table.

Button	Tool	Description
Draw ▾	Draw	Displays a menu with options to group, order, nudge, align, rotate or flip, edit control points, change an AutoShape, set AutoShape defaults, or create a grid
	Select Objects	Selects drawn objects
	Free Rotate	Rotates a drawing around a central point
AutoShapes ▾	AutoShapes	Displays a selection of predefined shapes
	Line	Draws a straight line
	Arrow	Draws an arrow
	Rectangle	Draws a rectangle (or square with SHIFT)
	Oval	Draws an ellipse (or circle with SHIFT)
	Text Box	Draws a text box for entering text
	Insert WordArt	Provides a selection of text styles
	Insert Clip Art	Provides access to numerous pieces of clip art
	Fill Color	Displays a palette of colors that fill closed shapes when they are clicked
	Line Color	Displays a palette of colors to apply to selected lines

Button	Tool	Description
![A]	Font Color	Displays a palette of colors to apply to selected text
![Line Style]	Line Style	Displays a selection of line styles to apply to selected lines
![Dash Style]	Dash Style	Displays a selection of dashed-line styles to apply to selected lines
![Arrow Style]	Arrow Style	Displays a selection of arrow styles to apply to selected arrows
![Shadow]	Shadow	Displays a selection of shadow styles to apply to selected objects
![3-D]	3-D	Displays a selection of 3-D styles to apply to selected objects.

 ## How can I protect my drawings from being changed or used by others?

You can apply password protection to a graphic in Excel and Word, just as you do to a spreadsheet cell or document. The procedure varies slightly for each application.

Word

In Word, to protect the graphic, you must protect the whole document, as follows:

1. From the Tools menu, select Protect Document. The Protect Document dialog box will be displayed.
2. Select Forms.
3. Enter a Password, and click OK.

Excel

In Excel, you protect the drawing as you do a cell, as follows:

1. Right-click the graphic.
2. From the context menu, select Format Object, and click the Protection tab.

 Note: *The Format option changes name according to what is selected and right-clicked. For a circle, the option is called Format AutoShape, for clip art it is Format Picture, and so on.*

3. Turn on the Locked option, and click OK.

4. From the Tools menu, select Protection and then Protect Sheet.

5. In the Protect Sheet dialog box, shown next, ensure Objects is selected, type in a password, and click OK.

When I work with a document with graphics in it, the response time is slow because of the time it takes to redraw the graphics. I want the graphics to be part of the document, but don't need to see them while I am working on the rest of the document. What can I do to speed up the handling of the document?

You can hide the graphics while you are working on a Word document or Excel spreadsheet by following these steps:

1. From the Tools menu, select Options.

2. In Word, on the View tab under Show, place a check mark on the items you want to show in the document. Under Print And Web Layout Options, remove the check mark for Drawings (and any other items you want to hide), as shown in Figure 11-2. Click OK.

   In Excel, in the View tab, click Hide All under Objects (or click Show Placeholders to display the placeholder graphics, which may be important while you are working).

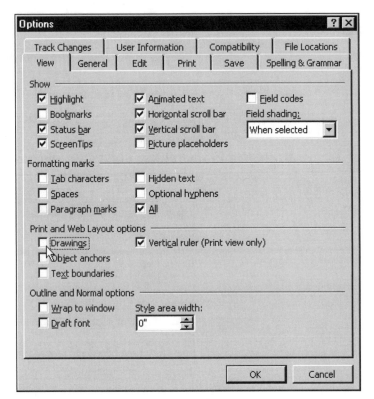

Figure 11-2 Hiding drawings in Word makes your response time faster

When you have finished working on the document or spreadsheet, you can reverse the process and place check marks next to the type of graphics you want to see, or next to Show All in Excel.

MICROSOFT GRAPH

How do I find and use Microsoft Graph? I don't know where it is or how to start.

You must be in Word, PowerPoint, or Access to use Microsoft Graph. (Excel has its own charting capability.) It is a subapplication that is used within the larger Office 2000 applications. However, it acts as if it were a part of the application, in terms of how the menus and dialog boxes are presented to you. That is, a separate application is not started

with its own environment, such as you might find with OLE. How you bring up the package and work with it varies slightly between the applications. The following lists explain how to bring up Graph from the various Office programs.

Note: The terms Chart and Graph are used interchangeably; they mean the same thing.

In Word

1. Initiate the Graph feature by selecting Object from the Insert menu, and then choosing Microsoft Graph 2000 Chart. A sample datasheet and sample chart will be displayed, as shown in Figure 11-3.

2. Replace the words and numbers in the datasheet that is displayed with the numbers and labels you want.

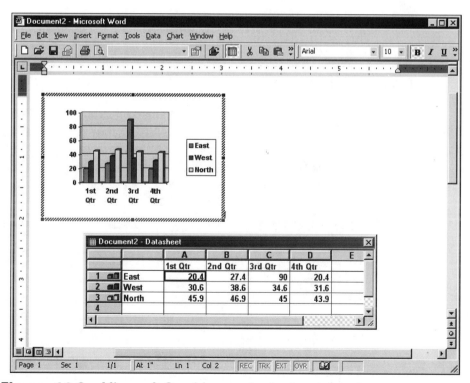

Figure 11-3 Microsoft Graph's sample chart and datasheet

 3. When you have finished, click the View Datasheet button in the toolbar, shown at left. This will close the datasheet until it is clicked again. You can also just click outside the datasheet area to clear it from the screen.

 Tip: *If the View Datasheet button is not showing, and you want to edit the data, right-click the chart, select Chart Object, and then select Edit. If you cannot get the Chart Object option on the context menu, double-click the chart first, and then right-click it and select Chart Object from the context menu. The Datasheet button will be redisplayed. See "Once it has been closed, how can I redisplay a chart datasheet?," later in this section, which covers this in more detail.*

4. From the Chart menu, select Chart Type to select the type of chart, and then select Chart Options to add titles and perform other fine-tuning of the chart.

 Tip: *If the Chart menu is not showing, right-click the chart and select Chart Object and then Edit. The Chart menu will reappear.*

In PowerPoint

In PowerPoint, you have a quicker way to get charts. When you are building a presentation and add a new slide, you will be given a choice of several AutoLayout styles, as shown here:

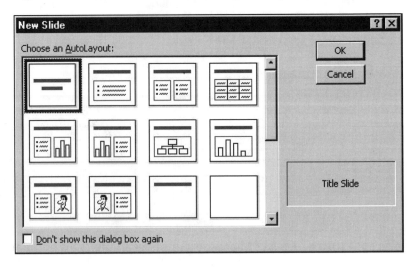

The second row contains three charting templates. Then follow these steps:

1. Select an AutoLayout slide with a chart placeholder, and click OK.

2. Double-click the chart placeholder to get the Microsoft Graph datasheet and chart, as described in the section "In Word," earlier in this question.

Tip: *If you are working with slides without chart placeholders, you can get to Microsoft Graph by clicking the Insert Chart icon on the toolbar, shown at left, or by opening the Insert menu and choosing Chart.*

In Access

In Access, you can create charts in either forms or reports. The chart's data is extracted from information in an Access table or query, rather than from a separate datasheet as in Word or PowerPoint. Follow these steps:

1. Open the form or report in Design view by either creating a new one or opening an existing one.

2. Open the Insert menu, and choose Chart.

3. Click the mouse pointer on the form or report where you want the chart placed, and the Chart Wizard will open. Follow the Chart Wizard's directions.

4. Switch to Print Preview or Form view to see the current chart.

 ### How do I add rows or columns to the Graph datasheet?

The original datasheet displayed when you first bring up Graph may appear to have a limited number of rows and columns. You can extend it by simply using the scroll bars on the bottom and right sides of the datasheet to scroll down to row 3999 or to scroll right to column EWU (which means

there are over 3,300 columns) to increase its size. If you need to add rows or columns in specific places, follow these steps:

1. Select a cell in the row below or the column to the right of where you want to add one.

 Note: *If you select the entire row or column, choosing Cells from the Insert menu adds another row or column without bringing up the Insert dialog box; if you only select a cell, then the dialog box is displayed.*

2. Select Cells from the Insert menu (or right-click the datasheet and select Insert).

3. In the Insert dialog box, click Entire Column or Entire Row, as shown next, and click OK.

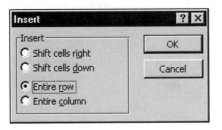

 Tip: *If you want to insert more than one row or column at a time, select the number of rows or columns you want inserted, and then choose Insert | Cells.*

Why is there more than one graph package? Which is the best graph package?

There are really only two graphing capabilities in Office 2000. One is the graphic feature within Excel and the other is Microsoft Graph, used within Word, PowerPoint, and Access.

The question of which is best is difficult to answer, because it depends on what you need graphing for and what your experience is. The Excel feature is more comprehensive and, consequently, more complex. The data to be graphed needs to be developed within Excel on a worksheet. This feature offers flexibility and capabilities not found in Graph. Graph, on the other hand, is easy to use, although limited in its capability.

If you want a quick chart or are new to graphing, Graph will serve you well. If you are comfortable with Excel and need a more comprehensive charting tool, Excel's charting features are best.

How can I change the size of a chart?

To change the size of a chart, follow these steps:

1. Click the chart to select it, causing control handles to appear.

2. Place your pointer on a corner control handle until a two-headed arrow (or a plus sign) appears. Drag the image in the direction you want the size to be changed.

   - If you drag toward the center of the graph, the image will be reduced; drag away from the center and the image size will be increased.

   - If you place the pointer somewhere within the graph, you can drag the chart wherever you want it.

Tip: To precisely size the chart using the keyboard in Word or PowerPoint, open the Format menu and choose Object. In the Size tab, you can enter precise measurements for the chart. Alternatively, you can precisely crop the graph in the Picture tab. You can use Reset in either the Size or Picture tabs to restore the original values while you get the measurements correct. In Access, display and select the chart in Design view. On the View menu, choose Properties, and then adjust the Width and Height values.

I have a graph in Word that I must insert into a document many times. What is an easy way to insert the same graph repeatedly?

The easiest way is to add the object to AutoText. Then, when you type its name and press F3, the graphic will automatically replace the name. Follow these steps to do it:

1. Select the graph.

2. Open the Insert menu fully, select AutoText, and then New from the submenu. The Create AutoText dialog box will be displayed, as shown here:

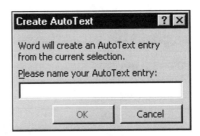

3. Type a name for the graph, and click OK.

The Basics of Graphing

Microsoft Graph offers 14 types of standard charts. These 14 types are then extended by several 3-D effects for each type, plus there are an additional 20 custom types. Each type of standard graph displays data in a slightly different way, allowing you to choose the type that is best for presenting your data. The standard types of charts are described in the table at the end of this sidebar.

Graphs display data on two or three axes, the latter of which is shown here:

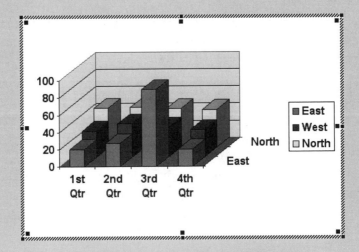

These axes and their reference names are as follows:

- The vertical axis, also called the Y axis, or the value axis
- The horizontal axis, also called the X axis, or the category axis
- The depth axis, which gives a 3-D appearance, also called the Z axis, or the series axis

Note: *The definition of which axis is used for values and which for categories can be changed.*

Using the options in the Chart Type and Chart Options dialog boxes, which are opened from the Chart menu as explained in the earlier question "How Do I Find And Use Microsoft Graph? . . .," you can define the appearance of your chart. You format a chart by opening the Chart Options dialog box and doing the following:

- Type the name for the chart and a title for each of the axes.
- Define which is the primary axis, and specify whether it is a category or time-scale axis, or whether Graph should assume the titles from the data.
- Designate whether major or minor gridlines are to be used for each axis.
- Stipulate where the legend is to be placed, or whether to hide it.
- Define whether to show data or value labels on the chart, or other measurements, such as percentages.
- Specify whether to show the data table where the values and labels are defined.

The standard types of charts are identified in the following table:

Sub-Types	Type of Chart	Description
	Column	Displays the data in vertical bars or columns; compares values in one category to those in another
	Bar	Displays data in horizontal bars; compares values in one category to those in another

Sub-Types	Type of Chart	Description
	Line	Displays data in lines with values plotted along the lines; used to show trends over time
	Pie	Displays the data as pieces of a pie, showing the relation of parts to the other pieces and to the whole
	XY (Scatter)	Compares pairs of values to show patterns or trends
	Area	Displays how a value contributes to a trend over time or categories
	Doughnut	Shows how a value compares to a whole; can display multiple series
	Radar	Connects values at various positions and frequencies compared with a central point and with each other
	Surface	3-D surface; shows how values in a continuous curve contribute to a trend
	Bubble	Compares sets of three values
	Stock	Displays four values of a stock's daily price: opening, high, low, and closing
	Cylinder	Same as Column, but displays the columns as cylinders
	Cone	Same as Column, but displays the columns as cones
	Pyramid	Same as Column, but displays the columns as pyramids

Once it has been closed, how can I redisplay a chart datasheet?

There are at least three ways to get the datasheet redisplayed, depending on what buttons and menus are available when you want to display it:

● Redisplay the graph datasheet by clicking the View Datasheet button on the toolbar.

● Select the chart by double-clicking it. This method selects the chart with a striped line surrounding it and black control handles, and may open the datasheet in the process. If the datasheet did not open, either right-click a clear area of the chart and select Datasheet from the context menu, as shown below, or select Datasheet from the View menu.

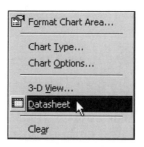

● Select the chart by clicking it once so that clear control handles are shown, and then right-click the chart and select Chart Object | Edit to see the datasheet.

How can I put tick marks on an axis?

You can insert tick marks on a selected axis so that it may be read more precisely. Follow these steps:

1. Ensure that the graph is selected, with the black striped line surrounding it. If not, double-click it to select it.

2. Select the axis by clicking it. Control handles will appear on each end of the axis. You must click the axis, but not on a corner.

3. Select Selected Axis from the Format menu. The Format Axis dialog box will open.

4. On the Patterns tab, click the type of tick mark you want in the Major Tick Mark Type, Minor Tick Mark Type, and Tick Mark Labels areas, as shown here:

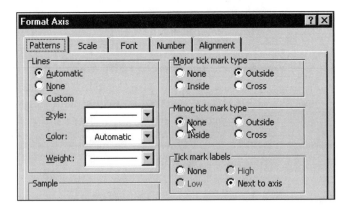

CLIP GALLERY

 ### How do I add clip art objects to the Clip Gallery?

In Word, Excel, Access, PowerPoint, and FrontPage, you can add new clip art objects to the Clip Gallery by importing them. First, bring up the Clip Gallery by selecting Picture from the Insert menu and then choosing Clip Art. The Clip Art Gallery window appears, as shown in Figure 11-4.

 Note: *The Clip Gallery window is titled differently in different products. In Word, Excel, and PowerPoint, it is Insert ClipArt; in Access, it is Microsoft Clip Gallery; and in FrontPage, it is Clip Art Gallery. In all cases, though, it is the same window.*

Now follow these steps:

1. Click the Import Clips button on the toolbar at the top of the Clip Gallery window.

2. In the Add Clip To Clip Gallery dialog box, find the file to be added and click Import.

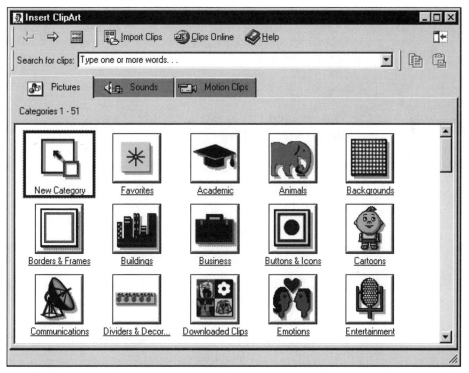

Figure 11-4   Clip Gallery window

3. In the Clip Properties dialog box, shown here, type a
   description for the object, enter one or more keywords,
   and choose a category under which it will be found.

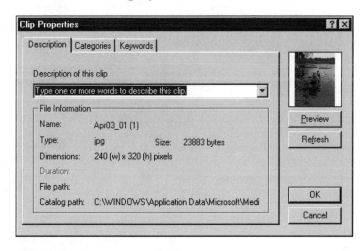

4. Click OK.

 Note: *In Access, you must be in Design view for a form or report, and then open the Insert menu and choose Object to open the dialog box in which Microsoft Clip Gallery can be selected.*

 ## I can't access the Clip Gallery. Why not?

You probably have not installed it correctly. Follow these steps to install it again:

1. Insert your Office 2000 CD into the CD-ROM drive.
2. From the Start menu, select Settings | Control Panel, and then double-click Add/Remove Programs.
3. On the Install/Uninstall tab, find and click Microsoft Office 2000 Premium, or one of the other Office 2000 editions, and click Add/Remove.
4. Click the Add Or Remove Features button in the Microsoft Office 2000 Setup dialog box.
5. In the Microsoft Office 2000: Update Features dialog box, expand Office Tools, and click Clip Gallery.
6. Click Run From My Computer, as shown in Figure 11-5, and click Update Now.
7. Click OK when told that Setup was completed successfully. Close the Add/Remove Programs dialog box.

 Tip: *In PowerPoint you can access the Clip Gallery quickly. You only need to insert a slide with an AutoLayout style containing a clip art placeholder, such as the one shown next, and then double-click it to open the Clip Gallery dialog box.*

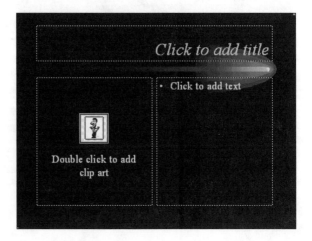

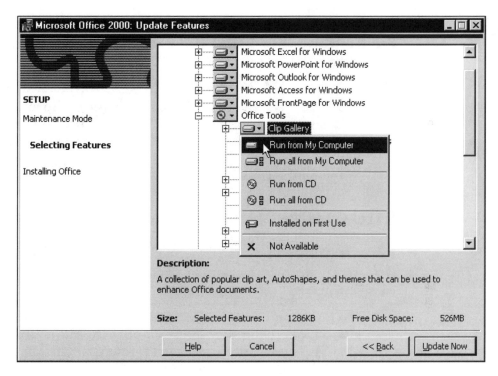

Figure 11-5   Installing the Microsoft Clip Gallery

Tip: *If you want clip art to be shown on all pages of a PowerPoint presentation, insert it on the Slide Master.*

How do I modify clip art?

If the image is composed of separate objects, and most clip art isn't, you can separate and change those elements. In all cases, you can add a background fill, lines, and callouts, all using the Drawing toolbar, but the operative word is "add." It is very hard to take away or change elements of a piece of clip art unless those elements are separate objects. However, you can paste clip art into Paint, modify it at the pixel level, and then save and import it back into the Clip Gallery.

 I want to try several clip art images in a presentation I'm building, but I find the process of repeatedly bringing up the Insert menu very laborious. Is there a quick way to replace clip art images?

 In Office 97, you could double-click a piece of clip art in a document and open the Clip Gallery. In Office 2000, that no longer works because a double-click now opens the Format Picture dialog box. The fastest way now is the Insert Clip Art button on the Drawing toolbar.

EQUATION EDITOR

 I would like to add equations to a document. Where do I find the symbols and tools for building a mathematical expression?

The Equation Editor is a separate application that works with Office products for that very purpose. However, as with OLE applications, you load it into your current Office application and the Equation Editor will appear with its own menus and toolbar. To get to it, follow these steps:

1. Open the Insert menu, select Object, and click the Create New tab (or option button, depending on the Office program) if it is not already selected.

2. Select Microsoft Equation, and click OK. The Equation toolbar will be displayed, as shown next. To see the contents of the toolbar menus, place the pointer over the icons and the detail list of symbols will appear.

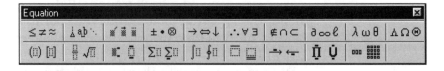

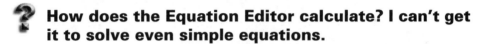

 Note: *If Microsoft Equation isn't available to you, you will need to install it using the Add / Remove Programs control panel and the Office 2000 CD.*

3. Construct the equation by clicking the toolbar menus to select the symbol and expression templates and typing variables and numbers in the Equation Editor text boxes.

 Tip: *A third-party product that significantly enhances the capabilities of Equation Editor is available. From the Equation Editor Help menu, select Equation Editor Help Topics, select the Contents tab, and then choose Upgrading Equation Editor to get additional information.*

How does the Equation Editor calculate? I can't get it to solve even simple equations.

The Equation Editor is not designed to perform calculations at all. It is simply a tool for typing complex equations with all the symbols and constructs needed.

When I want to change an equation in a document, is there a way to get the Equation Editor quickly without going through the Insert menu?

Yes, when you want the Equation Editor window to reappear, simply double-click the equation, and it will be displayed.

How do I change the font and font size used in equations?

There are three ways you can change fonts and sizes of equations:

● First, you can define the defaults for the fonts and sizes that will be used in equations. The fonts and sizes can be applied to the various parts of an equation (Text, Functions, Variables, Lower Case Greek, Upper Case

Greek, Symbols, Matrix-Vectors, and Numbers). To change the defaults for fonts, select Define from the Style menu. The Styles dialog box will be displayed, as shown here:

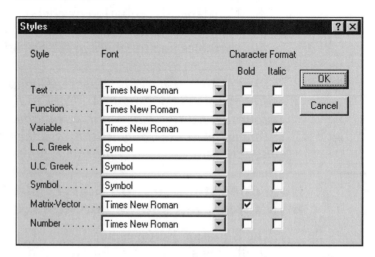

Select the font by clicking the down arrow and choosing the font you want. To specify bold or italic, click the relevant check box to place a check mark in it. To change the default for the size of font used, choose Define from the Size menu. A similar dialog box will allow you to change sizes for character variations.

● Second, you can change the font for an existing equation. Select the expression or the part you want to change, choose Other from the Style menu, and select the font you want. In the same way, you can change the size for an existing equation by selecting Other from the Size menu.

● Third, the Equation Editor assigns a standard size to elements of an equation—the equation templates have "slots" that define an element and, therefore, its size. For example, subscripts are smaller, and brackets around summations are larger. You can also change the size of an element by selecting a standard size from the Size menu. This assigns a standard size to a specific type of element:

- *Full* pertains to normal-size characters.
- *Subscript* is used for subscripts and superscripts next to normal numbers. It is one size smaller than Full size. It can also be used for other situations requiring that size of character.
- *Sub-Subscript* is used for subscripts and superscripts assigned to sub- or superscripts. It is two sizes smaller than Full size and can be used for other elements requiring the smaller-size characters.
- *Symbol* pertains to oversized symbols that are part of the equations and their templates.
- *Sub-Symbol* pertains to oversized symbols used in subscript-size positions.

 ### I find I am not as familiar with mathematical terminology as I need to be to use the Equation Editor easily. Where can I get some guidance?

The Equation Editor has a glossary you may find helpful. On the Help menu, select Equation Editor Help Topics. When the Help Topics dialog box opens, select the Contents tab, choose Reference Information, and then Definitions. The Definitions topic will be displayed, partially shown next. Click an item to see its definition.

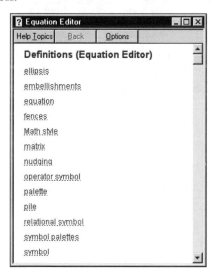

 There are parts of an equation that I want to move by small amounts, and I find it difficult. How can I enlarge the image and then move the components by small amounts?

When you want to make very precise changes to an equation's symbol and text positioning, you need to first increase the size of the image on the screen. Since you must be in the actual Equation Editor window, shown here, to have the magnification commands available to you, you can bring it up by right-clicking the equation and choosing Equation Object | Open.

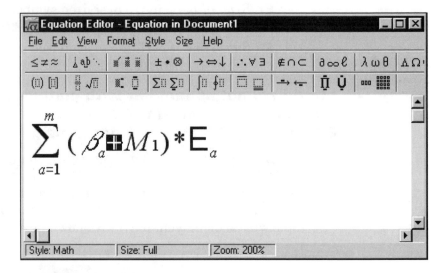

Then you can enlarge the image on the screen by selecting a magnification size from the View menu. For example, select 400% to see the image enlarged four times. Then select an element of the equation and use these commands to move it by one pixel:

- CTRL-LEFT ARROW to move left
- CTRL-RIGHT ARROW to move right
- CTRL-UP ARROW to move up
- CTRL-DOWN ARROW to move down

Tip: *Use Redraw in the View menu to redisplay the equation after you have made changes so that you can see where you are.*

BUILDING ORGANIZATION CHARTS

 ## What is a quick way to build an organization chart?

A separate mini-application works with Office to design organization charts. To use it, follow these steps:

1. Click where you want to insert the organization chart.

2. From the Insert menu, select Object, and then choose MS Organization Chart from the list. Click OK. The window shown in Figure 11-6 will be displayed.

 Note: *If MS Organization Chart isn't available to you, you will need to install it using the Add/Remove Programs control panel and the Office 2000 CD.*

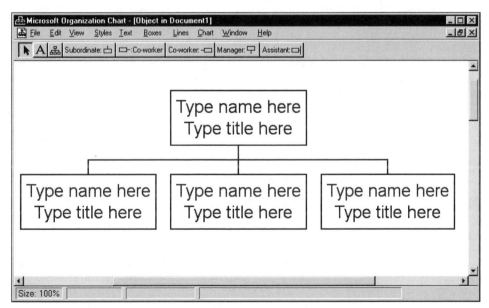

Figure 11-6   The Microsoft Organization Chart

3. Build the organization chart by using these tools:

- Select the style of chart by selecting an option from the Styles menu.
- Select the magnification of the chart with the View options.
- Replace the text in the default boxes with your own.
- Add boxes by clicking a position button, shown next, and then placing the resulting icon on the box you want it connected to.

- Add color, shadows, and borders to the boxes with the Boxes menu.
- Determine the thickness, color, and style of the box lines with the Lines menu.
- Use the Text menu to align the text and set its color and font.

4. Delete boxes by selecting them and selecting Cut from the Edit menu or pressing DEL.

❓ How can I change the initial default chart display?

You can only change a limited number of characteristics of the default organization chart that is first displayed. You can choose whether the number of boxes initially displayed for new charts will be the default 4-box template or a 1-box template. The 4-box template will always contain sample text to be replaced. You can choose between having one box with text to be replaced, or preset text that you have established. Finally, you can select the magnification that will be used to display the organization chart. Make your choices by following these steps:

1. Establish an organization chart as you would want to see it when the program is brought up each time.

2. From the Edit menu, select Options. The Options dialog box will be displayed like this:

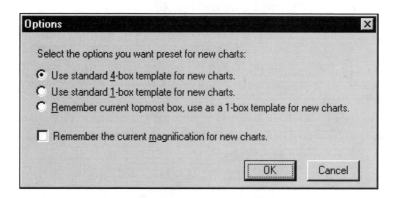

3. Select the options you want to retain.

Note: *Organization Chart is a simplified version of Org Plus for Windows. If you are interested in finding out about this enhanced organization chart program, look in the Help menu under About for additional information.*

How do I use color in an organization chart?

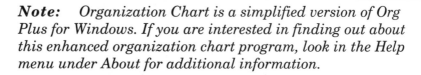

You can place color in the background of the chart, as well as within the boxes. You might, for example, want to give the chart a more readable format with all of the same positions in one color and a contrasting background.

- For background color, select Background Color from the Chart menu.

- For colored boxes, select the boxes, and then select Color from the Boxes menu. Select the boxes by clicking them, using SHIFT to select more than one box, or select specific positions from the Select option or levels from the Select Levels option, both in the Edit menu.

The boxes are so big on my screen that I cannot see them all. How do I reduce the size of an organization chart?

To reduce the size of the organization chart on the screen, select 50% Of Actual from the View menu. If that is still too large to see all of the page, select Size To Window. When you want to return to the normal size, select Actual Size.

When I revise my organization chart, I get some unexpected results. What are some guidelines for revising?

When an organization chart is revised, it must rebuild itself according to the information it has. So when you want to delete a line of positions, either horizontally or vertically, you must select all of them before deleting them. When you move a position from one level to another, you must move it precisely. Here are some guidelines:

- If you delete a managing position, the subordinate positions will be moved up one position in the organization chart, to the next managing position above. You can cut one box by right-clicking it and selecting Cut from the context menu, as shown here:

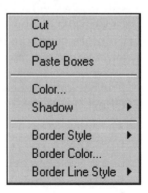

- To delete a manager and subordinates, you must select them all by selecting first the manager, and then choosing Select from the Edit menu, and then Branch. The whole line will be selected. Then select Cut from the Edit menu.

Tip: *If you select Group, a horizontal line of positions will be selected; if Branch, a vertical line.*

- To move subordinates from one position to another, select their boxes and drag them over the manager to which they will be subordinate.

ndex

To **speak to the support experts** who handle more than one million technical issues every month, call **Stream's** Microsoft® Office 2000® answer line! Trained specialists will answer your Microsoft® Office 2000® questions regarding Word for Windows®, Excel for Windows®, and PowerPoint for Windows®.

Have all your questions been answered?

1-800-477-7613

For Word for Windows and PowerPoint for Windows Questions:
$29.95 per problem (Charge to a major credit card.)

1-800-477-7614

For Excel for Windows Questions:
$29.95 per problem (Charge to a major credit card.)

1-900-555-2007

For Word for Windows and PowerPoint for Windows Questions:
$29.95 per problem (Charge to your phone bill.)

1-900-555-2006

For Excel for Windows Questions:
$29.95 per problem (Charge to your phone bill.)

Visit our web site at www.stream.com.

We help people use technology!